PSAT-NMSQT

PRELIMINARY SCHOLASTIC
APTITUDE TEST

NATIONAL MERIT SCHOLARSHIP
QUALIFYING TEST

PSAT-NMSQT

PRELIMINARY SCHOLASTIC APTITUDE TEST

NATIONAL MERIT SCHOLARSHIP QUALIFYING TEST

Eve P. Steinberg, M.A.

ARCO PUBLISHING, INC.
NEW YORK

Seventh Edition, Second Printing, 1985

Published by Arco Publishing, Inc.
215 Park Avenue South, New York, N.Y. 10003

Copyright © 1985 by Arco Publishing, Inc.

Library of Congress Cataloging in Publication Data

Steinberg, Eve P.
  PSAT/NMSQT: preliminary scholastic aptitude test.

  1. Preliminary scholastic aptitude test—Study guides.
2. National merit scholarship qualifying test—Study
guides. I. Title. II. Title: P.S.A.T./N.M.S.Q.T.
LB2353.56.S73   1985   378′.1664   84-6458
ISBN 0-668-06100-6 (Paper Edition)

Printed in the United States of America

CONTENTS

PSAT-NMSQT

PRELIMINARY SCHOLASTIC APTITUDE TEST

NATIONAL MERIT SCHOLARSHIP QUALIFYING TEST

WHY YOU SHOULD USE THIS BOOK

You are at the beginning of your junior year in high school. College still seems far away. The next two years will be filled with classes, papers and exams, with athletic contests and dramatic productions, with parties and a prom. They will also be filled with standardized tests, interviews and applications to colleges.

The first of the succession of tests is the Preliminary Scholastic Aptitude Test, the PSAT. You will take the PSAT at your high school in the fourth week of October. Your score on this exam will guide you as you begin to consider colleges.

One comforting aspect of the PSAT is that your scores do not count for admission to college. No admissions officer will receive your PSAT scores.

At this point you may ask yourself, "Why should I study for this exam?" There are a number of good reasons why you should prepare yourself to do your very best.

First of all, the PSAT is the qualifying exam for the National Merit Scholarship program. You may not consider yourself to be a potential scholarship winner, but don't sell yourself short. With solid preparation and calm self-confidence you may do surprisingly well. Even if you do not win a scholarship, there are other benefits which may result from a high score. The status of finalist, semi-finalist or commended student is a significant asset on your college application. It is worthwhile to try for national recognition in your PSAT performance.

In addition, you should consider the PSAT to be a "dress rehearsal" for the Scholastic Aptitude Test, the SAT. The SAT *does* count. Surely, you want the dress rehearsal to go very well, to go as smoothly and as professionally as the show itself.

This book will introduce you to each type of question you may expect on the exam. It will explain how to approach each of these question types. The book will also show you how the exam is organized: how many questions of each variety you may expect and how much time you will have to answer the questions.

Included in this book are four full-length simulated PSAT exams. These are not actual exams; the actual exams are copyrighted and cannot be reprinted. These exams are based upon information gathered after many years of research and experience. They have been created to be so similar to the "real thing" that they will give you excellent practice. By practicing with these exams you will learn to budget your own time, for you want to allow maximum time for the types of questions that give you the most difficulty. You will be able to build up your speed, accuracy and confidence. The answer to every question in each exam is fully explained so that you can learn from your errors and from your successes.

By the time you have completed this book, you will be ready—ready to earn the best score of which you are capable, ready to try for that scholarship, ready for a flawless dress rehearsal, without stage fright.

ABOUT THE EXAM

WHAT IS THE PSAT/NMSQT?

The Preliminary Scholastic Aptitude Test/National Merit Scholarship Qualifying Test (PSAT/NMSQT) is a two-hour multiple-choice type test offered by the Educational Testing Service on behalf of the College Entrance Examination Board and the National Merit Scholarship Corporation.

The PSAT provides a measure of the verbal and mathematical abilities important for success in college, and it is a necessary first step toward consideration for all scholarships administered by the National Merit Scholarship Corporation.

WHO TAKES THE EXAM?

Merit Scholarship candidates must take the PSAT in their Junior year of high school in order to be eligible for scholarships to be granted in the spring of their Senior year. If a student is to complete high school in three years, the exam may be taken in the Sophomore year.

Any high school Junior who expects to go on to college can profit by taking the PSAT. This exam gives the student an introduction to the type of test to be faced when taking the College Board Scholastic Aptitude Test (SAT) and provides an estimate of ability to do satisfactory work at various colleges and universities.

WHEN AND WHERE IT IS GIVEN

Every public, independent and parochial high school can administer the PSAT once each year, during the last week in October. Students who wish to take the exam must register for it in their school office. Once registered, each candidate will be provided with a Student Bulletin, which includes sample questions, helpful hints on preparing for the test and eligibility requirements for scholarships administered by the National Merit Scholarship Corporation.

FORMAT OF THE EXAMINATION

The PSAT is a test of general intellectual ability. It is divided into two fifty-minute sections, a Verbal section and a Mathematical section.

There are sixty-five questions in the Verbal section. These questions are of four different types, as follows:
- Twenty ANTONYMS to test the extent of your vocabulary;
- Ten SENTENCE COMPLETIONS to probe your in-depth comprehension of the meanings of sentences and your ability to maintain logic and consistency of style;
- Fifteen VERBAL ANALOGIES to test your understanding of the relationships between words;
- Twenty READING COMPREHENSION questions based upon four reading passages (five questions per passage) to assess your ability to understand and interpret what you read.

There are fifty questions in the Mathematical section. These questions test your ability to understand and solve problems in arithmetic, algebra and geometry. The questions are of two different styles:
- Thirty-three WORD PROBLEMS which you must read and solve. The Mathematical section begins and ends with word problems, fifteen at the beginning and eighteen at the end.
- Seventeen QUANTITATIVE COMPARISONS questions, in which you must compare two quantities in terms of size. These questions test your

understanding of mathematical concepts and the flexibility with which you can apply your understanding. The quantitative comparisons questions are in the middle of the Mathematical section.

NATURE OF THE QUESTIONS

The following questions are typical of those which you may expect on this exam. Each question is preceded by directions like the ones on the actual exam and followed by an explanation that indicates the kind of thinking involved.

ANTONYMS

DIRECTIONS: For each question, mark the letter preceding the word or phrase that is opposite or most nearly opposite in meaning to the capitalized word. Where more than one option appears to be correct, choose the *best* opposite.

Example:

BLACK

(A) gray
(B) bright
(C) white
(D) gaudy
(E) red

Ⓐ Ⓑ ● Ⓓ Ⓔ

(C) WHITE is the accepted opposite of BLACK. Red is only occasionally an opposite of black, as in checkers. Gray is a gradation between black and white, and bright and gaudy are qualities of color rather than colors.

1. IDYLLIC

(A) energetic
(B) lazy
(C) productive
(D) urban
(E) religious

Ⓐ Ⓑ Ⓒ Ⓓ Ⓔ

(D) URBAN, meaning related to the city, is the best opposite for IDYLLIC which means rural or pastoral or related to the country. Idyllic can also mean "peaceful." Were there no better opposite offered, energetic, (A), might be considered to be a near opposite. However, in this case, (D) is the *best* choice.

SENTENCE COMPLETIONS

DIRECTIONS: Each of the following questions consists of an incomplete sentence followed by five words or pairs of words. Choose that word or pair of words which, when substituted for the blank space or spaces, best completes the meaning of the sentence and mark the letter of your choice on your answer sheet.

Example:

A _____ person cannot be expected to resist _____.

(A) wealthy .. money
(B) religious .. temptation
(C) starving .. food
(D) peculiar .. quarreling
(E) witty .. tears

(C) The sentence implies that there is a necessary connection between something that cannot be resisted and an implied need. Of the five pairs of words, only (A) and (C) show a real, logical connection between the two words. Since a wealthy person has no need for money, clearly (C) is the *best* answer. A STARVING person cannot be expected to resist FOOD.

2. Those who feel that war is stupid and unnecessary think that to die on the battlefield is _____.

(A) courageous
(B) pretentious
(C) useless
(D) illegal
(E) impossible   Ⓐ Ⓑ Ⓒ Ⓓ Ⓔ

(C) The key to this answer is the attitude expressed—that war is stupid and unnecessary. Those who are antagonistic towards war would consider a battlefield death to be USELESS. While it is true that giving one's life on the field of battle is courageous, (A), that is not the answer in the context of this sentence.

VERBAL ANALOGIES

DIRECTIONS: Each of the following questions consists of a capitalized pair of words followed by five pairs of words lettered A to E. The capitalized words bear some meaningful relationship to each other. Choose the lettered pair of words whose relationship is most similar to that expressed by the capitalized pair and mark its letter on your answer sheet.

Example:

MYSTERY : CLUE ::

(A) book : reader
(B) fruit : bowl
(C) door : key
(D) detective : crime
(E) fry : pan

     Ⓐ Ⓑ ● Ⓓ Ⓔ

(C) A DOOR is unlocked by a KEY in the same way that a MYSTERY is unlocked by a CLUE. Detective and crime, (D), are somewhat related to mystery and clue, but the relationship between the two words within the pair does not parallel the relationship expressed by the original pair. A crime in no way unlocks a detective.

3. RACE : FATIGUE ::

(A) track : athlete
(B) contest : loser
(C) fast : hunger
(D) walking : running
(E) horse : sweaty   Ⓐ Ⓑ Ⓒ Ⓓ Ⓔ

(C) A FAST (a period of abstention from food) results in HUNGER; a RACE results in FATIGUE. The relationship is one of cause and effect. Choices (A) and (D) offer only an association relationship, not one of cause and effect. It is true that a horse becomes sweaty, (E), after a race, but a horse does not cause sweat. There is usually a loser in a contest, (B), but not necessarily—there could be a tie. Furthermore, fatigue and hunger are both states of being which result from an activity, whereas a loser is a person. (C) is clearly the best answer.

READING COMPREHENSION

DIRECTIONS: Below each of the following passages, you will find five questions or incomplete statements about the passage. Each statement or question is followed by five response options. Read the passage carefully. On the basis of what was stated or implied in the passage, select the option which *best* completes each statement or answers each question. You may refer to the passage as often as necessary. Mark the letter of your choice on your answer sheet.

During the past four decades the fishery scientists of the West have studied the dynamics of fish populations with the objective of determining the relation between the amount of fishing and the sustainable catch. They have developed a substantial body of theory that has been applied successfully to a large number of animal populations and has led to major improvement in the management of some of the major marine fisheries.

The theory has been developed for single-species (10) populations with man as a predator. Much of it is based on the Darwinian concept of a constant over-population of young that is reduced by density-dependent mortality resulting from intraspecific competition. The unfished population tends toward a maximum equilibrium size with a relatively high proportion of large, old individuals. As fishing increases, both population size and proportions of large, old individuals are reduced, but growth is

(20) increased and natural mortality is reduced. Fishing mortality eventually takes the place of most natural mortality. If the amount of fishing is increased too much, the individuals will tend to be taken before realizing their potential growth, and total yield will be reduced. The maximum sustainable yields can be taken at an intermediate population size that in some populations is about one-third to one-half the unfished population size.

(30) G. V. Nikolskii, of Moscow State University, develops his theory from a different approach. He is a non-Darwinian and is (he says) a non-mathematician; rather he considers himself an ecologist and a morphologist. He argues that Darwin's concept of constant overpopulation has led to neglect of the problem of protecting spawners and young fish. He argues also that Darwin's concept of a variety as an incipient species has led to extensive mathematical analysis of racial characteristics without understanding of the adaptive significance of the

(40) characters. Nikolskii considers the main laws of population dynamics to be concerned with the succession of generations: their birth, growth, and death. The details are governed by the relative rates of adaptation and environmental change. The mass and age structure of a population are the result of adaptation to the food supply. The rate of growth of individuals, the time of sexual maturity, and the accumulation of reserves vary according to the food supply. These factors in turn influence the success of

(50) reproduction in ways that tend to bring the size of the population into balance with its food supply.

4. The main concern of the researchers discussed in this passage is

(A) ecology as related to fishing
(B) effects of pollution on fish
(C) endangered species of fish
(D) commercial fishing
(E) development of fishing methods

(D) At first reading of this passage, one might get the impression that the researchers care about the fish. Careful reading of the first paragraph, especially ". . . the relation between the amount of fishing and the sustainable catch," reveals that the purpose of the research is commercial interest.

5. According to this passage, those theories based on Darwinian concepts assume fish population to be controlled mainly by the

(A) life expectancy within the species
(B) amount of fishing pressure on the species
(C) amount of food available to the species
(D) racial characteristics of the species
(E) size of the fish caught within a species

(B) The Darwinian theory is that overpopulation is controlled by natural mortality. The Darwinian theorists substitute fishing mortality for natural mortality and so attempt to control and manipulate population by controlling fishing pressure.

6. According to this passage, Nikolskii's theory is based on a concept that assumed fish population to be controlled mainly by the

(A) death rate within the species
(B) amount of fishing pressure on the species
(C) amount of food available to the species
(D) racial characteristics of the species
(E) size of the fish caught within a species

(C) Nikolskii feels that the food supply governs the success of reproduction, which he considers to be highly adaptive. See lines 46 to 49.

7. The author indicates that the main difference between the two theories is the

(A) amount of fish that can be harvested
(B) methods used to catch fish
(C) potential growth rate of fish
(D) cause of population variation in fish
(E) effect of food supply on the size of the fish

(D) The *cause* of population variation is a *theoretical* difference, hence (D) is the correct answer to the question. The other differences are practical and procedural.

8. Which of the following is NOT mentioned as affecting fish population?

(A) fishing pressure
(B) fishing methods
(C) food supply
(D) quality of environment
(E) management techniques

(B) The fishing method employed may well have an effect on the number of fish taken, but this article does not discuss fishing methods.

MATHEMATICS—PROBLEM SOLVING

Symbol references:

|| is parallel to   > is greater than
≦ is less than or equal to   < is less than
≧ is greater than or equal to   ⊥ is perpendicular to
∠ angle   △ triangle

DIRECTIONS: Solve each of the following problems, using available space on the page for your scratch work. Mark the letter of the correct answer on your answer sheet.

You may refer to the following data in solving the problems.

Notes: The diagrams which accompany problems should provide data helpful in working out the solutions. These diagrams are not necessarily drawn precisely to scale. Unless otherwise stated, all figures lie in the same plane. All numbers are real numbers.

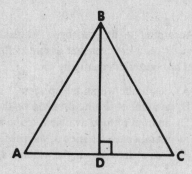

Triangle:

The angles of a triangle added together equal 180°. The angle BDC is a right angle; therefore,

(I) the area of triangle ABC = $\dfrac{AC \times BD}{2}$

(II) $AB^2 = AD^2 + DB^2$

Circle:

There are 360 degrees of arc in a circle.
The area of a circle of radius r = πr^2
The circumference of a circle = $2\pi r$
A straight angle has 180°.

9. In the figure, a rectangular piece of cardboard 18 inches by 24 inches is made into an open box by cutting a 5-inch square from each corner and building up the sides. What is the volume of the box in cubic inches?

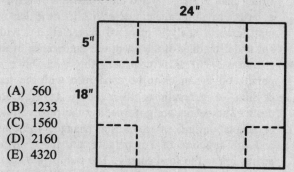

(A) 560
(B) 1233
(C) 1560
(D) 2160
(E) 4320

(A) The dimensions of the open box become:
length = 24 − 10 = 14 in.
width = 18 − 10 =   8 in.
height =   5 in.
 Hence, V = 14 · 8 · 5 = 560 cu. in.

MATHEMATICS—QUANTITATIVE COMPARISONS

DIRECTIONS: For each of the following questions, two quantities are given—one in Column A, the other in Column B. Compare the two quantities and mark your answer sheet as follows:
(A) if the quantity in Column A is greater
(B) if the quantity in Column B is greater
(C) if the two quantities are equal
(D) if the relationship cannot be determined from the information given.
NECESSARY INFORMATION:
• In each question, information concerning one or both of the quantities to be compared is centered above the entries in the two columns.

• A symbol that appears in any column represents the same thing in Column A as it does in Column B.

- All numbers used are real numbers; letters such as x, y, and t stand for real numbers.

- Assume that the position of points, angles, regions, and so forth are in the order shown and that all figures lie in a plane unless otherwise indicated.

- Figures are not necessarily drawn to scale.

Examples:

	Column A	Column B

E1. $a > 0$
$x > 0$

Column A: $a - x$

Column B: $a + x$

(B) The common information, $a > 0$ and $x > 0$, informs us that both a and x are positive numbers. The sum of two positive numbers is always greater than their difference.

E2. The average of
17, 19, 21, 23

The average of
16, 18, 20, 22

(A) The numbers in Column A are larger than the numbers in Column B, therefore their average must be greater.

E3.

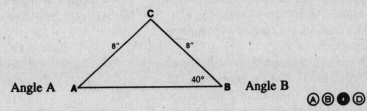

Angle A   Angle B

(C) $\triangle ABC$ is an isosceles $\triangle$. Since $\angle A$ is opposite a side which is equal in length to that side opposite $\angle B$, $\angle A$ must be equal to $\angle B$.

10.   *Column A*   *Column B*

$$x + y = -5$$
$$x - y = -1$$

$$x \qquad\qquad\qquad y$$

(B)

$$
\begin{array}{ll}
x + y = -5 & \text{substituting } x = -3 \\
x - y = -1 & x + y = -5 \\
2x = -6 & 3 + y = -5 \\
x = -3 & y = -2
\end{array}
$$

$$-2 > -3$$
$$\therefore \text{Column B} > \text{Column A}$$

SCORING AND REPORTING OF SCORES

Raw scores for each section of the PSAT are determined by recording one point for each question answered correctly and then subtracting from that total a fraction of the number of questions answered incorrectly. For most of the questions, all those with five answer choices, $\frac{1}{4}$ point is subtracted for each error. For Quantitative Comparisons, where there are only four response options, $\frac{1}{3}$ point is subtracted for each error.

The Educational Testing Service converts raw scores to scaled scores, which are reported on a scale of 20 to 80. The scaling of scores is meant to equalize for slight variations in difficulty for various editions of the exam. The booklet received by registrants for the PSAT includes a chart converting raw scores into scaled scores.

PSAT scaled scores are reported to high school principals about two months after the exam date. The principals, in turn, notify students of their scores. PSAT scores are also automatically reported to the National Merit Scholarship Corporation. No one else receives your scores without specific authorization from you. You may, at the time that you take the exam, request that your name be released to colleges which are actively recruiting students with your characteristics. This service is free. If you subscribe to it you may find yourself deluged with literature. You may also learn about some less well-known colleges which meet all of your requirements.

You will receive three separate PSAT scores—a Verbal score, a Mathematical score and a Selection Index score. The Selection Index score is the sum of twice the Verbal score plus the Mathematical score. The Selection Index is the score used to determine which candidates qualify as Semifinalists and Commended Students and also to screen candidates for special scholarships administered by the National Merit Scholarship Corporation.

CORRESPONDENCE ADDRESSES

Additional inquiries concerning the PSAT/NMSQT may be addressed to:

Educational Testing Service
Box 589
Princeton, NJ 08541

Inquiries regarding the scholarship programs should be addressed to:

National Merit Scholarship Corporation
One American Plaza
Evanston, IL 60201

HOW TO USE THIS BOOK

You will get the most benefit from this book if you use it with respect. By this we mean treat it seriously, follow instructions, observe time limits and do not cheat. We also mean that you should read every chapter and answer every question.

Find yourself a quiet spot with good light and a clear work space. Eliminate as many distractions as possible. Set aside specified periods of at least an hour for your PSAT preparation. In addition, reserve a number of two-hour stretches, for it is best to work straight through the two-hour exams.

Start at the beginning of the book. Read through each chapter carefully so that you can appreciate why you are studying, how to use the book and how to take the exam. Refer back to these chapters as needed. Be sure to reread the chapter on test-taking shortly before exam day.

Begin your active preparation by taking the Pretest in one two-hour sitting. Have your pencils sharpened beforehand so that you do not have to interrupt yourself. If you have a portable kitchen timer, bring it to your work area. If you have no timer, put a clock or watch in an easily visible spot. Tear out the answer sheet. Then, before you begin to read the directions for Section I, set the timer to fifty minutes or note the time. General instructions are given before the clock is started, but directions for answering questions must be read within the time limits. Allow yourself a very short, untimed break to stand up and stretch between sections.

If you finish a section before the time limit is up, check over your answers for that section. If the time runs out before you have completed a section, stop and mark the place where time ran out. Later on you will want to go back and answer the remaining questions just for the practice.

After you have devoted a full fifty minutes to each section of the exam, check your answers against the answer key. Calculate and enter your scores on the forms provided on the back of your answer sheet. Read the explanations which follow the answer key. Concentrate most on the explanations for those questions which you answered incorrectly and those questions which you got right by virtue of a lucky guess. But, be sure to read *all* of the explanations. By studying all the explanations, even for those questions you answered correctly, you may gain new insights into methods of reasoning out the answers.

Proceed through the entire book. Study the chapters which teach you how to answer the questions. Give extra time to those chapters dealing with the types of questions on which you showed weakness. Answer the practice questions and study the explanations.

Work with a dictionary. Look up *every* unfamiliar word in this book. If you run across a word you do not know while doing the exams, circle the word and look it up later. Look up words you find in the reading passages, new words from among answer choices, words you find in the explanations, words you meet in the study chapters. You are far more likely to remember a word which you have looked up for yourself than a word you have attempted to memorize from a long list. If you can understand every word used in this book, you have a broad-based vocabulary and are fully prepared for the verbal requirements of the exam.

Try another sample exam. After checking your answers, return to the study chapters that deal with the areas in which you still need help.

We strongly suggest that you plan to take at least two of these exams early in the morning. That is when the actual exam is given. If you are not a "morning person," that is, if you are usually at your best late in the day, then you should try to take all four sample exams in the morning. Set your alarm on a day when there is no school, eat a good breakfast and settle down to a practice exam. Train yourself to concentrate in the morning. Part of your preparation for the exam consists of gearing yourself to the early start.

Even if you feel that you have improved to the maximum of your ability, even if you are certain that you are ready, complete the book and read all of the explanations. The additional practice will add to your confidence and improve your scores.

TEST-TAKING TECHNIQUES

Your last minute preparations for the PSAT or for any exam are based strictly on common sense. They include assembling your materials the night before, getting a good night's sleep, awakening early enough so that you do not need to rush and eating a good breakfast. The only materials you need to bring to the PSAT are a few sharpened number two pencils with erasers. It is a good idea to wear a watch, as the room clock may be behind you or out of order.

Enter the room early enough to be able to choose a seat where you want to sit. Relax. The first half hour, or more, in the PSAT testing room will be spent filling out forms. You will be given detailed instructions for this procedure. Listen; read; follow the directions. The filling out of forms is not timed. Do not rush. The exam will not begin until everyone has finished these preliminary steps.

The test proctor will then give you general instructions for taking the exam. You will be told how to recognize the start and stop signals and how you will be notified of elapsed time. You will find out what to do if you have a problem, if all your pencils break or if a page is missing from your test booklet. Pay attention to the proctor's instructions. If you have any questions, ask them now.

When the signal is given, open your test booklet and READ.

- **READ** all directions carefully. The directions will probably be very similar to those in this book, but do not take anything for granted.

- **READ** every word of every question. Be alert for exclusionary words which might affect your answer—words like "not," "most," "all," "every," "except."

- **READ** all five choices before you mark your answer. It is statistically true that most errors are made when the correct answer is (E). Too many people mark the first answer that seems correct, without reading through all the choices to find out which answer is *best*.

If you read conscientiously, you are well on your way to mastering the exam. The following

suggestions comprise a comprehensive list for ready reference. Read them now before you attempt the practice exams in this book. Read them again before you take the PSAT. All are useful and important.

1. Mark your answers by completely blackening the oval of your choice.

2. Mark only ONE answer for each question, even if you think that more than one answer is correct. You must choose only one. If you mark more than one answer, the scoring machine will consider you wrong.

3. If you change your mind, erase completely. Leave no doubt as to which answer you mean.

4. Answer first the questions which you find easiest. Remember, you want to answer as many questions as possible. Put a mark in your test booklet next to the questions that you skipped so that you can find them quickly if you have time to go back to them.

5. If you skip a question, skip its answer space. Every question must be answered in the right place. Check often to be sure that your answer number corresponds to your question number. If you do find yourself "out of line" you must take the time to change your answers.

6. You are not required—or expected—to answer every question. You may leave any answer space blank, without penalty.

7. Guess if you wish. If you do not answer a question, you cannot earn any credit for it. An educated guess gives you a chance to get credit for a correct answer. However, an incorrect answer carries a $\frac{1}{4}$ point penalty ($\frac{1}{3}$ point for Quantitative Comparisons). You must weigh the odds.

8. Stay alert. Be aware of the risk of response errors, errors in which you mark the wrong answer because of a lapse in concentration.

Example: The correct answer to a Mathematics question is (B) d, and you mark (D) instead of (B).

9. Do not panic. If you do not finish Section I before time is called, do not worry. Many people do not finish, yet do very well on the questions they answer and earn high scores. At any rate, do not let your performance on Section I affect your performance on Section II.

10. Check and recheck. There is no bonus for leaving early. If you have completed the exam before the time is up, check Section II to be sure that each question is answered in the right space and that there is only one answer to each question. Return to the difficult questions which you skipped and try them again. Rethink those questions which you answered with some hesitancy.

Good luck!

PRETEST—MODEL EXAMINATION I

Section I
Time—50 minutes; 65 questions

DIRECTIONS: For each question, mark the letter preceding the word or phrase that is opposite or most nearly opposite in meaning to the capitalized word. Where more than one option appears to be correct, choose the *best* opposite.

Example:

HOT

(A) warm
(B) cool
(C) cold
(D) temperate
(E) humid

 Ⓐ Ⓑ ● Ⓓ Ⓔ

---

1. EULOGIZE

(A) bury
(B) engrave
(C) defend
(D) berate
(E) heal

2. DOUR

(A) gay
(B) engaged
(C) wealthy
(D) responsive
(E) gray

3. TRANQUILITY

(A) harm
(B) death
(C) concern
(D) discord
(E) knowledge

4. FORTUITOUS

(A) unfortunate
(B) strong
(C) designed
(D) fearful
(E) warlike

5. COGENT

(A) repetitive
(B) urgent
(C) complicated
(D) confused
(E) unconvincing

6. MUFTI

(A) scarf
(B) military
(C) irreligious
(D) necktie
(E) uniform

7. CANDID

(A) painted
(B) dishonest
(C) unimportant
(D) expected
(E) helpless

8. LOATHE

(A) reprieve
(B) formalize
(C) provoke
(D) eager
(E) love

9. PLACID

(A) rigid
(B) pliable
(C) impudent
(D) demure
(E) agitated

10. GRAPHIC

(A) tabular
(B) painted
(C) obscure
(D) incorrect
(E) inscribed

11. EXCISE

(A) forgive
(B) imprint
(C) produce
(D) insert
(E) deny

12. EMISSARY

(A) spy
(B) receptionist
(C) protector
(D) scribe
(E) dictator

13. PANACEA

(A) blessing
(B) poison
(C) triumph
(D) plunder
(E) confinement

14. SENTIMENTAL

(A) unwilling
(B) unequal
(C) unreliable
(D) unpardonable
(E) unresponsive

15. CLEFT

(A) lowered
(B) improved

(C) unmusical
(D) omitted
(E) unified

16. LEVITATE

(A) defend
(B) laugh at
(C) anchor
(D) criticize
(E) miniaturize

17. DIFFIDENT

(A) assertive
(B) interested
(C) happy
(D) companionable
(E) easy-going

18. USURP

(A) relinquish
(B) approach
(C) apologize
(D) motivate
(E) improve

19. DISCRETE

(A) orderly
(B) antisocial
(C) crude
(D) joking
(E) grouped

20. CHIMERICAL

(A) nimble
(B) realistic
(C) powerful
(D) underrated
(E) remarkable

DIRECTIONS: Each of the following questions consists of an incomplete sentence followed by five words or pairs of words. Choose that word or pair of words which, when substituted for the blank space or spaces, *best* completes the meaning of the sentence and mark the letter of your choice on your answer sheet.

(D) committees . . influenced
(E) solitude . . surrounded

Example:

In view of the extenuating circumstances and the defendant's youth, the judge recommended _____.

(A) conviction
(B) a defense
(C) a mistrial
(D) leniency
(E) life imprisonment   Ⓐ Ⓑ Ⓒ ● Ⓔ

25. A system of education should be _____ by the _____ of students it turns out, for quality is preferred to quantity.

(A) controlled . . intelligence
(B) justified . . number
(C) examined . . wealth
(D) judged . . caliber
(E) condemned . . ability

21. Custom has so _____ our language that we can _____ only what has been said before.

(A) freed . . write
(B) improved . . repeat
(C) changed . . understand
(D) enslaved . . say
(E) dominated . . hear

26. We seldom feel _____ when we are allowed to speak freely, but any _____ of our free speech brings anger.

(A) angry . . defense
(B) blessed . . restriction
(C) scholarly . . understanding
(D) enslaved . . misuse
(E) upset . . explanation

22. A few of the critics _____ the play, but in general they either disregarded or ridiculed it.

(A) mocked
(B) discredited
(C) criticized
(D) denounced
(E) appreciated

27. The worst team lost because it had many players who though not completely _____ were also not really _____.

(A) qualified . . agile
(B) clumsy . . incompetent
(C) inept . . proficient
(D) ungraceful . . amateurish
(E) experienced . . veterans

23. It is not the function of a newspaper to reflect on _____ but simply to record the _____, leaving conscience to the individual.

(A) morality . . present
(B) causes . . judgments
(C) deeds . . actions
(D) accuracy . . stories
(E) history . . events

28. Although the _____ of the legislature become law, the exact _____ of the law is the result of judicial interpretation.

(A) ideas . . enforcement
(B) bills . . wording
(C) works . . punishment
(D) words . . meaning
(E) ideals . . benefit

24. It is easier to formulate what is right in _____ than to carry out these ideas when _____ by people.

(A) abstraction . . encouraged
(B) theory . . effected
(C) general . . suggested

29. Since movies have become more _____, many people believe television to be _____.

(A) helpful . . utilitarian
(B) expensive . . necessary
(C) common . . inadequate
(D) costly . . useless
(E) exciting . . harmful

30. By suggesting that inmates be given some say in the operations of a prison, he certainly does not recommend that wardens should _____ authority and allow complete _____.

(A) renounce . . tyranny
(B) espouse . . freedom
(C) abandon . . repression
(D) personify . . chaos
(E) vacate . . anarchy

DIRECTIONS: Each of the following questions consists of a capitalized pair of words followed by five pairs of words lettered A to E. The capitalized words bear some meaningful relationship to each other. Choose the lettered pair of words whose relationship is most similar to that expressed by the capitalized pair and mark its letter on your answer sheet.

Example:

DAY : NIGHT ::

(A) sunlight : daylight
(B) solar : sun
(C) sun : moon
(D) hot : cool
(E) moon : star

31. CONTROL : ORDER ::

(A) joke : clown
(B) teacher : pupil
(C) disorder : climax
(D) anarchy : chaos
(E) government : legislator

32. WOOD : CARVE ::

(A) trees : sway
(B) paper : burn
(C) clay : mold
(D) pipe : blow
(E) statue : model

33. STATE : BORDER ::

(A) nation : state
(B) flag : loyalty
(C) Idaho : Montana
(D) planet : satellite
(E) property : fence

34. SOLDIER : REGIMENT ::

(A) navy : army
(B) lake : river
(C) star : constellation
(D) amphibian : frog
(E) flock : geese

35. APOGEE : PERIGEE ::

(A) dog : pedigree
(B) opposite : composite
(C) paradoxical : incredible
(D) effigy : statue
(E) inappropriate : apposite

36. ASYLUM : REFUGEE ::

(A) flight : escape
(B) peace : war
(C) lunatic : insanity
(D) accident : injury
(E) destination : traveler

37. WORRIED : HYSTERICAL ::

(A) hot : cold
(B) happy : ecstatic
(C) lonely : crowded
(D) happy : serious
(E) skilled : careful

38. PLAYER : TEAM ::

(A) fawn : doe
(B) book : story
(C) ball : bat
(D) fish : school
(E) tennis : racket

39. MOTH : CLOTHING ::

(A) egg : larva
(B) suit : dress
(C) hole : repair
(D) stigma : reputation
(E) mouse : closet

40. LINCOLN : NEBRASKA ::

(A) Washington : D.C.
(B) Trenton : New Jersey
(C) New York : U.S.
(D) Chicago : New York
(E) town : state

41. BOXER : GLOVES ::

(A) swimmer : mask
(B) librarian : glasses
(C) businessman : bills
(D) fruit : peddler
(E) bacteriologist : microscope

42. DECISION : CONSIDERATION ::

(A) gift : party
(B) plea : request
(C) greed : charity
(D) conference : constitution
(E) fulfillment : wish

43. DELUSION : MIRAGE ::

(A) haunter : specter
(B) imagination : concentration
(C) dream : reality
(D) mirror : glass
(E) desert : oasis

44. INSULT : INVULNERABLE ::

(A) success : capable
(B) poverty : miserable
(C) purchase : refundable
(D) assault : impregnable
(E) research : difficult

45. POISON : DEATH ::

(A) book : pages
(B) music : violin
(C) kindness : cooperation
(D) life : famine
(E) nothing : something

DIRECTIONS: Below each of the following passages, you will find five questions or incomplete statements about the passage. Each statement or question is followed by five response options. Read the passage carefully. On the basis of what was stated or implied in the passage, select the option which *best* completes each statement or answers each question. You may refer to the passage as often as necessary. Mark the letter of your choice on your answer sheet.

As befits a nation made up of immigrants from all over the Christian world, Americans have no distinctive Christmas symbols; but we have taken the symbols of all the nations and made them our own. The Christmas tree, the holly and the ivy, the mistletoe, the exchange of gifts, the myth of Santa Claus, the carols of all nations, the plum pudding and the wassail bowl are all elements in the American Christmas of the late twentieth century. Though we have no Christmas symbols of our own, the Ameri- (10) can Christmas still has a distinctive aura by virtue of two characteristic elements.

The first of these is that, as might be expected in a nation as dedicated to the carrying on of business as the American nation, the dominant role of the Christmas festivities has become to serve as a stimulus to retail business. The themes of Christmas advertising begin to appear as early as September, and the open season on Christmas shopping begins in November. Fifty years ago, Thanksgiving Day was (20) regarded as the opening day of the season for Christmas shopping; today, the season opens immediately after Halloween. Thus virtually a whole month has been added to the Christmas season—for shopping purposes.

Second, the Christmas season of festivities has insensibly combined with the New Year's celebration into one lengthened period of Saturnalia. This starts with the "office parties" a few days before Christmas, continues on Christmas Eve, now the (30) occasion in America of one of two large-scale revels that mark the season—save that the Christmas Eve revels are often punctuated by a visit to one of the larger churches for midnight Mass, which has increasingly tended to become blended into a part of the entertainment aspect of the season—and continues in spirited euphoria until New Year's Eve, the second of the large-scale revels. New Year's Day is spent resting, possibly regretting one's excesses, watching a football "bowl" game, and indulging in (40) the lenitive of one's choice. January 2 marks, for most, the return of temperance and decorum and business as usual.

46. The author's attitude toward the manner in which Christmas is celebrated in the United States is one of

(A) great disapproval
(B) humorous confusion
(C) laudatory acclaim
(D) objective appraisal
(E) great optimism

47. A statement which is most closely associated with the philosophy expressed in this passage is the following:

(A) In Puritan Massachusetts Bay Colony, it was a crime, punishable by the stocks, to observe Christmas.

(B) Christmas customs in Europe and America that are associated with the Feast of the Nativity were not originally Christian.

(C) Rudolph the Red Nosed Reindeer has become a traditional aspect of Christmas, yet he was created not long ago by commercial interests.

(D) The custom of wassailing continued well into the nineteenth century.

(E) In widely separated areas of the world, religious observances tend to cluster around striking natural phenomena.

48. According to the passage, Americans in regard to the Christmas season have

(A) demonstrated great originality

(B) little justification for merrymaking

(C) departed completely from the example of early settlers

(D) made little attempt to promote a variety of entertainment

(E) borrowed extensively from the traditions of other countries

49. Which of the following does the author point out as being distinctively American?

(A) The selling of Christmas artifacts as part of the season's activities.

(B) The extension of Christmas festivities from Thanksgiving to New Year's Eve.

(C) The extensive use of the Santa Claus myth.

(D) The attending of sports activities on New Year's Day.

(E) The spirited euphoria on New Year's Eve.

50. The "distinctive aura" mentioned in line 11 refers to

(A) the consistent depiction of the baby Jesus and the Holy Family with halos above their heads

(B) migraine headaches caused by the tension of Christmas shopping

(C) Christmas lights and decorations

(D) the unique atmosphere of Christmas in America

(E) the familiar sounds of Christmas, as, for instance, the Salvation Army bell

As America has grown in size and in diversity of population, political power is no longer wielded by one or two influential groups. Elected politicians appear to govern the land, but they are influenced and manipulated by a multitude of special interest groups. Some of these groups are highly organized and well financed. Since these groups tend to focus on one or two issues from the standpoint of their own self-interest, the pressure they exert can sometimes work against the national interest. (10)

One such pressure group is the National Rifle Association (NRA). Spokesmen for this influential lobby cite the Second Amendment to the Constitution, that which guarantees the right of all citizens to own and bear arms, as justification for their position. They claim that every citizen should be permitted to own a gun, provided that he or she can demonstrate proficiency in its care and use and familiarity with rules of safety. According to the NRA, a person has the *right* to own a gun even if he does not *need* to (20) own a gun. These spokesmen claim that if many people owned guns, criminals might be deterred because they could expect retaliatory fire at any time. A slogan of the NRA is, "If guns are outlawed, only outlaws will have guns."

The danger in this position is that guns, being easy to procure, fall into the hands of careless people. Thus, there are many accidental deaths occurring from mishandling of guns. The barrel may not be checked before cleaning. Children may find a loaded (30) gun and play with it.

More dangerous still are the crimes of passion which occur when a gun is readily available. An argument which might have led to shouts, curses and a fist fight, is quickly and tragically settled when a gun is in easy reach. True, knives will still be available, but a knife is a much more personal weapon. Assailant must come in physical contact with victim to do damage with a knife. Many a hot-head would become squeamish before plunging a (40) knife into another human being.

Most frightening to the nation at large is the availability of guns to the mentally unbalanced. These people are generally not criminals. They would not necessarily go to the trouble of acquiring guns illegally. However, to such persons, possession

of a gun is an overwhelming temptation to use it. Thus, snipers have murdered with no provocation. "Son of Sam" shot upon the urging of "voices."
(50) Civil rights leaders have been shot out of unleashed hatred for their causes. Public figures have been gunned down by fanatical foes. Innocent private citizens have been shot by "sick" persons with irrational grudges.

Despite all the evidence of the harm unrestricted gun ownership can cause, the NRA persists in its position. Furthermore, its influence seems out of proportion to its membership. In every session of Congress, the will of the NRA prevails. A majority
(60) of Congressmen is persuaded by the arguments and the show of political power and invariably defeats gun control legislation.

51. The author of this passage

(A) agrees with the position of the National Rifle Association
(B) disagrees in principle with the concept of lobbying
(C) would like to see the Second Amendment repealed
(D) is puzzled by the power of the NRA
(E) feels threatened by snipers

52. The purpose of this passage is to

(A) repeal gun control laws
(B) threaten lobbyists
(C) inform the public about the activities of lobbyists
(D) advocate a pending law
(E) state facts about gun ownership

53. The slogan "If guns are outlawed only outlaws will have guns" (line 24–25) means

(A) unlawful use of guns is a phenomenon of the old west
(B) gun control laws would legislate that only criminals could own guns
(C) out-of-season hunting regulations are sometimes violated
(D) policemen should not use guns
(E) if law-abiding citizens do not have guns, they will be vulnerable

54. The power of lobbyists is enhanced by
   I. Financial resources
   II. Political threats
   III. Articulate spokesmen.

According to the passage, which of the above is/are instrumental in helping the NRA to defeat gun control legislation?

(A) I alone
(B) I and III
(C) II and III
(D) I and II
(E) I, II and III

55. According to the NRA, a person should be able to own a gun if he

(A) knows how to use it
(B) works in a high-crime neighborhood
(C) likes to go hunting
(D) teaches riflery
(E) believes in the Constitution

Monseigneur, one of the great lords in power at the Court, held his fortnightly reception in his grand hotel in Paris. Monseigneur was in his inner room, his sanctuary of sanctuaries, the Holiest of Holiests to the crowd of worshippers in the suite of rooms without. Monseigneur was about to take his chocolate. Monseigneur could swallow a great many things with ease, and was by some few sullen minds supposed to be rather rapidly swallowing France; but, his morning's chocolate could not so much as (10) get into the throat of Monseigneur without the aid of four strong men besides the Cook.

Yes. It took four men, all four ablaze with gorgeous decoration, and the Chief of them unable to exist with fewer than two gold watches in his pocket, emulative of the noble and chaste fashion set by Monseigneur, to conduct the happy chocolate to Monseigneur's lips. One lackey carried the chocolate-pot into the sacred presence; a second milled and frothed the chocolate with the little in- (20) strument he bore for that function; a third presented the favoured napkin; a fourth (he of the two gold watches) poured the chocolate out. It was impossible for Monseigneur to dispense with one of these attendants on the chocolate and hold his high place under the admiring Heavens. Deep would have been the blot upon his escutcheon if his chocolate had been ignobly waited on by only three men; he must have died of two.

Monseigneur had been out at a little supper last (30) night, where the Comedy and the Grand Opera were charmingly represented. Monseigneur was out at a little supper most nights, with fascinating company.

So polite and so impressible was Monseigneur that the Comedy and the Grand Opera had far more influence with him in the tiresome articles of state affairs and state secrets than the needs of all France. A happy circumstance for France, as the like always is for all countries similarly favoured!—always was (40) for England (by way of example) in the regretted days of the merry Stuart who sold it.

Monseigneur had one truly noble idea of general public business which was to let everything go on in its own way; of particular public business Monseigneur had the other truly noble idea that it must all go his way—tend to his own power and pocket. Of his pleasures, general and particular, Monseigneur had the other truly noble idea that the world was made for them. The text of his order (altered from the (50) original by only a pronoun, which is not much) ran: ''The earth and the fulness thereof are mine, saith Monseigneur.''

56. The locale of this passage is

   (A) the opera
   (B) a sweet shop
   (C) the field of battle
   (D) an apartment
   (E) a church

57. The chronological placement is the

   (A) twentieth century
   (B) eighteenth century
   (C) sixteenth century
   (D) fourteenth century
   (E) indefinite past or future

58. Monseigneur represents

   (A) a person who elicits sympathy
   (B) a simpleton who cannot provide for himself
   (C) a profligate who cares little about others
   (D) an intellectual who dabbles in business matters
   (E) a miser who has moments of extravagance

59. The style of the passage suggests that it is part of

   (A) an historical document
   (B) a textbook on sociology
   (C) an essay against political favoritism
   (D) a magazine article on good etiquette
   (E) a story about abuse of power

60. The author is, with his reference to Monseigneur, using a literary device called

   (A) onomatopoeia
   (B) denouement
   (C) symbolism
   (D) psychogenesis
   (E) euphemism

However important we may regard school life to be, there is no gainsaying the fact that children spend more time at home than in the classroom. Therefore, the great influence of parents cannot be ignored or discounted by the teacher. They can become strong allies of the school personnel or they can consciously or unconsciously hinder and thwart curricular objectives.

Administrators have been aware of the need to keep parents apprised of the newer methods used in (10) schools. Many principals have conducted workshops explaining such matters as the reading readiness program, manuscript writing and developmental mathematics.

Moreover, the classroom teacher, with the permission of the supervisors, can also play an important role in enlightening parents. The informal tea and the many interviews carried on during the year, as well as new ways of reporting pupils' progress, can significantly aid in achieving a harmonious interplay (20) between school and home.

To illustrate, suppose that a father has been drilling Junior in arithmetic processes night after night. In a friendly interview, the teacher can help the parent sublimate his natural paternal interest into productive channels. He might be persuaded to let Junior participate in discussing the family budget, buying the food, using a yardstick or measuring cup at home, setting the clock, calculating mileage on a trip and engaging in scores of other activities that (30) have a mathematical basis.

If the father follows the advice, it is reasonable to assume that he will soon realize his son is making satisfactory progress in mathematics and, at the same time, enjoying the work.

Too often, however, teachers' conferences with parents are devoted to petty accounts of children's misdemeanors, complaints about laziness and poor work habits, and suggestions for penalties and rewards at home. (40)

What is needed is a more creative approach in which the teacher, as a professional adviser, plants ideas in parents' minds for the best utilization of the many hours that the child spends out of the class-room.

In this way, the school and the home join forces in fostering the fullest development of youngsters' capacities.

61. The author directly discusses the fact that

   (A) parents drill their children too much in arithmetic
   (B) principals have explained the new art programs to parents
   (C) a father can have his son help him construct articles at home
   (D) a parent's misguided efforts can be properly directed
   (E) there is not sufficient individual instruction in the classroom

62. It can reasonably be inferred that the author

   (A) is satisfied with present relationships between home and school
   (B) feels that the traditional program in mathematics is slightly superior to the developmental program
   (C) believes that schools are woefully lacking in guidance personnel
   (D) feels that parent-teacher interviews can be made much more constructive than they are at present
   (E) is of the opinion that teachers of this generation are inferior to those of the last generation

63. The author implies that

   (A) participation in interesting activities relating to a subject improves one's achievement in that area
   (B) too many children are lazy and have poor work habits
   (C) school principals do more than their share in interpreting the curriculum to the parents
   (D) only a small part of the school day should be set apart for drilling in arithmetic
   (E) teachers should occasionally make home visits to parents

64. The author's attitude toward supervisors is one of

   (A) disdain
   (B) indifference
   (C) indecision
   (D) suspicion
   (E) approval

65. We may infer that the writer of the article does not favor

   (A) a father's helping his son with the latter's studies
   (B) suggestions by the teacher to a parent in regard to improving the student's scholastic average
   (C) written communications to the parent from the teacher
   (D) having the parent observe lessons which the children are being taught
   (E) principal-parent conferences rather than teacher-parent conferences

END OF SECTION I

IF YOU COMPLETE THIS SECTION BEFORE TIME IS UP, CHECK OVER YOUR WORK.

Section II
Time—50 minutes; 50 questions

DIRECTIONS: Solve each of the following problems, using available space on the page for your scratch work. Mark the letter of the correct answer on your answer sheet.
   You may refer to the following data in solving the problems.

Triangle:

The angles of a triangle added together equal 180°.
The angle BDC is a right angle; therefore,

   (I) the area of triangle ABC $= \dfrac{AC \times BD}{2}$

   (II) $AB^2 = AD^2 + DB^2$

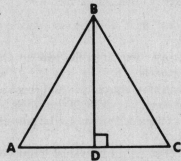

Circle:

There are 360° of arc in a circle.
The area of a circle of radius r $= \pi r^2$
The circumference of a circle $= 2\pi r$
A straight angle has 180°.

Symbol references:

∥ is parallel to	> is greater than
≦ is less than or equal to	< is less than
≧ is greater than or equal to	⊥ is perpendicular to
∠ angle	△ triangle

Notes: The diagrams which accompany problems should provide data helpful in working out the solutions. These diagrams are not necessarily drawn precisely to scale. Unless otherwise stated, all figures lie in the same plane. All numbers are real numbers.

1. Of the following the one that is *not* a meaning of $\frac{2}{3}$ is

   (A) 1 of the 3 equal parts of 2
   (B) 2 of the 3 equal parts of 1
   (C) 2 divided by 3
   (D) a ratio of 2 to 3
   (E) 4 of the 6 equal parts of 2

2. If the average weight of boys of John's age and height is 105 lbs. and if John weighs 110% of average, then John weighs

   (A) 110 lbs.
   (B) 110.5 lbs.
   (C) 106.05 lbs.
   (D) 126 lbs.
   (E) 115½ lbs.

3. On a house plan on which 2 inches represents 5 feet, the length of a room measures 7½ inches. The actual length of the room is

   (A) 12½ feet
   (B) 15¾ feet
   (C) 17½ feet
   (D) 18¾ feet
   (E) 13¾ feet

Questions 4–7 are to be answered with reference to the following diagram.

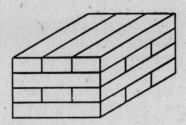

The figure shown in the diagram is made of pieces of plastic, each piece half a centimeter thick and one centimeter wide.

4. What is the volume of the figure?

   (A) 12 cu cm
   (B) 18 cu cm
   (C) 27 cu cm
   (D) 36 cu cm
   (E) cannot be determined from the given information

5. How many pieces are touched by at least 8 other pieces?

   (A) 1
   (B) 2
   (C) 3
   (D) 4
   (E) 5

6. If all pieces had been cut from one strip of plastic, how long a piece of $\frac{1}{2}$ cm × 1 cm material would have been required?

   (A) 15 cm
   (B) 18 cm
   (C) 27 cm
   (D) 12 cm
   (E) 36 cm

7. What is the total surface in square centimeters of all the pieces?

   (A) 10
   (B) 18
   (C) 72
   (D) 120
   (E) 42

8. ABCD is a parallelogram, and DE = EC

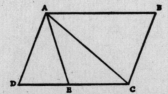

What is the ratio of triangle ADE to the area of the parallelogram?

(A) 1:2
(B) 1:3
(C) 2:5
(D) 1:4
(E) cannot be determined from the given information

9. If pencils are bought at 35 cents per dozen and sold at 3 for 10 cents the total profit on 5½ dozen is

(A) 25 cents
(B) 27½ cents
(C) 28½ cents
(D) 31½ cents
(E) 35 cents

10. Of the following, the one which may be used correctly to compute $26 \times 3\frac{1}{2}$ is

(A) $(26 \times 30) + (26 \times \frac{1}{2})$
(B) $(20 \times 3) + (6 \times 3\frac{1}{2})$
(C) $(20 \times 3\frac{1}{2}) + (6 \times 3)$
(D) $(20 \times 3) + (26 \times \frac{1}{2}) + (6 \times 3\frac{1}{2})$
(E) $(26 \times \frac{1}{2}) + (20 \times 3) + (6 \times 3)$

Questions 11 to 15 are to be answered with reference to the following explanation and table.

Ten judges were asked to judge the relative sweetness of five compounds (A, B, C, D, and E) by the method of paired comparisons. In judging each of the possible pairs they were required to state unequivocally which of the two compounds was the sweeter—a judgment of equality or no difference was not permitted.

The results of their judgments are summarized in the table below. In studying the table, note that each cell entry shows the number of comparisons in which the "row" compound was judged to be sweeter than the "column" compound.

	A	B	C	D	E
A		5	8	10	2
B	5		3	9	6
C	2	7		7	8
D	0	1	3		4
E	8	4	2	6	

11. How many comparisons did each judge make?

(A) 5
(B) 10
(C) 15
(D) 20
(E) 25

12. Which compound was judged to be sweetest?

(A) A
(B) B
(C) C
(D) D
(E) E

13. Which compound was judged to be least sweet?

(A) A
(B) B
(C) C
(D) D
(E) E

14. Which of the following statements is most nearly correct?

(A) There was almost perfect agreement among the ten judges.
(B) The clearest discrimination was between B and C.
(C) The judges were not expert in discriminating sweetnesses.
(D) Compound D was most clearly discriminated from the other four compounds.
(E) Compounds C and E were judged to have the same sweetness.

15. Between which two compounds was the discrimination least consistent?

(A) A and D
(B) B and E
(C) C and E
(D) C and D
(E) A and B

DIRECTIONS: For each of the following questions, two quantities are given—one in Column A, the other in Column B. Compare the two quantities and mark your answer sheet as follows:
(A) if the quantity in Column A is greater
(B) if the quantity in Column B is greater
(C) if the quantities are equal
(D) if the relationship cannot be determined from the information given.

NECESSARY INFORMATION:
• In each question, information concerning one or both of the quantities to be compared is centered above the entries in the two columns.

• A symbol that appears in any column represents the same thing in Column A as it does in Column B.

• All numbers used are real numbers; letters such as x, y and t stand for real numbers.

• Assume that the position of points, angles, regions and so forth are in the order shown and that all figures lie in a plane unless otherwise indicated.

• Figures are not necessarily drawn to scale.

Column A	Column B

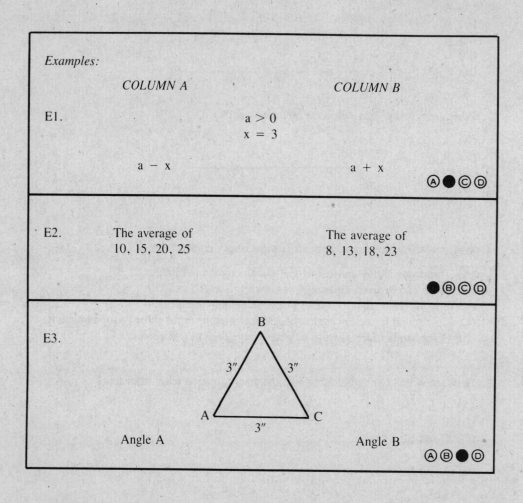

Examples:

	COLUMN A	COLUMN B
E1.	$a > 0$ $x = 3$	
	$a - x$	$a + x$ Ⓐ ● Ⓒ Ⓓ
E2.	The average of 10, 15, 20, 25	The average of 8, 13, 18, 23 ● Ⓑ Ⓒ Ⓓ
E3.	Angle A	Angle B Ⓐ Ⓑ ● Ⓓ

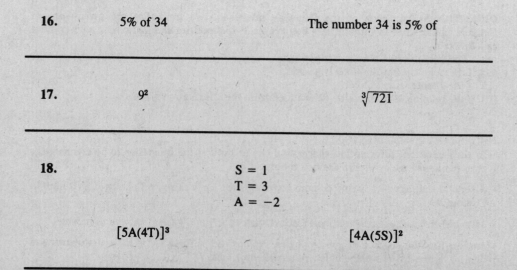

16.	5% of 34	The number 34 is 5% of

17.	9^2	$\sqrt[3]{721}$

18.

$$S = 1$$
$$T = 3$$
$$A = -2$$

$[5A(4T)]^3$	$[4A(5S)]^2$

	Column A	Column B

19.

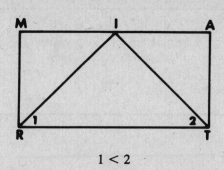

$$1 < 2$$

IR   IT

20. $$4 > x > -3$$

$x/3$ $3/x$

21. $\frac{2}{3} + \frac{3}{7}$ $\frac{16}{21} - \frac{3}{7}$

22.

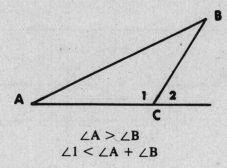

$$\angle A > \angle B$$
$$\angle 1 < \angle A + \angle B$$

$\angle A + \angle B$ $\angle 2$

23. $$Y = \text{an odd integer}$$

The numerical value of Y^2 The numerical value of Y^3

Column A	*Column B*

24. $8 + 6 \div 3 - 7(2)$ $\qquad\qquad$ $6 + 8 \div 2 - 7(3)$

25.

$$N * A = 1/N^2 + A/2$$

Substitute the following values of
N * A into the equation.

$\frac{2}{3} * \frac{1}{3}$ $\qquad\qquad\qquad\qquad\qquad$ $\frac{1}{5} * \frac{3}{5}$

---

26. $\frac{3}{4}$ of $\frac{9}{9}$ $\qquad\qquad\qquad\qquad\qquad$ $\frac{9}{9} \cdot \frac{3}{4}$

27.

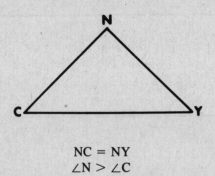

NC = NY
$\angle N > \angle C$

NC $\qquad\qquad\qquad\qquad\qquad$ CY

28.

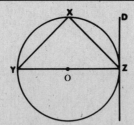

XYZ is inscribed in circle O and
DZ is tangent to circle O.

$\angle$YXZ $\qquad\qquad\qquad\qquad\qquad$ $\angle$DZY

---

29. A given chord in $\qquad\qquad$ The radius of the same
a given circle. $\qquad\qquad\qquad$ circle.

---

30. $9^{-\frac{1}{2}}$ $\frac{1}{3}$

---

31. $5(\frac{2}{3})^{\circ}$ $(25)^{\frac{1}{2}}$

---

32. $1/\sqrt{3}$ $\frac{1}{3}\sqrt{3}$

DIRECTIONS: Solve each of the following problems, using available space on the page for your scratch work. Mark the letter of the correct answer on your answer sheet.

33. A piece of wood 35 feet, 6 inches long was used to make 4 shelves of equal length. The length of each shelf was

(A) 9 feet, $1\frac{1}{2}$ inches
(B) 8 feet, $10\frac{1}{2}$ inches
(C) 7 feet, $10\frac{1}{2}$ inches
(D) 7 feet, $1\frac{1}{2}$ inches
(E) 6 feet, $8\frac{1}{2}$ inches

34. A class punch ball team won 2 games and lost 10. The fraction of its games won is correctly expressed as

(A) $\frac{1}{6}$
(B) $\frac{1}{5}$
(C) $\frac{4}{5}$
(D) $\frac{5}{6}$
(E) $\frac{1}{10}$

35. 10 to the fifth power may correctly be expressed as

(A) 10×5
(B) 5^{10}
(C) $5\sqrt{10}$
(D) $10 \times 10 \times 10 \times 10 \times 10$
(E) $10^{10} \div 10^2$

36. The total number of eighths in two wholes and three fourths is

(A) 11
(B) 14
(C) 19
(D) 22
(E) 24

37. The difference between one hundred five thousand eighty-four and ninety-three thousand seven hundred nine is

    (A) 37,215
    (B) 12,131
    (C) 56,294
    (D) 56,375
    (E) 11,375

38. A recipe for a cake calls for $2\frac{1}{2}$ cups of milk and 3 cups of flour. With this recipe, a cake was baked using 14 cups of flour. How many cups of milk were required?

    (A) $10\frac{1}{3}$
    (B) $10\frac{3}{4}$
    (C) 11
    (D) $11\frac{3}{5}$
    (E) $11\frac{2}{3}$

39. If the profit gained on the sale of an article is 10% of the selling price, and the original cost of the article is $12.60, the article must be marked for sale at

    (A) $13.66
    (B) $13.86
    (C) $11.34
    (D) $12.48
    (E) $14.00

40. A certain type of board is sold only in lengths of multiples of 2 feet from 6 ft. to 24 ft. A builder needs a large quantity of this type of board in $5\frac{1}{2}$ foot lengths. For minimum waste, the lengths to be ordered should be

    (A) 6 ft.
    (B) 12 ft.
    (C) 24 ft.
    (D) 22 ft.
    (E) 18 ft.

41. The tiles in the floor of a bathroom are $\frac{15}{16}$-inch squares. The cement between the tiles is $\frac{1}{16}$ inch. There are 3,240 individual tiles in this floor. The area of the floor is

    (A) 225 sq. yds.
    (B) 2.5 sq. yds.
    (C) 250 sq. ft.
    (D) 22.5 sq. yds.
    (E) 225 sq. ft.

42. A group of 15 children received the following scores in a reading test: 36 36 30 30 30 29 27 27 27 26 26 26 26 18 13. What was the median score?

    (A) 25.4
    (B) 26
    (C) 27
    (D) 30
    (E) 24.5

43. Of the following the one that is *not* equivalent to 376 is

(A) (3 × 100) + (6 × 10) + 16
(B) (2 × 100) + (17 × 10) + 6
(C) (3 × 100) + (7 × 10) + 6
(D) (2 × 100) + (16 × 10) + 6
(E) (2 × 100) + (7 × 10) + 106

44. A man bought a TV set that was listed at $160. He was given successive discounts of 20% and 10%. The price he paid was

(A) $112.00
(B) $115.20
(C) $119.60
(D) $129.60
(E) $118.20

45. In the figure, ST is tangent to the circle at T. RT is a diameter. If RS = 12, and ST = 8, what is the area of the circle?

(A) 5π
(B) 8π
(C) 20π
(D) 40π
(E) 9π

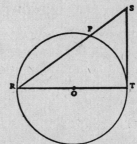

46. The radius of a circle which has a circumference equal to the perimeter of a hexagon whose sides are each 22 inches long is closest in length to which one of the following?

(A) 7
(B) 21
(C) 14
(D) 28
(E) 24

47. If a plane starts from New York at 11 P.M. Eastern Daylight Saving Time and travels for 6 hours to California, the time of arrival in Pacific Standard Time is

(A) 12 midnight
(B) 1 A.M.
(C) 2 A.M.
(D) 3 A.M.
(E) 4 A.M.

48. $1\frac{1}{4}$ subtracted from its reciprocal is

(A) $\frac{1}{5}$
(B) $-\frac{1}{5}$
(C) $\frac{9}{20}$
(D) $-\frac{9}{20}$
(E) $-\frac{1}{20}$

49. If each of the dimensions of a rectangle is increased 100%, the area is increased

(A) 100%
(B) 200%
(C) 300%
(D) 400%
(E) 500%

50. The total number of feet in x yards, y feet and z inches is

(A) $3x + y + \dfrac{z}{12}$

(B) $12(x + y + z)$

(C) $x + y + z$

(D) $\dfrac{x}{36} + \dfrac{y}{12} + z$

(E) $x + 3y + 36z$

END OF EXAMINATION

IF YOU FINISH BEFORE TIME IS CALLED, CHECK OVER YOUR WORK ON SECTION II. DO NOT RETURN TO SECTION I.

MODEL EXAMINATION I—ANSWER KEY

Section I

1. D	14. E	27. C	40. B	53. E
2. A	15. E	28. D	41. E	54. B
3. D	16. C	29. B	42. E	55. A
4. C	17. A	30. E	43. A	56. D
5. E	18. A	31. D	44. D	57. B
6. E	19. E	32. C	45. C	58. C
7. B	20. B	33. E	46. D	59. E
8. E	21. D	34. C	47. C	60. C
9. E	22. E	35. E	48. E	61. D
10. C	23. A	36. E	49. B	62. D
11. D	24. E	37. B	50. D	63. A
12. B	25. D	38. D	51. D	64. E
13. B	26. B	39. D	52. C	65. E

Section II

1. E	11. B	21. A	31. C	41. B
2. E	12. A	22. C	32. C	42. C
3. D	13. D	23. D	33. B	43. D
4. B	14. D	24. A	34. A	44. B
5. B	15. E	25. B	35. D	45. C
6. E	16. B	26. C	36. D	46. B
7. D	17. A	27. B	37. E	47. B
8. D	18. B	28. C	38. E	48. D
9. B	19. A	29. D	39. E	49. C
10. E	20. D	30. C	40. D	50. A

EXPLANATORY ANSWERS

SECTION I

1. **(D)** BERATE means to scold. EULOGIZE means to praise.

2. **(A)** GAY means bright and lively. DOUR means gloomy and sullen.

3. **(D)** DISCORD means strife and contention. TRANQUILITY means serenity and calm.

4. **(C)** DESIGNED means intended or planned. FORTUITOUS means accidental or occurring by chance. The usual connotation of "fortuitous" is "lucky accident," but fortuitous does not necessarily mean lucky. Therefore, while (A), unfortunate, might be a correct answer, (C), designed, is the *best* answer.

5. **(E)** UNCONVINCING. COGENT means convincing.

6. **(E)** UNIFORM. Mufti means civilian clothes.

7. **(B)** DISHONEST. CANDID means frank, open and honest.

8. **(E)** LOVE. LOATHE means hate. Eager, (D), is the opposite of *loath*, which means reluctant.

9. **(E)** AGITATED means shaken and excited. PLACID means undisturbed and calm.

10. **(C)** OBSCURE means indistinct or vague. GRAPHIC means sharply defined or clearly described.

11. **(D)** INSERT means to put in. EXCISE means to cut out. Imprint, (B), means to put *on*, rather than *in*. The *best* opposite of *out* is *in*.

12. **(B)** A RECEPTIONIST is employed to stay within limited confines and to *receive* callers. An EMISSARY is *sent out* on missions as an agent of his employers.

13. **(B)** A POISON harms, injures or makes ill. A PANACEA is a remedy or cure.

14. **(E)** UNRESPONSIVE means insensitive in perception or feeling. SENTIMENTAL means highly sensitive and deeply emotional.

15. **(E)** UNIFIED. CLEFT means divided.

16. **(C)** ANCHOR means to secure firmly. LEVITATE means to rise or float in the air.

17. **(A)** ASSERTIVE means aggressive. DIFFIDENT means timid.

18. **(A)** RELINQUISH means to give up power. USURP means to seize power without the right to it.

19. **(E)** GROUPED. DISCRETE means separate. Crude, (C), is the opposite of *discreet*, which means unobtrusive and modest.

20. **(B)** REALISTIC. CHIMERICAL means imaginary.

21. **(D)** The sense of the sentence calls for a word with a negative connotation in the first blank; therefore we need consider only (D) and (E). Of these choices, ENSLAVED .. SAY, (D) is clearly the better completion.

22. **(E)** Since it is stated that most critics disregarded or ridiculed the play, the few critics remaining must have done the opposite, or APPRECIATED the work.

23. **(A)** Since conscience (the internal faculty that decides on the moral quality of one's deeds) is left to the individual, the newspaper should not reflect on MORALITY (conformity to the rules of right conduct), but simply record the PRESENT.

24. **(E)** Deciding what is right when one is alone (in SOLITUDE) is easier than doing the right thing when others are all around you (when SURROUNDED by people).

25. **(D)** If "quality is preferred to quantity" in an educational system, then the measure by which that system should be JUDGED is the CALIBER (degree of ability or merit) of the students it produces.

26. **(B)** Freedom of speech is something we take for granted, so we do not feel BLESSED when

allowed to exercise this freedom; however, we do become angry when any RESTRICTION (limit) is imposed on our right to speak freely.

27. **(C)** The qualities attributed to the players on the worst team must be opposites for comparison and adjectives for parallelism within the sentence. INEPT which means awkward and PROFICIENT which means skilled comprise the only choice which meets both requirements.

28. **(D)** It is the function of the legislature to write laws (their WORDS become law). It is the function of the judiciary to interpret the words of the law (to determine their MEANING).

29. **(B)** Movies and television are both media of entertainment. The sentence compares the two media in terms of their cost, stating that many people believe television (which is free after the initial investment in the set) is NECESSARY because movies have become so EXPENSIVE (and therefore out of reach for many people.)

30. **(E)** Saying that prisoners should have a voice in the operation of the prison is not saying that prison officials should VACATE (give up and leave) authority and allow ANARCHY (chaos resulting from lack of governmental rule or control) to reign.

31. **(D)** ANARCHY (lack of government or control) results in CHAOS (disorder); CONTROL of a group results in ORDER. The relationship is one of *cause and effect*.

32. **(C)** One may MOLD CLAY to create an object just as one may CARVE WOOD to create an object. One may also blow a pipe, but the element of creation is lacking from choice (D). Likewise, one may model a statue, but choice (E) is lacking the medium of creation. The relationship is of both *function* and *purpose*.

33. **(E)** A FENCE separates one PROPERTY from another; a BORDER separates one STATE from another. This is a *functional* relationship.

34. **(C)** A STAR is a member of a CONSTELLATION; a SOLDIER is a member of his REGIMENT. The relationship is that of part to whole. Do not be misled by choice (E) in which the relationship is that of *whole to part*.

35. **(E)** INAPPROPRIATE is the opposite of APPOSITE (appropriate); APOGEE (the point in its orbit at which a satellite is farthest from the earth) is the opposite of PERIGEE (that point in a satellite's orbit at which it is closest to the earth). The relationship is that of *antonyms*.

36. **(E)** His DESTINATION is the goal of a TRAVELER; ASYLUM is the goal of the REFUGEE. This is a *purposeful relationship*.

37. **(B)** One who is HAPPY may become ECSTATIC (overwhelmed by joy); one who is WORRIED may become HYSTERICAL (overwhelmed by fear). The relationship is one of *degree*.

38. **(D)** A FISH is part of a SCHOOL; a PLAYER is part of the TEAM. This is a *part to whole* relationship.

39. **(D)** A STIGMA (a mark of discredit or shame) can ruin one's REPUTATION; a MOTH can ruin CLOTHING. The relationship is *cause to effect*.

40. **(B)** TRENTON is the capital city of the state of NEW JERSEY; LINCOLN is the capital city of the state of NEBRASKA. It is a *functional* relationship.

41. **(E)** A BACTERIOLOGIST must use a MICROSCOPE as a tool of his trade; a BOXER must use GLOVES as a tool of his trade. This is a *functional* relationship which requires necessity as well. Thus, while a librarian might wear glasses, this is not necessarily true for all librarians; likewise, not all professional swimmers wear masks.

42. **(E)** Reading in reverse: a WISH precedes the FULFILLMENT of that wish; CONSIDERATION of a matter occurs before the DECISION is reached. This is a *sequential* relationship.

43. **(A)** A HAUNTER is a SPECTER (both mean "ghost"); a DELUSION is an illusion, hallucination or MIRAGE. The relationship is that of *synonyms*.

44. **(D)** ASSAULT cannot hurt an IMPREGNABLE (well-fortified) city; INSULT cannot hurt an INVULNERABLE (morally fortified) person. This is a variation on the *cause and effect* relationship.

45. **(C)** KINDNESS may produce COOPERATION; POISON is likely to lead to DEATH. This is a *cause and effect* relationship.

46. **(D)** The passage is a description of the "American" way of celebrating Christmas. The depiction is hardly complimentary and is, in fact, somewhat sarcastic, but great disapproval, (A), is too strong and too negative a term to describe the author's attitude.

47. **(C)** The second paragraph makes clear that Christmas is an extension of the American "dedication to business."

48. **(E)** The first paragraph enumerates some of the Christmas symbols of other countries which have been adopted into our own culture. While it is surely true that the modern American celebration of Christmas bears no resemblance to that of the early settlers, (C), that point is not made in the passage.

49. **(B)** The author makes much of the lengthening of the Christmas season in America. The shopping season extends from Halloween to Christmas and the season of celebration includes the entire month of December. Spirited euphoria on New Year's Eve, (E), may be found in other parts of the world, but the month-long "Saturnalia" is strictly American.

50. **(D)** The "distinctive aura" of the American Christmas is that unique atmosphere created by the over-commercialization, the long shopping season and the prolonged season of celebration.

51. **(D)** The author of this passage, after citing so many well-known arguments against unrestricted gun ownership, is clearly puzzled that the NRA holds power over Congress to the extent of blocking restrictive legislation. Secondarily, the author may feel threatened by snipers and may have some argument with lobbyists in general, but (D) is the *best* answer.

52. **(C)** The purpose of this passage is to inform the public about the status of gun control and why it is needed, and to explain the role of lobbyists in thwarting gun control. Its tone goes beyond mere stating of facts (E). The passage does not cite the details of any pending law (D).

53. **(E)** The point of the NRA is that if possession of guns by private citizens is made illegal, criminals who break other laws will break the gun restriction law as well. Law-abiding citizens, on the other hand, will be defenseless against gun-toting criminals.

54. **(B)** The passage states that the NRA is typical of well-financed pressure groups. It goes on to paraphrase some of the NRA's well-articulated arguments. Nowhere does it suggest that the NRA resorts to political threats.

55. **(A)** The only restriction placed by the NRA on gun ownership is proficiency in the use of the weapon and awareness of safety precautions. The NRA feels that need for a gun or even specific use for a gun are irrelevant to gun ownership.

56. **(D)** Monseigneur is drinking hot chocolate in his suite of rooms at a grand hotel in Paris. A suite of rooms is an apartment.

57. **(B)** The House of Stuart ruled in England from 1603 to 1649 and from 1660 to 1714, basically in the seventeenth century. Thus, the passage is pinpointed in time as occurring in the seventeenth century or later. By the twentieth century, France was a republic. There was no Court, so there were no lords holding power at the Court. Among the choices offered, the passage must be placed in the eighteenth century.

58. **(C)** A "profligate" is a self-indulgent, wasteful individual. This term is very appropriate to Monseigneur. A person who is so thoroughly devoted to his own selfish pleasures cannot spare any concern for others.

59. **(E)** The narrative, sarcastic style of the passage immediately rules out the possibility that it is part of either a historical document, (A), or a textbook on sociology, (B). The subject matter, which has nothing to do with political favoritism, (C), or etiquette, (D), rules out those choices as well. The style of the passage is that of a story and the subject of the story is Monseigneur's use of power for his own pleasure.

60. **(C)** Monseigneur is a "symbol" of the corruption and debauchery of the eighteenth century French court. "Onomatopoeia," (A), is the use of words whose sounds enhance their meaning, such as "ooze." The "denouement," (B), is the final unraveling of the plot of a drama or mystery. "Psychogenesis," (D), is the process by which the mind creates physical symptoms. A "euphemism," (E), is a polite word or expression used in place of a stronger or more offensive word or expression.

61. **(D)** In the fourth paragraph, the author discusses the possibility of suggesting newer and more interesting ways in which a parent might assist a child's academic development. The fifth paragraph then implies that parent, child and school will all benefit and be satisfied if the parent accepts the teacher's direction.

62. **(D)** The author clearly feels disgusted with the usual course of teacher-parent conferences (paragraph 6), but offers specific suggestions for making these conferences more worthwhile (paragraph 7).

63. **(A)** In the discussion of how the parent can improve his son's arithmetic by assigning him mathematical tasks instead of rote drill, the author is implying that learning can occur during pleasurable activities which have some relevance to the subject matter or skill area.

64. **(E)** The author appears to approve of administrators, of their awareness of a need to keep parents informed of new methods and of the parent workshops which they have developed (paragraph 2).

65. **(E)** It is unlikely that the author would prefer principal-parent conferences to teacher-parent conferences. The principal can explain overall philosophies, methods and curricula, but the teacher, in order to enlist parent cooperation, must tailor suggestions to the specific needs of each individual child.

SECTION II

1. **(E)** 4 of the 6 equal parts of 2 means $\frac{4}{6} \times 2$, or $\frac{4}{3}$.

2. **(E)** 110% of 105 is 1.1×105, or 115.5.

3. **(D)** This is a proportion: 2 inches: $7\frac{1}{2}$ inches = 5 feet: x, so $x = 18\frac{3}{4}$ feet.

4. **(B)** The horizontal edges are each 3 cm. long, and the vertical edges are 2 cm. long. Therefore, the volume is $3 \times 3 \times 2$, or 18 cc.

5. **(B)** The only pieces that touch eight other pieces are the shaded ones in this diagram:

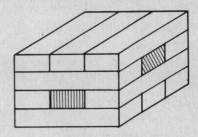

6. **(E)** In order to have a volume of 18 cc., the piece of material must be $\frac{1}{2}$ cm. $\times$ 1 cm. $\times$ 36 cm.

7. **(D)** Each piece has two faces which are 1 cm. $\times \frac{1}{2}$ cm., or $\frac{1}{2}$ sq. cm., two faces which are 1 cm. $\times$ 3 cm., or 3 sq. cm., and two faces which are $\frac{1}{2}$ cm. $\times$ 3 cm., or $1\frac{1}{2}$ sq. cm. The surface area of each piece is therefore 10 sq. cm. Since there are 12 such pieces, the total area is 120 sq. cm.

8. **(D)** The area of triangle ADE equals the area of triangle AEC, since they have the same base and altitude. The area of triangle ABC equals that of triangle ADC, since the diagonal of a parallelogram divides it equally.

9. **(B)** At 3 for 10¢, one dozen pencils cost 40¢, so the profit on each dozen is 5¢. With $5\frac{1}{2}$ dozen, the profit is $27\frac{1}{2}$¢.

10. **(E)** $26 \times 3\frac{1}{2} = (26 \times 3) + (26 \times \frac{1}{2})$ by the distributive law. $26 \times 3 = (20 \times 3) + (6 \times 3)$ by the distributive law. Therefore, $26 \times 3\frac{1}{2} = (26 \times \frac{1}{2}) + (20 \times 3) + (6 \times 3)$.

11. **(B)** Each compound is compared with all the others, giving 20, but since each comparison has been counted twice, we divide by 2 to give 10.

12. **(A)** A was judged sweeter 25 times.

13. **(D)** D was judged sweeter only 8 times.

14. **(D)** The other compounds were judged sweeter 25, 23, 24, and 20 times, while D was judged sweeter only 8 times.

15. **(E)** 5 judges called A sweeter, and 5 called B sweeter.

16. **(B)**

$$\frac{5}{100} = \frac{x}{34} \qquad \frac{5}{100} = \frac{34}{x}$$
$$100x = 170 \qquad 5x = 3400$$
$$x = 1.7 \qquad x = 680$$

17. (A)

$$9^2 = 81$$
$$\sqrt[3]{721} < 9$$

18. (B)

$$[5A(4T)]^3 = [-10(12)]^3$$
$$= (-120)^3$$
$$= \text{negative answer}$$
$$[4A(5S)]^2 = [-8(1)]^2$$
$$= (-8)^2$$
$$= \text{positive answer}$$

∴ A positive product is greater than a negative one

19. (A)

$$\angle 2 > \angle 1 \quad \text{(given)}$$
∴IR > IT   (in a triangle the greater side lies opposite the greater angle)

20. (D)

Since x could be any integer from −2 to 3, the values of the fractions are impossible to determine.

21. (A)

$$\tfrac{2}{3} + \tfrac{3}{7} = \tfrac{14}{21} + \tfrac{9}{21} \qquad \tfrac{16}{21} - \tfrac{3}{7} = \tfrac{16}{21} - \tfrac{9}{21}$$
$$= \tfrac{23}{21} \qquad\qquad\qquad = \tfrac{7}{21}$$

22. (C)

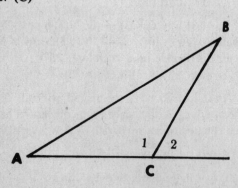

$$\angle 2 = \angle A + \angle B$$ (an exterior angle of a triangle is equal to the sum of the two interior remote angles)

23. (D)

There is not enough information, as Y could equal 1, which would make both quantities equal; or Y could be greater than 1, which would make Y^3 greater than Y^2. If Y were a negative integer, then Y^2 would be greater than Y^3.

24. (A)

$$8 + 6 \div 3 - 7(2) = 8 + 2 - 14$$
$$= 10 - 14$$
$$= -4$$
$$6 + 8 \div 2 - 7(3) = 6 + 4 - 21$$
$$= 10 - 21$$
$$= -11$$

25. (B)

$$N * A = \frac{1}{n^2} + \frac{a}{2}$$

$$\frac{2}{3} + \frac{1}{3} = \frac{1}{(\frac{2}{3})^2} + \frac{\frac{1}{3}}{2} \qquad \frac{1}{5} * \frac{3}{5} = \frac{1}{(\frac{1}{5})^2} + \frac{\frac{3}{5}}{2}$$

$$= \frac{1}{\frac{4}{9}} + \frac{1}{6} \qquad\qquad = \frac{1}{\frac{1}{25}} + \frac{3}{10}$$

$$= \frac{9}{4} + \frac{1}{6} \qquad\qquad = 25 + \tfrac{3}{10}$$

$$= \frac{27}{12} + \frac{2}{12} \qquad\qquad = 25\tfrac{3}{10}$$

$$= \frac{29}{12} = 2\tfrac{5}{12}$$

26. (C)

$$\tfrac{3}{4} \times \tfrac{9}{9} = \tfrac{3}{4} \qquad \tfrac{9}{9} \times \tfrac{3}{4} = \tfrac{3}{4}$$

27. (B)

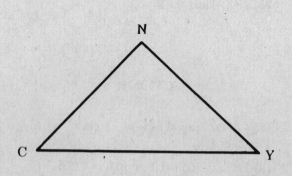

NC = NY   (given)
∠C = ∠Y   (angles opposite equal sides are equal)

∠N > ∠C   (given)
∠N > ∠Y   (substitution)
CY > NC   (the greater side lies opposite the greater angle)

28. (C)

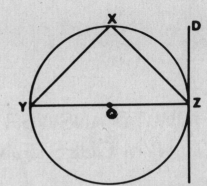

$\angle YXZ = 90°$ (an angle inscribed in a semicircle equals 90°)

$\angle DZY = 90°$ (a radius is perpendicular to a tangent at their point of contact)

29. (D)
Impossible to determine from the information given. The radius could be less than, equal to, or greater than the chord.

30. (C)
$$9^{-\frac{1}{2}} = \frac{1}{\sqrt{9}} = \frac{1}{3}$$

31. (C)
$$5(\tfrac{2}{3})^0 = 5(1) \qquad (25)^{\frac{1}{2}} = \sqrt{25}$$
$$= 5 \qquad\qquad = 5$$

32. (C)
$$\frac{1}{\sqrt{3}} = \frac{1}{\sqrt{3}}\left(\frac{\sqrt{3}}{\sqrt{3}}\right)$$
$$= \frac{1}{3}\sqrt{3}$$
$$= \tfrac{1}{3}\sqrt{3}$$

33. (B) 35 feet, 6 inches equals 426 inches. One-fourth of this is $106\frac{1}{2}$ inches, or 8 feet, $10\frac{1}{2}$ inches.

34. (A) Out of 12 total games, two were won. Thus, the fraction is $\frac{2}{12}$, or $\frac{1}{6}$.

35. (D) 10^5 is defined as $10 \times 10 \times 10 \times 10 \times 10$, or 100,000. $10 \times 5 = 50$; $5^{10} = 25^5$; $5\sqrt{10}$ is between 1 and 2; and $10^{10} \div 10^2 = 10^8$.

36. (D) $2\frac{3}{4} \div \frac{1}{8} = \frac{11}{4} \div \frac{1}{8} = \frac{11}{4} \times 8 = 22.$

37. (E) $105{,}084 - 93{,}709 = 11{,}375.$

38. (E) This is a proportion $\rightarrow 2\frac{1}{2} : 3 = x : 14$; $x = \frac{35}{3}$, or $11\frac{2}{3}$.

39. (E) If the gain was 10% of the selling price, then $12.60 was 90% so 100% was equal to $14.00.

40. (D) There will be no waste if the lengths are multiples of $5\frac{1}{2}$ feet. This occurs between 6 and 24 only for 22 feet.

41. (B) Each tile, including half of the cement around it, has an area of 1 square inch. 3,240 square inches equals 22.5 square feet, or 2.5 square yards.

42. (C) A median score is the middle score when all scores are arranged in ascending or descending order. This is 27 here.

43. (D) $(2 \times 100) + (16 \times 10) + 6 = 200 + 160 + 6 = 366.$

44. (B) After the 20% discount, the price was $128. After the 10% discount, the price was $115.20.

45. (C) Angle T is a right angle. By the Pythagorean Theorem, $RT^2 + ST^2 = RS^2$. Since $RS = 12$ and $ST = 8$, RT must equal $\sqrt{80}$, so $OT = \frac{1}{2}\sqrt{80}$. By the formula for area of a circle $(A = \pi r^2)$, our area equals $(\pi)(\frac{1}{2})^2(\sqrt{80})^2$, or $(\pi)(\frac{1}{4})(80)$, which equals 20π.

46. (B) A hexagon with 22-inch sides has a perimeter of 6×22, or 132 inches. The circumference of a circle with a 21-inch radius is (assuming that $\pi = 3.14$) $2 \times 3.14 \times 21$, or 131.88, but the answer is actually slightly greater, since π is actually greater than 3.14.

47. (B) 11 P.M. Eastern Daylight Time is the same as 10 P.M. Eastern Standard Time. Since there is a three-hour difference between E.S.T. and Pacific Standard Time, this is the same as 7 P.M. P.S.T. 6 hours later, the time will be 1:00 A.M. P.S.T.

48. (D) The reciprocal of $1\frac{1}{4}$ is $\frac{4}{5}$. $\frac{4}{5} - \frac{5}{4} = \frac{16}{20} - \frac{25}{20} = -\frac{9}{20}.$

49. (C) If each of the dimensions is doubled, the area of the new rectangle is four times the size of the original one. The increase is three times, or 300%.

50. (A) x yards = 3x feet; y feet = y feet; z inches = z/12 feet. Therefore, x yards + y feet + z inches = 3x feet + y feet + z/12 feet, or 3x + y + z/12 feet.

ANTONYMS

DIRECTIONS: For each question, mark the letter preceding the word or phrase that is opposite or most nearly opposite in meaning to the capitalized word. Where more than one option appears to be correct, choose the *best* opposite.

Example:

WET

(A) humid
(B) damp
(C) acrid
(D) dry
(E) dusty

(D) DRY is the opposite of WET. *Humid* and *damp* are degrees of wetness and are not true opposites. *Arid* is a synonym for *dry,* but the word at (C) is *acrid,* which means *bitter.* Something that is *dusty* is probably *dry,* but *dry* itself is a much better antonym for *wet.*

The above directions challenge you to demonstrate your verbal skills and your mental flexibility. Initially, the task appears to be a simple one: define the capitalized word and pick its opposite. However, as you approach the questions, the task becomes more complicated. Where there is no true opposite, you must choose that word or phrase which is *most nearly opposite.* Where there appear to be two or more opposites, you must choose the *best* opposite. You must be on guard against choosing an associated word or phrase which is different in meaning but is not a true opposite. After struggling to define a word, you must take care not to then choose the word or phrase which is most similar in meaning.

HOW TO ANSWER ANTONYM QUESTIONS

Read each word and its five possible answers very carefully. Then follow a step-by-step approach to find your answer. This approach may lead you through a number of different procedures depending on your initial reaction to the word.

Possibility #1. You know the meaning of the capitalized word. You read all five choices and the *best* opposite is clear to you. Mark it quickly and go on. You will need more time for questions which are more difficult for you.

Possibility #2. You know the meaning of the word, but no answer choice seems correct.

- Perhaps you misread the word. Does it have a close look-alike with a different meaning? For example, did you read REVELATION for REVALUATION or COMPLIMENT for COMPLEMENT?

- Perhaps you read the word correctly but accented the wrong syllable. Some words have alternative pronunciations with vastly different meanings. Consider de-sert' and de'sert.

- Perhaps you are dealing with a single word which can be used as two different parts of speech and has two entirely unrelated meanings. A MOOR (noun) is a boggy wasteland. To MOOR (verb) is to tie up a vessel. The proper noun MOOR refers to the Moslem conquerors of Spain.

- Perhaps the word can appear as a number of parts of speech with numerous meanings and shades of meaning within each of these. FANCY (noun) can mean: inclination, love, notion, whim, taste, judgment, imagination. FANCY (verb) can mean: to like, to imagine, to think. FANCY (adjective) can mean: whimsical, ornamental, extravagant. Your task is to choose from among the five choices one word or phrase which is opposite to *one* of these meanings of the word FANCY.

Possibility #3. You do not know the meaning of the word, but it appears to contain prefix, suffix or root clues. Let us suppose that the question looks like this:

INAUDIBLE

    (A) dark
    (B) invisible
    (C) bright
    (D) loud
    (E) clear

You do not know the meaning of the word INAUDIBLE, but you recognize a part of "audio" and you know that the audio of your TV is the sound. You also know that the prefix "in" generally means "not." You might also see "able" in "ible" and thereby reconstruct "not soundable" or "not heard."

NOW BEWARE—This is the point at which your reasoning can easily lead you astray. If you associate with your TV, you may think, "The opposite of 'not heard' is 'not seen' or (B), invisible." Wrong. These are not true opposites. Or, you might associate "not heard" with "not seen" and choose the opposite of "not seen," (C), bright. Wrong again. Or, you might think of "inaudible" as "hard to hear" and choose (E), clear. "Clear" would not be a bad answer, but (D), loud, is better and is indeed the *best* answer. The *best* opposite of INAUDIBLE is LOUD.

Possibility #4. You do not know the meaning of the word, can see no clues, but have a feeling that the word has some specific connotation, be it sinister, gloomy or positive. Play your hunch. Choose a word with the opposite connotation.

Possibility #5. You are stumped. You may guess. If you guess correctly you will get credit for a right answer. If you guess wrong, you will lose ¼ point. Or, you may skip the question. There is no penalty for the omission, but of course no chance of getting the answer right. The choice is yours.

PRACTICE WITH ANTONYMS

Directions: For each question, mark the letter preceding the word or phrase that is opposite or most nearly opposite in meaning to the capitalized word. Where more than one option appears to be correct, choose the *best* opposite.

SET ONE

1. QUERY

    (A) argument
    (B) answer
    (C) square
    (D) loner
    (E) ordinary

2. VITRIOLIC

    (A) benevolent
    (B) vanquished
    (C) invisible
    (D) alcoholic
    (E) reformed

3. MYOPIC

    (A) poisonous
    (B) toadstool
    (C) froglike
    (D) genuine
    (E) open-minded

4. NAPPED

    (A) awake
    (B) tired
    (C) soft
    (D) smooth
    (E) open

5. OBSEQUIOUS

    (A) haughty
    (B) frightened
    (C) perseverant
    (D) phobic
    (E) friendly

6. ICONOCLAST

    (A) criminal
    (B) priest
    (C) warrior
    (D) custodian
    (E) conformist

7. PLACATE

    (A) amuse
    (B) antagonize
    (C) embroil
    (D) pity
    (E) reject

8. RETICENT

   (A) fidgety
   (B) repetitious
   (C) talkative
   (D) restful
   (E) truthful

9. ECLECTIC

   (A) brilliant
   (B) exclusive
   (C) prosaic
   (D) conclusive
   (E) reproaching

10. QUEASY

   (A) nautical
   (B) partial
   (C) broken
   (D) confident
   (E) regal

11. INDIGENT

   (A) healthy
   (B) wealthy
   (C) wise
   (D) active
   (E) interested

12. SANGUINE

   (A) pink
   (B) belligerent
   (C) dry
   (D) peaceful
   (E) pessimistic

13. AUSPICIOUS

   (A) condemnatory
   (B) conspicuous
   (C) unfavorable
   (D) questionable
   (E) spicy

14. EXPUNGE

   (A) clarify
   (B) embroil
   (C) perpetuate
   (D) investigate
   (E) underline

15. AMBULATORY

   (A) supine
   (B) influential
   (C) injured
   (D) quarantined
   (E) suffering

16. SPECIOUS

   (A) scanty
   (B) particular
   (C) genuine
   (D) suspicious
   (E) vigorous

17. RANCOR

   (A) dignity
   (B) affection
   (C) odor
   (D) disorder
   (E) suspicion

18. CATHOLIC

   (A) irreligious
   (B) irreverant
   (C) heretic
   (D) Jewish
   (E) intolerant

19. CUPIDITY

   (A) infatuation
   (B) restraint
   (C) foolishness
   (D) anger
   (E) harshness

20. ORTHODOX

   (A) irreligious
   (B) conservative
   (C) catholic
   (D) unconventional
   (E) reform

21. INDOLENT

   (A) hypnotized
   (B) rich
   (C) happy
   (D) generous
   (E) ambitious

22. PROCRASTINATE

    (A) eulogize
    (B) invest
    (C) expedite
    (D) insinuate
    (E) mediate

23. SYCOPHANCY

    (A) colloquialism
    (B) innuendo
    (C) nihilism
    (D) frankness
    (E) ignorance

24. ESCHEW

    (A) swallow
    (B) vomit
    (C) greet
    (D) perform
    (E) subvert

25. INTREPID

    (A) surreptitious
    (B) monotonous
    (C) theocratic
    (C) paranoid
    (E) pedestrian

SET TWO

1. CAUSE

    (A) affect
    (B) result
    (C) question
    (D) matter
    (E) accident

2. PITHY

    (A) wooden
    (B) boring
    (C) inane
    (D) bareheaded
    (E) virtuous

3. PROGRESS

    (A) halt
    (B) change
    (C) invert
    (D) follow
    (E) lead

4. RURAL

    (A) suburban
    (B) exurban
    (C) arid
    (D) urban
    (E) watery

5. ATTRITION

    (A) partition
    (B) subjugation
    (C) death
    (D) decision
    (E) adding on

6. ARCHAIC

    (A) novel
    (B) dug up
    (C) buried
    (D) pointed
    (E) satanic

7. ELAN

    (A) horror
    (B) fear
    (C) bravery
    (D) depth
    (E) apathy

8. PROFIT

    (A) ratio
    (B) gross
    (C) net
    (D) loss
    (E) mark-down

9. REST

    (A) sleep
    (B) activity
    (C) wake
    (D) speak
    (E) snore

10. BIRTH

    (A) life
    (B) age
    (C) youth
    (D) childlessness
    (E) death

11. MEND

   (A) give back
   (B) pray
   (C) change
   (D) destroy
   (E) clean

12. BRAVADO

   (A) scrawny
   (B) shortness
   (C) humility
   (D) bowleggedness
   (E) discord

13. HUMANE

   (A) bestial
   (B) ill-mannered
   (C) ill-tempered
   (D) anthropomorphic
   (E) anti-vivisection

14. HARD

   (A) crisp
   (B) soft
   (C) wet
   (D) nut
   (E) weak

15. ACID

   (A) sweet
   (B) bitter
   (C) bland
   (D) alkaline
   (E) saline

16. BRUSQUE

   (A) patient
   (B) clean
   (C) dirty
   (D) dusty
   (E) dim

17. ALLY

   (A) fight
   (B) resist
   (C) separate
   (D) hate
   (E) win

18. ABSTRACT

   (A) art
   (B) absurd
   (C) sculpture
   (D) concrete
   (E) asphalt

19. ANOREXIA

   (A) brazenness
   (B) gluttony
   (C) disrespect
   (D) anarchy
   (E) performance

20. CEILING

   (A) roof
   (B) wall
   (C) cellar
   (D) floor
   (E) foundation

21. DEAR

   (A) ugly
   (B) decaying
   (C) coarse
   (D) cloying
   (E) cheap

22. ENCLOSED

   (A) naked
   (B) stripped
   (C) aired
   (D) cut
   (E) freed

23. FISSION

   (A) fusion
   (B) rendition
   (C) confiscation
   (D) absolution
   (E) ablution

24. FREEZE

   (A) hot
   (B) bend
   (C) slow
   (D) water
   (E) skate

25. INSIDIOUS

(A) inquiring
(B) obsolete
(C) obvious
(D) oblivious
(E) innocent

SET THREE

1. TITAN

(A) warrior
(B) sage
(C) pit
(D) dwarf
(E) buffoon

2. RAMBUNCTIOUS

(A) lazy
(B) friendly
(C) calm
(D) fearful
(E) unpleasant

3. ADDLE

(A) detoxify
(B) clarify
(C) persuade
(D) subtract
(E) detract

4. INVALID

(A) alert
(B) trusting
(C) brave
(D) careful
(E) true

5. PROVINCIAL

(A) urbane
(B) rootless
(C) untroubled
(D) temporary
(E) permanent

6. SECULAR

(A) whole
(B) combined
(C) clerical
(D) educational
(E) pointed

7. ARTICULATE

(A) decisive
(B) direct
(C) general
(D) silent
(E) common

8. DISCORD

(A) reward
(B) music
(C) punishment
(D) abutment
(E) harmony

9. VERVE

(A) cowardice
(B) ability
(C) lethargy
(D) litany
(E) philanthropy

10. GLUTINOUS

(A) slick
(B) swollen
(C) hungry
(D) lurid
(E) livid

11. ITINERANT

(A) careless
(B) sedentary
(C) disorganized
(D) bossy
(E) loud

12. GROTTO

(A) giant
(B) child
(C) desert
(D) mound
(E) pastel

13. VERDANT

  (A) barren
  (B) untruthful
  (C) reckless
  (D) obnoxious
  (E) passionate

14. AFFLUENT

  (A) glamorous
  (B) scanty
  (C) stable
  (D) charitable
  (E) clogged

15. TREPIDATION

  (A) fearlessness
  (B) anger
  (C) honesty
  (D) vigor
  (E) enormity

16. COMMODIOUS

  (A) disengaged
  (B) rich
  (C) mourned
  (D) small
  (E) empty

17. ENDEARMENT

  (A) attachment
  (B) strangeness
  (C) welcome
  (D) thriftiness
  (E) hostility

18. CREDULITY

  (A) doubt
  (B) understanding
  (C) muscularity
  (D) commendation
  (E) misery

19. ALIENATE

  (A) unfurl
  (B) banish

  (C) encourage
  (D) remain
  (E) befriend

20. FRIVOLITY

  (A) distraction
  (B) seriousness
  (C) warmth
  (D) exactness
  (E) decoration

21. ESTRANGE

  (A) allow
  (B) recognize
  (C) release
  (D) remember
  (E) reconcile

22. GARISH

  (A) dull
  (B) damp
  (C) sweet
  (D) closed
  (E) holy

23. GREGARIOUS

  (A) sour
  (B) free
  (C) shortened
  (D) quiet
  (E) unsociable

24. DIVERSE

  (A) happy
  (B) definite
  (C) understandable
  (D) similar
  (E) boring

25. LUMINOUS

  (A) solar
  (B) unimaginative
  (C) unknown
  (D) dim
  (E) stellar

SET FOUR

1. RESCIND

   (A) provide
   (B) reinstate
   (C) cancel
   (D) mutilate
   (E) correct

2. AFFABLE

   (A) unbent
   (B) untruthful
   (C) unfriendly
   (D) unable
   (E) unreliable

3. CAUSTIC

   (A) sleepy
   (B) cleansing
   (C) unintelligent
   (D) resultant
   (E) soothing

4. ADAMANT

   (A) effeminate
   (B) prayerful
   (C) yielding
   (D) courageous
   (E) reluctant

5. AFFECTATION

   (A) hatred
   (B) security
   (C) cause
   (D) result
   (E) modesty

6. VULNERABLE

   (A) reverent
   (B) innocent
   (C) unassailable
   (D) inflated
   (E) playful

7. ABATEMENT

   (A) addition
   (B) guarantee
   (C) denial
   (D) danger
   (E) flood

8. PERTURBED

   (A) disrespectful
   (B) penetrable
   (C) tractable
   (D) cheerful
   (E) relaxed

9. AVARICE

   (A) kindness
   (B) detriment
   (C) starvation
   (D) sorrow
   (E) generosity

10. ABHORRENCE

    (A) revelation
    (B) detachment
    (C) engagement
    (D) admiration
    (E) avoidance

11. UNKEMPT

    (A) tied
    (B) tidy
    (C) enclosed
    (D) supervised
    (E) alone

12. RECTITUDE

    (A) dishonesty
    (B) disillusionment
    (C) decisiveness
    (D) wholesomeness
    (E) left-handedness

13. OFFICIOUS

    (A) informal
    (B) illegal
    (C) aloof
    (D) bureaucratic
    (E) unsigned

14. DOVE

    (A) eagle
    (B) hawk
    (C) turkey
    (D) ostrich
    (E) elephant

15. MUNDANE

   (A) livable
   (B) unprotected
   (C) critical
   (D) childish
   (E) ethereal

16. ADULTERATED

   (A) immature
   (B) disgraced
   (C) pure
   (D) destroyed
   (E) committed

17. STAMINA

   (A) fatigue
   (B) nerve
   (C) pistil
   (D) disgrace
   (E) failure

18. SUPPLE

   (A) soft
   (B) stale
   (C) lazy
   (D) rigid
   (E) generous

19. CONTORT

   (A) answer
   (B) deny
   (C) stretch
   (D) swell
   (E) smile

20. SPURT

   (A) spill
   (B) seep

   (C) stream
   (D) stalk
   (E) supply

21. CATHARSIS

   (A) rowboat
   (B) argument
   (C) success
   (D) repression
   (E) analysis

22. CULPABLE

   (A) courteous
   (B) childless
   (C) trustworthy
   (D) free
   (E) innocent

23. PARSIMONIOUS

   (A) obdurate
   (B) extravagant
   (C) carnivorous
   (D) officious
   (E) illegal

24. TIMOROUS

   (A) timid
   (B) punctual
   (C) tardy
   (D) bold
   (E) false

25. NEPOTISM

   (A) impartiality
   (B) demagogy
   (C) indifference
   (D) apathy
   (E) benevolence

ANSWER KEY FOR
PRACTICE ANTONYMS

SET ONE

1. B	6. E	11. B	16. C	21. E
2. A	7. B	12. E	17. B	22. C
3. E	8. C	13. C	18. E	23. D
4. D	9. B	14. C	19. B	24. C
5. A	10. D	15. A	20. D	25. D

SET TWO

1. B	6. A	11. D	16. A	21. E
2. C	7. E	12. C	17. C	22. E
3. A	8. D	13. A	18. D	23. A
4. D	9. B	14. B	19. B	24. B
5. E	10. E	15. D	20. D	25. C

SET THREE

1. D	6. C	11. B	16. D	21. E
2. C	7. D	12. D	17. E	22. A
3. B	8. E	13. A	18. A	23. E
4. E	9. C	14. B	19. E	24. D
5. A	10. A	15. A	20. B	25. D

SET FOUR

1. B	6. C	11. B	16. C	21. D
2. C	7. A	12. A	17. A	22. E
3. E	8. E	13. C	18. D	23. B
4. C	9. E	14. B	19. C	24. D
5. E	10. D	15. E	20. B	25. A

EXPLANATORY ANSWERS
FOR PRACTICE ANTONYMS

SET ONE

1. **(B)** ANSWER. A QUERY is a question.

2. **(A)** BENEVOLENT means full of generous and kind feelings. VITRIOLIC means caustic and bitter in feeling or speech.

3. **(E)** OPEN-MINDED. MYOPIC means narrow-minded or shortsighted.

4. **(D)** SMOOTH. NAPPED means having a hairy or downy surface, as suede.

5. **(A)** HAUGHTY means arrogant or proud. OB-SEQUIOUS means servile and subservient.

6. **(E)** A CONFORMIST is one who adapts to prevailing standards or customs. An ICONO-

CLAST is one who attacks established beliefs and institutions.

7. **(B)** ANTAGONIZE means to provoke hostility. PLACATE means to soothe or mollify.

8. **(C)** TALKATIVE. RETICENT means uncommunicative in speech.

9. **(B)** EXCLUSIVE means limiting or restricting. ECLECTIC means accepting from many different sources.

10. **(D)** CONFIDENT. QUEASY means full of doubt.

11. **(B)** WEALTHY. INDIGENT means poor.

12. **(E)** PESSIMISTIC. SANGUINE means cheerful and optimistic.

13. **(C)** UNFAVORABLE. AUSPICIOUS means favorable or accompanied by a good omen.

14. **(C)** PERPETUATE means to cause to last indefinitely. EXPUNGE means to destroy.

15. **(A)** SUPINE means lying flat on the back. AMBULATORY means walking about.

16. **(C)** GENUINE means authentic. SPECIOUS means having a deceptive appearance of truthfulness.

17. **(B)** AFFECTION means fondness. RANCOR means bitter ill-will.

18. **(E)** INTOLERANT. CATHOLIC means broad in sympathies, tastes and interests.

19. **(B)** RESTRAINT means reserve and self-control. CUPIDITY means lust or greed.

20. **(D)** UNCONVENTIONAL. ORTHODOX is a word meaning conventional and conformist.

21. **(E)** AMBITIOUS. INDOLENT means lazy.

22. **(C)** EXPEDITE means to execute promptly. PROCRASTINATE means to put off intentionally.

23. **(D)** FRANKNESS means openness and directness of speech. SYCOPHANCY means servile flattery.

24. **(C)** GREET means to welcome. ESCHEW means to avoid.

25. **(D)** PARANOID means suspicious. INTREPID means fearless.

SET TWO

1. **(B)** RESULT. The RESULT is the end product of a CAUSE. A synonym for RESULT is *effect*. Do not confuse *effect* with *affect*, which means influence.

2. **(C)** That which is INANE is empty and pointless. That which is PITHY has substance and point.

3. **(A)** HALT. To PROGRESS is to move forward.

4. **(D)** URBAN means pertaining to a city or town. RURAL pertains to the country, especially agricultural areas. *Suburban* and *exurban* fall between the opposites.

5. **(E)** ADDING ON. ATTRITION means the wearing away.

6. **(A)** NOVEL, meaning new. ARCHAIC means ancient.

7. **(E)** APATHY. ELAN refers to eagerness for action.

8. **(D)** LOSS is the true opposite of PROFIT.

9. **(B)** ACTIVITY is motion. REST is freedom from activity.

10. **(E)** DEATH. BIRTH is the beginning of a continuum that ends in DEATH.

11. **(D)** DESTROY. To MEND is to repair.

12. **(C)** HUMILITY. BRAVADO is boasting.

13. **(A)** BESTIAL means as brutal as an animal. HUMANE means kind and benevolent.

14. **(B)** SOFT. *Weak* might also be considered an antonym for HARD, but it is not as clear and definite an antonym as SOFT. You must choose the *best* answer.

15. **(D)** ALKALINE is the chemical opposite of ACID. ALKALIS neutralize ACIDS.

16. **(A)** PATIENT. BRUSQUE means abrupt and short in manner.

17. **(C)** SEPARATE. To ALLY is to join.

18. **(D)** CONCRETE means specific or particular. ABSTRACT means general or theoretical.

19. **(B)** GLUTTONY means excessive eating. ANOREXIA means self-starvation.

20. **(D)** FLOOR. The *roof* and *foundation* are opposites, being the extreme outer limits of a building. The FLOOR and CEILING are opposites within a room.

21. **(E)** CHEAP means inexpensive. DEAR means costly.

22. **(E)** FREED. ENCLOSED means shut up or shut in.

23. **(A)** FUSION means blending together. FISSION means breaking into parts. The two processes, while total opposites, can both create nuclear energy.

24. **(B)** BEND. To FREEZE is to stiffen. The antonym you choose must be the same part of speech as the original word. The antonym of the verb to *freeze*, meaning to chill, would be to *heat*.

25. **(C)** OBVIOUS. INSIDIOUS means hidden.

SET THREE

1. **(D)** DWARF. A TITAN is a giant.

2. **(C)** CALM. RAMBUNCTIOUS means boisterous and unruly.

3. **(B)** CLARIFY. To ADDLE means to confuse.

4. **(E)** TRUE. INVALID means not valid or not true.

5. **(A)** URBANE. PROVINCIAL means unsophisticated.

6. **(C)** CLERICAL means related to the clergy or to the church. SECULAR means civil and in no way connected to a church.

7. **(D)** SILENT. ARTICULATE means spoken.

8. **(E)** HARMONY. DISCORD means deep disagreement. Music may be either harmonious or discordant.

9. **(C)** LETHARGY is inaction or indifference. VERVE is great vitality.

10. **(A)** SLICK. GLUTINOUS means sticky or gummy.

11. **(B)** SEDENTARY means stationary. ITINERANT means travelling.

12. **(D)** MOUND. A GROTTO is a cave.

13. **(A)** BARREN. VERDANT means green and lush with vegetation.

14. **(B)** SCANTY. AFFLUENT means abundant.

15. **(A)** FEARLESSNESS. TREPIDATION means fear.

16. **(D)** SMALL. COMMODIOUS means spacious.

17. **(E)** HOSTILITY. ENDEARMENT means affection.

18. **(A)** DOUBT. CREDULITY means unquestioning belief.

19. **(E)** BEFRIEND. To ALIENATE is to estrange.

20. **(B)** SERIOUSNESS. FRIVOLITY is lightness or triviality.

21. **(E)** RECONCILE. To ESTRANGE is to separate by enmity.

22. **(A)** DULL. GARISH means gaudy and glaring.

23. **(E)** UNSOCIABLE. GREGARIOUS means habitually moving in large groups.

24. **(D)** SIMILAR. DIVERSE means different.

25. **(D)** DIM. LUMINOUS means shining or brilliant.

SET FOUR

1. **(B)** REINSTATE. To RESCIND is to take back, so the *best* antonym is a reversal of the process. PROVIDE might serve as an antonym if there were no better choice.

2. **(C)** UNFRIENDLY. AFFABLE means sociable.

3. **(E)** SOOTHING. CAUSTIC means sharp or abrasive.

4. **(C)** YIELDING. ADAMANT means impenetrable and firm.

5. **(E)** MODESTY. AFFECTATION refers to a putting on of airs.

6. **(C)** UNASSAILABLE. VULNERABLE means susceptible to attack or wounds.

7. **(A)** ADDITION. ABATEMENT means diminution.

8. **(E)** RELAXED. One who is PERTURBED is agitated.

9. **(E)** GENEROSITY. AVARICE is greed.

10. **(D)** ADMIRATION. ABHORRENCE is loathing or hatred.

11. **(B)** TIDY. One who is UNKEMPT is sloppy.

12. **(A)** DISHONESTY. RECTITUDE is uprightness and honesty.

13. **(C)** ALOOF. One who is OFFICIOUS is meddlesome and bossy. One who is ALOOF takes no interest in the affairs of others.

14. **(B)** HAWK. Birds cannot be opposites of one another, nor can one really say that a bird is the opposite of an animal. To answer this antonym question, you must think of the birds as symbols. The DOVE is a symbol of peace; its opposite is the HAWK, a symbol of war.

15. **(E)** ETHEREAL relates to the celestial or spiritual; MUNDANE relates to worldly things.

16. **(C)** PURE. ADULTERATED means corrupt.

17. **(A)** FATIGUE. STAMINA is endurance.

18. **(D)** RIGID. SUPPLE means flexible.

19. **(C)** STRETCH. To CONTORT is to twist or bend out of shape.

20. **(B)** SEEP. To SPURT is to burst forth.

21. **(D)** REPRESSION. CATHARSIS is emotional release.

22. **(E)** INNOCENT. CULPABLE means guilty.

23. **(B)** EXTRAVAGANT. PARSIMONIOUS means stingy.

24. **(D)** BOLD. TIMOROUS means frightened. *Temerity* is a synonym for boldness.

25. **(A)** IMPARTIALITY. NEPOTISM is favoritism shown to relatives.

SENTENCE COMPLETIONS

DIRECTIONS: Each of the following questions consists of an incomplete sentence followed by five words or pairs of words. Choose that word or pair of words which, when substituted for the blank space or spaces, *best* completes the meaning of the sentence and mark the letter of your choice on your answer sheet.

Example:

The _____ on the letter indicated that it had been mailed in Chicago three weeks _____.

(A) address . . ago
(B) stamp . . in advance
(C) postmark . . previously
(D) envelope . . from tomorrow
(E) water stains . . late

(C) The sentence clearly asks which clue tells the date that a letter was mailed. The only possible answer to fill the first blank is POSTMARK. Since the second blank is easily filled by PREVIOUSLY, this question is an easy one to answer.

These directions introduce you to a difficult type of question. The sentence completion question is at once a test of your reading comprehension and of your vocabulary. It is a measure of your understanding of shades of meaning and of the connotations of words and of your ability to readily grasp ideas and to use your verbal imagination. In a typical sentence completion question, *any* of the answer choices might be inserted into the blank spaces and the sentence would be technically correct; but, it might not make sense. Usually more than one choice would make sense, but only one choice completely carries out the full meaning of the sentence. There is one *best* answer.

HOW TO ANSWER SENTENCE COMPLETION QUESTIONS

1. Read the sentence. Try to figure out what it means.

2. Look at the blank or blanks with relation to the meaning of the sentence. Is a negative connotation called for, or a positive one? If there are two blanks, should the pair be comparative, contrasting or complementary? Are you looking for the term which best defines a phrase in the sentence?

3. Eliminate those answer choices which do not meet the criteria you established in step two.

4. Read the sentence to yourself, trying out each of the remaining choices, one by one. Which of the choices does the *best* job of carrying the message of the sentence? Choose the one which makes the *best* sense.

A SAMPLE QUESTION EXPLAINED

An unruly person may well become _____ if he is treated with _____ by those around him.

(A) angry . . kindness
(B) calm . . respect
(C) peaceful . . abuse
(D) interested . . medicine
(E) dangerous . . love

1. This sentence is about a person's behavior and how it is affected by the way he is treated.

2. "Unruly" is a word with a negative connotation, but this unruly person may become _____. The implication is that the person will change for the better, so the first blank should be filled by a word with a positive connotation. The sentence further implies a cause and effect relationship. Positive treatment logically results in a positive change in behavior, so the second blank should also be filled by a word with a positive connotation.

3. Choices (A), (C), and (E) all contain words which have a negative connotation.

4. Of the remaining choices, (B) makes much better sense than (D).

PRACTICE WITH SENTENCE COMPLETIONS

SET ONE

DIRECTIONS: Each of the following questions consists of an incomplete sentence followed by five words or pairs of words. Choose that word or pair of words which, when substituted for the blank space or spaces, best completes the meaning of the sentence and mark the letter of your choice on your answer sheet.

1. Although fortunetellers claim to _____ future happenings, there is no scientific evidence of their _____.

(A) understand . . intelligence
(B) cloud . . ability
(C) effect . . knowledge
(D) foretell . . fees
(E) predict . . accuracy

2. Great ideas have _____ youth: they are _____.

(A) no . . petrified
(B) eternal . . immortal
(C) constant . . ephemeral
(D) little . . frivolous
(E) exaggerated . . wasted

3. Each human relationship is unique, and the lovers who think there never was a love like theirs are _____.

(A) proud
(B) foolish
(C) blind
(D) prejudiced
(E) right

4. Rats give some _____ as scavengers, but this is over-balanced by their _____ activities.

(A) help . . useful
(B) service . . harmful
(C) problems . . nocturnal
(D) trouble . . breeding
(E) uneasiness . . dynamic

5. Ancient societies gave authority to those who knew and preserved _____, for the idea of what was right lay in the past.

(A) order
(B) law
(C) intelligence
(D) tradition
(E) freedom

6. The rare desert rains often come in _____, causing loss of life and property, thus people living in an oasis think of rain with _____.

(A) floods . . longing
(B) torrents . . terror
(C) sprinkles . . fear
(D) winter . . snow
(E) summer . . desire

7. His admirers were not _____, for his essays were not widely known.

(A) respected
(B) numerous
(C) ardent
(D) interested
(E) educated

8. Archeologists found ruins of temples and palaces but no _____; it was as though these people never _____.

(A) food . . lived
(B) tombs . . died

(C) books . . thought
(D) plans . . built
(E) monasteries . . worshipped

9. Safe driving prevents _____ and the endless _____ of knowing you have caused others pain.

(A) recklessness . . dream
(B) disease . . reminder
(C) tragedy . . remorse
(D) accidents . . hope
(E) lawsuits . . expense

10. A true amateur plays because he _____ the game and will not cheat because that would _____ the game.

(A) wins . . destroy
(B) studies . . lose
(C) understands . . improve
(D) knows . . forfeit
(E) loves . . degrade

11. Companies have found it pays to have _____ handy when a meeting is likely to be _____.

(A) food . . prolonged
(B) secretaries . . enjoyable
(C) telephones . . successful
(D) money . . interesting
(E) officials . . prompt

12. He _____ apart, for he prefers _____ to the company of others.

(A) lives . . books
(B) falls . . animals
(C) stays . . throngs
(D) remains . . hibernation
(E) dwells . . solitude

13. The Constitutional duty to "take care that the laws be faithfully executed" make the President the head of law _____.

(A) development
(B) interpretation
(C) education
(D) enforcement
(E) reform

14. A reduction of the work week to four days would certainly _____ the _____ industry.

(A) decrease . . service
(B) destroy . . automobile
(C) stimulate . . steel
(D) improve . . electrical
(E) benefit . . leisure

15. History tells us it took Athens less than a generation to change from a champion of _____ into a ruthless _____.

(A) democracy . . republic
(B) freedom . . tyrant
(C) independence . . commonwealth
(D) dictatorship . . liberator
(E) expansion . . warmonger

16. The society was not _____ and required much outside aid.

(A) philanthropic
(B) destitute
(C) democratic
(D) self-sufficient
(E) moral

17. The _____ climate of the country _____ the delicate electronic equipment.

(A) intolerable . . restored
(B) dry . . vaporized
(C) changeable . . demoralized
(D) humid . . corroded
(E) parched . . hydrated

18. The value of _____ science to modern progress is _____.

(A) research . . unimportant
(B) physical . . unquestionable
(C) medical . . unlikely
(D) statistical . . unreliable
(E) industrial . . unnecessary

19. The final end of a nonadapting society is the same as for a nonadapting animal, _____.

(A) admiration
(B) resignation
(C) extinction
(D) immortality
(E) evolution

20. Some temperamental actresses fail to understand that a director's criticism is aimed at their _____ and not at their _____.

   (A) weaknesses . . conduct
   (B) stupidity . . graciousness
   (C) performance . . personality
   (D) prosperity . . inability
   (E) deportment . . attitude

21. The greater the _____ of a mineral in an ore, the less it costs to refine it.

   (A) volatility
   (B) expense
   (C) weight
   (D) oxidation
   (E) concentration

22. The church had traditionally served as a _____ for debtors, and those _____ it were safe from prosecution.

   (A) prison . . leaving
   (B) blessing . . obeying
   (C) court . . denying
   (D) sanctuary . . entering
   (E) prosecutor . . defending

23. Today's students are encouraged to absorb facts rather than to apply _____. Education is becoming _____.

   (A) understanding . . regrettable
   (B) intelligence . . invaluable
   (C) knowledge . . passive
   (D) formulas . . extensive
   (E) memories . . active

24. Man's survival is a result of mutual assistance, since he is essentially _____ rather than _____.

   (A) superior . . inferior
   (B) cooperative . . competitive
   (C) individualistic . . gregarious
   (D) physical . . mental
   (E) selfish . . stingy

25. Ancient Greeks were not only concerned with the development of the _____ but also felt training of the body was of _____ importance.

   (A) muscles . . equal
   (B) psyche . . little
   (C) mind . . prime
   (D) physical . . vital
   (E) ego . . greater

SET TWO

1. His theory is not _____; it only sounds plausible to the uninformed because he _____ several facts and fails to mention the mountain of evidence that contradicts his ideas.

   (A) tenable . . distorts
   (B) pliable . . pursued
   (C) predominant . . embellished
   (D) prejudiced . . included
   (E) sufficient . . invokes

2. That organization _____ its concern for endangered species of wildlife by encouraging congressmen to pass laws that _____ these animals.

   (A) imposes . . promote
   (B) manipulates . . defend
   (C) manifests . . protect
   (D) supplants . . prohibit
   (E) exposes . . destroy

3. His filing system was so _____ that no one else in the department could locate material quickly.

   (A) alphabetical

   (B) specific
   (C) appropriate
   (D) intense
   (E) peculiar

4. When the last item on the _____ had been taken care of, the meeting was _____.

   (A) roster . . called to order
   (B) itinerary . . finalized
   (C) table . . sequestered
   (D) agenda . . adjourned
   (E) list . . postponed

5. It has been predicted that the new _____ barring discrimination in employment on the basis of sexual orientation will dramatically _____ hiring practices.

   (A) morality . . effect
   (B) permissiveness . . reflect
   (C) legislation . . affect
   (D) rulings . . reset
   (E) procedures . . determine

6. The Navy scoured the area for over a month, but the _____ search turned up no clues.

 (A) temporary
 (B) cursory
 (C) fruitful
 (D) present
 (E) painstaking

7. Although her personality is sometimes _____, she is a conscientious worker and is _____ better treatment than she has received.

 (A) pleasing . . conscious of
 (B) abrasive . . entitled to
 (C) gloomy . . eligible for
 (D) cheerful . . granted
 (E) ingratiating . . denied

8. _____ manipulation of the stock market and other _____ practices in security sales resulted in the 1933 legislation for the control of security markets.

 (A) Meticulous . . legal
 (B) Degenerate . . lucrative
 (C) Economic . . useless
 (D) Continual . . productive
 (E) Unscrupulous . . unethical

9. The handbook _____ for beginners was written in an elementary style.

 (A) bound
 (B) intended
 (C) paged
 (D) authored
 (E) predicted

10. When a job becomes too _____, workers get _____, their attention wanders, and they start to make careless errors.

 (A) diverse . . busy
 (B) hectic . . lazy
 (C) tedious . . bored
 (D) fascinating . . interested
 (E) detailed . . angry

11. Because of her uncompromising stands on divisive issues, she was unable to _____ broad support among the voters; however, the minority who did support her were exceptionally _____.

 (A) alienate . . many
 (B) survey . . divided

(C) cut across . . quiet
(D) amass . . loyal
(E) withstand . . vocal

12. His remarks were too _____ to be taken seriously.

 (A) germane
 (B) crucial
 (C) timely
 (D) pointed
 (E) insipid

13. No training course can operate to full advantage without job descriptions, which _____ those parts of the job that require the most training before the training course is _____.

 (A) list . . improved
 (B) identify . . implemented
 (C) teach . . predicted
 (D) ignore . . met
 (E) insulate . . finished

14. Since the course was not only _____ but also had a reputation for being extremely difficult, _____ students registered for it.

 (A) operational . . male
 (B) enjoyable . . many
 (C) required . . some
 (D) useful . . practical
 (E) optional . . few

15. The new secretary has a more businesslike manner than her _____ in the job.

 (A) precedent
 (B) ancestor
 (C) successor
 (D) predecessor
 (E) antecedent

16. Because of the _____ hazard, regulations forbid the use of highly _____ materials in certain items such as children's pajamas.

 (A) health . . synthetic
 (B) fire . . flammable
 (C) drug . . inflammatory
 (D) chemical . . flame-retardant
 (E) sleep . . toxic

17. The _____ report was submitted, subject to such _____ as would be made before the final draft.

    (A) preliminary . . revisions
    (B) ubiquitous . . submissions
    (C) ultimate . . editions
    (D) obsolete . . alterations
    (E) committee's . . references

18. _____ action on the part of a passerby revived the victim before brain damage could occur.

    (A) Physical
    (B) Prompt
    (C) Violent
    (D) Delayed
    (E) Brave

19. As the workload _____, she _____ responsibility for many routine tasks to an assistant.

    (A) evolved . . preserved
    (B) changed . . handled
    (C) increased . . delegated
    (D) steadied . . abased
    (E) lessened . . optioned

20. For many years _____ have been recognized as breeding disease, juvenile delinquency, and crime, which not only threaten the health and welfare of people who live there, but also _____ the structure of society as a whole.

    (A) prisons . . rebuild
    (B) swamps . . bolster
    (C) schools . . disengage
    (D) colonialization . . alienate
    (E) slums . . weaken

21. As citizens we would be _____ if we did not make these facts public.

    (A) entitled

(B) nominative
(C) elective
(D) derelict
(E) private

22. A _____ in the diplomatic service, she had not yet _____ such a question of protocol.

    (A) success . . dispatched
    (B) volunteer . . avoided
    (C) veteran . . bantered
    (D) novice . . encountered
    (E) participant . . warranted

23. Excessive fatigue can _____ be attributed to _____ working conditions such as poor lighting.

    (A) inevitably . . archaic
    (B) occasionally . . inadequate
    (C) always . . obsolete
    (D) never . . demoralizing
    (E) aggressively . . unpleasant

24. The company received a _____ from the government to help develop new sources of energy.

    (A) reward
    (B) compendium
    (C) memorandum
    (D) subsidy
    (E) honorarium

25. The _____ with which the agent calmed the anxieties and soothed the tempers of the travelers _____ by the delay was a mark of frequent experience with similar crises.

    (A) evasiveness . . angered
    (B) reverence . . pleased
    (C) facility . . inconvenienced
    (D) mannerism . . destroyed
    (E) vitality . . exhausted

SET THREE

1. Although for years _____ resources had been devoted to alleviating the problem, a satisfactory solution remained _____.

    (A) natural . . costly
    (B) adequate . . probable
    (C) substantial . . elusive
    (D) capital . . decisive
    (E) inadequate . . unlikely

2. The police department will not accept for _____ a report of a person missing from his residence if such _____ is located outside of the city.

    (A) foreclosure . . person
    (B) convenience . . location
    (C) control . . report
    (D) filing . . department
    (E) investigation . . residence

3. The treaty cannot go into effect until it has been
_____ by the Senate.

   (A) considered
   (B) debated
   (C) ratified
   (D) shelved
   (E) amended

4. His _____ of practical experience and his psychological acuity more than _____ his lack of formal academic training.

   (A) dearth . . concede to
   (B) claims . . comprise
   (C) background . . educate for
   (D) brief . . account for
   (E) wealth . . compensate for

5. Because I wanted to use a(n) _____, I looked the word up in the _____.

   (A) synonym . . thesaurus
   (B) homonym . . directory
   (C) antonym . . encyclopedia
   (D) pseudonym . . dictionary
   (E) syllable . . atlas

6. You will have to speak to the head of the department; I am not _____ to give out that information.

   (A) willing
   (B) authorized
   (C) programmed
   (D) happy
   (E) going

7. Research in that field has become so _____ that researchers on different aspects of the same problem may be _____ each other's work.

   (A) secure . . bombarded with
   (B) partial . . surprised at
   (C) departmental . . inimical to
   (D) specialized . . unfamiliar with
   (E) complete . . duplicating

8. She _____ the way things were done, but many of the _____ for which she broke ground were left to be fully realized by others.

   (A) disliked . . provocations

   (B) continued . . initiations
   (C) eliminated . . foundations
   (D) implemented . . buildings
   (E) revolutionized . . innovations

9. A change in environment is very likely to _____ a change in one's work habits.

   (A) affect
   (B) inflict
   (C) propose
   (D) effect
   (E) prosper

10. A shift to greater use of _____ or inexhaustible resources in the production of power would slow the depletion of _____ fuel materials.

   (A) synthetic . . regional
   (B) cleaner . . irradiated
   (C) natural . . chemical
   (D) renewable . . irreplaceable
   (E) unknown . . fossil

11. A _____ is likely to give you _____ advice.

   (A) fool . . useful
   (B) thief . . profitable
   (C) doctor . . lethal
   (D) friend . . harmful
   (E) charlatan . . unreliable

12. An accident report should be written as soon as possible after the necessary _____ has been obtained.

   (A) bystander
   (B) formulation
   (C) information
   (D) permission
   (E) certificate

13. To protect the respondents' _____, names and social security numbers are _____ the questionnaires before the results are tabulated.

   (A) privilege . . referred to
   (B) privacy . . deleted from
   (C) information . . retained in
   (D) rights . . appended to
   (E) health . . coded to

14. While fewer documents are being kept, the usefulness of those _____ is now _____ by an improved cataloguing system.

   (A) printed . . documented
   (B) discarded . . concurred
   (C) read . . emblazoned
   (D) retained . . insured
   (E) purchased . . corroborated

15. The man _____ the speaker at the meeting by shouting false accusations.

   (A) corrected
   (B) interfered with
   (C) disconcerted
   (D) acknowledged
   (E) pleased

16. For the sake of public _____, public officials should avoid even the _____ of a conflict of interest.

   (A) confidence . . appearance
   (B) competence . . resistance
   (C) relations . . actuality
   (D) appearances . . apparition
   (E) commotion . . hint

17. A professional journalist will attempt to _____ the facts learned in an interview by independent _____.

   (A) retell . . videotape
   (B) endorse . . questions
   (C) query . . situation
   (D) garnish . . sources
   (E) verify . . investigation

18. The _____ of the award stopped by the financial aid office to pick up his check.

   (A) recipient
   (B) subject
   (C) donor
   (D) sponsor
   (E) officer

19. He often, out of modesty, _____ his own contribution; without his efforts, _____, the program would still be in the planning stage.

   (A) affirms . . therefore
   (B) represses . . notwithstanding
   (C) belittles . . however

   (D) rescinds . . moreover
   (E) trumpets . . meanwhile

20. The committee was so _____ about the legitimate sources of the students' unrest that its recommendations were _____ value.

   (A) incensed . . of moderate
   (B) uninformed . . devoid of
   (C) uninterested . . depreciating in
   (D) blasé . . of incontestable
   (E) upset . . little

21. Unfortunately, these favorable influences can be expected to _____ or even disappear within the next few years.

   (A) defray
   (B) recur
   (C) intensify
   (D) vanish
   (E) abate

22. Although she was otherwise efficient and responsible, _____ was not one of her virtues, and she was _____ in the office by nine.

   (A) conscientiousness . . often
   (B) tardiness . . never
   (C) politeness . . always
   (D) punctuality . . rarely
   (E) neatness . . frequently

23. A string of lies had landed her in such a hopeless _____ that she didn't know how to _____ herself.

   (A) status . . clear
   (B) pinnacle . . explain
   (C) enigma . . help
   (D) predicament . . extricate
   (E) confusion . . fool

24. In an attempt to _____ a strike, the parties agreed to negotiate through the night.

   (A) trigger
   (B) avert
   (C) arbitrate
   (D) herald
   (E) mediate

25. Because of their _____ exposure to this strain of influenza, they are fortunately _____ to the current outbreak.

(A) previous . . immune
(B) frequent . . oblivious
(C) recent . . not liable
(D) lack of . . vulnerable
(E) recent . . prone

SET FOUR

1. A survey to determine the school subjects that have helped students most in their jobs shows that _____ leads all other subjects in the _____ group.

(A) chemistry . . professional
(B) history . . service
(C) typewriting . . business
(D) mathematics . . legal
(E) spelling . . nursing

2. Many industrial processes are dangerous to the _____ of workers and give rise to occupational _____.

(A) lives . . benefits
(B) stability . . factors
(C) marriages . . dislocation
(D) health . . diseases
(E) leisure . . hazards

3. A telegram should be clear yet _____.

(A) compendious
(B) concise
(C) colloquial
(D) correct
(E) communicative

4. Statutes to _____ adulteration of foods and to _____ for sanitary food preparation are in force in every state.

(A) cause . . penalize
(B) abet . . arrange
(C) police . . sterilize
(D) propose . . legislate
(E) prevent . . provide

5. _____, in almost every community there are some men and women who are known to be _____.

(A) Sadly . . philanthropic
(B) Obviously . . sadistic
(C) Fortunately . . public spirited
(D) Fortuitously . . misanthropic
(E) Reluctantly . . impoverished

6. Specialization in industry creates workers who lack _____.

(A) versatility
(B) employment
(C) intelligence
(D) ability
(E) expertise

7. During World War I, the government decided to relieve _____ congestion by reviving use of the _____.

(A) highway . . mails
(B) traffic . . airways
(C) slum . . national guard
(D) harbor . . ocean
(E) railroad . . waterways

8. The increasing size of business organizations has resulted in less personal contact between _____ and _____.

(A) workers . . the final product
(B) salespeople . . customers
(C) superiors . . subordinates
(D) men . . their families
(E) one worker . . another

9. Because of a death in the family, the soldier's leave was _____.

(A) denied
(B) extended
(C) postponed
(D) publicized
(E) corroborated

10. The _____ hat she wore gave her a _____ appearance.

(A) flowery . . florid
(B) peculiar . . comical
(C) tiny . . imposing
(D) fashionable . . dowdy
(E) unbecoming . . handsome

11. Farm life was too _____ an existence for the _____ young man.

 (A) interesting . . dull
 (B) active . . energetic
 (C) boring . . tall
 (D) tough . . frail
 (E) demanding . . sullen

12. The carpenter was criticized for his _____ work.

 (A) original
 (B) careful
 (C) recent
 (D) projected
 (E) slipshod

13. Most of the time, the three divisions of the Federal government tend to _____; in crises they tend to _____.

 (A) check . . balance
 (B) balance . . check
 (C) convene . . collide
 (D) convict . . absolve
 (E) compete . . cooperate

14. There exists a _____ but _____ idea that a clue is a mysterious fact that most people overlook.

 (A) false . . popular
 (B) private . . well-known
 (C) harmless . . true
 (D) frightening . . pleasant
 (E) useful . . helpful

15. With a full month for vacation, we made a very _____ trip to California.

 (A) unforgettable
 (B) tiresome
 (C) perfunctory
 (D) leisurely
 (E) unexpected

16. Scientific judgments as _____ legal judgments are more _____.

 (A) supported by . . accurate
 (B) compared to . . opinionated
 (C) proposed by . . verifiable
 (D) contrasted with . . supportable
 (E) opposed to . . objective

17. The amount that the government can spend is limited by the people's _____ and _____ to pay taxes.

 (A) candidates . . voting
 (B) desire . . objection
 (C) Federal . . local
 (D) capacity . . willingness
 (E) faith . . opportunity

18. The study produced a _____ amount of data, so much in fact that it will take several weeks to prepare the report.

 (A) considerate
 (B) minuscule
 (C) considerable
 (D) constant
 (E) useful

19. Doctors recommend that those who normally use _____ salt _____ their salt consumption in hot weather, when salt is depleted through perspiration.

 (A) iodized . . cut out
 (B) sea salt . . dilute
 (C) ample . . decrease
 (D) seasoned . . alter
 (E) little . . increase

20. The police powers of the state provide for ____ designed to _____ the health and general welfare of the people.

 (A) legislation . . promote
 (B) prosecution . . convict
 (C) arrests . . punish
 (D) warrants . . search
 (E) jails . . protect

21. _____ recommendations are generally more constructive than vague complaints.

 (A) Justified
 (B) Nebulous
 (C) Sweeping
 (D) Specific
 (E) Repetitious

22. The team attributes its _____ season to a number of _____ factors.

 (A) losing . . propitious
 (B) long . . irrelevant
 (C) winning . . favorable
 (D) embarrassing . . optimistic
 (E) championship . . unknown

23. Although mental growth ceases between the ages of fourteen and sixteen, a(n) _____ in ability to meet novel situations is _____ by experience.

(A) increase . . gained
(B) growth . . negated
(C) loss . . explained
(D) drop . . countered
(E) proficiency . . declined

24. The teachers of foreign languages were asked to _____ their conversation courses with written grammar reviews.

(A) substantiate
(B) formulate
(C) supplement
(D) abridge
(E) exercise

25. A suggestion system allows for the _____ of employees to be used for _____ of expenses.

(A) expertise . . expansion
(B) suggestions . . aggravation
(C) antagonism . . elimination
(D) ideas . . instigation
(E) abilities . . reduction

ANSWER KEY FOR
PRACTICE SENTENCE COMPLETIONS

SET ONE

1. E	6. B	11. A	16. D	21. E
2. B	7. B	12. E	17. D	22. D
3. E	8. B	13. D	18. B	23. C
4. B	9. C	14. E	19. C	24. B
5. D	10. E	15. B	20. C	25. C

SET TWO

1. A	6. E	11. D	16. B	21. D
2. C	7. B	12. E	17. A	22. D
3. E	8. E	13. B	18. B	23. B
4. D	9. B	14. E	19. C	24. D
5. C	10. C	15. D	20. E	25. C

SET THREE

1. C	6. B	11. E	16. A	21. E
2. E	7. D	12. C	17. E	22. D
3. C	8. E	13. B	18. A	23. D
4. E	9. D	14. D	19. C	24. B
5. A	10. D	15. C	20. B	25. A

SET FOUR

1. C	6. A	11. D	16. E	21. D
2. D	7. E	12. E	17. D	22. C
3. B	8. C	13. E	18. C	23. A
4. E	9. B	14. A	19. E	24. C
5. C	10. B	15. D	20. A	25. E

EXPLANATORY ANSWERS FOR PRACTICE
SENTENCE COMPLETIONS

SET ONE

1. **(E)** The first blank must be filled with what it is that fortunetellers do. This narrows your choice to (D) or (E). There being no scientific evidence of their fees makes no sense, so the answer is (E).

2. **(B)** The sentence calls for synonyms, as the second clause merely expands upon the first. ETERNAL and IMMORTAL both mean everlasting.

3. **(E)** The second clause of the sentence is meant

to corroborate the first. Since each human relationship is unique, the lovers who assume the uniqueness of their own relationship are RIGHT.

4. **(B)** The word "but" gives the clue that the blanks must be filled with contrasting terms. (B) best meets this condition.

5. **(D)** If the idea of what was right lay in the past, then authority would have to be given to those who knew and preserved ancient lore and habits, i.e., TRADITION.

6. **(B)** Since the desert rains cause loss of life and property, people in an oasis must think of rain with TERROR, (B), or fear, (C). The word which best fills the second blank will determine whether the correct answer is (B) or (C). Sprinkles, (C), would be unlikely to cause loss of life and property; TORRENTS, (B), is more appropriate.

7. **(B)** If the essayist's essays were not widely known, he would have few (not NUMEROUS) admirers.

8. **(B)** In light of the fact that archeologists found palaces, (A), (C) and (D) cannot be correct. The people clearly lived, thought and built. Temples are places of worship, so (E) is also incorrect. (B) presents a mystery, but it does create a logically correct sentence.

9. **(C)** Safe driving prevents TRAGEDY, (C), accidents, (D), and lawsuits, (E). The second part of the sentence, however, is reasonably completed only with (C).

10. **(E)** The purpose of amateur sports is recreation; the amateur participates for fun, for LOVE of the sport. (The word "amateur" is derived directly from Latin and means "lover.") Cheating is DEGRADING; it makes an activity less desirable.

11. **(A)** If there is to be a meeting, it might be well to have FOOD, (A), secretaries, (B), and telephones, (C), available. However, none of these is specifically needed at an enjoyable, (B), meeting or at a successful, (C), meeting. If the meeting is likely to be PROLONGED, (A), then it is worthwhile to provide FOOD.

12. **(E)** Both (A) and (E) form excellent completions for this sentence. (E) is the *best* answer because

SOLITUDE is in direct contrast to the company of others.

13. **(D)** Executing the laws requires law ENFORCEMENT.

14. **(E)** A four-day work week would give workers much more LEISURE time, which would, in turn, greatly BENEFIT the LEISURE industry.

15. **(B)** The adjective "ruthless" (cruel) aptly describes a TYRANT. Since the sense of the sentence calls for contrast, a change from champion of DEMOCRACY to ruthless TYRANT fulfills the requirement.

16. **(D)** The reason that a society would need outside aid would be that the society was not SELF-SUFFICIENT.

17. **(D)** The sentence requires that there be a cause and effect relationship between the two words which fill the blanks. Only (D) meets this requirement.

18. **(B)** The meaning of any one of the choices would be equally appropriate for filling the first blank, though (A) would be grammatically incorrect. The words "value" and "progress" are positive words, suggesting the need for a positive completion for the second blank. The only positive second term is in choice (B).

19. **(C)** The final end is EXTINCTION.

20. **(C)** The role of a director is to perfect the PERFORMANCE through necessary criticism. A temperamental actress might misinterpret direction as PERSONAL criticism.

21. **(E)** It is reasonable to assume that a more CONCENTRATED ore would yield a greater quantity of the mineral and would thus be more cost efficient.

22. **(D)** The word "and" connecting the two clauses implies that safety from prosecution applies to the church. A SANCTUARY is a place for refuge and protection and all who ENTER it are safe.

23. **(C)** Absorption of facts is PASSIVE, as opposed to the more active mode of education, the application of KNOWLEDGE.

24. **(B)** The sentence, by the words "rather than," requires that the two words filling the blanks be

opposites. Only (E) does not meet this requirement. However, mutual assistance implies COOPERATION, hence (B) is the correct answer.

25. **(C)** The sentence requires that the first blank be filled by a word which contrasts with body. Of the choices, MIND, (C), best meets this criterion.

SET TWO

1. **(A)** The first blank might be filled equally well by the first term of choice (A) or choice (E); however, the coordinating ''and'' implies that the second blank must be filled with something negative that he does to the facts. DISTORTS is the best word here.

2. **(C)** Choices (D) and (E) make no sense. ''Encouraging'' is not a coercive type of activity, so (A) and (B) would be too forceful as completions in the first blank.

3. **(E)** If no one else could locate the material, you may be pretty sure that his filing system was PECULIAR.

4. **(D)** The list of items for consideration at a meeting is the AGENDA. When the business is completed, one might as well ADJOURN the meeting.

5. **(C)** The barring of discrimination is an official act, so only (C) or (D) could fill the first blank. The second blank is best filled with the idiomatic ''AFFECT hiring practices.''

6. **(E)** A search that lasts more than a month is most certainly a PAINSTAKING one.

7. **(B)** The first blank calls for a negative trait to contrast with her conscientiousness. (B) or (C) might both be correct, but ENTITLED TO better fits the informality of the sentence. ''Eligible for'' implies a legal requirement.

8. **(E)** The coordinating ''and'' in the compound subject requires that both words have the same connotation. Since these acts led to the imposition of controls, we must assume that they were negative acts.

9. **(B)** The style of a manual must be appropriate to the audience for which it is INTENDED.

10. **(C)** The key here is that the workers' attention wanders. Attention wanders when one is BORED. One becomes BORED when the work is TEDIOUS.

11. **(D)** Only AMASS really makes sense in the first blank.

12. **(E)** Any remarks other than stupid or INSIPID ones should be taken seriously.

13. **(B)** The second blank can be filled only by (B) or (E). (E) makes no sense in the first blank.

14. **(E)** The ''not only . . . but also'' construction implies two complementary reasons why a classification of students might register for the course. Only (E) really fits this requirement. A course that is OPTIONAL and very difficult will draw FEW registrants.

15. **(D)** The person who held this job before the current secretary was her PREDECESSOR.

16. **(B)** Only (A) or (B) makes sense in the first blank. Synthetics are not in themselves a health hazard.

17. **(A)** The report was submitted before the final draft. Only (A) or (E) can describe the report. A report is not made subject to references; it is made subject to REVISIONS before the final draft.

18. **(B)** Since the action was taken before brain damage could occur, the *best* completion implies speed.

19. **(C)** The best thing to do with excess responsibility is to DELEGATE it.

20. **(E)** The second blank must be filled by a negative word. This limits the answer to (C), (D) or (E). Of the three first-term choices, only SLUMS are recognized as the breeding grounds of disease, juvenile delinquency and crime.

21. **(D)** The structure of the sentence leaves only (D) as a sensible completion.

22. **(D)** The words ''not yet'' imply that she was new to or a NOVICE in the diplomatic service. (B) is a possible answer as well, but (D) is better.

23. **(B)** Excessive fatigue can often be attributed to factors other than inhospitable working conditions, but OCCASIONALLY, INADEQUATE working conditions are its cause.

24. **(D)** Money helps in the development of new processes and products. A SUBSIDY is money received in advance of the work. Rewards and honoraria follow a service.

25. **(C)** The blanks could be filled with choices (A), (C) or (E). However, frequent experience should lead to FACILITY in soothing INCONVENIENCED travelers, so (C) is the *best* answer.

SET THREE

1. **(C)** The construction of the sentence demands that the first blank be filled with a positive word while the second is filled with a less positive word. (C) best fits these requirements.

2. **(E)** A missing person report demands INVESTIGATION.

3. **(C)** All the consideration, amendment and debate will not put a treaty into effect until it is RATIFIED.

4. **(E)** The words in the blanks should contrast with his lack of formal academic training.

5. **(A)** The THESAURUS is a book of SYNONYMS.

6. **(B)** All choices except (C) might be correct, but the imperative of "you will *have* to" implies that I am not AUTHORIZED.

7. **(D)** No enmity is implied in this sentence, so (D) is a better answer than (C).

8. **(E)** One might break ground for (C), (D), or (E), but only INNOVATIONS for which one breaks ground are fully realized by others.

9. **(D)** To EFFECT is to cause. *Inflict* has a negative connotation that is uncalled for in this sentence.

10. **(D)** Fuel materials that could be depleted are either (D) or (E). Only (D) fits into the first blank. The use of RENEWABLE resources would slow the depletion of IRREPLACEABLE fuel materials.

11. **(E)** The type of advice must be appropriate to the giver. The advice of a CHARLATAN or imposter is likely to be UNRELIABLE.

12. **(C)** An accident report should be dependent only upon INFORMATION and not upon permission or certificates.

13. **(B)** DELETION of identification insures PRIVACY.

14. **(D)** If fewer documents are being kept, we are probably discussing those that are RETAINED. Their usefulness is INSURED by an improved cataloguing system.

15. **(C)** The man would have interfered with the speaker even if he had shouted words of agreement. Since the point is made that the man shouted false accusations, the *best* answer is that he DISCONCERTED the speaker.

16. **(A)** The second blank could be filled with (A) or (E); however, the first term of (E) makes no sense in the first blank.

17. **(E)** VERIFICATION is at the heart of professionalism.

18. **(A)** Only the RECIPIENT would pick up the check.

19. **(C)** Modesty would lead one to BELITTLE his role. The connective HOWEVER makes the best transition between the two clauses.

20. **(B)** The second blank might be filled by all choices except (C). However, the two terms of (D) make no sense in apposition. (A) and (E) are not the correct answers. The committee might have been incensed or upset about the students' unrest but it would be unlikely to be upset or incensed about the legitimate causes of that unrest. If it were UNINFORMED of the legitimate causes, its recommendations would be DEVOID OF value.

21. **(E)** The word in the blank must be a precursor to or a lesser degree of disappearance. *Vanish* is a synonym.

22. **(D)** Since getting into the office by nine is a factor, the sentence clearly refers to time. *Tardiness* is not a virtue. PUNCTUALITY is the virtue that she lacked, and she was RARELY in the office on time.

23. **(D)** Choice (C) might also be correct, but (D) is the more idiomatic expression, and EXTRICATE is the more expressive word for describing the manner in which one emerges from a tangle or PREDICAMENT.

24. **(B)** Negotiation is the stage at which the parties to a dispute talk to each other and try to reach their own solution. If they are successful, they AVERT the strike. Mediation and arbitration are later steps taken if negotiation fails.

25. **(A)** The word "fortunately" leads to the conclusion that they are IMMUNE to the flu.

SET FOUR

1. **(C)** Since the survey determined the school subjects that were most useful to students in their jobs, there must be a necessary connection between the subject and the occupation. That connection exists between TYPEWRITING and BUSINESS.

2. **(D)** Since the industrial processes are dangerous, the second blank must be filled with a negative word. There must be some logical connection between the words that fill the two blanks. Conditions that are dangerous to HEALTH lead to DISEASES.

3. **(B)** Your understanding of the function of a telegram should help you answer this question. (D) and (E) are so obvious as to represent tautologies.

4. **(E)** (A), (B) and (D) would all be ridiculous in the first blank. The second blank could not be filled by the second term of choice (C).

5. **(C)** Choices (A) and (D) lead to internally contradictive statements. While the sentiment of choice (E) is reasonable, the first term does not serve as an effective connecting word. Choice (C) makes a more logical statement than does (B).

6. **(A)** Specialization creates workers with ability and expertise in specific, narrow applications and with a consequent lack of VERSATILITY. Only if and when these specialities are no longer in demand will such workers lack employment.

7. **(E)** Choices (C) and (D) make no sense. The clue to the answer is found in the words "reviving use of." Use of the mails never declined, and, during World War I, there was no prior use of the airways to revive. On the other hand, in its heyday the RAILROAD was used to the exclusion of the WATERWAYS.

8. **(C)** The key words "personal contact" eliminate choice (A). Salespeople deal directly with customers regardless of the size of the business organization, and men still come home to their families. The size of the organization does, however, create distance between top management, SUPERIORS, and rank-and-file workers, SUBORDINATES.

9. **(B)** This is a simple cause and effect statement. The soldier's leave was EXTENDED because of a death in the family.

10. **(B)** There must be a logical connection between some aspect of the hat and her appearance. A PECULIAR hat might give her a COMICAL appearance.

11. **(D)** Again, look for a necessary connection between some aspect of farm life and a characteristic of the young man. (C) and (E) make no connection at all. (A) and (B) make for illogical connections. A FRAIL person might well find farm life too TOUGH.

12. **(E)** Any one of the choices could be used to fill the blank, so you must find a reason for the criticism.

13. **(E)** The blanks must be filled by true opposites. If you fill the second blank first, you realize that it must be filled with a very positive word. In times of crisis, COMPETING forces tend to COOPERATE.

14. **(A)** The two terms that fill the blanks must be complementary, neither contrasting nor synonymous. (B) and (D) are contrasting. (E) is synonymous. (C) is correct but meaningless, leaving (A) as the *best* answer.

15. **(D)** The time aspect gives the clue here. With a full month, the trip could be very LEISURELY.

16. **(E)** Fill the second blank first and eliminate (B). The first terms of (A) and (C) make no sense in the first blank. (D) in itself represents a value judgment. (E) is a noncontroversial, correct answer.

17. **(D)** Choices (A) and (C) make no sense. The two terms connected by "and" should be of equal impact and parallel construction. Remember that you must choose the *best* answer.

18. **(C)** So much data is a CONSIDERABLE amount.

19. **(E)** Since salt is depleted through perspiration, it is logical that doctors recommend an INCREASE in consumption in hot weather.

20. **(A)** Only (A) and (E) make any sense at all. Jails do not promote the health of the people.

21. **(D)** What could be more constructive than a SPECIFIC recommendation?

22. **(C)** There must be a logical connection between the kind of season and the named factors. The

team would be able to name the factors that led to a championship season.

23. **(A)** The negative first clause introduced by "although" leads us to expect a positive statement in the main clause. The need for a positive word in the first blank eliminates choices (C) and (D). The word in the second blank must support the word in the first. As one GAINS in experience, one INCREASES one's ability to meet novel situations.

24. **(C)** Grammar review SUPPLEMENTS conversation in the study of a foreign language.

25. **(E)** Clearly a suggestion system should have a positive effect on expenses. This eliminates (A), (B) and (D). Antagonism is not likely to lead to constructive suggestions.

VERBAL ANALOGIES

Example:

SHOE : LEATHER ::

(A) moccasin : trail
(B) tree : leaf
(C) sky : stars
(D) highway : asphalt
(E) postcard : picture

(D) A *shoe* is a manufactured product made of *leather;* a *highway* is man-made and is constructed of *asphalt.* While *leaves, stars* and *pictures* are component parts of, respectively, *trees, the sky* and *postcards,* they are not the main, man-made structural parts.

The analogy question tests your ability to see a relationship between words and to apply that relationship to other words. It is both a measure of your vocabulary and a test of your ability to think things out. Its most important function is to spotlight your ability to think clearly and to sidestep confusion of ideas. If you are inexperienced with it, the analogy question is difficult. The form in which it is put is sometimes complex. And it requires thought. If you know something of the mechanics and the structure

of analogies, you have taken a big step in the direction of expertise.

A popular form of analogy is that used on both the PSAT (Preliminary Scholastic Aptitude Test) and the SAT (Scholastic Aptitude Test). Two words are given. They bear a certain, meaningful relationship to each other. The first pair is followed by five pairs of words. You are asked to select the pair which is related in the same way as the words of the first pair are related to each other. This type of analogy question is often written in the form of a mathematical proportion, with the symbol ":" standing for "is to" and the symbol "::" standing for "as." Thus, a simple completed analogy MAN : BOY :: WOMAN : GIRL would be read: MAN is to BOY as WOMAN is to GIRL. A WOMAN is an adult GIRL in the same way that a MAN is an adult BOY.

HOW TO ANSWER ANALOGY QUESTIONS

The first step in approaching an analogy question is to define the capitalized words. The vocabulary of analogy questions is not usually too difficult, but occasionally an unfamiliar word will appear. If you cannot define both words of the initial pair, you cannot identify their relationship. Do not waste your time puzzling over such a question; skip it.

Most often you will know the meanings of both words. Your next step is to determine how those words are related to each other. First define a general relationship, then narrow it to a more specific relationship. Suppose you are confronted with an analogy question which begins: BRIM : HAT :: __. BRIM and HAT are immediately associated in your mind; therefore the first relationship which comes to mind is that of association. More specifically, a BRIM is a part of a HAT, so your relationship is more specifically that of a part to the whole.

Once you have isolated the relationship between

the first two words, you must find among the choices another pair of words which bear the same relation to one another. This is best done through a process of elimination. Let us further analyze the analogy question which we met above.

BRIM : HAT ::

   (A) hand : glove
   (B) spoke : umbrella
   (C) skirt : hem
   (D) snood : hood
   (E) lace : shoe

Consider each answer choice in turn.

Hand is certainly associated with glove. If you had not narrowed your relationship to part/whole, you might now consider (A) to be the correct answer. Do not totally discount (A) until you look over the remaining choices. However, since the initial relationship lends itself best to the part/whole classification, you should be looking for a better answer than (A).

A spoke is part of an umbrella. (B) is a likely answer choice. However, you must ALWAYS look at all five choices before marking your answer.

Skirt and hem are associated. In fact, a hem is part of a skirt, but BEWARE. The relationship in (C) is that of a whole to its part, which is the reverse of the initial relationship. Your answer must maintain the same relationship in the same sequence as the original pair.

If you know the meaning of the word "snood," you know that a snood is a hair net. Snood, hood and hat are all related, are all a form of headgear. However, a snood is not a part of a hood, hence (D) is incorrect. If you do not know the meaning of one word among the answer choices, do not fall into the trap of choosing the unfamiliar because of lack of self-confidence. Consider all the choices very carefully before you mark the unknown as the only possibility.

A lace is a part of a shoe. (E) appears to be a perfectly good answer.

Having found at least two part/whole choices, you may now eliminate (A) as a possible answer. And, having followed this process of elimination, you are now faced with two very likely answers, (B) and (E).

Return to the original pair and determine its other distinguishing characteristics. A brim is a part of a hat, but it is not a necessary part. Not all hats have brims. A lace is a part of a shoe, but it is not a

necessary part. Some shoes have buckles, some are slip-ons. A spoke, however, is a necessary part of an umbrella. Furthermore, a brim is part of a hat, which is wearing apparel. A lace is a part of a shoe, also wearing apparel. But one does not wear an umbrella. There are thus two counts (wearing apparel and necessity of the part) on which to eliminate (B) and to choose (E) as the *best* answer.

And so the process is:
1. Define the initial terms.
2. Describe the initial relationship.
3. Eliminate incorrect answers.
4. Refine the initial relationship.
5. Choose the *best* answer.

Usually your problem will be that of narrowing to the *best* answer. Sometimes, however, your difficulty will be in finding even one correct answer. If this happens, you may have to shift gears and completely redefine your initial relationship. Consider an analogy which begins, LETTER : WORD ::. Initially, you will probably think, "A LETTER is part of a WORD, therefore the relationship is that of part to whole." If you can find a pair of words with a part/whole relationship, all is well. However, suppose the question looks like this:

LETTER : WORD ::

   (A) procession : parade
   (B) dot : dash
   (C) whisper : orate
   (D) song : note
   (E) spell : recite

Not one of these choices offers a true part to whole relationship. Returning to the original pair, you must then consider other relationships between LETTER and WORD. If "letter" is not "letter of the alphabet," but rather "written communication," then a WORD is part of a LETTER and the relationship becomes that of the whole to its part. The answer is immediately clear, (D). A SONG is the whole of which a NOTE is a part.

Analogy questions are a real challenge and can even be fun. They also offer many opportunities for errors if every answer is not given careful consideration. A few of the most common pitfalls to avoid are:

• Reversal of sequence of the relationship
   Part to whole is *not* the same as whole to part.
   Cause to effect is *not* the same as effect to its cause.

Smaller to larger is *not* the same as larger to smaller.

Action to object is *not* the same as object to action.

- Confusion of relationship

    Part to Part (geometry : calculus) with Part to Whole (verb : grammar)

    Cause and Effect (fire : smoke) with Association (man : woman)

    Degree (drizzle : downpour) with Antonyms (dry : wet)

    Association (walk : limp) with Synonyms (eat : consume)

- Grammatical inconsistency

    The grammatical relationship of the first two words must be retained throughout the analogy. A wrong analogy would be IMPRISONED : LION :: CAGE : PARROT. While the meaningful relationship exists, the analogy is not parallel in construction. A correct analogy of this sort would have to read: PRISON : LION :: CAGE : PARROT or IMPRISONED : LION :: CAGED : PARROT. In analogy questions, you have to choose that pair which is grammatically consistent as well as meaningfully correct.

- Concentration on the meanings of words instead of on their relationships

    In this type of error, you see FEATHERS : BEAK and you think "bird" instead of part to part relationship. Then, you choose as your answer WING : BIRD instead of FIN : GILL.

REMEMBER: THE KEY TO ANSWERING ANALOGY QUESTIONS LIES IN THE RELATIONSHIP BETWEEN THE FIRST TWO WORDS!

If you are having trouble determining the relationship between the words of the initial pair, you might find it useful to mentally reverse their order. If the relationship becomes clear when you effect this reversal, you must then remember to mentally reverse the order of the option pairs as well, so as to maintain parallelism in your answer.

Note: Defining a relationship is a personal process. As long as you understand the relationship, the terminology used to describe it is unimportant. At no time must you *state* the nature of the relationship; you need only understand it and apply it to the choices. With our explanations of the answers to analogy questions in this book, we have offered you our rough classification of the nature of the relationship. You may disagree; you must often further refine. However, our manner of analyzing may give you insight and assistance in solving your own analogy questions.

A few of the most common, very general relationships are:

Part to whole, e.g., BRANCH : TREE
Whole to part, e.g., OCEAN : WATER
Cause and effect, e.g., GERM : DISEASE
Effect and cause, e.g., HONORS : STUDY
Association, e.g., BAT : BALL
Degree; e.g., HUT : MANSION
Sequence, e.g., ELEMENTARY : SECONDARY
Function, e.g., TEACHER : STUDENT
Characteristic, e.g., WISE : OWL
Antonym, e.g., BAD : GOOD
Synonym, e.g., SPRING : JUMP
Purpose, e.g., MASK : PROTECTION

PRACTICE WITH VERBAL ANALOGIES

SET ONE

DIRECTIONS: Each of the following questions consists of a capitalized pair of words followed by five pairs of words lettered A to E. The capitalized words bear some meaningful relationship to each other. Choose the lettered pair of words whose relationship is most similar to that expressed by the capitalized pair and mark its letter on your answer sheet.

1. INTIMIDATE : FEAR ::

    (A) maintain : satisfaction
    (B) astonish : wonder
    (C) soothe : concern
    (D) feed : hunger
    (E) awaken : tiredness

2. STOVE : KITCHEN ::

    (A) window : bedroom
    (B) sink : bathroom
    (C) television : living room
    (D) trunk : attic
    (E) pot : pan

3. MARGARINE : BUTTER ::

   (A) cream : milk
   (B) lace : cotton
   (C) nylon : silk
   (D) egg : chicken
   (E) oak : acorn

4. GAZELLE : SWIFT ::

   (A) horse : slow
   (B) wolf : sly
   (C) swan : graceful
   (D) elephant : gray
   (E) lion : tame

5. SATURNINE : MERCURIAL ::

   (A) Saturn : Venus
   (B) Appenines : Alps
   (C) redundant : wordy
   (D) allegro : adagio
   (E) heavenly : starry

6. ORANGE : MARMALADE ::

   (A) potato : vegetable
   (B) jelly : jam
   (C) tomato : ketchup
   (D) cake : picnic
   (E) sandwich : ham

7. AFFIRM : HINT ::

   (A) say : deny
   (B) assert : convince
   (C) confirm : reject
   (D) charge : insinuate
   (E) state : relate

8. SPEEDY : GREYHOUND ::

   (A) innocent : lamb
   (B) animate : animal
   (C) voracious : tiger
   (D) clever : fox
   (E) sluggish : sloth

9. TRIANGLE : PYRAMID ::

   (A) cone : circle
   (B) corner : angle
   (C) tube : cylinder
   (D) pentagon : quadrilateral
   (E) square : box

10. IMPEACH : DISMISS ::

   (A) arraign : convict
   (B) exonerate : charge
   (C) imprison : jail
   (D) plant : bear
   (E) president : Johnson

11. HAND : NAIL ::

   (A) paw : claw
   (B) foot : toe
   (C) head : hair
   (D) ear : nose
   (E) jaw : tooth

12. WOODSMAN : AXE ::

   (A) mechanic : wrench
   (B) soldier : gun
   (C) draftsman : ruler
   (D) doctor : prescription
   (E) carpenter : saw

13. BIGOTRY : HATRED ::

   (A) sweetness : bitterness
   (B) segregation : integration
   (C) equality : government
   (D) sugar : grain
   (E) fanaticism : intolerance

14. DOUBLEHEADER : TRIDENT ::

   (A) twin : troika
   (B) ballgame : three bagger
   (C) chewing gum : toothpaste
   (D) freak : zoo
   (E) two : square

15. BOUQUET : FLOWER ::

   (A) key : door
   (B) air : balloon
   (C) skin : body
   (D) chain : link
   (E) eye : pigment

16. LETTER : WORD ::

   (A) club : people
   (B) homework : school
   (C) page : book
   (D) product : factory
   (E) picture : crayon

17. GERM : DISEASE : :

(A) trichinosis : pork
(B) men : woman
(C) doctor : medicine
(D) war : destruction
(E) biologist : cell

18. WAVE : CREST : :

(A) pinnacle : nadir
(B) mountain : peak
(C) sea : ocean
(D) breaker : swimming
(E) island : archipelago

19. ROCK : SLATE : :

(A) wave : sea
(B) mineral : ore
(C) swimmer : male
(D) lifeguard : beach
(E) boat : kayak

20. LAW : CITIZEN : :

(A) democracy : communism
(B) weapon : peace
(C) reins : horse
(D) gangster : policeman
(E) tyranny : despot

21. JOY : ECSTASY : :

(A) admiration : love
(B) weather : humidity

(C) happiness : sorrow
(D) life : hope
(E) youth : frolic

22. ANTISEPTIC : GERMS : :

(A) bullet : death
(B) mosquitoes : disease
(C) lion : prey
(D) doctor : medicine
(E) nose : throat

23. EXAMINATION : CHEAT : :

(A) lawyer : defendant
(B) compromise : principles
(C) army : gripe
(D) swindle : business
(E) politics : graft

24. GARBAGE : SQUALOR : :

(A) filth : cleanliness
(B) fame : knowledge
(C) diamonds : magnificence
(D) color : brush
(E) mayor : governor

25. MYTH : STORY : :

(A) fiction : reality
(B) bonnet : hat
(C) literature : poetry
(D) flower : redness
(E) stencil : paper

SET TWO

1. LINEAR : CURVILINEAR : :

(A) throw : reach
(B) sunrise : sunset
(C) absolute : relative
(D) arrow : bow
(E) bow : arrow

2. ALLAY : PAIN : :

(A) damp : noise
(B) create : noise
(C) regain : consciousness
(D) fray : edge
(E) stimulate : nerves

3. CANDID : DEVIOUS : :

(A) unnerved : unhinged
(B) unruffled : unnerved
(C) unhinged : unspoken
(D) unsullied : unruffled
(E) upright : underhanded

4. FRENETIC : SANGUINE : :

(A) cool : hot
(B) ardent : involved
(C) frantic : unruffled
(D) unharried : unsullied
(E) uncouth : rude

5. BONES : LIGAMENTS ::

(A) break : stretch
(B) muscles : tendons
(C) fat : cells
(D) knuckles : fingers
(E) knees : joints

6. SPICY : INSIPID ::

(A) pepper : salt
(B) hot : creamy
(C) exciting : dull
(D) cucumber : pickle
(E) bland : sharp

7. BURL : TREE ::

(A) silver : ore
(B) bronze : copper
(C) plank : wood
(D) glass : sand
(E) pearl : oyster

8. YEAST : LEAVEN ::

(A) soda : bubble
(B) iodine : antiseptic
(C) aspirin : medicine
(D) flour : dough
(E) penicillin : plant

9. READ : BOOK ::

(A) taste : salty
(B) attend : movie
(C) smell : odor
(D) listen : record
(E) touch : paper

10. EXPURGATE : PASSAGES ::

(A) defoliate : leaves
(B) cancel : checks
(C) incorporate : ideas
(D) invade : privacy
(E) till : fields

11. PHARMACIST : DRUGS ::

(A) psychiatrist : ideas
(B) mentor : drills
(C) mechanic : troubles
(D) chef : foods
(E) nurse : diseases

12. CONQUER : SUBJUGATE ::

(A) esteem : respect
(B) slander : vilify
(C) discern : observe
(D) ponder : deliberate
(E) freedom : slavery

13. ENGRAVING : CHISEL ::

(A) printing : paper
(B) photography : camera
(C) lithography : stone
(D) printing : ink
(E) etching : acid

14. DECIBEL : SOUND ::

(A) calorie : weight
(B) volt : electricity
(C) temperature : weather
(D) color : light
(E) area : distance

15. HOMONYM : SOUND ::

(A) synonym : same
(B) antonym : meaning
(C) acronym : ideas
(D) pseudonym : fake
(E) synopsis : summary

16. PARROT : SPARROW ::

(A) dog : poodle
(B) elephant : ant
(C) goldfish : guppy
(D) lion : cub
(E) eagle : butterfly

17. VALUELESS : INVALUABLE

(A) miserly : philanthropic
(B) frugality : wealth
(C) thriftiness : cheap
(D) costly : cut-rate
(E) cheap : unsalable

18. TRIANGLE : PRISM ::

(A) sphere : earth
(B) square : rhomboid
(C) rectangle : building
(D) circle : cylinder
(E) polygon : diamond

19. YOKE : OX ::

(A) saddle : stallion
(B) stall : cow
(C) herd : sheep
(D) brand : steer
(E) harness : horse

20. COW : BUTTER ::

(A) chicken : omelets
(B) tree : fruit
(C) steer : mutton
(D) water : ice
(E) grape : raisin

21. GOLD : PROSPECTOR ::

(A) medicine : doctor
(B) prayer : preacher
(C) wood : carpenter
(D) clue : detective
(E) iron : machinist

22. COUPLET : POEM ::

(A) page : letter
(B) sentence : paragraph

(C) number : address
(D) epic : poetry
(E) biography : novel

23. OIL : WELL ::

(A) water : faucet
(B) iron : ore
(C) silver : mine
(D) gas : tank
(E) lumber : yard

24. RUDDER : SHIP ::

(A) wheel : car
(B) motor : truck
(C) row : boat
(D) kite : string
(E) wing : plane

25. STALLION : ROOSTER ::

(A) buck : doe
(B) filly : colt
(C) horse : chicken
(D) foal : calf
(E) mare : hen

SET THREE

1. WHALE : FISH ::

(A) collie : dog
(B) fly : insect
(C) bat : bird
(D) clue : detective
(E) mako : shark

2. LUTE : STRING ::

(A) flute : treble
(B) xylophone : percussion
(C) drum : rhythm
(D) violin : concert
(E) piano : octave

3. FEATHERS : PLUCK ::

(A) goose : duck
(B) garment : weave
(C) car : drive
(D) wool : shear
(E) duck : down

4. MODESTY : ARROGANCE ::

(A) debility : strength
(B) cause : purpose
(C) passion : emotion
(D) finance : Wall Street
(E) practice : perfection

5. WATER : SWIMMING ::

(A) egg : breaking
(B) fire : flaming
(C) chair : sitting
(D) learning : knowledge
(E) deed: owning

6. BAY : SEA ::

(A) mountain : valley
(B) plain : forest
(C) peninsula : land
(D) cape : reef
(E) island : sound

7. DECEMBER : WINTER ::

    (A) April : showers
    (B) September : summer
    (C) June : fall
    (D) March : spring
    (E) February : autumn

8. SENSATION : ANESTHETIC ::

    (A) breath : lung
    (B) drug : reaction
    (C) satisfaction : disappointment
    (D) poison : antidote
    (E) observation : sight

9. ASTUTE : STUPID ::

    (A) scholar : idiotic
    (B) agile : clumsy
    (C) lonely : clown
    (D) dance : ignorant
    (E) intelligent : smart

10. INTERRUPT : SPEAK ::

    (A) shout : yell
    (B) intrude : enter
    (C) assist : interfere
    (D) telephone : telegraph
    (E) concede : defend

11. ENCOURAGE : RESTRICT ::

    (A) gain : succeed
    (B) deprive : supply
    (C) see : believe
    (D) detain : deny
    (E) finish : complete

12. BEFOUL : TIDY ::

    (A) animate : inanimate
    (B) extricate : intricate
    (C) introvert : extrovert
    (D) cloth : clergy
    (E) indict : acquit

13. ITALY : MILAN ::

    (A) Paris : Moscow
    (B) Moscow : Russia
    (C) Spain : Madrid
    (D) Manhattan : New York
    (E) Norway : Sweden

14. MIST : RAIN ::

    (A) wind : hurricane
    (B) hail : thunder
    (C) snow : freeze
    (D) clouds : sky
    (E) sun : warm

15. GUN : HOLSTER ::

    (A) shoe : soldier
    (B) sword : warrior
    (C) ink : pen
    (D) books : school bag
    (E) cannon : plunder

16. MACE : MAJESTY ::

    (A) king : crown
    (B) sword : soldier
    (C) diploma : knowledge
    (D) book : knowledge
    (E) house : security

17. VIXEN : SCOLD ::

    (A) wound : scar
    (B) hero : winner
    (C) bee : sting
    (D) pimple : irritate
    (E) duck : walk

18. DEBATE : SOLILOQUY ::

    (A) crowd : mob
    (B) Hamlet : Macbeth
    (C) Lincoln : Douglas
    (D) group : hermit
    (E) fight : defend

19. THREAT : INSECURITY ::

    (A) challenge : fight
    (B) reason : anger
    (C) thunder : lightning
    (D) speed : acceleration
    (E) discipline : learning

20. LARGE : ENORMOUS ::

    (A) cat : tiger
    (B) warmth : frost
    (C) plump : fat
    (D) royal : regal
    (E) happy : solemn

21. NECK : NAPE ::

    (A) foot : heel
    (B) head : forehead
    (C) arm : wrist
    (D) stomach : back
    (E) eye : lid

22. UNFRIENDLY : HOSTILE ::

    (A) weak : ill
    (B) weak : strong
    (C) blaze : flame
    (D) useful : necessary
    (E) violence : danger

23. RADIUS : CIRCLE ::

    (A) rubber : tire
    (B) bisect : angle
    (C) equator : earth
    (D) cord : circumference
    (E) spoke : wheel

24. PROTEIN : MEAT ::

    (A) calories : cream
    (B) energy : sugar
    (C) cyclamates : diet
    (D) starch : potatoes
    (E) fat : cholesterol

25. GOBBLE : TURKEY ::

    (A) poison : cobra
    (B) bark : tree
    (C) trunk : elephant
    (D) twitter : bird
    (E) king : lion

SET FOUR

1. FIN : FISH ::

    (A) engine : auto
    (B) propeller : airplane
    (C) five : ten
    (D) teeth : stomach
    (E) leg : chair

2. RESTRAIN : REPRESS ::

    (A) advance : capitulate
    (B) surround : surrender
    (C) march : refrain
    (D) retire : battle
    (E) urge : spur

3. CONCERT : MUSIC ::

    (A) performance : artist
    (B) exhibition : art
    (C) play : actor
    (D) operetta : singer
    (E) flute : soloist

4. KEY : DOOR ::

    (A) combination : safe
    (B) keyhole : porthole
    (C) lock : key
    (D) opening : closing
    (E) bolt : safety

5. GOOD FRIDAY : CHRISTMAS ::

    (A) opening : closing
    (B) holiday : school
    (C) end : beginning
    (D) New Year : Christmas
    (E) Veterans Day : Memorial Day

6. AFTERNOON : DUSK ::

    (A) breakfast : dinner
    (B) yesterday : tomorrow
    (C) Sunday : Saturday
    (D) night : dawn
    (E) age : youth

7. STUDYING : LEARNING ::

    (A) running : jumping
    (B) investigating : discovering
    (C) reading : writing
    (D) dancing : singing
    (E) feeling : thinking

8. PULP : PAPER ::

    (A) rope : hemp
    (B) box : package
    (C) fabric : yarn
    (D) paper : package
    (E) cellulose : rayon

9. RUN : RACE ::

(A) walk : pogo stick
(B) swim : boat
(C) fly : kite
(D) sink : bottle
(E) repair : automobile

10. OBSTRUCTION : BUOY ::

(A) construction : building
(B) boy : girl
(C) danger : red light
(D) iceberg : Titanic
(E) barricade : wall

11. EXPEDITE : HASTEN ::

(A) illuminate : disturb
(B) refine : refute
(C) inflate : distend
(D) scour : squeeze
(E) augment : lessen

12. VIBRATION : SOUND ::

(A) gravity : pull
(B) watercolor : paint
(C) accident : death
(D) worm : reptile
(E) drought : plague

13. WRITE : LETTER ::

(A) pen : paper
(B) drink : glass
(C) act : part
(D) rhyme : poem
(E) memorize : book

14. PAMPHLET : BOOK ::

(A) dress : sweater
(B) discomfort : pain
(C) height : weight
(D) swimming : wading
(E) epilogue : summary

15. SKIN : MAN ::

(A) scaled : fur
(B) hide : hair
(C) walls : room
(D) window : house
(E) clothes : lady

16. ELIXIR : PILL ::

(A) life : health
(B) water : ice
(C) bottle : box
(D) mystery : medicine
(E) nurse : doctor

17. FRUGAL : ECONOMICAL ::

(A) fragile : solid
(B) prosperous : wealthy
(C) fruitful : sunny
(D) regal : comical
(E) spendthrift : miser

18. CONSTELLATION : STARS ::

(A) state : country
(B) library : book
(C) archipelago : islands
(D) continent : peninsula
(E) dollar : penny

19. CLARINET : MUSIC ::

(A) symbol : sign
(B) chalk : writing
(C) daughter : father
(D) pencil : pen
(E) bread : flour

20. FURIOUS : ANGRY ::

(A) cold : frozen
(B) love : like
(C) embrace : hug
(D) slap : hit
(E) wish : fulfillment

21. RAIN : DROPS ::

(A) ice : water
(B) cloud : sky
(C) flake : snow
(D) ocean : stream
(E) mankind : men

22. PAPER : REAM ::

(A) eggs : dozen
(B) newspaper : stand
(C) apartment : room
(D) candy : wrapper
(E) gaggle : geese

23. HORSE : CENTAUR ::

 (A) stable : barn
 (B) decade : century
 (C) pig : sty
 (D) fish : mermaid
 (E) hydra : chimera

24. MODEST : QUIET ::

 (A) cynical : determined
 (B) conceited : loquacious

 (C) capable : stubborn
 (D) egocentric : reserved
 (E) demure : brash

25. IMPORTANT : CRUCIAL ::

 (A) orange : lemon
 (B) sorrow : death
 (C) misdemeanor : felony
 (D) poverty : uncleanliness
 (E) axiom : hypothesis

ANSWER KEY FOR
PRACTICE VERBAL ANALOGIES

SET ONE

1. B	6. C	11. A	16. C	21. A
2. B	7. D	12. E	17. D	22. C
3. C	8. E	13. E	18. B	23. E
4. C	9. E	14. A	19. E	24. C
5. D	10. A	15. D	20. C	25. B

SET TWO

1. D	6. C	11. D	16. C	21. D
2. A	7. E	12. B	17. A	22. B
3. E	8. B	13. E	18. D	23. C
4. C	9. D	14. B	19. E	24. A
5. B	10. A	15. B	20. A	25. E

SET THREE

1. C	6. C	11. B	16. C	21. A
2. B	7. D	12. E	17. C	22. C
3. D	8. D	13. C	18. D	23. E
4. A	9. B	14. A	19. A	24. D
5. C	10. B	15. D	20. C	25. D

SET FOUR

1. B	6. D	11. C	16. B	21. E
2. E	7. B	12. A	17. B	22. A
3. B	8. E	13. C	18. C	23. D
4. A	9. C	14. B	19. B	24. B
5. C	10. C	15. C	20. B	25. C

EXPLANATORY ANSWERS
FOR PRACTICE VERBAL ANALOGIES

SET ONE

1. **(B)** To ASTONISH is to inspire WONDER; to INTIMIDATE is to inspire FEAR. The relationship is that of *cause and effect*.

2. **(B)** A SINK is a necessary part of a BATH-ROOM; a STOVE is a necessary part of a KITCHEN. The relationship is that of *part to whole*, with the additional element of necessity. A window is commonly a part of a bedroom, but a windowless bedroom is possible. The

correct answer is further affirmed by the parts, in both instances, being fixtures.

3. **(C)** NYLON is a SILK substitute; MARGARINE is a BUTTER substitute. The relationship is one of *association*.

4. **(C)** A commonly used simile is "GRACEFUL as a SWAN"; also commonly used as a simile is "SWIFT as a GAZELLE." The relationship is one of *association*. An elephant is usually gray, but the common verbal association with an elephant has to do with its size or strength. No one says "gray as an elephant."

5. **(D)** ALLEGRO (a musical term meaning "briskly") is the opposite of ADAGIO (a musical term meaning "slowly"); SATURNINE (moody and sullen) is the opposite of MERCURIAL (subject to rapid changes in mood). The relationship is one of *antonyms*.

6. **(C)** A TOMATO is a component of KETCHUP; an ORANGE is a component of MARMALADE. The relationship is that of *part to whole*.

7. **(D)** To CHARGE is to make a direct accusation, while to INSINUATE is to accuse indirectly; to AFFIRM is to make a direct statement, while to HINT is to make an indirect statement. The relationship is one of *degree*.

8. **(E)** A SLOTH is a slow-moving, SLUGGISH animal that hangs upside down from tropical trees; a GREYHOUND is a swift, SPEEDY dog. The relationship is one of *association*. However, (A), (C) and (D) all offer associations involving animals and their characteristics, so in solving this analogy question you must further refine the relationship to determine the nature of the associated relationship, that is, associated speed.

9. **(E)** A SQUARE is a plane figure, while a BOX is a solid figure; a TRIANGLE is a plane figure, while a PYRAMID is a solid figure. The relationship is one of *degree*. *Sequence* is a consideration too, since (A) offers the same relationship, but in reverse order.

10. **(A)** The ARRAIGNment is the accusation or beginning stage of a criminal procedure which may result in CONVICTion; IMPEACHment is the accusation phase of a judicial procedure which may result in DISMISSal. The relationship is a *sequential association*.

11. **(A)** A CLAW is the nail at the end of a digit on an animal's PAW; a NAIL is at the end of a digit on a person's HAND. The relationship is a *functional* one. Choices (B), (C) and (E) all include a larger part of the body followed by a smaller part which is directly attached to it, but the correct answer (A) offers the closest possible parallel in function.

12. **(E)** A CARPENTER uses a SAW to cut; a WOODSMAN uses an AXE to cut. The relationship is a *functional* one. In all the other choices we are offered a worker and the tool of his trade, but none of those encompasses the essential function of cutting.

13. **(E)** FANATICISM leads to INTOLERANCE; BIGOTRY leads to HATRED. The relationship is that of *cause to effect*.

14. **(A)** TWIN has to do with *two* identical units, while TROIKA has to do with a group of *three* related persons or things; a DOUBLEHEADER has to do with *two* ballgames, while a TRIDENT has *three* teeth. The relationship can best be called *association*.

15. **(D)** A CHAIN is made up of a succession of LINKs; a BOUQUET is made up of a number of FLOWERs. The relationship is that of a *whole to its parts*.

16. **(C)** A PAGE is a part of a BOOK; a LETTER is a part of a WORD. The relationship is that of *part to whole*.

17. **(D)** WAR leads to DESTRUCTION; a GERM leads to DISEASE. The relationship is that of *cause and effect*.

18. **(B)** A PEAK is the top of a MOUNTAIN; a CREST is the top of a WAVE. The relationship is that of the *whole to its part*.

19. **(E)** A KAYAK is a kind of BOAT, a member of the larger class of boats; SLATE is a kind of ROCK, a member of the larger class of rocks. The relationship is that of the *whole to a part*.

20. **(C)** REINS control a HORSE; LAWS control the CITIZEN. The relationship is one of *function*.

21. **(A)** ADMIRATION is a mild emotion, a stronger form of which is LOVE; JOY is a mild emotion, a stronger form of which is ECSTASY. The relationship is one of *degree*.

22. **(C)** A LION kills his PREY; an ANTISEPTIC kills GERMS. The relationship is *functional*.

23. **(E)** In POLITICS it is dishonest to take GRAFT (kickbacks); in an EXAMINATION it is dishonest to CHEAT. The relationship is a specific type of *association*. (D) has the same meaning, but the sequence of the relationship is reversed.

24. **(C)** DIAMONDS contribute to MAGNIFICENCE; GARBAGE contributes to SQUALOR (filth). The relationship is that of *part to whole*.

25. **(B)** A BONNET is a kind of HAT; a MYTH is a kind of STORY. The relationship is that of a *part* (or kind) *to the whole* (or larger classification). Do not allow yourself to be misled by choice (A). While a myth is always fictitious, a story may be fiction or reality, so (A) is not analogous to the initial pair.

SET TWO

1. **(D)** LINEAR and CURVILINEAR refer to equations which, when graphed, describe straight and curved lines respectively. The only answer choice that suggests first a straight and then a curved line is ARROW : BOW. Choice (E) is incorrect because the order of the shapes is reversed. The relationship is one of *characteristics*.

2. **(A)** One ALLAYS (reduces) PAIN; one DAMPS (reduces) NOISE. There is a *functional* relationship.

3. **(E)** CANDID and DEVIOUS are *antonyms*. Both (B) and (E) provide antonym pairs; however, (E) is the better match for the key pair because UPRIGHT means the same as candid and UNDERHANDED means the same as devious.

4. **(C)** FRENETIC and SANGUINE are *opposites* meaning the same as FRANTIC and UNRUFFLED respectively. Choice (A) is incorrect because the opposites are in reverse order.

5. **(B)** MUSCLES are connected to bone by TENDONS just as BONES are connected to bones by LIGAMENTS. The relationship is one of *function*.

6. **(C)** Food that is INSIPID is DULL and uninteresting, whereas SPICY food can be said to be EXCITING. The relationship is that of *opposites*. While (E) also reflects an opposite relationship, the order is reversed.

7. **(E)** A BURL is an outgrowth of a TREE, and a PEARL is an outgrowth of an OYSTER. The relationship is of *part to whole*.

8. **(B)** YEAST is used as a LEAVEN, and IODINE as an ANTISEPTIC. These *functions* are more specific than aspirin's function as a medicine.

9. **(D)** We assimilate a BOOK through READING, and a RECORD through LISTENING. The relationship is one of *function*.

10. **(A)** One can EXPURGATE (eliminate) PASSAGES as one can DEFOLIATE LEAVES. The relationship is of *action to object*.

11. **(D)** The basic materials of a PHARMACIST are DRUGS; the basic materials of a CHEF are FOODS. The relationship is one of *necessary association*.

12. **(B)** To CONQUER someone is to SUBJUGATE him. To SLANDER someone is to VILIFY him. In both cases, the subject is hostile toward the object. The relationship is one of *synonyms connoting hostility*.

13. **(E)** A CHISEL can be used to cut out an ENGRAVING. ACID can be used to cut through a surface to create an ETCHING. The relationship is one of *function* or *purpose*.

14. **(B)** SOUND is measured in DECIBELS, and ELECTRICITY in VOLTS. The relationship is one of *function*.

15. **(B)** SOUND determines whether two words are HOMONYMS. MEANING determines whether two words are ANTONYMS. The relationship is one of *association*.

16. **(C)** A PARROT and a SPARROW are two very different sorts of birds. A GOLDFISH and a GUPPY are two very different sorts of fish. The relationship can only be described as *definition*.

17. **(A)** At one extreme something can be VALUELESS, and at another extreme something can be

INVALUABLE. At one extreme an individual can be MISERLY, and at another extreme, PHILANTHROPIC. The relationship is that of *antonyms*.

18. **(D)** A TRIANGLE is a three-sided plane figure, and a PRISM is a three-sided solid figure. A CIRCLE is a plane figure, and a CYLINDER is a circular solid figure. The relationship is one of *characteristics*.

19. **(E)** An OX is controlled by means of a YOKE. A HORSE is controlled by means of a HARNESS. The relationship is one of *function*.

20. **(A)** Both a COW and a CHICKEN are animals. Indirectly, BUTTER is a product from the former and OMELETS are products from the latter. The relationship is loosely *cause and effect*.

21. **(D)** A PROSPECTOR seeks GOLD, and a DETECTIVE seeks a CLUE. The relationship is one of *purpose*.

22. **(B)** A COUPLET makes up part of a POEM, and a SENTENCE makes up part of a PARAGRAPH. The relationship is that of a *part to the whole*.

23. **(C)** OIL is extracted from the earth by means of a WELL, and SILVER by means of a MINE. The relationship is one of *function*.

24. **(A)** A RUDDER is used in directing a SHIP. A WHEEL is used in directing a CAR. The relationship is one of *purpose*.

25. **(E)** A STALLION and a ROOSTER are two different animals of the same sex, as are a MARE and a HEN. The relationship is one of *definition*. You might restate this analogy as male : male :: female : female.

SET THREE

1. **(C)** A WHALE is a mammal that is mistakenly thought to be a FISH, and a BAT is a mammal that is mistakenly thought to be a BIRD. The relationship is one of *mistaken definition*.

2. **(B)** The LUTE is a STRING instrument just as the XYLOPHONE is a PERCUSSION instrument. The relationship is one of *definition*.

3. **(D)** One PLUCKs FEATHERS and SHEARs WOOL. The relationship is one of *product to action* involved in taking that product from an animal.

4. **(A)** MODESTY is the *opposite* of ARROGANCE; DEBILITY is the *opposite* of STRENGTH.

5. **(C)** WATER is for SWIMMING; a CHAIR is for SITTING. The relationship is one of *purpose*. Learning is for knowledge but "learning" is not a concrete noun as are "water" and "chair," so the analogy is imperfect and (C) is the *best* answer.

6. **(C)** A BAY is smaller than a SEA and an extension of it, just as a PENINSULA is smaller than the LAND mass from which it protrudes. The relationship is one of *part to whole*.

7. **(D)** DECEMBER is the first month of WINTER; MARCH is the first month of SPRING. The relationship is *part to whole*.

8. **(D)** One can counteract a SENSATION with an ANESTHETIC and a POISON with an ANTIDOTE. This is a *functional* relationship.

9. **(B)** As ASTUTE is in emphatic *opposition* to STUPID, so is AGILE in *opposition* to CLUMSY.

10. **(B)** When you SPEAK at the wrong time, you might INTERRUPT; when you ENTER at the wrong time, you might INTRUDE. The relationship is that of the *effect to its cause*.

11. **(B)** ENCOURAGE is the *opposite* of RESTRICT. DEPRIVE is the *opposite* of SUPPLY.

12. **(E)** The key words are *opposites* as are answer choices (A), (C) and (E). BEFOUL is strongly negative in feeling, while TIDY is decidedly positive. Only INDICT : ACQUIT conveys the same negative-positive relationship.

13. **(C)** ITALY is the country where MILAN is located. Similarly, SPAIN is the country where MADRID is located. The relationship is that of the *whole to its part*. (B) is a reversal of the order of the relationship.

14. **(A)** MIST is a minor kind of RAIN, just as WIND is a lesser kind of HURRICANE. The relationship is one of *degree*.

15. **(D)** A HOLSTER is used to carry a GUN; a SCHOOL BAG is used to carry BOOKS. This is a *functional* or *purposeful* relationship.

16. **(C)** A MACE is an ornamental staff borne as a symbol of authority or MAJESTY; a DIPLOMA is a symbol of educational achievement or the

acquisition of KNOWLEDGE. (A) reverses the order of the *symbolic* relationship.

17. **(C)** A VIXEN attacks by SCOLDING; a BEE attacks by STINGING. The relationship is that of *actor to action*.

18. **(D)** A DEBATE involves two or more people; a SOLILOQUY, only one. A GROUP consists of several people; a HERMIT lives alone. The relationship is one of *plural to singular*.

19. **(A)** A THREAT often results in INSECURITY; a CHALLENGE often results in a FIGHT. The relationship is one of *cause and effect*.

20. **(C)** ENORMOUS means very LARGE; FAT means very PLUMP. The relationship is one of *degree*.

21. **(A)** The NAPE is the back of the NECK, and the

HEEL is the back of the FOOT. This is a *part to whole* relationship in which location of the part is a crucial refinement.

22. **(C)** UNFRIENDLY and HOSTILE are *synonyms*, as are BLAZE and FLAME.

23. **(E)** The RADIUS extends from the center of the CIRCLE to the edge, as the SPOKE extends from the center of the WHEEL to the edge. The relationship is one of a *specific part to the whole*.

24. **(D)** MEAT is a food that supplies us with PROTEIN; POTATOES are a food that supplies us with STARCH. The relationship is that of the *supplied to its supplier*.

25. **(D)** A TURKEY GOBBLES; some other BIRDS TWITTER. The relationship is that of the *sound to its producer* or *action to actor*.

SET FOUR

1. **(B)** A FIN is the external part that propels a FISH; a PROPELLER is the external part that propels an AIRPLANE. (E) provides an external part/whole relationship without propulsion; (A) provides a part/whole relationship with propulsion, but the part is internal.

2. **(E)** RESTRAIN and REPRESS are *synonyms*, as are URGE and SPUR.

3. **(B)** You hear MUSIC at a CONCERT; you see ART at an EXHIBITION. The relationship is one of *purpose*.

4. **(A)** The right KEY opens the DOOR; the right COMBINATION opens the SAFE. The relationship is *functional*.

5. **(C)** GOOD FRIDAY commemorates the death of Christ; CHRISTMAS commemorates the birth of Christ. The answer hinges on the relationship of end to beginning, in other words, *sequence*.

6. **(D)** In this *sequence relationship*, AFTERNOON precedes DUSK as NIGHT precedes DAWN. In (A) and (B) there is an intervening time; (E) is reversed.

7. **(B)** STUDYING is required for LEARNING; INVESTIGATING is required for DISCOVERING. The relationship is *cause and effect*.

8. **(E)** PULP is used in making PAPER; CELLULOSE is used in making RAYON. You might call this a *part to whole* relationship. (A) and (C) are reversals.

9. **(C)** One RUNS a RACE and FLIES a KITE. The relationship is one of *action to object*.

10. **(C)** A BUOY warns of an OBSTRUCTION; a RED LIGHT warns of DANGER. The relationship is *purposeful*.

11. **(C)** EXPEDITE and HASTEN are *synonyms*, as are INFLATE and DISTEND.

12. **(A)** SOUND is caused by VIBRATION; PULL is caused by GRAVITY. The relationship is one of *cause and effect*.

13. **(C)** One WRITES a LETTER and ACTS a PART in this *action-to-object* relationship.

14. **(B)** A PAMPHLET is a short printed work; a BOOK is longer. DISCOMFORT is a milder form of PAIN. The relationship is one of *degree*.

15. **(C)** SKIN encloses a MAN; WALLS enclose a ROOM. The relationship is one of *function*.

16. **(B)** An ELIXIR is a liquid medicine; a PILL is a solid medicine. WATER is liquid; ICE is solid. The relationship may be stated as liquid : solid.

17. **(B)** FRUGAL and ECONOMICAL are *synonyms*, as are PROSPEROUS and WEALTHY.

18. **(C)** A group of STARS make up a CONSTELLATION; a group of ISLANDS make up an ARCHIPELAGO. The relationship is that of *whole to parts*. (B) and (E) are incorrect because the second term is expressed in the singular.

19. **(B)** A CLARINET is used to produce MUSIC; CHALK is used for WRITING. The relationship is one of *purpose*.

20. **(B)** Being FURIOUS is a more intense emotion than being ANGRY; LOVE is a more intense emotion than LIKE. The relationship is one of *degree*.

21. **(E)** RAIN is made up of DROPS; MANKIND is made up of MEN. The relationship is that of *whole to parts*.

22. **(A)** PAPER is counted by the REAM; EGGS are counted by the DOZEN. The relationship is one of *item to unit of measure*.

23. **(D)** A CENTAUR has as its upper part a man and as its lower part a HORSE; a MERMAID is part woman and part FISH. Both a centaur and a mermaid are legendary. The relationship is that of a *component part to the whole legendary creature*.

24. **(B)** A MODEST person is usually QUIET; a CONCEITED person is usually LOQUACIOUS. The relationship is one of *characteristic*.

25. **(C)** In this analogy of *degree* something that is CRUCIAL is very IMPORTANT; a FELONY is a more serious offense than a MISDEMEANOR.

READING COMPREHENSION

Reading Comprehension questions are an integral component of almost all standardized examinations. Reading is, of course, basic to scholarship. Proficiency in reading serves as proof of achievement and as prediction of future achievement. On your PSAT you will find four reading passages with five questions based upon each passage. These questions will test not only how well you understand what you read, but also how well you can interpret the meaning of the passage and the intent of the author.

Reading speed is vital for success with Reading Comprehension questions. You cannot even attempt to answer questions based upon a passage if you have not had time to read it. In budgeting your time within the Verbal section of the PSAT, you will want to allot the bulk of the time for Reading Comprehension.

HOW TO PREPARE FOR READING COMPREHENSION QUESTIONS

Read, Read, Read! The best way to increase your reading speed is to read. Read everything in sight between now and the test. Newspaper reading is an

Adapted from LAW SCHOOL ADMISSION TEST, Candrilli & Slawsky, ARCO Publishing, Inc., New York, NY: © 1978, by permission of the authors.

especially good way to improve your reading skills. Don't be satisfied with just the opening paragraph of each article. Push yourself to read the whole story and give it your full attention as you read. If your mind wanders, you will not comprehend what you read.

Expand Your Peripheral Vision. You have probably heard about speed readers who can race down a page, consuming it almost instantaneously. Unfortunately, that technique works for very few people. To read with understanding your eyes must fixate (i.e., stop). Most people fixate on each word because that is the way reading is taught. However, this method wastes a great deal of time.

The key to increasing your reading speed is to take in more words each time your eyes stop. If a line has ten words in it and you are able to read the line by stopping only twice instead of ten times, you would be reading five times as fast as you do now. For example, if you are now reading at about 200 words per minute, by stopping only twice per line you would increase your speed to 1,000 words per minute.

Don't Subvocalize. If you can hear every word you read, you are subvocalizing. No matter how fast you can talk, you can read faster if you stop subvocalizing. Reading teachers have employed many tricks to stop people from subvocalizing. They may ask students to put pebbles in their mouths or to chew on pencils. We ask only that you be aware that you may be subvocalizing. Reading is a very psychological thing; if you become aware of your bad habits, you may be able to correct them.

Become More Aware of Words. You cannot build a good vocabulary in a day or even a week. However, you can increase your knowledge of words by stopping to look up each new word you run across and by systematic study of those prefixes, suffixes and roots which make up the greater part of the English language.

Use Your Hand. Here is a simple technique for you to try: when you read, move your hand or your pen underneath the line you are reading. Because your eyes tend to move as quickly as your pen, you will not stop on every word, you will not regress, and you probably will not subvocalize. However, what you may do is concentrate on your pen and not on the reading passage. This is why you must practice this technique before using it on your test. Start your hand or your pen at the second or third word in the line and stop it before the last word in the line. Your peripheral vision will pick up the first and last words in the lines and you will save time by not having to focus on them.

Try the SQ2R Method. The SQ2R method of reading was developed by the government during World War II in an attempt to advance men to officer rank as quickly as possible. The method used may be helpful to you and so it is presented here.

1. Before you read, scan the material (S). Once you have scanned the passage, you should be aware of the type of passage you are about to read and the logical structure of the passage.
2. Scanning the passage should bring questions to mind (Q).
3. Now read the passage (R1), trying to answer your own questions. By using this question and answer method you will become involved in what you are reading and consequently you will remember more of it. As you read, stop briefly at the end of each paragraph and think about what you have read. If you cannot remember what you have read, reread the paragraph immediately. Don't wait until the end of the passage expecting that understanding will come later.
4. After you have read the passage, reread it quickly (R2). In other words, scan it a second time. This second scanning should give you additional information and allow you to fill in gaps in your understanding of the passage.

Keep Track of Your Time. Timing is an essential element of this test. That is why it is important that you wear a watch while taking the exam. You may think the suggestions given here will slow you down. On the contrary, if you practice these techniques before taking the test, you will actually finish the readings faster and your score will be higher.

SPEED READING TESTS

DIRECTIONS: Read the following passage as quickly as possible, timing yourself as you read. When you are finished, divide the number of minutes it took you to read the passage into the number of words in the

passage (435). This will give you the number of words you are reading per minute. Next, answer the questions following the reading passage. Multiply the number of words you are reading per minute by the number of questions which you answered correctly and divide by the number of questions in the test (5). This will give you your Real Reading Speed. To illustrate, if you read 200 words per minute and answered three questions correctly, your Real Reading Speed would be:

$$\frac{200 \text{ words per minute} \times 3 \text{ correct answers}}{5 \text{ questions}}$$

= 120 words per min.

SAMPLE READING PASSAGE

The supernatural world was both real and awesome to early man, as it still is in primitive societies, and heavy dependency was put upon it in worshipping and propitiating the gods. It is more than likely the degree to which our ancestral homo sapiens relied upon telepathic communication instead of articulate speech would today fill us with both amazement and disbelief. Certainly human beings who populated the earth prior to the fourteenth century are well documented as having had a keen interest in the spirit world, thought transference, witches, premonitions and so forth.

In order to conjure up departed spirits, make predictions or go into a trance, a variety of drugs existing since antiquity (many of which are now classed as hallucinogens) were used by witch doctors, alchemists, shamen and cultist tribesmen throughout the world, and seemed to buttress natural powers. Yage, a drug related to LSD and known under several different names (including "telepathine"), is from a vine native to the Amazon Basin and is identical with harmine, an alkaloid from the seeds of wild rice. Both are reputed to aid in locating missing objects, in transporting users to distant lands and times, and in communicating with the dead. Greatly favored in Europe at witches' sabbaths are bufotenin (related to serotonin and first obtained from toad skins), scopolamine and henbane.

However, by Savonarola's time the church itself had declared magic and witchcraft evil. After the witch hunts and witch burnings that continued for three centuries, the supernatural world with its ghosts, demons and human emissaries was in a state of subjugation. It was not until the nineteenth century that there was any open revival of interest in "seers" and "spooks" or acceptance of their possible validity.

Those who pioneered the re-exploration of what is now called "psi phenomena," or all things pertaining to the psychic world, were considered crazy, pathetic, eccentric and ridiculous. They were sneered at for their sacrilegious superstition and made to feel uncomfortable among their fellow men. Sir Oliver Lodge and a handful of others did succeed, however, in establishing the Society for Psychical Research in London in 1882, and gradually interest in spiritualism, clairvoyance and mental telepathy seeped out of its small confines and spread elsewhere. The American Society for Psychic Research was founded in 1906; however, the psi subject did not gain much public ground until the 1930s and it is still far from respected despite the efforts of such men as Drs. J.B. Rhine and Gardner Murphy, who have approached it scientifically and have been steadily working at it in conjunction with their European colleagues. (435)

1. The author's attitude toward telepathic communication is one of

(A) disbelief
(B) skepticism
(C) acceptance
(D) inquisitiveness
(E) reserved judgment

2. All of the following groups were mentioned by the author as using drugs of ancient origin except

I. witch doctors
II. voodooists
III. alchemists
IV. shamen

(A) I only
(B) I and II only
(C) II, III, and IV only
(D) II only
(E) IV only

3. Another name for the drug known as telepathine is

(A) marijuana
(B) LSD
(C) wild rice
(D) yage
(E) harmine

4. Harmine is reputed to have the ability to

(A) aid in locating missing objects
(B) transport users to distant lands and aid in communication with the dead
(C) enable one to communicate with spirits
(D) help the user find his directions
(E) transport the users to distant lands, aid in locating missing objects, and help the user communicate with the dead.

5. During what period of time, approximately, did the church declare magic and witchcraft evil?

(A) 1400s
(B) 1500s
(C) 1600s
(D) 1800s
(E) 1900s

ANSWERS TO SPEED READING TEST

1. C   2. D   3. D   4. E   5. A

The same reading techniques apply to all types of reading passages. However, due to the nature of the passage some may have to be read more slowly than others.

The reading passages may be very general or they may be highly specific and full of detail. Some of these readings may be self-contained; that is, all the information on which you will be questioned is stated in the passage. Others are idea oriented and may require that you draw conclusions from the information given in order to answer the questions.

TYPES OF QUESTIONS YOU MAY BE ASKED

1. *General Question.* These questions are usually based on the main idea of the passage, its purpose or the best title for it. To answer this type of question, look for the choice which takes in the greatest amount of information. Wrong answers are usually too limited or too vague.

2. *Inclusive Question.* These questions often contain the phrase "all of the following EXCEPT" and are best answered by attempting to eliminate all the alternatives that do not fit first. This narrows the field considerably, increasing your chances for choosing the right answer.

3. *Comparison Question.* If the passage mentions both nineteenth- and twentieth-century authors, for example, you can expect to be quizzed on comparisons between the two. Try to spot these obvious sources of comparison as you read.

4. *Detail Question.* These questions refer to a fact or statistic given in the reading. Don't try to memorize these specifics. A glance back at the reading will enable you to answer this type of question.

HOW TO ANSWER READING COMPREHENSION QUESTIONS

1. Skim the passage to get a general idea of the subject matter and of the point that is being made.

2. Reread the passage, giving attention to details and point of view. Be alert for the author's hints as to what he or she thinks is important. Phrases such as "Note that . . ." "Of importance is . . ." and "Do not overlook . . ." give clues to what the writer is stressing.

3. If the author has quoted material from another source, be sure that you understand the purpose of the quote. Does the author agree or disagree?

4. Read and answer one question at a time. Read the question or incomplete statement. Determine exactly what is being asked. Watch for negatives or all-inclusive words such as, "always," "never," "all," "only," "every," "absolutely," "completely," "none," "entirely," "no." These words can affect your choice of answer.

5. Read all five answer choices. Eliminate those which are obviously incorrect. Reread the remaining options and refer to the passage, if necessary, to determine the *best* answer.

6. Avoid inserting your own judgments into your answers. Even if you disagree with the author or

even if you spot a factual error in the passage, you must answer on the basis of what is stated or implied in the passage.

7. Do not allow yourself to spend too much time on any one question. If looking back at the passage does not help you to find or figure out the answer, move on to the next question or next reading passage.

PRACTICE WITH READING COMPREHENSION

SET ONE

DIRECTIONS: Below each of the following passages, you will find five questions or incomplete statements about the passage. Each statement or question is followed by five response options. Read the passage carefully. On the basis of what was stated or implied in the passage, select the option which best completes each statement or answers each question. You may refer to the passage as often as necessary. Mark the letter of your choice on your answer sheet.

A rosebud holds the entire flower in miniature. The unfolding petals reveal nothing which they did not harbor in microcosmic existence. They merely exemplify more fully the nature of the beauty which is indigenous to them. When we view the ages of man unfolding through the centuries, we see not a Utopian fulfillment of idealistic beginnings, but we are brought vis-a-vis the perennial problem of man's enduring fallibility in approaching and handling the enigmas that face him. (10)

If we turn back several centuries of the corona of civilization, we may find the same dichotomy of values as are inherent in twentieth century mortals. English kings of the fourteenth century kept the people preoccupied with foreign wars in order to mollify them at home. The Magna Carta had been no panacea for the ills of the land, and the seeds of rebellion came to fruition in the Peasants' Revolt of 1381. The Plague has already ravaged the country and subsequent disruption of labor practices left the land (20) in utter chaos. Although Christianity had preserved civilization and fostered education throughout the "Dark Ages," nevertheless, Wycliffe led the Lollards in protest against Church weaknesses, such as those which allowed pardoners to prey upon the poor, and which permitted a Western Schism and an Avignon Papacy to occur.

(30) Several epidemics of the Black Death caused a mushroom-like cloud to hang over the populace. The tavern became the temple where the gods Bacchus and Venus were diligently worshipped. The liturgical theme was "Eat, drink and be merry, for tomorrow we die"—and again, ironically, the horror of death was palliated by a *Danse Macabre*. There was no other paladin for the peasantry than their own timorously bold, superstitiously impotent affront to personified Death.

Folks in medieval times were well aware of the paradox of the mutability of time and the perma-
(40) nence of human nature. They looked to the heavens both for eternal salvation and for astrological guidance, but whereas religion could bring the former, science strove in vain to achieve the latter. Twentieth century man has his wars, poverty, sickness, and disenchantment with efforts of his leaders, but while death constantly pursues him, he ignores the Bomb and puts his sights on the moon and stars. The rose opens continuously, revealing beauty alongside the thorns.

1. The basic idea which the article develops is that

   (A) the "Dark Ages" evidenced both strength and weakness in Church policies
   (B) medieval kings were notorious for their self-aggrandizement
   (C) Wycliffe hoped to develop a Utopia
   (D) the development of civilization is an expansion of primitive beginnings
   (E) roses, mushrooms, and bombs are all literary figures of death

2. The author implies that the direction which civilization is taking is

   (A) despair
   (B) indifference
   (C) skepticism
   (D) optimism
   (E) resignation

3. In comparing medieval man with modern man the author finds

   (A) medieval man more interesting
   (B) medieval man more frightened
   (C) very little difference

   (D) modern man more scientific
   (E) modern man more interesting

4. It can be inferred from the passage that

   (A) medieval people had no fear of death
   (B) European kings used war as a way of lining their own pockets
   (C) the Black Death brought the same fear as does the Atomic Bomb of today
   (D) we can learn much of history by studying the development of roses
   (E) man will eventually overcome the evils that persist in following him

5. With which of the following statements would the author be most likely to agree?

   (A) Man has in the past shown his fallibility but often surmounts his weaknesses.
   (B) The Church of the Middle Ages suffered from abuses which Wycliffe and the Lollards cured.
   (C) Astrology brought no relief or comfort to medieval people because they regarded it as a pseudo-science.
   (D) The Magna Carta solved most of the ills of the English peasants and led to the renunciation of despotism.
   (E) Medieval people were inspired to worship in the taverns when churches became corrupt.

It is almost a definition of a gentleman to say he is one who never inflicts pain. This description is both refined and, as far as it goes, accurate. He is mainly occupied in merely removing the obstacles which hinder the free and unembarrassed action of those about him; and he concurs with their movements rather than taking the initiative himself. His benefits may be considered as parallel to what are called comforts or conveniences in arrangements of a personal nature: like an easy chair or a good fire, which (10) do their part in dispelling cold and fatigue, though nature provides both means of rest and animal heat without them. The true gentleman, in like manner, carefully avoids whatever may cause a jar or a jolt in the minds of those with whom he is cast—all clashing of opinion, or collision of feeling, all restraint, or suspicion, or gloom, or resentment; his great concern being to make everyone at his ease and at home. He has his eyes on all his company; he is tender towards the bashful, gentle towards the dis-

tant, and merciful towards the absurd; he can recollect to whom he is speaking; he guards against unseasonable allusions, or topics which may irritate; he is seldom prominent in conversation and never wearisome. He makes light of favors while he does them, and seems to be receiving when he is conferring. He never speaks of himself except when compelled, never defends himself by a mere retort. He has no ears for slander or gossip, is scrupulous in
(30) imputing motives to those who interfere with him, and interprets everything for the best. He is never mean or little in his disputes, never takes unfair advantage, never mistakes personalities or sharp sayings for arguments, or insinuates evil which he dare not say out. From a longsighted prudence, he observes the maxim of the ancient sage, that we should ever conduct ourselves towards our enemy as if he were one day to be our friend. He has too much good sense to be affronted at insults; he is too well
(40) employed to remember injuries, and too indolent to bear malice. He is patient, forbearing, and resigned, on philosophical principles; he submits to pain, because it is inevitable, to bereavement, because it is irreparable, and to death, because it is his destiny. If he engages in controversy of any kind, his disciplined intellect preserves him from the blundering discourtesy of better, perhaps, but less educated minds, who, like blunt weapons, tear and hack instead of cutting clean, who mistake the point in
(50) argument, waste their strength on trifles, misconceive their adversary to leave the question more involved than they find it. He may be right or wrong in his opinion, but he is too clear-headed to be unjust; he is as simple as he is forcible, and as brief as he is decisive. Nowhere shall we find greater candor, consideration, indulgence: he throws himself into the minds of his opponents; he accounts for their mistakes. He knows the weakness of human reason as well as its strength, its province, and its limits. If
(60) he be an unbeliever, he will be too profound and large-minded to ridicule religion or to act against it; he is too wise to be a dogmatist or fanatic in his infidelity. He respects piety and devotion; he even supports institutions as venerable, beautiful, or useful, to which he does not assent; he honors the ministers of religion, and it contents him to decline its mysteries without assailing or denouncing them. He is a friend of religious toleration not only because his philosophy has taught him to look on all forms of
(70) faith with an impartial eye, but also from the gentleness and effeminacy of feeling, which is the attendant on civilization.

6. According to the passage, the gentleman when engaged in debate is

   (A) soothing and conciliatory
   (B) brilliant and insightful
   (C) opinionated and clever
   (D) concise and forceful
   (E) quiet and charming

7. A gentleman, here, is equated with

   (A) a jar or jolt
   (B) an easy chair or a good fire
   (C) a blunt weapon
   (D) a sharp saying
   (E) collisions and restraints

8. A person who is "scrupulous in imputing motives" is

   (A) careful about accusing others
   (B) eager to prove another guilty
   (C) willing to falsify
   (D) unable to make decisions
   (E) suspicious concerning the actions of others

9. This passage does *not* take into account a commonly held concept of a gentleman—namely,

   (A) consideration for others
   (B) refusal to slander
   (C) leniency toward the stupid
   (D) neatness in attire
   (E) willingness to forgive

10. The word "effeminacy" as used in this selection really means

   (A) femininity
   (B) childishness
   (C) cowardice
   (D) indecision
   (E) delicacy

The Rhinegold's malignity seems to have leaped from Valhalla's legendary realms to the sphere of humans. Wieland Wagner was to have produced *Der Ring des Nibelungen* in Geneva, with the gifted young Christian Vöchting conducting; both died within a year of each other, Vöchting this past November. Undaunted, the Grand Theatre's director, Herbert Graf, met the first challenge by producing *Das Rheingold* himself, conceiving both stage effects and costumes. The second problem was solved (10) through the courtesy of Rudolf Bing, who lent Metropolitan conductor Ignace Strasfogel for the emergency. Then there was the formidable hurdle of molding in three weeks a green cast (only John Modenos as Alberich having been in *Das Rheingold* before) and a green orchestra, the opera not having been played in Geneva for forty years.

The result was an admirable production, given six performances in January and February. Through (20) some adroit lighting, Graf emphasized the characters without resorting to the starkness of the modern Bayreuth stage. A film projection on a fine-net screen seemed to submerge the audience in the Rhine's rippling current: also through film, Valhalla was projected in the background as a massive but nebulous bastion of stone blocks. For clangorous Nibelheim's obscurity, a large shaft of rock sufficed. In long robes, with cuirass-like decor, the gods lent visual warmth in rich blue, Nile green and saffron; (30) Loge's flame-red cape glistened with flecks of gold, and the giants wore garb of vertical gray slabs, suggesting their Valhalla.

An exceptionally homogeneous cast included the mature mezzo of Sandra Warfield as Fricka, the ringing soprano of Jeanne Cook as Freia and the somewhat light baritone of Ramon Vinay as an imperious Wotan. Glade Peterson's flickering, mercurial Loge was a delight. Portraying the giants were lumbering Franz Petri and Manfred Schenk, with (40) Modenos and Fritz Peter as Alberich and Mimme, Michel Bouvier and Thomas Page as Donner and Froh. Strasfogel made *Das Rheingold* stirringly eloquent, and at the end he, Graf, and the cast were rewarded with shouts of enthusiasm.

11. The reviewer's reactions to this performance of *Das Rheingold* could best be described as

(A) filled with awe
(B) genuinely affirmative
(C) completely noncommittal
(D) somewhat negative
(E) completely unhappy

12. The author implies that the person most responsible for the performance was

(A) Wieland Wagner
(B) Christian Vöchting
(C) Herbert Graf
(D) Rudolf Bing
(E) Ignace Strasfogel

13. All of the following difficulties in preparing this performance were mentioned *except* the

(A) unexpected death of the producer
(B) unexpected death of the conductor
(C) lack of money for proper staging
(D) lack of needed practice time
(E) relative unfamiliarity of singers and musicians with the work

14. The author implied that the *least impressive* of the singers was

(A) John Modenos
(B) Sandra Warfield
(C) Jeanne Cook
(D) Ramon Vinay
(E) Glade Peterson

15. This passage suggests that Valhalla was

(A) cheerful
(B) majestic
(C) unimpressive
(D) dreary
(E) ominous

Once upon a time, little girls treasured their Raggedy Ann dolls and boys their teddy bears throughout childhood. The playthings were symbols of a simpler and perhaps happier time, an era in which dolls and toys had a special, lasting meaning.

The last decade has brought about a startling revolution in the dollhouse. Parents still can buy Raggedy Ann and charming baby dolls which just sit and smile. But these venerable standbys are being nudged aside by the "action" dolls, fashion figurines such as Barbie, and adventure heroes of the G. I. Joe genre.

Some see the new look in dolls as a long-overdue sign that reality finally has found its way into the toy store; others regard it as a perplexing deviation from the traditional role of dolls as children's play pals. Even the men who make them do not agree.

"Dolls are a manifestation of the child's view of the adult world, and the best are mechanical ones that establish a feeling of give and take between the doll and child," contends Chicago toy designer, Marvin Glass. "For example, consider the Kissy Doll that I designed several years ago. Kids had been kissing dolls for so long that I felt it was time the dolls reciprocated."

Edwin Nelson, President of Toy Manufacturers of America, sharply disagrees. "A simple doll gives a girl a greater opportunity to express her own personality. The real trouble with these gimmicky, animated dolls is that they don't offer the child a chance to participate."

Most psychologists, psychiatrists, and pediatricians tend to side with the latter. Many professionals are disturbed by the transition of dolls from meaningful playthings into automatons. They see them reflecting some of the less desirable traits of American life, and they view the relentless television promotion of toys as a means of introducing the young to too much, too soon.

One of the many medical experts who dislike performing dolls says, "I'm concerned that mechanical dolls may be providing children with a substitute for real play with real children. It suggests a breakdown in interpersonal relationships. A doll is of little value unless the child can enliven it with her own fantasies."

16. The main purpose of this passage is to

   (A) alert parents to the dangers of modern dolls
   (B) plead for the return to a simpler and happier era
   (C) help set standards of decency for doll manufacturers
   (D) discuss the impact of action dolls on children
   (E) compare modern dolls with dolls of the past

17. The passage implies that Marvin Glass would dislike teddy bears mainly because they

   (A) do not look like real people
   (B) do not attempt to return a child's affection
   (C) are from another era
   (D) would remind children of a fairy tale world
   (E) could not fool a child into thinking they were real

18. This passage implies that those experts who dislike modern mechanical dolls might like teddy bears mainly because they

   (A) have no moving parts
   (B) remind them of their own childhood
   (C) do not look realistic
   (D) help children to get along better with each other
   (E) give a child a chance to use his imagination

19. In this passage, which of the following was *not* used as an attack on modern mechanical dolls?

   (A) They are more interesting to adults than to children.
   (B) They might keep children from developing friendships.
   (C) They cause children to become interested in things that are too mature for them.
   (D) They prevent a child from using fantasies.
   (E) They lend themselves to high-pressure advertising.

20. On which of the following statements would both those opposed to modern mechanical dolls and those in favor of them most likely agree?

   (A) It is important that dolls represent the best image of adult life.
   (B) The dolls of past eras can no longer fulfill the needs of modern children.
   (C) It is important that quality dolls be made as realistic as possible.
   (D) Dolls should not only be fun but should be helpful to a child's development.
   (E) Both modern mechanical dolls and dolls of the past provide wholesome experiences for young children.

I had never shared in the general vituperation which greeted *Leaves of Grass* when it appeared in an English dress under the auspices of Dante Gabriel Rossetti, much as there was repulsive even in that expurgated edition. There seemed to me flashes of genius and clear insight which no age, least of all our own, can afford to despise. The man who wrote "Whispers of Heavenly Death" could not be a mere licentious charlatan. The revolt of Whitman against rhyme is like the revolt of Wagner against stereotyped melody, and in his way he seemed to me to be in search of a freer and more adequate method for conveying the intimate and rapid interior changes of the soul. Over and above this, Whitman's wild stanzas, with their lists of carpenters' tools and "barbaric yawps," their delight in the smoke and roar of cities as well as in the solitudes of woods and the silence of mountains and seas of prairies, seemed to me to breathe something distinctive, national, American, with all his confusion of mind. I could hardly read his superb prose description of the Federal battlefields and those matchless pages on the assassination of President Lincoln (of which he was an eyewitness), without feeling that Whitman was no figurehead—one more monkey, in fact—but a large and living soul, with a certain width of aboriginal sympathy too rare in these days of jejune thought and palsied heart.

21. According to the passage, when *Leaves of Grass* was published

    (A) Walt Whitman was acclaimed as a great philosopher
    (B) Walt Whitman became famous and important in England
    (C) it was written completely in prose form
    (D) it started a revolution against rhyme
    (E) it was generally very poorly received

22. The author seemed to be most impressed with Whitman's

    (A) insight into the nature of death
    (B) logical development of his philosophy
    (C) willingness to express his ideas and emotions freely
    (D) choice of subject matter
    (E) knowledge of American history

23. The author suggests that Whitman's reason for not using rhyme was

    (A) to enable him to better express his feelings
    (B) so that he might better aid the revolutionary movement
    (C) a result of his clear insight into the real nature of poetry
    (D) a flash of genius
    (E) to show his disdain for tradition

24. The author used all the following characteristics in describing Whitman *except*

    (A) his ability to see beneath the surface of a problem
    (B) that he often acted like a monkey on a string
    (C) that much of what he wrote was terrible
    (D) his lack of logic in developing ideas
    (E) his willingness to ignore tradition when it didn't help him

25. The tone of this passage could best be described as

    (A) bitter
    (B) defensive
    (C) noncommittal
    (D) angry
    (E) filled with awe

SET TWO

As recently as the 1860s, most people believed that the earth, and man with it, was created a mere 6000 to 7000 years ago. For centuries, beautifully worked flints were regarded as the work of elves, a notion once far more plausible than the idea that man roamed the world's wildernesses in small bands long before the days of Greece and Rome. Even when these stones were accepted as man-made tools, they were attributed to the Romans or early Britons.

(10)   Today we think in wider terms. The earliest dated works of man have been found on the floor of Oldeiwai Gorge, a miniature Grand Canyon in East Africa, and include carefully made stone tools about 2,000,000 years old. Furthermore, fossil evidence suggests that members of the family of man used tools millions of years before that.

Opposition to these ideas began to fade during the late eighteenth and early nineteenth centuries. Excavators, mainly enthusiastic amateurs, pointed to ma-
(20) terial associated with the tools—fossil remains of men and extinct animals. Most geologists still thought in Biblical terms, maintaining that such associations were accidental, that the Flood had mixed the bones of ancient animals with the tools and remains of recent men. But their last-ditch defenses crumbled with the finding of bones and tools together in unflooded and undisturbed deposits, including a number of important sites on the banks of the Somme River. British investigators came to check the French deposits, were convinced, and announced their conclusions in 1859, (30) the year that saw publication of Darwin's *On the Origin of Species*. This date marks the beginning of modern research into human evolution.

1. All of the following kinds of archaeological information were mentioned except

    (A) carbon dating
    (B) fossils
    (C) flints
    (D) extinct animals
    (E) man-made objects

2. According to the article, man has lived on earth for

   (A) 6000 years or less
   (B) about 7000 years
   (C) between 7000 and 100,000 years
   (D) about 2,000,000 years
   (E) far more than 2,000,000 years

3. The scientific turning point in theories about the age of man's existence was the

   (A) publication of *On the Origin of Species*
   (B) discovery in France of the remains of extinct animals and men together
   (C) new theological research of the Bible
   (D) new theories about the Flood and its effects on mankind
   (E) evidence left by the Greeks, Romans, and early Britons

4. The oldest dated works of man have been found in

   (A) East Africa
   (B) the Grand Canyon
   (C) Greece
   (D) Rome
   (E) Britain

5. In the early nineteenth century

   (A) elves made flints in caves
   (B) small bands of Romans roamed the earth
   (C) geologists dated man's existence back 2,000,000 years
   (D) the stones were accepted as ancient tools
   (E) most people believed that man's existence was 6000–7000 years old

The police department of New York City has one branch which many do not know about, although it was established a century ago. This is the harbor precinct's fourteen-boat fleet of police launches, which patrols 578 miles of waters around the city, paying particular attention to the areas containing 500 piers and some ninety boat clubs.

The boats are equipped for various jobs. One boat is an icebreaker; another is equipped to render aid in the event of an airplane crash at La Guardia Airport. All of the boats are equipped with lifeline guns, heavy grappling irons to raise sunken automobiles, and lasso-sticks to rescue animals in the water. They have power pumps to bail out sinking craft, first-aid kits, extra life preservers, signal flags, and searchlights.

The force of 183 men have all had previous experience with boats. Many of the harbor policemen have ocean-going Master's or Harbor Captain's licenses. All are highly trained in the care and handling of engines and in navigation. All are skilled in giving first-aid, and each man is a qualified radio operator and a trained marksman with a revolver.

The work of the police includes many tasks. One duty of this force is to check the operation of the fleet of forty-three junk boats that ply their trade in the harbor, buying scrap, rope, and other items for resale ashore. These boats could just as easily be used to smuggle narcotics, gems, aliens, or spies into the country, so they are watched closely by the city's harbor police force. During last summer the police launches towed 450 disabled boats and gave some kind of help to thousands of others. The officers also arrested those who broke navigation laws, or who endangered the safety of bathers by approaching too near the shore in speed boats.

6. The harbor police were

   (A) introduced during the depression
   (B) first used in the twentieth century
   (C) in use before the Civil War
   (D) introduced by veterans of World War II
   (E) in full force almost 100 years ago

7. The boats used

   (A) are uniform in design
   (B) can all serve as icebreakers
   (C) are all equipped with deck guns
   (D) work at Kennedy Airport
   (E) vary in function

8. The harbor police

   (A) arrest any man found on a junk boat
   (B) prevent the resale of scrap material
   (C) regulate the admission of spies
   (D) ensure legal traffic in junk
   (E) regulate disabled boats

9. The services provided by the harbor police include

   (A) towing, life-saving, and salvage
   (B) customs collection, towing, and the sending of radio messages
   (C) first aid, the rescue of animals, and fire fighting

(D) icebreaking, the collection of junk, and the transportation of aliens

(E) smuggling, first aid, and rescue

10. The police boats

(A) have no responsibility for bathers
(B) unload ships at the piers
(C) assist boats of all kinds
(D) warn offenders but do not make arrests
(E) cannot detain other boats

A knowledge of atomic structure provides an understanding of how various atoms combine. They form compounds. One group of the atoms (the positive atoms) tends to give up one or more planetary electrons, transferring the electrons to the planets of atoms of another group (negative atoms), which have a tendency to gain planetary atoms. When such an exchange occurs, the participating atoms tend to cling together to form a molecule. The number of planetary (10) electrons which can be gained or lost during such a union is specified as the valence of the particular atom involved.

What causes atoms to combine? The electrons in the outermost shell of an atom play a very important part in the formation of compounds. For this reason the electrons in an incomplete outer shell are called valence electrons. The remainder of the atom, excluding valence electrons, is called the "kernel" of the atom. In the formation of compounds from ele-(20) ments, the valence electrons are either transferred from the outer shell of one atom to the outer shell of another atom, or shared among the outer shells of the combining atoms. This produces a chemical bond, with all the atoms involved attaining a stable outer shell.

The types of chemical bonding that are generally recognized are "ionic bonding" and "covalent bonding." In the formation of a compound by ionic bonding, electrons are actually transferred from the outer shell of one atom to the outer shell of a second atom. (30) By this process, both atoms attain stable outer shells containing eight electrons. In the second type of bonding, covalent bonding, the electrons are not transferred from one atom to another, but the two atoms each share one of their electrons with the other. These two shared electrons effectively fill the outer shell in each element. It is important to note that while atoms transfer or share electrons to form chemical bonds, there are still equal numbers of protons and electrons in the group of atoms forming the molecule.

11. The last sentence of this passage implies that

(A) a molecule of all compounds is electrically neutral
(B) a molecule of all compounds has an electrically positive charge
(C) a molecule of all compounds has an electrically negative charge
(D) the "kernel" of all molecules is electrically neutral
(E) none of the above

12. Valence electrons refer to

(A) the number of electrons in the outer ring of an atom
(B) the number of electrons in the incomplete outer ring of an atom
(C) the total number of electrons in an atom
(D) the number of electrons in the kernel of an atom
(E) none of the above

13. The part(s) of the atom involved in chemical bonding is (are) the

(A) kernel
(B) nucleus
(C) valence electrons
(D) protons
(E) neutron

14. If we let "V" represent the number of valence electrons in an atom, and "T" represent the total number of planetary electrons, and "K" represent the number of electrons in the kernel of the atom, then the formula that would best represent the kernel would be

(A) $K = V - T$
(B) $K = V + T$
(C) $K = T - V$
(D) $K = TV$
(E) $K = T/V$

15. According to this passage, ionic bonding differs from covalent bonding because

(A) in ionic bonding, the number of electrons in the outer shell of the resulting compound is different from the number in a compound formed by covalent bonding
(B) in ionic bonding, the nucleus of the compound differs from the nucleus of a com-

pound formed by covalent bonding by the addition of one or more protons

(C) in ionic bonding, the number of valence electrons in the outer shell is different from the number of valence electrons in covalent bonding

(D) in ionic bonding, electrons are actually given up or received, whereas in covalent bonding atoms have mutual electrons

(E) none of the above

In August of 1814, when news came that the British were advancing on Washington, three State Department clerks stuffed all records and valuable papers—including the Articles of Confederation, the Declaration of Independence, and the Constitution—into coarse linen sacks and smuggled them in carts to an unoccupied gristmill on the Virginia side of the Potomac. Later, fearing that a cannon factory nearby might attract a raiding party of the enemy, the clerks procured wagons from neighboring farmers, took the papers thirty-five miles away to Leesburg, and locked them in an empty house. It was not until the British fleet had left the waters of the Chesapeake that it was considered safe to return the papers to Washington.

On December 26, 1941, the five pages of the Constitution together with the single leaf of the Declaration of Independence were taken from the Library of Congress, where they had been kept for many years, and were stored in the vaults of the United States Bullion Depository at Fort Knox, Kentucky. Here they "rode out the war" safely.

Since 1952, visitors to Washington may view these historic documents at the Exhibition Hall of the National Archives. Sealed in bronze and glass cases filled with helium, the documents are protected from touch, light, heat, dust, and moisture. At a moment's notice, they can be lowered into a large safe that is bombproof, shockproof, and fireproof.

16. The title that best expresses the main idea of this selection is

(A) Three Courageous Clerks
(B) The Constitution and Other Documents
(C) How to Exhibit Valuables
(D) Preserving America's Documents of Freedom
(E) Washington In War and Peace

17. Before the War of 1812, the Constitution and the Declaration of Independence were apparently kept in

(A) Independence Hall
(B) Fort Knox, Kentucky
(C) the office of the State Department
(D) a gristmill in Virginia
(E) the National Archives

18. Nowadays, these documents are on view in the

(A) National Archives Exhibition Hall
(B) Library of Congress
(C) United States Bullion Depository
(D) United States Treasury Building
(E) White House

19. An important reason for the installation of a device to facilitate the quick removal of the documents is the

(A) increasing number of tourists
(B) need for more storage space
(C) lack of respect for the documents
(D) need to protect them from dust and moisture
(E) possibility of a sudden disaster

20. The documents have been removed from Washington at least twice in order to preserve them from

(A) dust, heat, and moisture
(B) careless handling
(C) possible war damage
(D) sale to foreign governments
(E) unscrupulous thieves

The First Brigade, after pushing its way through the throng at the river with the point of the bayonet, was already forming on the crest of the hill. Now and then we heard the pattering sounds of bullets, stragglers from the leaden storm above, falling upon the roofs of the boats. Our horses were quickly disembarked, and with the First Brigade in columns closed in mass, leaving orders for the rest of the Division to follow as soon as landed, we moved toward the point indicated by the firing. Directly we saw evidence of close and terrible fighting. Artillery horses dead, cannon dismounted, accouterments torn and bloody, appeared everywhere. The first dead soldier we saw had fallen in the road; our artillery had crushed and mangled his limbs, and ground him into the mire. He lay a bloody, loathsome mass, the scraps of his blue uniform furnishing the only distinguishable evidence that a hero there had died. At this sight, I saw a manly fellow gulp down his heart, which swelled too closely into his throat. Near him lay a slender rebel boy—his face in the mud, his brown hair floating in a bloody pool. Soon a dead Major, then a Colonel, then the lamented Wallace, yet alive, were passed in quick and sickening succession. The gray gleaming of the misty morning gave a ghostly pallor to the faces of the dead. The disordered hair, dripping from the night's rain, the distorted and passion-marked faces, the stony, glaring eyes, the blue lips, the glistening teeth, the shriveled and contracted hands, the wild agony of pain and passion in the attitudes of the dead—all the horrid circumstances with which death surrounds the brave when torn from life in the whirlwind of battle—were seen as we marched over the field, the beseeching cries of the wounded from their bloody and miry beds meanwhile saluting our ears and cutting to our hearts.

Daniel McCook, *The Second Division at Shiloh*

21. At the beginning of this selection, the First Brigade

(A) has just come ashore from landing craft
(B) is retreating
(C) has spent the night in battle
(D) has been wiped out
(E) has killed some Union soldiers

22. The author's attitude toward the dead soldiers he sees

(A) reflects pity and sorrow
(B) shows disgust and hatred

(C) indicates scorn and revulsion
(D) is full of humor and delight
(E) indicates none of the above

23. It is apparent that

(A) the battle is over
(B) the battle has just begun
(C) the First Brigade has been fighting for hours
(D) the battle has been going on for some time
(E) none of the above has happened

24. The reader can infer from the author's choice of language that

(A) he glories in combat
(B) war disgusts and horrifies him
(C) he regards battle as a comic adventure
(D) he wants to desert
(E) the Union must be preserved

25. The dead and wounded on the field are

I. Union soldiers
II. Confederate soldiers
III. civilians

(A) I only
(B) II only
(C) III only
(D) I and II only
(E) I, II, and III

SET THREE

Like the United States today, Athens had courts where a wrong might be righted. Since any citizen might accuse another of a crime, the Athenian courts of law were very busy. In fact, unless a citizen was unusually peaceful or very unimportant, he would be sure to find himself in the courts at least once every few years.

At a trial both the accuser and the person accused were allowed a certain time to speak. The length of (10) time was marked by a water clock. Free men testified under oath as they do today, but the oath of a slave was counted as worthless.

To judge a trial, a jury was chosen from the members of the assembly who had reached 30 years of age. The Athenian juries were very large, often consisting of 201, 401, 501, 1,001 or more men, depending upon the importance of the case being tried.

The juryman swore by the gods to listen carefully to both sides of the question and to give his honest opinion of the case. Each juryman gave his decision by (20) depositing a white or black stone in a box. To keep citizens from being too careless in accusing each other, there was a rule that if the person accused did not receive a certain number of negative votes, the accuser was condemned instead.

1. The title that best expresses the main idea of this selection is

(A) Athens and the United States
(B) Justice in Ancient Athens
(C) Testifying Under Oath
(D) The Duties of Juries
(E) Choosing A Jury

2. People in Athens were frequently on trial in a law court because

   (A) they liked to serve on juries
   (B) a juryman agreed to listen to both sides
   (C) any person might accuse another of a crime
   (D) the slaves were troublesome
   (E) it was a time of violence

3. An Athenian was likely to avoid accusing another without a good reason because

   (A) the jury might condemn the accuser instead of the accused
   (B) the jury might be very large
   (C) cases were judged by men over 30 years old
   (D) there was a limit on the time a trial could take
   (E) the Athenian courts were very busy

4. Which statement is *true* according to the selection?

   (A) An accused person was denied the privilege of telling his side of the case.
   (B) A jury's decision was handed down in writing.
   (C) A citizen had to appear in court every few years.
   (D) Important men were seldom accused of crimes.
   (E) The importance of the case determined the number of jurors.

5. The testimony of which of the following was timed?

   I. the accused
   II. the accuser
   III. slaves

   (A) I only
   (B) I and II only
   (C) III only
   (D) II and III only
   (E) I, II and III

In 1979, Americans consumed about eight billion pounds of red meat that had been cured with nitrites and/or nitrates. Smaller amounts of poultry and fish contained these preservatives, which are now the subject of bitter legal, public relations, and regulatory battles being waged between the meat industry and some consumer groups. The controversy was sparked by the disclosure that nitrosamines, which are suspected of causing cancer, formed in some cured meats (10) under certain conditions, including frying bacon with very high heat. Since then, government and industry have taken a number of steps to mitigate the danger from these pre-formed nitrosamines. These steps include lowering the level of nitrite used, and adding sodium ascorbate or sodium erythorbate, both of which are believed to retard the formation of nitrosamines from nitrites. Even if these pre-formed nitrosamines are eliminated, the scientific question remains: does the human body form nitrosamines from the nitrites or nitrates in cured foods? If so, are these additives (20) more dangerous than the nitrites which are found in human saliva, or the nitrates which come from vegetables?

Both industry and government contend that the use of nitrites is an important protection against botulism, the most deadly food-borne toxin. Some consumer groups contend that the botulism threat is overstated, and that the toxin will not form in meats which are properly processed and kept under refrigeration. Consumer activists contend that the talk of botulism is a (30) smoke screen to protect the industry reliance on long shelf life. Food scientists point out that the botulism spore (the inactive stage of the bacteria's life) is notoriously difficult to kill. Heat sufficient to destroy it would alter the flavor and texture of meat products.

6. A proper title for this paragraph might be:

   (A) The Problem of Nitrosamines—the Consumer's Dilemma
   (B) Big Business Wins Again
   (C) Cancer and the Problem of Big Business
   (D) Botulism: A Deadly Poison
   (E) Protecting the Meat-Eater

7. In this section, the reader is given information about the "botulism threat." When one talks about botulism, one means

   (A) a bacterial food poisoning
   (B) a chemical food poisoning
   (C) a food spoilage retardant
   (D) sodium erythorbate
   (E) an antitoxin produced by the body

8. The botulism spore could be killed by heat but that process would

   (A) cost too much
   (B) endanger the lives of workers
   (C) lower the processor's profits
   (D) change the flavor and texture of the meat
   (E) cause cancer cells to grow

9. Consumer groups complain that the use of nitrites is an excuse

   (A) to keep old products on store shelves
   (B) to allow industry to use cheap meat
   (C) to change the meat's flavor and texture
   (D) to substitute cheap meat for fresh meat
   (E) to allow canned meat into the country

10. Nitrates occur naturally in

    (A) fish
    (B) vegetables
    (C) fried bacon
    (D) nitrosamines
    (E) human saliva

The crimson hand, which at first had been strongly visible upon the marble paleness of Georgiana's cheek, now grew more faintly outlined. She remained not less pale than ever; but the birthmark, with every breath that came and went, lost somewhat of its former distinctness. Its presence had been awful; its departure was more awful still. Watch the stain of the rainbow fading out of the sky, and you will know how the mysterious symbol passed away.

"By Heaven! it is well-nigh gone!" said Aylmer to himself, in almost irrepressible ecstasy. "I can scarcely trace it now. Success! Success! And now it is like the faintest rose color. The lightest flush of blood across her cheek would overcome it. But she is so pale!"

He drew aside the window curtain and suffered the light of natural day to fall into the room and rest upon her cheek. At the same time he heard a gross, hoarse chuckle, which he had long known as his servant Aminadab's expression of delight.

"Ah, clod! ah, earthly mass!" cried Aylmer, laughing in a sort of frenzy. "You have served me well! Matter and spirit—earth and heaven—have both done their part in this! Laugh, thing of the senses! You have earned the right to laugh."

These exclamations broke Georgiana's sleep. She slowly unclosed her eyes and gazed into the mirror which her husband had arranged for that purpose. A faint smile flitted over her lips when she recognized how barely perceptible was now that crimson hand which had once blazed with such disastrous brilliancy as to scare away all their happiness. But then her eyes sought Aylmer's face with a trouble and anxiety that he could by no means account for.

"My poor Aylmer!" murmured she.

"Poor? Nay, richest, happiest, most favored!" ex-claimed he. "My peerless bride, it is successful! You are perfect!"

"My poor Aylmer," she repeated with a more than human tenderness, "you have aimed loftily; you have done nobly. Do not repent that with so high and pure a feeling, you have rejected the best the earth could offer. Aylmer, dearest Aylmer, I am dying!"

from "The Birthmark" by Nathaniel Hawthorne

11. From these paragraphs, the reader can infer that Aylmer

    (A) does not love Georgiana
    (B) is trying to kill his wife
    (C) is disappointed at the result
    (D) has done some operation on his wife
    (E) has caused his wife to commit suicide

12. The birthmark on Georgiana is in the shape of

    (A) a crimson hand
    (B) a pale rose
    (C) a rainbow
    (D) a butterfly
    (E) none of the above

13. The mysterious symbol on her cheek

    (A) is immutable
    (B) becomes redder
    (C) is beginning to fade
    (D) begins to return
    (E) is completely obliterated

14. In Aylmer's view, Georgiana now is

    (A) beyond redemption
    (B) flawless
    (C) a termagant
    (D) ready to die
    (E) unappreciative

15. The moral of this selection is

    (A) perfection cannot be achieved on earth
    (B) power can be abused
    (C) do not try to change what is
    (D) love conquers all
    (E) none of the above

One of the most important experiments in photosynthesis was performed by the English scientist Jo-

seph Priestley. Priestley believed that mint could restore oxygen to an atmosphere from which this gas had been removed. To test this he placed a burning candle in a closed jar. Quickly the flame went out. A mouse was then placed in the jar; it, too, quickly died. From this Priestley concluded that a burning candle and a living mouse both extracted the same substance
(10) from the air. Priestley observed by chance that a sprig of mint had the effect of restoring the injured air to a normal state. A mouse now placed in the jar thrived as though it were breathing atmospheric air.

The experiment made by Priestley was soon followed by others. Other plants besides mint were tested and were found to have the same effect on the atmosphere as mint. It was later found that it was only the green parts of plants which possessed the ability to produce oxygen. Moreover, it was found that the for-
(20) mation of oxygen occurred only in the presence of sunlight. It was further shown that in the process of adding oxygen to the air, plants simultaneously extracted another gaseous material, a substance we now know as carbon dioxide. In addition to the exchange of gases with the surrounding air, there was the growth of the plant itself. From the above it was confirmed that plants consumed carbon dioxide in the production of organic material and oxygen. The plant gained considerable weight during the process. It was later es-
(30) tablished that the overall gain in weight, together with the weight of oxygen given off, equaled the weight of all the raw materials consumed by the plant. These raw materials consisted partly of the carbon dioxide removed from the air but largely of water, incorporated by the plant through a number of complex chemical processes.

16. If in Priestley's experiment the sprig of mint had been replaced by blades of grass, the results would most likely have been

(A) inconclusive
(B) reversible
(C) changed
(D) unchanged
(E) irrelevant

17. "Priestley believed that mint could restore oxygen to an atmosphere from which this gas had been removed," can best be described as a statement of

(A) an observation
(B) a conclusion
(C) a hypothesis

(D) an analysis
(E) a hypothecation

18. According to this passage, oxygen concentration would be greatest in which of the following areas?

(A) a desert
(B) a cave
(C) a wheat field
(D) a frozen lake
(E) an animal cage

19. We may conclude from reading this passage that oxygen is produced

(A) independently of sunlight
(B) only in the presence of sunlight
(C) at any time of day
(D) by the brown stems of the plant
(E) all of the above

20. Which of the following statements is most essential for the conclusion that "plants consume carbon dioxide in photosynthesis"?

(A) plants extracted another gaseous material
(B) only the green parts of plants produce oxygen
(C) mint restored the injured air
(D) the plant gained considerable weight
(E) the mouse was able to breathe in the jar that contained the mint

The two-career marriage, in which both the husband and the wife work, is becoming the accepted norm in American society. Although it has not radically altered mankind's most basic and oldest social unit, the family, there have been some painful adjustments to accommodate the dual-career concept. More than half the nation's mothers work outside the home. The traditional American family, still portrayed in advertising, children's literature, and popular movies as a working father, a stay-at-home mother, and one or (10) more children, represents a scant 13 percent of the nation's families. The apparent reason for this dual-career family is the need for increased income. The more than nineteen million families that had at least two wage earners in 1979 made an average of $509 a week—more than $26,000 a year—compared with $305 a week for families with single breadwinners. Does the dual-career family hurt the child? According to one prominent sociologist, current research indicates that a working mother does not either hurt or (20) help the child. "They grow up just like everybody else." However, more traditional minded scholars take a wait-and-see position, noting that it may take years for the long-term effects of family work habits to become clear.

21. According to this paragraph, the basic social unit of American life is

(A) changing drastically
(B) relatively unchanged
(C) made up of a growing number of children
(D) caused by the liberation of women
(E) a good idea

22. The basic family unit, in the popular media if not in reality, consists of

(A) two working parents and two teenage children
(B) a working husband, a nonworking wife, and children
(C) a group that goes bowling together
(D) a hardworking mother who does not believe in divorce
(E) a poor but honest group that is upwardly mobile

23. In the paragraph, the word "scant" means

(A) incredible
(B) mere
(C) large
(D) unusual
(E) heavy

24. The chief reason why so many women seek employment outside the home is

(A) boredom
(B) lack of volunteer opportunities
(C) desire for a career
(D) economic necessity
(E) dissatisfaction with traditional roles

25. The effect upon children of having both parents work is

(A) beneficial
(B) harmful
(C) insignificant one way or the other
(D) not yet determined
(E) not addressed in the article

SET FOUR

Can you spot a criminal by his physical characteristics? When the science of criminology was founded in the nineteenth century, an imaginative Italian observer decided that criminals are born that way and are distinguished by certain physical marks. They are, he claimed, "a special species, a subspecies having distinct physical and mental characteristics. In general, all criminals have long, large, protruding ears, abundant hair, a thin beard, prominent frontal sinuses, (10) a protruding chin, large cheekbones." Rapists, he argued, have "brilliant eyes, delicate faces" and murderers may be distinguished by "cold, glassy eyes, nose always large and frequently aquiline; jaws strong; cheekbones large, hair curly, dark and abundant."

Around the turn of the century, a British physician made a detailed study of the faces of three thousand convicts and compared them with a like number of English college students, measuring the noses, ears, eyebrows, and chins of both groups. He could find (20) no correlation between physical types and criminal behavior.

But the myth doesn't die easily. During the 1930s, a German criminologist Gustav Aschaffenburg, declared that stout, squat people with large abdomens are more likely to be occasional offenders, while slender builds and slight muscular development are common among habitual offenders. In the 1940s, according to writer Jessica Mitford, a group of Harvard sociologists decided that criminals are most likely to be "mesomorphs, muscular types with large trunks (30) who walk assertively, talk noisily, and behave aggressively. Watch out for those."

1. The earliest criminologist mentioned in this selection believed that

(A) bald men commit no crimes
(B) rapists had strong, immobile facial expressions
(C) large-nosed people were apt to be murderers
(D) criminals had distinct physical characteristics
(E) a protruding chin was a sign of mental illness

2. According to the German criminologist, habitual criminals are likely to be

(A) quick-witted and glassy-eyed
(B) a scholarly English sort
(C) marked by aggressive behavior
(D) short and squat
(E) slender and flabby

3. The "scientific" attempt to discover if criminals

are a specific physical type has been going on

(A) since the 1940s
(B) since the turn of the century
(C) since criminology began
(D) since the 1930s
(E) since Biblical times

4. The writer of this selection has, through irony, indicated that he believes

(A) science does not make many mistakes
(B) criminology is an exact science
(C) women do not make good crooks
(D) criminals represent no physical type
(E) stereotypes are accurate

5. A British physician at the turn of the century discovered that

(A) college students are likely to be criminals
(B) for each criminal there is a college student with corresponding characteristics
(C) some criminals are college students
(D) college students may be useful in the identification of criminals
(E) there is no apparent correlation between physical type and criminality

The history of modern pollution problems shows that most have resulted from negligence and ignorance. We have an appalling tendency to interfere with nature before all of the possible consequences of our actions have been studied in depth. We produce and distribute radioactive substances, synthetic chemicals, and many other potent compounds before fully comprehending their effects on living organisms. Our education is dangerously incomplete.

It will be argued that the purpose of science is to move into unknown territory, to explore, and to discover. It can be said that similar risks have been taken before, and that these risks are necessary to technological progress.

These arguments overlook an important element. In the past, risks taken in the name of scientific progress were restricted to a small place and a brief period of time. The effects of the processes we now strive to master are neither localized nor brief. Air pollution covers vast urban areas. Ocean pollutants have been discovered in nearly every part of the world. Synthetic chemicals spread over huge stretches of forest and farmland may remain in the soil for decades. Radioactive pollutants will be found in the biosphere for

generations. The size and persistence of these problems have grown with the expanding power of modern science.

One might also argue that the hazards of modern pollutants are small compared to the dangers associated with other human activity. No estimate of the actual harm done by smog, fallout, or chemical residues can obscure the reality that the risks are being taken before being fully understood.

The importance of these issues lies in the failure of science to predict and control human intervention into natural processes. The true measure of the danger is represented by the hazards we will encounter if we enter the new age of technology without first evaluating our responsibility to the environment.

6. According to the author, the major cause of pollution is the result of

(A) designing synthetic chemicals to kill living organisms
(B) a lack of understanding of the history of technology
(C) scientists who are too willing to move into unknown territory
(D) changing our environment before understanding the effects of these changes
(E) not passing enough laws

7. The author believes that the risks taken by modern science are greater than those taken by earlier scientific efforts because

(A) the effects may be felt by more people for a longer period of time
(B) science is progressing faster than ever before
(C) technology has produced more dangerous chemicals
(D) the materials used are more dangerous to scientists
(E) the problems are greater

8. The author apparently believes that the problem of finding solutions to pollution depends on

(A) the removal of present hazards to the environment
(B) the removal of all potential pollutants from their present uses
(C) overcoming technical difficulties
(D) the willingness of scientists to understand possible dangers before using new products in the environment

(E) a new age of science that will repair the faults of our present technology

9. The author seems to feel that the attitude of scientists toward pollution has been

(A) naive
(B) concerned
(C) confused
(D) ignorant
(E) nonchalant

10. The word "synthetic" means

(A) new
(B) unsafe
(C) polluting
(D) man-made
(E) progressive

From this time I was most narrowly watched. If I was in a separate room any considerable length of time, I was sure to be suspected of having a book, and was at once called to give an account of myself. All this, however, was too late. The first step had been taken. Mistress, in teaching me the alphabet, had given me the inch, and no precaution could prevent me from taking the ell.

The plan which I adopted, and the one by which I was most successful, was that of making friends of all the little white boys whom I met in the street. As many of these as I could, I converted into teachers. With their kindly aid, obtained at different times and in different places, I finally succeeded in learning to read. When I was sent on errands, I always took my book with me, and by doing one part of my errand quickly, I found time to get a lesson before my return. I used also to carry bread with me, enough of which was always in the house, and to which I was always welcome; for I was much better off in this regard than many of the poor white children in our neighborhood. This bread I used to bestow upon the hungry little urchins, who, in return, would give me the more valuable bread of knowledge.

I am strongly tempted to give the names of two or three of those little boys, as a testimonial of the gratitude and affection I bear them; but prudence forbids;—not that it would injure me, but it might embarrass them; for it is almost an unpardonable offense to teach slaves to read in this Christian country. It is enough to say of the dear little fellows that they lived on Philpot Street, very near Durgin and Bailey's shipyard. I used to talk this matter of slavery over with them. I would sometimes say to them, I wished I could be as free as they would be when they got to be men. "You will be free as soon as you are twenty-one, but I am a slave for life! Have not I as good a right to be free as you have?" These words seemed to trouble them; they would express for me the liveliest sympathy, and console with the hope that something would occur by which I might be free.

from *Narrative of the Life of Frederick Douglass*

11. Based on information in this selection, Frederick Douglass' *Narrative* was written

(A) before the Civil War
(B) between 1880 and 1900
(C) after 1900
(D) during the Middle Ages
(E) none of the above

12. Douglass learned to read

(A) by his own efforts
(B) from his mistress
(C) with the help of young white boys
(D) by using his time in a clever way
(E) all of the above

13. The title which one might give this selection is

(A) The Yearning for Freedom
(B) The Burning for Success
(C) As the World Turns
(D) How I Learned to Read
(E) Youthful Pranks

14. The reason Douglass does not give the names of young white friends is

(A) they asked him not to
(B) they might be embarrassed
(C) he never learned their names
(D) he had forgotten their names
(E) all of the above

15. Judging from this selection, a reader might sum up Douglass' character as

(A) brave but unforgiving
(B) courageous and determined
(C) cowardly and bitter
(D) a seeker after knowledge
(E) lazy and selfish

Many men can be of greatest service to a company by remaining in the laboratory. A single outstanding discovery may have a far greater impact on the company's profit picture five years hence than the activities of even the most able administrator. It is simply good sense—and good economics—to allow qualified researchers to continue their work. Granting these men maximum freedom to explore their scientific ideas is also eminently good sense.

Some years ago, the theory was rampant that after the age of about 40, the average researcher began losing his creative spark. The chance of his making a major discovery was believed to drop off sharply. Hence, there really wasn't much point to encouraging a man of 45 or 50 to do research.

In recent years, however, this theory has fallen into wide disrepute. Companies find that many researchers continue to be highly productive throughout their careers. There is every reason to allow these men to continue their pioneering work.

Companies are also convinced that the traditional guideposts in establishing salaries are not completely valid. In former years, the size of a man's paycheck was determined primarily by such factors as the number of men he supervised or the size of his annual budget. On this basis, the researcher—however brilliant—who had perhaps one assistant and never spent much money made an extremely poor showing. Companies now realize that the two very important criteria that must also be considered are a man's actual contributions to the company and his creative potential.

In today's era of scientific manpower shortages, companies have more reason than ever to encourage scientists to do the work for which they are most qualified. They also have greater reason than ever to provide within the laboratory the environment in which the creative processes of research can be carried out most effectively.

16. According to the passage, research workers need

(A) less supervision by administrators
(B) good working conditions
(C) smaller budgets
(D) more assistants
(E) equal share in the company's profits

17. The author implies that administrators are

(A) underpaid
(B) envious of the research workers
(C) well appreciated by the company

(D) able to hire sufficient research workers
(E) participating actively in research projects

18. Which factor once helped to determine the salary a research worker received?

(A) his contributions to research
(B) the profits made on his discovery
(C) administrative considerations
(D) his creativeness
(E) the number of administrators

19. The author's purpose in writing this passage is to

(A) describe a significant new concept in industry
(B) explore scientific ideas
(C) gain administrative responsibility for research workers
(D) encourage further education for research workers
(E) defend the company administrators

20. Scientists are most creative and productive

    I. before the age of 40
    II. between the ages of 45 and 50
    III. after the age of 50

(A) I only
(B) II only
(C) III only
(D) I and II only
(E) I, II, and III

The ear is indeed a remarkable mechanism; it is so complicated that its operation is not well-understood. Certainly it is extremely sensitive. At the threshold of audibility, the power requirement is inconceivably tiny. If all the people in the United States were listening simultaneously to a whisper (20 decibels), the power received by all their collective eardrums would total only a few millionths of a watt—far less than the power generated by a single flying mosquito.

This aural organ is also remarkable for its ability (10) to distinguish various pitches and other qualities of sound. In the range of frequencies where the ear is most sensitive (between 500 and 4000 vibrations per second), changes in pitch of only .3 percent can be detected. Thus, if a singer trying to reach the octave above middle C (512 vibrations per second) is off-key by only 1.5 vibrations per second, the fault can be detected.

The normal ear can respond to frequencies ranging

(20) from 20 to 20,000 vibrations per second. In this range, it is estimated that the ear can distinguish more than half a million separate pure tones; that is, 500,000 differences in frequency or loudness. The range varies somewhat from ear to ear and becomes somewhat shorter for low-intensity sounds. Above the audible range, air vibrations similar to sound are called super-sonic vibrations. These may be generated and detected by electrical devices and are useful particularly for depth sounding at sea. The time for the waves to travel
(30) from the generator to the bottom of the ocean and back again is a measure of the depth of that particular spot. Supersonic vibrations apparently can be heard by some animals—notably bats. It is believed that bats are guided during flight by supersonic sounds (supersonic only to humans) which they emit and which are reflected back to their ears in a kind of natural radar.

Humans can tell approximately where a sound comes from because we have two ears, not one. The sound
(40) arriving at one ear a split second before or after its arrival at the second ear gives the brain information, which the latter organ interprets to note the direction from which the sound originally came.

The ear is divided into three parts: the outer ear, the middle ear, and the inner ear. The outer ear con-sists of a canal closed at the inner end by a membrane, the eardrum. The middle ear contains a system of three bone levers, known as the hammer, the anvil, and the stirrup. These bones serve to transmit the sound vi-
(50) brations from the eardrum to the membrane-window covering the inner ear. The principal feature of the inner ear is the cochlea, a peculiar spiral bony enclo-sure that looks much like a snail shell. Contained in the cochlea is the vital organ of hearing, the basilar membrane of the organ of corti.

Surrounding the basilar membrane is a liquid. The sound vibrations are transmitted to this liquid, and then, apparently, through the liquid for a distance which is dependent on the frequency of the sound
(60) vibration. Lower frequencies are transmitted to the farther end of the basilar membrane; higher frequen-cies are able to penetrate only a short distance through the liquid. Along the basilar membrane are located the auditory nerve endings. When a particular portion of the basilar membrane is stimulated by the sound vibrations, the brain records the disturbance as a cer-tain pitch. More vigorous oscillation is interpreted as a louder sound.

21. Which of the following statements about normal human hearing is true?

(A) All ear vibrations occur at frequencies be-tween 2000 and 20,000 vibrations per second.
(B) Vibrations below 20 or above 20,000 per second cannot be detected.
(C) All human beings can hear sounds if the vibrations are within a range of between 2 and 200,000 vibrations per second.
(D) Many women can detect vibrations below 4 per second.
(E) The cochlea is in the middle ear.

22. The amount of wattage received by the normal eardrum

(A) indicates high electrical energy
(B) is extremely sensitive to heat
(C) is extraordinarily small
(D) can be harnessed to do useful work
(E) cannot be measured

23. A sound coming from a person's left side would

(A) hit the right ear first
(B) irritate the cortex
(C) hit both ears at the same time
(D) not be perceived by a brain-damaged child
(E) hit the left ear first

24. Which of the following would cause the most vigorous vibration in the human ear?

(A) supersonic vibration
(B) police whistle
(C) loud bass drum
(D) shot from a canon
(E) cat's meow

25. Sound is transmitted immediately past the ear-drum by

(A) a series of bone levers
(B) nerve endings
(C) cochlea
(D) membranes
(E) basilar liquids

ANSWER KEY FOR
PRACTICE READING COMPREHENSION

SET ONE

1. D	6. D	11. B	16. D	21. E
2. E	7. B	12. C	17. B	22. C
3. C	8. A	13. C	18. E	23. A
4. C	9. D	14. D	19. A	24. B
5. A	10. E	15. E	20. D	25. B

SET TWO

1. A	6. E	11. A	16. D	21. A
2. E	7. E	12. B	17. C	22. A
3. B	8. D	13. C	18. A	23. D
4. A	9. A	14. C	19. E	24. B
5. E	10. C	15. D	20. C	25. D

SET THREE

1. B	6. A	11. D	16. D	21. B
2. C	7. A	12. A	17. C	22. B
3. A	8. D	13. C	18. C	23. B
4. E	9. A	14. B	19. B	24. D
5. E	10. B	15. C	20. A	25. D

SET FOUR

1. D	6. D	11. A	16. B	21. B
2. E	7. A	12. C	17. C	22. C
3. C	8. D	13. D	18. C	23. E
4. D	9. E	14. B	19. A	24. D
5. E	10. D	15. B	20. E	25. A

EXPLANATORY ANSWERS FOR PRACTICE
READING COMPREHENSION

SET ONE

1. **(D)** The metaphor of the rose, in the opening sentences, is the means by which the topic is introduced. The theme of development is then expanded with respect to mankind and civilization.

2. **(E)** The author suggests that modern man understands and accepts all that is wrong in modern society, yet surges on to explore new frontiers. This means that man is resigned to the ills of life even while pursuing new goals. Optimism, (D), would not be as good an answer because it suggests an attitude and expectation that improvement will occur.

3. **(C)** The parallel drawn in the final paragraph shows that there is really very little difference between medieval man and modern man. The awarenesses and the aspirations of mankind have not altered appreciably over the centuries.

4. **(C)** The author makes very graphic his equation of the Black Death with the Atomic Bomb by describing the specter of the Black Death as a "mushroom-like cloud" (line 29).

5. **(A)** Returning to the metaphor of the rose, the author sums up his attitude in his final sentence, ". . . beauty alongside the thorns."

6. **(D)** "If he engages in controversy . . . he is as simple as he is forcible, and as brief as he is decisive" (lines 44 and 54).

7. **(B)** The analogy here is an interesting and unusual one. The gentleman is said to provide extra comfort and convenience to those about him just as an easy chair or good fire provides extra comfort and convenience to the householder. The benefits are not necessities, but are very pleasant.

8. **(A)** A scrupulous person has a great deal of moral integrity and is very exacting of his own behavior. "Imputing" is insinuating or accusing, often without basis in fact. Our gentleman would go out of his way to avoid even implying that another might have hidden motives.

9. **(D)** The passage defines a gentleman in terms of his attitudes and behavior. Manner of dress is not discussed.

10. **(E)** The word "effeminacy" appears in line 71. The term is used in a positive sense ". . . gentleness and effeminacy of feeling, which is the attendant on civilization." Of the five answer choices, (B), childishness, (C) cowardice, and (D), indecision, all have negative connotations. (A), femininity, would be irrelevant to the meaning of the statement. (E), delicacy of feeling, is a characteristic of a refined person.

11. **(B)** The reviewer first cites the difficulties involved in mounting the production and then describes the results in such genuinely affirmative terms as "admirable" and "stirringly eloquent."

12. **(C)** The third sentence states that Herbert Graf, Director of the Grand Theatre, produced *Das Rheingold* himself and that he was responsible for the stage effects and costumes as well. Rudolf Bing does get credit for lending Strasfogel, who is in turn praised for his performance, but the major credit must go to Graf.

13. **(C)** Whether or not money was an additional problem in preparing this production, it is not mentioned in the passage.

14. **(D)** In the last paragraph, ". . . the somewhat light baritone of Ramon Vinay . . ." may be taken as mildly critical. The author roundly praises the performances of Sandra Warfield, Jeanne Cook and Glade Peterson. John Modenos is mentioned uncritically as having played in *Das Rheingold* before.

15. **(E)** The "massive but nebulous bastion of stone blocks" (lines 25–6) certainly sounds ominous (foreboding evil).

16. **(D)** The passage describes changes in the concept of dolls and discusses differing attitudes toward "action dolls." While the viewpoint expressed is mainly negative, it is not judgmental, hence the passage cannot really be considered to be a plea for the simpler dolls.

17. **(B)** Marvin Glass suggests that there should be give and take between doll and child, hence he would dislike the passive teddy bear.

18. **(E)** The argument against mechanical toys is that their activity is pre-structured. Teddy bears, on the other hand, allow the child to actively participate in the play, to use his imagination and to endow the plaything with his own fantasies.

19. **(A)** The author comments about the impact of mechanical dolls upon children, but does not appear to be concerned about adults invading the nursery to play with the toys.

20. **(D)** While the "experts" may disagree on what constitutes fun with respect to a doll, or as to what makes a doll helpful to a child's development, they certainly all agree that the purpose of the doll is to provide fun and to aid in the child's development.

21. **(E)** In the first sentence, the author speaks of the general vituperation (verbal abuse) which greeted *Leaves of Grass*. He means that the book was not well liked.

22. **(C)** The author suggests, in an admiring tone, that Whitman ". . . seemed to me to be in search of a freer and more adequate method for conveying the intimate and rapid interior changes of the soul."

23. **(A)** While Whitman was most certainly an anti-traditionalist, the author's feeling is that there was a positive reason for Whitman to avoid rhyme. According to the author, it was necessary for Whitman to break away from the strictures of rhyme patterns in order to fully express his variety of emotions.

24. **(B)** The author makes a point of Whitman's independence of thought, sentiment and expression. This is the antithesis of a monkey on a string.

25. **(B)** The passage defends that which the author considers worthwhile in Whitman's writing.

SET TWO

1. **(A)** While the article does talk about "dated works of man," it does not specifically mention carbon dating.

2. **(E)** Fossil evidence suggests that man used tools millions of years before the dated tools 2,000,000 years old.

3. **(B)** See line 25.

4. **(A)** The Oldeiwai Gorge looks like a miniature Grand Canyon. It is in East Africa.

5. **(E)** See the first sentence.

6. **(E)** See the first sentence.

7. **(E)** The second paragraph describes some of the varying functions of the boats.

8. **(D)** In checking the operation of junk boats, the harbor police ensure that all their activities arc legal.

9. **(A)** If you got this wrong, reread the passage and the answer choices very carefully. Choice (C) gives the appearance of being correct, but while the harbor police will certainly report any fire they spot, the firefighting is left to the fireboats of the fire department. (You will note that firefighting is not mentioned in the passage as a function of the harbor police.)

10. **(C)** All other choices are wrong.

11. **(A)** Protons are positively charged particles. Electrons are negatively charged particles. If the molecule has "equal numbers of protons and electrons," it is electrically neutral.

12. **(B)** See line 15.

13. **(C)** See the third paragraph.

14. **(C)** The kernel includes all of the planetary electrons *except* the valence electrons. Therefore K = T − V.

15. **(D)** See lines 27 and 31.

16. **(D)** The selection describes efforts to protect the documents named in the first sentence.

17. **(C)** The answer to this question must be inferred from the information given. In August 1814, when the British were advancing on Washington, three State Department clerks took the documents across the river into Virginia.

18. **(A)** See the last paragraph.

19. **(E)** Again the answer is to be found in the last paragraph.

20. **(C)** The second paragraph describes efforts to preserve the documents during the Second World War.

21. **(A)** The third sentence mentions that the horses were disembarked; that means they were taken off the boats.

22. **(A)** Throughout the paragraph the author expresses pity and sorrow for the fallen men.

23. **(D)** The number of dead indicates that the battle began some time ago. The sounds of bullets landing on the roofs of the boats indicate that the battle is not entirely over.

24. **(B)** Clearly the war horrifies and disgusts the author.

25. **(D)** The scene is a battlefield, and civilians are unlikely to be among the casualties. The first dead soldier is wearing a blue uniform (a Union soldier) and near him is a rebel boy.

SET THREE

1. **(B)** The entire selection is about jury trials in ancient Athens.

2. **(C)** See the second sentence.

3. **(A)** This is an interesting feature of the Athenian system. See the last sentence.

4. **(E)** See line 15.

5. **(E)** The testimony of both accused and accuser was timed. Since slaves were permitted to testify, even though not under oath, their testimony as accuser or accused was timed just as was that of citizens.

6. **(A)** The selection tries to balance the danger from the carcinogen nitrosamine against the danger of the food poison botulism.

7. **(A)** The next-to-last sentence speaks of the botulism spore as the inactive stage of the bacteria's life.

8. **(D)** See the last sentence.

9. **(A)** Since nitrites retard spoilage, they permit foodstuffs to remain on store shelves longer than foods that have not been treated.

10. **(B)** See line 20.

11. **(D)** Aylmer's cry of "Success! Success!" indicates that he is pleased with something he has done. The operation is clearly not a surgical one as the birthmark is fading and has not been excised. More likely the deed has been done with potions and, perhaps, a pact with the Devil.

12. **(A)** See the first sentence.

13. **(C)** The fading progresses throughout the selection, but when Georgiana looks at her cheek the birthmark is still barely perceptible and not totally obliterated.

14. **(B)** In the next-to-last paragraph Aylmer tells his wife that she is perfect, hence flawless.

15. **(C)** Both (A) and (B) have a ring of truth to them, but the moral of the selection is that near perfection is good enough, and one should leave well enough alone.

16. **(D)** See lines 15 through 17.

17. **(C)** A hypothesis is a tentative assumption to be tested.

18. **(C)** A wheat field provides ideal conditions for the production of oxygen—green plants in the sunlight.

19. **(B)** See line 21.

20. **(A)** Carbon dioxide is a gas. Therefore "to consume carbon dioxide" is synonymous with "to extract a gaseous material."

21. **(B)** See the second sentence.

22. **(B)** See lines 7 through 12.

23. **(B)** *Scant* means *not quite* or *barely*.

24. **(D)** See lines 12 through 13.

25. **(D)** See the last sentence.

SET FOUR

1. **(D)** See the second sentence.

2. **(E)** See lines 25 through 27. Persons with slight muscular development are likely to be flabby.

3. **(C)** Criminology is by definition the scientific study of criminals.

4. **(D)** In line 22 the author makes his view clear.

5. **(E)** See lines 19 through 21.

6. **(D)** The answer is found in the first and last paragraphs.

7. **(A)** The third paragraph spells out the problems created by persistent pollutants.

8. **(D)** See the last sentence.

9. **(E)** *Nonchalant* means *indifferent* or *unconcerned*. That scientists are willing to take risks that are not fully understood indicates that their attitude is nonchalant.

10. **(D)** Synthetic chemicals are chemicals made by man.

11. **(A)** Black slavery as described in the selection was a feature of American life before the Civil War.

12. **(C)** While Douglass' mistress gave him his start by teaching him the alphabet, it was the young white boys in the street who actually taught him to read.

13. **(D)** These paragraphs are about learning to read.

14. **(B)** In the third paragraph Douglass tells us that he would like to publicly acknowledge the help of these boys but fears doing so lest he embarrass them.

15. **(B)** The tone of the whole passage indicates a strong and indomitable spirit. Seeking knowledge is not a character trait.

16. **(B)** The answer is stated in the last sentence.

17. **(C)** A company shows its appreciation in the paycheck. The article tells us that traditionally the size of the paycheck is determined by the number of people supervised. Since administrators tend to supervise many people, they are well paid and much appreciated by their companies.

18. **(C)** There was a time when salary was based simply upon administrative duties and not upon contributions to the company. See the fourth paragraph.

19. **(A)** The author is contrasting old notions of research workers with new ones.

20. **(E)** The third paragraph tells us that research workers tend to be equally productive throughout their working years.

21. **(B)** See lines 19–20.

22. **(C)** See the first paragraph, especially the last sentence.

23. **(E)** The fourth paragraph tells us that sound arrives at one ear a split second before it arrives at the other. Common sense indicates that the sound would arrive first at the ear closest to it.

24. **(D)** The louder the sound, the more vigorous the vibration. See the last sentence.

25. **(A)** Transmission of sound is described in the fifth paragraph.

MATHEMATICAL PROBLEMS

DIRECTIONS: Solve each of the following problems, using available space on the page for your scratch work. Mark the letter of the correct answer on your answer sheet.

You may refer to the following data in solving the problems.

Triangle:

The angles of a triangle added together equal 180°.
The angle BDC is a right angle; therefore,

(I) the area of triangle ABC = $\dfrac{AC \times BD}{2}$

(II) $AB^2 = AD^2 + DB^2$

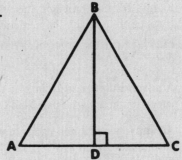

Circle:

There are 360° of arc in a circle.
The area of a circle of radius r = πr^2
The circumference of a circle = $2\pi r$
A straight angle has 180°.

Symbol references:

∥ is parallel to	> is greater than
≦ is less than or equal to	< is less than
≧ is greater than or equal to	⊥ is perpendicular to
∠ angle	△ triangle

Notes: The diagrams which accompany problems should provide data helpful in working out the solutions. These diagrams are not necessarily drawn precisely to scale. Unless otherwise stated, all figures lie in the same plane. All numbers are real numbers.

The instructions above introduce you to the mathematical problem-solving questions of the PSAT. These questions require you to read the question carefully, to determine just what the question asks, to solve the problem and to mark the letter of the correct answer. You will find some of the problems easy enough to answer without computation. Most of the questions, however, will require you to reason and calculate in the space provided on the page. The computations are not so complicated as to require the use of a calculator or a slide rule. If you find yourself involved with very "difficult" numbers or complex operations, you have probably made a mistake earlier in the problem. Look back and try to spot your error before you spend too much time in intricate computations.

A thorough familiarity with arithmetic, algebra and geometry is essential for success with the mathematical section of the PSAT. For this reason, we offer you in the following pages a refresher course in the mathematics you need to know.

FRACTIONS

Fractions and Mixed Numbers

1. A **fraction** is part of a unit.

   a. A fraction has a **numerator** and a **denominator**.

   Example: In the fraction $\frac{3}{4}$, 3 is the numerator and 4 is the denominator.

   b. In any fraction, the numerator is being divided by the denominator.

   Example: The fraction $\frac{2}{7}$ indicates that 2 is being divided by 7.

   c. In a fraction problem, the whole quantity is 1, which may be expressed by a fraction in which the numerator and denominator are the same number.

   Example: If the problem involves $\frac{1}{8}$ of a quantity, then the whole quantity is $\frac{8}{8}$, or 1.

2. A **mixed number** is an integer together with a fraction, such as $2\frac{3}{5}$, $7\frac{3}{8}$, etc. The integer is the integral part, and the fraction is the fractional part.

3. An **improper fraction** is one in which the numerator is equal to or greater than the denominator, such as $\frac{19}{6}$, $\frac{25}{4}$, or $\frac{10}{10}$.

4. To change a mixed number to an improper fraction:

   a. Multiply the denominator of the fraction by the integer.

   b. Add the numerator to this product.

   c. Place this sum over the denominator of the fraction.

   Illustration: Change $3\frac{4}{7}$ to an improper fraction.

   SOLUTION:
   $$7 \times 3 = 21$$
   $$21 + 4 = 25$$
   $$3\frac{4}{7} = \frac{25}{7}$$

   Answer: $\frac{25}{7}$

5. To change an improper fraction to a mixed number:

   a. Divide the numerator by the denominator. The quotient, disregarding the remainder, is the integral part of the mixed number.

   b. Place the remainder, if any, over the denominator. This is the fractional part of the mixed number.

   Illustration: Change $\frac{36}{13}$ to a mixed number.

   SOLUTION:
   $$\begin{array}{r} 2 \\ 13 \overline{)\ 36} \\ 26 \\ \hline 10 \ \text{remainder} \end{array}$$
   $$\frac{36}{13} = 2\frac{10}{13}$$

   Answer: $2\frac{10}{13}$

116

6. The numerator and denominator of a fraction may be changed by multiplying both by the same number, without affecting the value of the fraction.

   Example: The value of the fraction $\frac{2}{5}$ will not be altered if the numerator and the denominator are multiplied by 2, to result in $\frac{4}{10}$.

7. The numerator and the denominator of a fraction may be changed by dividing both by the same number, without affecting the value of the fraction. This process is called **reducing the fraction**. A fraction that has been reduced as much as possible is said to be in **lowest terms**.

   Example: The value of the fraction $\frac{3}{12}$ will not be altered if the numerator and denominator are divided by 3, to result in $\frac{1}{4}$.

   Example: If $\frac{6}{30}$ is reduced to lowest terms (by dividing both numerator and denominator by 6), the result is $\frac{1}{5}$.

8. As a final answer to a problem:

   a. Improper fractions should be changed to mixed numbers.

   b. Fractions should be reduced as far as possible.

Addition of Fractions

9. Fractions cannot be added unless the denominators are all the same.

   a. If the denominators are the same, add all the numerators and place this sum over the common denominator. In the case of mixed numbers, follow the above rule for the fractions and then add the integers.

   Example: The sum of $2\frac{3}{8} + 3\frac{1}{8} + \frac{3}{8} = 5\frac{7}{8}$.

   b. If the denominators are not the same, the fractions, in order to be added, must be converted to ones having the same denominator. To do this, it is first necessary to find the lowest common denominator.

10. The **lowest common denominator** (henceforth called the L.C.D.) is the lowest number that can be divided evenly by all the given denominators. If no two of the given denominators can be divided by the same number, then the L.C.D. is the product of all the denominators.

    Example: The L.C.D. of $\frac{1}{2}$, $\frac{1}{3}$, and $\frac{1}{5}$ is $2 \times 3 \times 5 = 30$.

11. To find the L.C.D. when two or more of the given denominators can be divided by the same number:

    a. Write down the denominators, leaving plenty of space between the numbers.

    b. Select the smallest number (other than 1) by which one or more of the denominators can be divided evenly.

    c. Divide the denominators by this number, copying down those that cannot be divided evenly. Place this number to one side.

    d. Repeat this process, placing each divisor to one side until there are no longer any denominators that can be divided evenly by any selected number.

e. Multiply all the divisors to find the L.C.D.

Illustration: Find the L.C.D. of $\frac{1}{5}$, $\frac{1}{7}$, $\frac{1}{10}$, and $\frac{1}{14}$.

SOLUTION:

$$
\begin{array}{c|cccc}
2 & 5 & 7 & 10 & 14 \\ \hline
5 & 5 & 7 & 5 & 7 \\ \hline
7 & 1 & 7 & 1 & 7 \\ \hline
& 1 & 1 & 1 & 1
\end{array}
$$

$7 \times 5 \times 2 = 70$

Answer: The L.C.D. is 70.

12. To add fractions having different denominators:

a. Find the L.C.D. of the denominators.

b. Change each fraction to an equivalent fraction having the L.C.D. as its denominator.

c. When all of the fractions have the same denominator, they may be added, as in the example following item 9a.

Illustration: Add $\frac{1}{4}$, $\frac{3}{10}$, and $\frac{2}{5}$.

SOLUTION: Find the L.C.D.:

$$
\begin{array}{c|ccc}
2 & 4 & 10 & 5 \\ \hline
2 & 2 & 5 & 5 \\ \hline
5 & 1 & 5 & 5 \\ \hline
& 1 & 1 & 1
\end{array}
$$

L.C.D. $= 2 \times 2 \times 5 = 20$

$$
\begin{aligned}
\frac{1}{4} &= \frac{5}{20} \\
\frac{3}{10} &= \frac{6}{20} \\
+ \frac{2}{5} &= + \frac{8}{20} \\
\hline
&\quad \frac{19}{20}
\end{aligned}
$$

Answer: $\frac{19}{20}$

13. To add mixed numbers in which the fractions have different denominators, add the fractions by following the rules in item 12 above, then add the integers.

Illustration: Add $2\frac{5}{7}$, $5\frac{1}{2}$, and 8.

SOLUTION: L.C.D. $= 14$

$$
\begin{aligned}
2\frac{5}{7} &= 2\frac{10}{14} \\
5\frac{1}{2} &= 5\frac{7}{14} \\
+ 8 &= + 8 \\
\hline
&\quad 15\frac{17}{14} = 16\frac{3}{14}
\end{aligned}
$$

Answer: $16\frac{3}{14}$

Subtraction of Fractions

14. a. Unlike addition, which may involve adding more than two numbers at the same time, subtraction involves only two numbers.

    b. In subtraction, as in addition, the denominators must be the same.

15. To subtract fractions:

    a. Find the L.C.D.

    b. Change both fractions so that each has the L.C.D. as the denominator.

    c. Subtract the numerator of the second fraction from the numerator of the first, and place this difference over the L.C.D.

    d. Reduce, if possible.

    Illustration: Find the difference of $\frac{5}{8}$ and $\frac{1}{4}$.

    SOLUTION: L.C.D. = 8

    $$\begin{array}{r} \frac{5}{8} = \frac{5}{8} \\ -\frac{1}{4} = -\frac{2}{8} \\ \hline \frac{3}{8} \end{array}$$

    Answer: $\frac{3}{8}$

16. To subtract mixed numbers:

    a. It may be necessary to "borrow," so that the fractional part of the first term is larger than the fractional part of the second term.

    b. Subtract the fractional parts of the mixed numbers and reduce.

    c. Subtract the integers.

    Illustration: Subtract $16\frac{4}{5}$ from $29\frac{1}{3}$.

    SOLUTION: L.C.D. = 15

    $$\begin{array}{r} 29\frac{1}{3} = 29\frac{5}{15} \\ -16\frac{4}{5} = -16\frac{12}{15} \end{array}$$

    Note that $\frac{5}{15}$ is less than $\frac{12}{15}$. Borrow 1 from 29, and change to $\frac{15}{15}$.

    $$\begin{array}{r} 29\frac{5}{15} = 28\frac{20}{15} \\ -16\frac{12}{15} = -16\frac{12}{15} \\ \hline 12\frac{8}{15} \end{array}$$

    Answer: $12\frac{8}{15}$

Multiplication of Fractions

17. a. To be multiplied, fractions need not have the same denominators.

    b. A whole number has the denominator 1 understood.

18. To multiply fractions:

    a. Change the mixed numbers, if any, to improper fractions.

    b. Multiply all the numerators, and place this product over the product of the denominators.

    c. Reduce, if possible.

Illustration: Multiply $\frac{2}{3} \times 2\frac{4}{7} \times \frac{5}{9}$.

SOLUTION:
$$2\frac{4}{7} = \frac{18}{7}$$
$$\frac{2}{3} \times \frac{18}{7} \times \frac{5}{9} = \frac{180}{189}$$
$$= \frac{20}{21}$$

Answer: $\frac{20}{21}$

19. a. **Cancellation** is a device to facilitate multiplication. To cancel means to divide a numerator and a denominator by the same number in a multiplication problem.

    Example: In the problem $\frac{4}{7} \times \frac{5}{6}$, the numerator 4 and the denominator 6 may be divided by 2.

$$\frac{\overset{2}{\cancel{4}}}{7} \times \frac{5}{\underset{3}{\cancel{6}}} = \frac{10}{21}$$

    b. The word "of" is often used to mean "multiply."

    Example: $\frac{1}{2}$ of $\frac{1}{2} = \frac{1}{2} \times \frac{1}{2} = \frac{1}{4}$

20. To multiply a whole number by a mixed number:

    a. Multiply the whole number by the fractional part of the mixed number.

    b. Multiply the whole number by the integral part of the mixed number.

    c. Add both products.

Illustration: Multiply $23\frac{3}{4}$ by 95.

SOLUTION:
$$\frac{95}{1} \times \frac{3}{4} = \frac{285}{4}$$
$$= 71\frac{1}{4}$$
$$95 \times 23 = 2185$$
$$2185 + 71\frac{1}{4} = 2256\frac{1}{4}$$

Answer: $2256\frac{1}{4}$

Division of Fractions

21. The **reciprocal** of a fraction is that fraction inverted.

    a. When a fraction is inverted, the numerator becomes the denominator and the denominator becomes the numerator.

    Example: The reciprocal of $\frac{3}{8}$ is $\frac{8}{3}$.

    Example: The reciprocal of $\frac{1}{3}$ is $\frac{3}{1}$, or simply 3.

    b. Since every whole number has the denominator 1 understood, the reciprocal of a whole number is a fraction having 1 as the numerator and the number itself as the denominator.

    Example: The reciprocal of 5 (expressed fractionally as $\frac{5}{1}$) is $\frac{1}{5}$.

22. To divide fractions:

    a. Change all the mixed numbers, if any, to improper fractions.

    b. Invert the second fraction and multiply.

    c. Reduce, if possible.

    Illustration: Divide $\frac{2}{3}$ by $2\frac{1}{4}$.

    SOLUTION:
    $$2\frac{1}{4} = \frac{9}{4}$$
    $$\frac{2}{3} \div \frac{9}{4} = \frac{2}{3} \times \frac{4}{9}$$
    $$= \frac{8}{27}$$

    Answer: $\frac{8}{27}$

23. A **complex fraction** is one that has a fraction as the numerator, or as the denominator, or as both.

    Example: $\dfrac{\frac{2}{3}}{5}$ is a complex fraction.

24. To clear (simplify) a complex fraction:

    a. Divide the numerator by the denominator.

    b. Reduce, if possible.

    Illustration: Clear $\dfrac{\frac{3}{7}}{\frac{5}{14}}$.

    SOLUTION:
    $$\frac{3}{7} \div \frac{5}{14} = \frac{3}{7} \times \frac{14}{5} = \frac{42}{35}$$
    $$= \frac{6}{5}$$
    $$= 1\frac{1}{5}$$

    Answer: $1\frac{1}{5}$

Comparing Fractions

25. If two fractions have the same denominator, the one having the larger numerator is the greater fraction.

    Example: $\frac{3}{7}$ is greater than $\frac{2}{7}$.

26. If two fractions have the same numerator, the one having the larger denominator is the smaller fraction.

    Example: $\frac{5}{12}$ is smaller than $\frac{5}{11}$.

27. To compare two fractions having different numerators and different denominators:

    a. Change the fractions to equivalent fractions having their L.C.D. as their new denominator.

b. Compare, as in the example following item 25.

Illustration: Compare $\frac{4}{7}$ and $\frac{5}{8}$.

SOLUTION: L.C.D. $= 7 \times 8 = 56$

$$\frac{4}{7} = \frac{32}{56}$$
$$\frac{5}{8} = \frac{35}{56}$$

Answer: Since $\frac{35}{56}$ is larger than $\frac{32}{56}$, $\frac{5}{8}$ is larger than $\frac{4}{7}$.

Fraction Problems

28. Most fraction problems can be arranged in the form: "What fraction of a number is another number?" This form contains three important parts:

   • The fractional part
   • The number following "of"
   • The number following "is"

   a. If the fraction and the "of" number are given, multiply them to find the "is" number.

Illustration: What is $\frac{3}{4}$ of 20?

SOLUTION: Write the question as "$\frac{3}{4}$ of 20 is what number?" Then multiply the fraction $\frac{3}{4}$ by the "of" number, 20:

$$\frac{3}{\overset{}{\underset{1}{4}}} \times \overset{5}{\cancel{20}} = 15$$

Answer: 15

   b. If the fractional part and the "is" number are given, divide the "is" number by the fraction to find the "of" number.

Illustration: $\frac{4}{5}$ of what number is 40?

SOLUTION: To find the "of" number, divide 40 by $\frac{4}{5}$:

$$40 \div \frac{4}{5} = \frac{\overset{10}{\cancel{40}}}{1} \times \frac{5}{\underset{1}{\cancel{4}}}$$
$$= 50$$

Answer: 50

   c. To find the fractional part when the other two numbers are known, divide the "is" number by the "of" number.

Illustration: What part of 12 is 9?

SOLUTION: $9 \div 12 = \frac{9}{12}$
$$= \frac{3}{4}$$

Answer: $\frac{3}{4}$

Practice Problems Involving Fractions

1. Reduce to lowest terms: $\frac{60}{108}$.
   (A) $\frac{1}{48}$
   (C) $\frac{5}{9}$
   (B) $\frac{1}{3}$
   (D) $\frac{10}{18}$

2. Change $\frac{27}{7}$ to a mixed number.
   (A) $2\frac{1}{7}$
   (C) $6\frac{1}{3}$
   (B) $3\frac{6}{7}$
   (D) $7\frac{1}{2}$

3. Change $4\frac{2}{3}$ to an improper fraction.
   (A) $\frac{10}{3}$
   (C) $\frac{14}{3}$
   (B) $\frac{11}{3}$
   (D) $\frac{42}{3}$

4. Find the L.C.D. of $\frac{1}{6}$, $\frac{1}{10}$, $\frac{1}{18}$, and $\frac{1}{21}$.
   (A) 160
   (C) 630
   (B) 330
   (D) 1260

5. Add $16\frac{3}{8}$, $4\frac{1}{5}$, $12\frac{3}{4}$, and $23\frac{5}{6}$.
   (A) $57\frac{91}{120}$
   (C) 58
   (B) $57\frac{1}{4}$
   (D) 59

6. Subtract $27\frac{5}{14}$ from $43\frac{1}{6}$.
   (A) 15
   (C) $15\frac{8}{21}$
   (B) 16
   (D) $15\frac{17}{21}$

7. Multiply $17\frac{5}{8}$ by 128.
   (A) 2200
   (C) 2356
   (B) 2305
   (D) 2256

8. Divide $1\frac{2}{3}$ by $1\frac{1}{9}$.
   (A) $\frac{2}{3}$
   (C) $1\frac{23}{27}$
   (B) $1\frac{1}{2}$
   (D) 6

9. What is the value of $12\frac{1}{6} - 2\frac{3}{8} - 7\frac{2}{3} + 19\frac{3}{4}$?
   (A) 21
   (C) $21\frac{1}{8}$
   (B) $21\frac{7}{8}$
   (D) 22

10. Simplify the complex fraction $\dfrac{\frac{4}{9}}{\frac{2}{5}}$
    (A) $\frac{1}{2}$
    (C) $\frac{2}{5}$
    (B) $\frac{9}{10}$
    (D) $1\frac{1}{9}$

11. Which fraction is largest?
    (A) $\frac{9}{16}$
    (C) $\frac{5}{8}$
    (B) $\frac{7}{10}$
    (D) $\frac{4}{5}$

12. One brass rod measures $3\frac{5}{16}$ inches long and another brass rod measures $2\frac{3}{4}$ inches long. Together their length is
    (A) $6\frac{9}{16}$ in.
    (C) $6\frac{1}{16}$ in.
    (B) $5\frac{1}{8}$ in.
    (D) $5\frac{1}{16}$ in.

13. The number of half-pound packages of tea that can be weighed out of a box that holds $10\frac{1}{2}$ lb. of tea is
    (A) 5
    (C) $20\frac{1}{2}$
    (B) $10\frac{1}{2}$
    (D) 21

14. If each bag of tokens weighs $5\frac{3}{4}$ pounds, how many pounds do 3 bags weigh?
    (A) $7\frac{1}{4}$
    (C) $16\frac{1}{2}$
    (B) $15\frac{3}{4}$
    (D) $17\frac{1}{4}$

15. During one week, a man traveled $3\frac{1}{2}$, $1\frac{1}{4}$, $1\frac{1}{4}$, and $2\frac{3}{8}$ miles. The next week he traveled $\frac{1}{4}$, $\frac{3}{8}$, $\frac{9}{16}$, $3\frac{1}{16}$, $2\frac{5}{8}$, and $3\frac{3}{16}$ miles. How many more miles did he travel the second week than the first week?
    (A) $1\frac{37}{48}$
    (C) $1\frac{3}{4}$
    (B) $1\frac{1}{2}$
    (D) 1

16. A certain type of board is sold only in lengths of multiples of 2 feet. The shortest board sold is 6 feet and the longest is 24 feet. A builder needs a large quantity of this type of board in $5\frac{1}{2}$-foot lengths. For minimum waste the lengths to be ordered should be
    (A) 6 ft
    (C) 22 ft
    (B) 12 ft
    (D) 24 ft

17. A man spent $\frac{15}{16}$ of his entire fortune in buying a car for $7500. How much money did he possess?
    (A) $6000
    (C) $7000
    (B) $6500
    (D) $8000

18. The population of a town was 54,000 in the last census. It has increased $\frac{2}{3}$ since then. Its present population is
    (A) 18,000
    (C) 72,000
    (B) 36,000
    (D) 90,000

19. If one third of the liquid contents of a can evaporates on the first day and three fourths of the remainder evaporates on the second day, the fractional part of the original contents remaining at the close of the second day is
   (A) $\frac{5}{12}$ (C) $\frac{1}{6}$
   (B) $\frac{7}{12}$ (D) $\frac{1}{2}$

20. A car is run until the gas tank is $\frac{1}{8}$ full. The tank is then filled to capacity by putting in 14 gallons. The capacity of the gas tank of the car is
   (A) 14 gal   (C) 16 gal
   (B) 15 gal   (D) 17 gal

Fraction Problems — Correct Answers

1. **(C)**	6. **(D)**	11. **(D)**	16. **(C)**
2. **(B)**	7. **(D)**	12. **(C)**	17. **(D)**
3. **(C)**	8. **(B)**	13. **(D)**	18. **(D)**
4. **(C)**	9. **(B)**	14. **(D)**	19. **(C)**
5. **(A)**	10. **(D)**	15. **(A)**	20. **(C)**

Problem Solutions — Fractions

1. Divide the numerator and denominator by 12:
$$\frac{60 \div 12}{108 \div 12} = \frac{5}{9}$$

One alternate method (there are several) is to divide the numerator and denominator by 6 and then by 2:
$$\frac{60 \div 6}{108 \div 6} = \frac{10}{18}$$
$$\frac{10 \div 2}{18 \div 2} = \frac{5}{9}$$

Answer: **(C)** $\frac{5}{9}$

2. Divide the numerator (27) by the denominator (7):

$$7\overline{)27}$$
$$\underline{21}$$
$$6 \quad \text{remainder}$$
$$\tfrac{27}{7} = 3\tfrac{6}{7}$$

Answer: **(B)** $3\frac{6}{7}$

3.
$$4 \times 3 = 12$$
$$12 + 2 = 14$$
$$4\tfrac{2}{3} = \tfrac{14}{3}$$

Answer: **(C)** $\frac{14}{3}$

4.
$$2\,\overline{)6 \quad 10 \quad 18 \quad 21}$$ (2 is a divisor of 6, 10, and 18)

$$3\,\overline{)3 \quad 5 \quad 9 \quad 21}$$ (3 is a divisor of 3, 9, and 21)

$$3\,\overline{)1 \quad 5 \quad 3 \quad 7}$$ (3 is a divisor of 3)

$$5\,\overline{)1 \quad 5 \quad 1 \quad 7}$$ (5 is a divisor of 5)

$$7\,\overline{)1 \quad 1 \quad 1 \quad 7}$$ (7 is a divisor of 7)

$$1 \quad 1 \quad 1 \quad 1$$

L.C.D. $= 2 \times 3 \times 3 \times 5 \times 7 = 630$

Answer: **(C)** 630

5. L.C.D. = 120

$$16\tfrac{3}{8} = 16\tfrac{45}{120}$$
$$4\tfrac{4}{5} = 4\tfrac{96}{120}$$
$$12\tfrac{3}{4} = 12\tfrac{90}{120}$$
$$+\ 23\tfrac{5}{6} = +\ 23\tfrac{100}{120}$$
$$55\tfrac{331}{120} = 57\tfrac{91}{120}$$

Answer: **(A)** $57\tfrac{91}{120}$

6. L.C.D. = 42

$$43\tfrac{1}{6} = 43\tfrac{7}{42} = 42\tfrac{49}{42}$$
$$-\ 27\tfrac{5}{14} = -\ 27\tfrac{15}{42} = -\ 27\tfrac{15}{42}$$
$$15\tfrac{34}{42} = 15\tfrac{17}{21}$$

Answer: **(D)** $15\tfrac{17}{21}$

7.
$$17\tfrac{5}{8} = \tfrac{141}{8}$$
$$\tfrac{141}{8} \times \tfrac{16}{1} = 2256$$

Answer: **(D)** 2256

8.
$$1\tfrac{2}{3} \div 1\tfrac{1}{9} = \tfrac{5}{3} \div \tfrac{10}{9}$$
$$= \tfrac{5}{3} \times \tfrac{9}{10}$$
$$= \tfrac{3}{2}$$
$$= 1\tfrac{1}{2}$$

Answer: **(B)** $1\tfrac{1}{2}$

9. L.C.D. = 24

$$12\tfrac{1}{6} = 12\tfrac{4}{24} = 11\tfrac{28}{24}$$
$$-\ 2\tfrac{3}{8} = -\ 2\tfrac{9}{24} = -\ 2\tfrac{9}{24}$$
$$9\tfrac{19}{24} = 9\tfrac{19}{24}$$
$$-\ 7\tfrac{2}{3} = -\ 7\tfrac{16}{24}$$
$$2\tfrac{3}{24} = 2\tfrac{3}{24}$$
$$+\ 19\tfrac{3}{4} = +\ 19\tfrac{18}{24}$$
$$21\tfrac{21}{24}$$

$$21\tfrac{21}{24} = 21\tfrac{7}{8}$$

Answer: **(B)** $21\tfrac{7}{8}$

10. To simplify a complex fraction, divide the numerator by the denominator:

$$\tfrac{4}{9} \div \tfrac{2}{5} = \tfrac{4}{9} \times \tfrac{5}{2}$$
$$= \tfrac{10}{9}$$
$$= 1\tfrac{1}{9}$$

Answer: **(D)** $1\tfrac{1}{9}$

11. Write all of the fractions with the same denominator. L.C.D. = 80

$$\tfrac{9}{16} = \tfrac{45}{80}$$
$$\tfrac{7}{10} = \tfrac{56}{80}$$
$$\tfrac{5}{8} = \tfrac{50}{80}$$
$$\tfrac{4}{5} = \tfrac{64}{80}$$

Answer: **(D)** $\tfrac{4}{5}$

12.
$$3\tfrac{5}{16} = 3\tfrac{5}{16}$$
$$+\ 2\tfrac{3}{4} = +\ 2\tfrac{12}{16}$$
$$5\tfrac{17}{16}$$
$$= 6\tfrac{1}{16}$$

Answer: **(C)** $6\tfrac{1}{16}$ in.

13.
$$10\tfrac{1}{2} \div \tfrac{1}{2} = \tfrac{21}{2} \div \tfrac{1}{2}$$
$$= \tfrac{21}{2} \times \tfrac{2}{1}$$
$$= 21$$

Answer: **(D)** 21

14.
$$5\tfrac{3}{4} \times 3 = \tfrac{23}{4} \times \tfrac{3}{1}$$
$$= \tfrac{69}{4}$$
$$= 17\tfrac{1}{4}$$

Answer: **(D)** $17\tfrac{1}{4}$

15. First week:
L.C.D. = 24

$$3\tfrac{1}{2} = 3\tfrac{12}{24} \text{ miles}$$
$$1\tfrac{1}{4} = 1\tfrac{6}{24}$$
$$1\tfrac{1}{6} = 1\tfrac{4}{24}$$
$$+\ 2\tfrac{3}{8} = +\ 2\tfrac{9}{24}$$
$$7\tfrac{31}{24} = 8\tfrac{7}{24} \text{ miles}$$

Second week:
L.C.D. = 16

$$\tfrac{1}{4} = \tfrac{4}{16} \text{ miles}$$
$$\tfrac{3}{8} = \tfrac{6}{16}$$
$$\tfrac{9}{16} = \tfrac{9}{16}$$
$$3\tfrac{1}{16} = 3\tfrac{1}{16}$$
$$2\tfrac{5}{8} = 2\tfrac{10}{16}$$
$$+\ 3\tfrac{3}{16} = +\ 3\tfrac{3}{16}$$
$$8\tfrac{33}{16} = 10\tfrac{1}{16} \text{ miles}$$

L.C.D. = 48

$$10\tfrac{1}{16} = 9\tfrac{51}{48} \text{ miles second week}$$
$$-\ 8\tfrac{7}{24} = -\ 8\tfrac{14}{48} \text{ miles first week}$$
$$1\tfrac{37}{48} \text{ miles more traveled}$$

Answer: **(A)** $1\tfrac{37}{48}$

16. Consider each choice:

    Each 6-ft board yields one $5\frac{1}{2}$-ft board with $\frac{1}{2}$ ft waste.

    Each 12-ft board yields two $5\frac{1}{2}$-ft boards with 1 ft waste. $(2 \times 5\frac{1}{2} = 11; 12 - 11 = 1$ ft waste$)$

    Each 24-ft board yields four $5\frac{1}{2}$-ft boards with 2 ft waste. $(4 \times 5\frac{1}{2} = 22; 24 - 22 = 2$ ft waste$)$

    Each 22 ft board may be divided into four $5\frac{1}{2}$-ft boards with no waste. $(4 \times 5\frac{1}{2} = 22$ exactly$)$

    Answer: **(C)** 22 ft

17. $\frac{15}{16}$ of fortune is $7500.

    Therefore, his fortune $= 7500 \div \frac{15}{16}$

    $$= \frac{\overset{500}{\cancel{7500}}}{1} \times \frac{16}{\cancel{15}}$$

    $$= 8000$$

    Answer: **(D)** $8000

18. $\frac{2}{3}$ of 54,000 = increase

    $$\text{Increase} = \frac{2}{\cancel{3}} \times \overset{18,000}{\cancel{54,000}}$$

    $$= 36,000$$

    $$\text{Present population} = 54,000 + 36,000$$
    $$= 90,000$$

    Answer: **(D)** 90,000

19. First day: $\frac{1}{3}$ evaporates
                   $\frac{2}{3}$ remains

    Second day: $\frac{3}{4}$ of $\frac{2}{3}$ evaporates
                  $\frac{1}{4}$ of $\frac{2}{3}$ remains

    The amount remaining is

    $$\frac{1}{\underset{2}{\cancel{4}}} \times \overset{1}{\cancel{\frac{2}{3}}} = \frac{1}{6} \text{ of original contents}$$

    Answer: **(C)** $\frac{1}{6}$

20. $\frac{7}{8}$ of capacity $= 14$ gal

    therefore, capacity $= 14 \div \frac{7}{8}$

    $$= \frac{\overset{2}{\cancel{14}}}{1} \times \frac{8}{\cancel{7}}$$

    $$= 16 \text{ gal}$$

    Answer: **(C)** 16 gal

DECIMALS

1. A **decimal**, which is a number with a decimal point (.), is actually a fraction, the denominator of which is understood to be 10 or some power of 10.

   a. The number of digits, or places, after a decimal point determines which power of 10 the denominator is. If there is one digit, the denominator is understood to be 10; if there are two digits, the denominator is understood to be 100, etc.

   Example: $.3 = \frac{3}{10}$, $.57 = \frac{57}{100}$, $.643 = \frac{643}{1000}$

   b. The addition of zeros after a decimal point does not change the value of the decimal. The zeros may be removed without changing the value of the decimal.

   Example: $.7 = .70 = .700$ and vice versa, $.700 = .70 = .7$

   c. Since a decimal point is understood to exist after any whole number, the addition of any number of zeros after such a decimal point does not change the value of the number.

   Example: $2 = 2.0 = 2.00 = 2.000$

Addition of Decimals

2. Decimals are added in the same way that whole numbers are added, with the provision that the decimal points must be kept in a vertical line, one under the other. This determines the place of the decimal point in the answer.

   Illustration: Add 2.31, .037, 4, and 5.0017

   SOLUTION:
   $$
   \begin{array}{r}
   2.3100 \\
   .0370 \\
   4.0000 \\
   + 5.0017 \\
   \hline
   11.3487
   \end{array}
   $$

   Answer: 11.3487

Subtraction of Decimals

3. Decimals are subtracted in the same way that whole numbers are subtracted, with the provision that, as in addition, the decimal points must be kept in a vertical line, one under the other. This determines the place of the decimal point in the answer.

   Illustration: Subtract 4.0037 from 15.3

   SOLUTION:
   $$
   \begin{array}{r}
   15.3000 \\
   - \quad 4.0037 \\
   \hline
   11.2963
   \end{array}
   $$

   Answer: 11.2963

Multiplication of Decimals

4. Decimals are multiplied in the same way that whole numbers are multiplied.

   a. The number of decimal places in the product equals the sum of the decimal places in the multiplicand and in the multiplier.

   b. If there are fewer places in the product than this sum, then a sufficient number of zeros must be added in front of the product to equal the number of places required, and a decimal point is written in front of the zeros.

Illustration: Multiply 2.372 by .012

SOLUTION:

$$
\begin{array}{rl}
2.372 & \text{(3 decimal places)} \\
\times \quad .012 & \text{(3 decimal places)} \\
\hline
4744 & \\
2372 \quad\; & \\
\hline
.028464 & \text{(6 decimal places)}
\end{array}
$$

Answer: .028464

5. A decimal can be multiplied by a power of 10 by moving the decimal point to the *right* as many places as indicated by the power. If multiplied by 10, the decimal point is moved one place to the right; if multiplied by 100, the decimal point is moved two places to the right; etc.

Example:
$$.235 \times 10 \quad = \quad 2.35$$
$$.235 \times 100 \quad = \quad 23.5$$
$$.235 \times 1000 = 235$$

Division of Decimals

6. There are four types of division involving decimals:
   - When the dividend only is a decimal.
   - When the divisor only is a decimal.
   - When both are decimals.
   - When neither dividend nor divisor is a decimal.

   a. When the dividend only is a decimal, the division is the same as that of whole numbers, except that a decimal point must be placed in the quotient exactly above that in the dividend.

Illustration: Divide 12.864 by 32

SOLUTION:

$$
\begin{array}{r}
.402 \\
32\ \overline{)\ 12.864} \\
\underline{12\ 8\quad\;} \\
64 \\
\underline{64} \\
\end{array}
$$

Answer: .402

b. When the divisor only is a decimal, the decimal point in the divisor is omitted and as many zeros are placed to the right of the dividend as there were decimal places in the divisor.

Illustration: Divide 211327 by 6.817

$$
\begin{array}{r}
31000 \\
\text{SOLUTION:} \quad 6.817\,\overline{)\,211327} = 6817\,\overline{)\,211327000} \\
(3 \text{ decimal places}) \qquad 20451 \qquad (3 \text{ zeros added}) \\
6817 \\
6817
\end{array}
$$

Answer: 31000

c. When both divisor and dividend are decimals, the decimal point in the divisor is omitted and the decimal point in the dividend must be moved to the right as many decimal places as there were in the divisor. If there are not enough places in the dividend, zeros must be added to make up the difference.

Illustration: Divide 2.62 by .131

$$
\begin{array}{r}
20 \\
\text{SOLUTION:} \quad .131\,\overline{)\,2.62} = 131\,\overline{)\,2620} \\
262
\end{array}
$$

Answer: 20

d. In instances when neither the divisor nor the dividend is a decimal, a problem may still involve decimals. This occurs in two cases: when the dividend is a smaller number than the divisor; and when it is required to work out a division to a certain number of decimal places. In either case, write in a decimal point after the dividend, add as many zeros as necessary, and place a decimal point in the quotient above that in the dividend.

Illustration: Divide 7 by 50.

$$
\begin{array}{r}
.14 \\
\text{SOLUTION:} \quad 50\,\overline{)\,7.00} \\
5\,0 \\
\hline
2\,00 \\
2\,00 \\
\hline
\end{array}
$$

Answer: .14

Illustration: How much is 155 divided by 40, carried out to 3 decimal places?

$$
\begin{array}{r}
3.875 \\
\text{SOLUTION:} \quad 40\,\overline{)\,155.000} \\
120 \\
\hline
35\,0 \\
32\,0 \\
\hline
3\,00 \\
2\,80 \\
\hline
200
\end{array}
$$

Answer: 3.875

7. A decimal can be divided by a power of 10 by moving the decimal to the *left* as many places as indicated by the power. If divided by 10, the decimal point is moved one place to the left; if divided by 100, the decimal point is moved two places to the left; etc. If there are not enough places, add zeros in front of the number to make up the difference and add a decimal point.

Example: .4 divided by 10 = .04
.4 divided by 100 = .004

Rounding Decimals

8. To round a number to a given decimal place:

a. Locate the given place.

b. If the digit to the right is less than 5, omit all digits following the given place.

c. If the digit to the right is 5 or more, raise the given place by 1 and omit all digits following the given place.

Examples: 4.27   = 4.3 to the nearest tenth
.71345 = .713 to the nearest thousandth

9. In problems involving money, answers are usually rounded to the nearest cent.

Conversion of Fractions to Decimals

10. A fraction can be changed to a decimal by dividing the numerator by the denominator and working out the division to as many decimal places as required.

Illustration: Change $\frac{5}{11}$ to a decimal of 2 places.

$$
SOLUTION: \quad \frac{5}{11} = 11 \overline{)\,5.00} \quad .45\tfrac{5}{11}
$$

$$
\begin{array}{r}
.45\tfrac{5}{11} \\
11\,)\overline{5.00} \\
4.44 \\
\hline
60 \\
55 \\
\hline
5
\end{array}
$$

Answer: $.45\tfrac{5}{11}$

11. To clear fractions containing a decimal in either the numerator or the denominator, or in both, divide the numerator by the denominator.

Illustration: What is the value of $\dfrac{2.34}{.6}$?

SOLUTION:
$$\frac{2.34}{.6} = .6\overline{)2.34} = 6\overline{)23.4}$$

$$\begin{array}{r} 3.9 \\ 6\overline{)23.4} \\ \underline{18} \\ 5\,4 \\ \underline{5\,4} \end{array}$$

Answer: 3.9

Conversion of Decimals to Fractions

12. Since a decimal point indicates a number having a denominator that is a power of 10, a decimal can be expressed as a fraction, the numerator of which is the number itself and the denominator of which is the power indicated by the number of decimal places in the decimal.

Example: $.3 = \frac{3}{10}$, $.47 = \frac{47}{100}$

13. When the decimal is a mixed number, divide by the power of 10 indicated by its number of decimal places. The fraction does not count as a decimal place.

Illustration: Change $.25\frac{1}{3}$ to a fraction.

SOLUTION:
$$\begin{aligned} .25\tfrac{1}{3} &= 25\tfrac{1}{3} \div 100 \\ &= \tfrac{76}{3} \times \tfrac{1}{100} \\ &= \tfrac{76}{300} = \tfrac{19}{75} \end{aligned}$$

Answer: $\frac{19}{75}$

14. When to change decimals to fractions:

a. When dealing with whole numbers, do not change the decimal.

Example: In the problem $12 \times .14$, it is better to keep the decimal:
$$12 \times .14 = 1.68$$

b. When dealing with fractions, change the decimal to a fraction.

Example: In the problem $\frac{3}{5} \times .17$, it is best to change the decimal to a fraction:
$$\tfrac{3}{5} \times .17 = \tfrac{3}{5} \times \tfrac{17}{100} = \tfrac{51}{500}$$

15. Because decimal equivalents of fractions are often used, it is helpful to be familiar with the most common conversions.

$\frac{1}{2} = .5$		$\frac{1}{3} = .3333$	
$\frac{1}{4} = .25$		$\frac{2}{3} = .6667$	
$\frac{3}{4} = .75$		$\frac{1}{6} = .1667$	
$\frac{1}{5} = .2$		$\frac{1}{7} = .1429$	
$\frac{1}{8} = .125$		$\frac{1}{9} = .1111$	
$\frac{1}{16} = .0625$		$\frac{1}{12} = .0833$	

Note that the left column contains exact values. The values in the right column have been rounded to the nearest ten-thousandth.

Practice Problems Involving Decimals

1. Add 37.03, 11.5627, 3.4005, 3423, and 1.141.
   (A) 3476.1342   (C) 3524.4322
   (B) 3500   (D) 3424.1342

2. Subtract 4.64324 from 7.
   (A) 3.35676   (C) 2.45676
   (B) 2.35676   (D) 2.36676

3. Multiply 27.34 by 16.943.
   (A) 463.22162   (C) 462.52162
   (B) 453.52162   (D) 462.53162

4. How much is 19.6 divided by 3.2, carried out to 3 decimal places?
   (A) 6.125   (C) 6.123
   (B) 6.124   (D) 5.123

5. What is $\frac{5}{11}$ in decimal form (to the nearest hundredth)?
   (A) .44   (C) .40
   (B) .55   (D) .45

6. What is $.64\frac{2}{3}$ in fraction form?
   (A) $\frac{97}{120}$ (C) $\frac{97}{130}$
   (B) $\frac{97}{150}$ (D) $\frac{98}{130}$

7. What is the difference between $\frac{3}{5}$ and $\frac{9}{8}$ expressed decimally?
   (A) .525   (C) .520
   (B) .425   (D) .500

8. A boy saved up $4.56 the first month, $3.82 the second month, and $5.06 the third month. How much did he save altogether?
   (A) $12.56   (C) $13.44
   (B) $13.28   (D) $14.02

9. The diameter of a certain rod is required to be 1.51 ± .015 inches. The rod would not be acceptable if the diameter measured
   (A) 1.490 in   (C) 1.510 in
   (B) 1.500 in   (D) 1.525 in

10. After an employer figures out an employee's salary of $190.57, he deducts $3.05 for social security and $5.68 for pension. What is the amount of the check after these deductions?
    (A) $181.84   (C) $181.93
    (B) $181.92   (D) $181.99

11. If the outer diameter of a metal pipe is 2.84 inches and the inner diameter is 1.94 inches, the thickness of the metal is
    (A) .45 in   (C) 1.94 in
    (B) .90 in   (D) 2.39 in

12. A boy earns $20.56 on Monday, $32.90 on Tuesday, $20.78 on Wednesday. He spends half of all that he earned during the three days. How much has he left?
    (A) $29.19   (C) $34.27
    (B) $31.23   (D) $37.12

13. The total cost of $3\frac{1}{2}$ pounds of meat at $1.69 a pound and 20 lemons at $.60 a dozen will be
    (A) $6.00   (C) $6.52
    (B) $6.40   (D) $6.92

14. A reel of cable weighs 1279 lb. If the empty reel weighs 285 lb and the cable weighs 7.1 lb per foot, the number of feet of cable on the reel is
    (A) 220   (C) 140
    (B) 180   (D) 100

15. 345 fasteners at $4.15 per hundred will cost
    (A) $ .1432   (C) $ 14.32
    (B) $1.4320   (D) $143.20

Decimal Problems — Correct Answers

1.	(A)	6.	(B)	11.	(A)
2.	(B)	7.	(A)	12.	(D)
3.	(A)	8.	(C)	13.	(D)
4.	(A)	9.	(A)	14.	(C)
5.	(D)	10.	(A)	15.	(C)

Problem Solutions — Decimals

1. Line up all the decimal points one under the other. Then add:

    ```
         37.03
         11.5627
          3.4005
       3423.0000
    +     1.141
       ─────────
       3476.1342
    ```

    Answer: **(A)** 3476.1342

2. Add a decimal point and five zeros to the 7. Then subtract:

    ```
       7.00000
    -  4.64324
      ─────────
       2.35676
    ```

    Answer: **(B)** 2.35676

3. Since there are two decimal places in the multiplicand and three decimal places in the multiplier, there will be 2 + 3 = 5 decimal places in the product.

    ```
           27.34
        ×  16.943
        ─────────
           8202
         1 0936
        24 606
       164 04
       273 4
       ─────────
       463.22162
    ```

    Answer: **(A)** 463.22162

4. Omit the decimal point in the divisor by moving it one place to the right. Move the decimal point in the dividend one place to the right and add three zeros in order to carry your answer out to three decimal places, as instructed in the problem.

    ```
                6.125
       3.2. ) 19.6.000
              19 2
              ────
               4 0
               3 2
               ───
                 80
                 64
                ───
                160
                160
    ```

    Answer: **(A)** 6.125

5. To convert a fraction to a decimal, divide the numerator by the denominator:

    ```
             .454
       11 ) 5.000
            4 4
            ───
             60
             55
             ──
             50
             44
             ──
              6
    ```

    Answer: **(D)** .45 to the nearest hundredth

6. To convert a decimal to a fraction, divide by the power of 10 indicated by the number of decimal places. (The fraction does not count as a decimal place.)

$$64\tfrac{2}{3} \div 100 = \tfrac{194}{3} \div \tfrac{100}{1}$$
$$= \tfrac{194}{3} \times \tfrac{1}{100}$$
$$= \tfrac{194}{300}$$
$$= \tfrac{97}{150}$$

Answer: **(B)** $\tfrac{97}{150}$

7. Convert each fraction to a decimal and subtract to find the difference:

$$\tfrac{9}{8} = 1.125 \qquad \tfrac{3}{5} = .60$$

$$\begin{array}{r} 1.125 \\ -\ .60 \\ \hline .525 \end{array}$$

Answer: **(A)** .525

8. Add the savings for each month:

$$\begin{array}{r} \$4.56 \\ 3.82 \\ +\ 5.06 \\ \hline \$13.44 \end{array}$$

Answer: **(C)** $13.44

9.

$$\begin{array}{r} 1.51 \\ +\ .015 \\ \hline 1.525 \end{array} \qquad \begin{array}{r} 1.510 \\ -\ .015 \\ \hline 1.495 \end{array}$$

The rod may have a diameter of from 1.495 inches to 1.525 inches inclusive.

Answer: **(A)** 1.490 in.

10. Add to find total deductions:

$$\begin{array}{r} \$3.05 \\ +\ 5.68 \\ \hline \$8.73 \end{array}$$

Subtract total deductions from salary to find amount of check:

$$\begin{array}{r} \$190.57 \\ -\ 8.73 \\ \hline \$181.84 \end{array}$$

Answer: **(A)** $181.84

11. The difference of the two diameters equals the total thickness of the metal on both ends of the inner diameter.

$$\begin{array}{r} 2.84 \\ -1.94 \\ \hline .90 \end{array} \qquad .90 \div 2 = .45 = \text{thickness of metal}$$

Answer: **(A)** .45 in.

12. Add daily earnings to find total earnings:

$$\begin{array}{r} \$20.56 \\ 32.90 \\ +\ 20.78 \\ \hline \$74.24 \end{array}$$

Divide total earnings by 2 to find out what he has left:

$$2 \overline{)\ \$74.24} \quad \$37.12$$

Answer: **(D)** $37.12

13. Find cost of $3\tfrac{1}{2}$ pounds of meat:

$$\begin{array}{r} \$1.69 \\ \times\ 3.5 \\ \hline 845 \\ 5\ 07 \\ \hline \$5.915 \end{array} = \$5.92 \text{ to the nearest cent}$$

Find cost of 20 lemons:
$.60 \div 12 = \$.05$ (for 1 lemon)
$.05 \times 20 = \$1.00$ (for 20 lemons)

Add cost of meat and cost of lemons:

$$\begin{array}{r} \$5.92 \\ +\ 1.00 \\ \hline \$6.92 \end{array}$$

Answer: **(D)** $6.92

14. Subtract weight of empty reel from total weight to find weight of cable:

$$\begin{array}{r} 1279 \text{ lb} \\ -\ 285 \text{ lb} \\ \hline 994 \text{ lb} \end{array}$$

Each foot of cable weighs 7.1 lb. Therefore, to find the number of feet of cable on the reel, divide 994 by 7.1:

$$
\begin{array}{r}
14\,0. \\
7.1\,)\overline{\,994.0.} \\
71 \\
\overline{284} \\
284 \\
\overline{0\,0}
\end{array}
$$

Answer: **(C)** 140

15. Each fastener costs:

$$\$4.15 \div 100 = \$.0415$$

345 fasteners cost:

$$
\begin{array}{r}
345 \\
\times\ .0415 \\
\hline
1725 \\
345 \\
13\ 80 \\
\hline
14.3175
\end{array}
$$

Answer: **(C)** $14.32

PERCENTS

1. The **percent symbol** (%) means "parts of a hundred." Some problems involve expressing a fraction or a decimal as a percent. In other problems, it is necessary to express a percent as a fraction or a decimal in order to perform the calculations.

2. To change a whole number or a decimal to a percent:

   a. Multiply the number by 100.

   b. Affix a % sign.

   Illustration: Change 3 to a percent.

   SOLUTION: $3 \times 100 = 300$

   $$3 = 300\%$$

   Answer: 300%

   Illustration: Change .67 to a percent.

   SOLUTION: $.67 \times 100 = 67$

   $$.67 = 67\%$$

   Answer: 67%

3. To change a fraction or a mixed number to a percent:

   a. Multiply the fraction or mixed number by 100.

   b. Reduce, if possible.

   c. Affix a % sign.

   Illustration: Change $\frac{1}{7}$ to a percent.

   SOLUTION: $\frac{1}{7} \times 100 = \frac{100}{7}$

   $$= 14\tfrac{2}{7}$$

   $$\tfrac{1}{7} = 14\tfrac{2}{7}\%$$

   Answer: $14\tfrac{2}{7}\%$

   Illustration: Change $4\tfrac{2}{3}$ to a percent.

   SOLUTION: $4\tfrac{2}{3} \times 100 = \frac{14}{3} \times 100 = \frac{1400}{3}$

   $$= 466\tfrac{2}{3}$$

   $$4\tfrac{2}{3} = 466\tfrac{2}{3}\%$$

   Answer: $466\tfrac{2}{3}\%$

4. To remove a % sign attached to a decimal, divide the decimal by 100. If necessary, the resulting decimal may then be changed to a fraction.

Illustration: Change .5% to a decimal and to a fraction.

SOLUTION: .5% = .5 ÷ 100 = .005

$$.005 = \frac{5}{1000} = \frac{1}{200}$$

Answer: .5% = .005

.5% = $\frac{1}{200}$

5. To remove a % sign attached to a fraction or mixed number, divide the fraction or mixed number by 100, and reduce, if possible. If necessary, the resulting fraction may then be changed to a decimal.

Illustration: Change $\frac{3}{4}$% to a fraction and to a decimal.

SOLUTION: $\frac{3}{4}$% = $\frac{3}{4}$ ÷ 100 = $\frac{3}{4}$ × $\frac{1}{100}$

$$= \frac{3}{400}$$

$$\frac{3}{400} = 400 \overline{)3.0000} \quad .0075$$

Answer: $\frac{3}{4}$% = $\frac{3}{400}$

$\frac{3}{4}$% = .0075

6. To remove a % sign attached to a decimal that includes a fraction, divide the decimal by 100. If necessary, the resulting number may then be changed to a fraction.

Illustration: Change .5$\frac{1}{3}$% to a fraction.

SOLUTION: .5$\frac{1}{3}$% = .005$\frac{1}{3}$

$$= \frac{5\frac{1}{3}}{1000}$$

$$= 5\frac{1}{3} ÷ 1000$$

$$= \frac{16}{3} × \frac{1}{1000}$$

$$= \frac{16}{3000}$$

$$= \frac{2}{375}$$

Answer: .5$\frac{1}{3}$% = $\frac{2}{375}$

7. Some fraction-percent equivalents are used so frequently that it is helpful to be familiar with them.

$\frac{1}{25}$ = 4%	$\frac{1}{5}$ = 20%
$\frac{1}{20}$ = 5%	$\frac{1}{4}$ = 25%
$\frac{1}{12}$ = 8$\frac{1}{3}$%	$\frac{1}{3}$ = 33$\frac{1}{3}$%
$\frac{1}{10}$ = 10%	$\frac{1}{2}$ = 50%
$\frac{1}{8}$ = 12$\frac{1}{2}$%	$\frac{2}{3}$ = 66$\frac{2}{3}$%
$\frac{1}{6}$ = 16$\frac{2}{3}$%	$\frac{3}{4}$ = 75%

Solving Percent Problems

8. Most percent problems involve three quantities:
    - The rate, R, which is followed by a % sign.
    - The base, B, which follows the word "of."
    - The amount or percentage, P, which usually follows the word "is."

    a. If the rate (R) and the base (B) are known, then the percentage (P) = R × B.

Illustration: Find 15% of 50.

SOLUTION: Rate = 15%
            Base = 50
              P = R × B
              P = 15% × 50
                = .15 × 50
                = 7.5

Answer: 15% of 50 is 7.5.

b. If the rate (R) and the percentage (P) are known, then the base (B) = $\frac{P}{R}$.

Illustration: 7% of what number is 35?

SOLUTION: Rate = 7%
           Percentage = 35
              B = $\frac{P}{R}$
              B = $\frac{35}{7\%}$
                = 35 ÷ .07
                = 500

Answer: 7% of 500 is 35.

c. If the percentage (P) and the base (B) are known, the rate (R) = $\frac{P}{B}$.

Illustration: There are 96 men in a group of 150 people. What percent of the group are men?

SOLUTION: Base = 150
        Percentage (amount) = 96
              Rate = $\frac{96}{150}$
                = .64
                = 64%

Answer: 64% of the group are men.

Illustration: In a tank holding 20 gallons of solution, 1 gallon is alcohol. What is the strength of the solution in percent?

SOLUTION: Percentage (amount) = 1 gallon
              Base = 20 gallons
              Rate = $\frac{1}{20}$
                = .05
                = 5%

Answer: The solution is 5% alcohol.

9. In a percent problem, the whole is 100%.

Example: If a problem involves 10% of a quantity, the rest of the quantity is 90%.

Example: If a quantity has been increased by 5%, the new amount is 105% of the original quantity.

Example: If a quantity has been decreased by 15%, the new amount is 85% of the original quantity.

Practice Problems Involving Percents

1. 10% written as a decimal is
   (A) 1.0   (C) 0.001
   (B) 0.01   (D) 0.1

2. What is 5.37% in fraction form?
   (A) $\frac{537}{10,000}$ (C) $\frac{537}{1000}$
   (B) $5\frac{37}{10,000}$ (D) $5\frac{37}{100}$

3. What percent of $\frac{5}{8}$ is $\frac{3}{4}$?
   (A) 75%   (C) 80%
   (B) 60%   (D) 90%

4. What percent is 14 of 24?
   (A) $62\frac{1}{4}$%   (C) $41\frac{2}{3}$%
   (B) $58\frac{1}{3}$%   (D) $33\frac{3}{5}$%

5. 200% of 800 equals
   (A) 2500   (C) 1600
   (B) 16   (D) 4

6. If John must have a mark of 80% to pass a test of 35 items, the number of items he may miss and still pass the test is
   (A) 7   (C) 11
   (B) 8   (D) 28

7. The regular price of a TV set that sold for $118.80 at a 20% reduction sale is
   (A) $148.50   (C) $138.84
   (B) $142.60   (D) $ 95.04

8. A circle graph of a budget shows the expenditure of 26.2% for housing, 28.4% for food, 12% for clothing, 12.7% for taxes, and the balance for miscellaneous items. The percent for miscellaneous items is
   (A) 31.5   (C) 20.7
   (B) 79.3   (D) 68.5

9. Two dozen shuttlecocks and four badminton rackets are to be purchased for a playground. The shuttlecocks are priced at $.35 each and the rackets at $2.75 each. The playground receives a discount of 30% from these prices. The total cost of this equipment is
   (A) $ 7.29   (C) $13.58
   (B) $11.43   (D) $18.60

10. A piece of wood weighing 10 ounces is found to have a weight of 8 ounces after drying. The moisture content was
    (A) 25%   (C) 20%
    (B) $33\frac{1}{3}$%   (D) 40%

11. A bag contains 800 coins. Of these, 10 percent are dimes, 30 percent are nickels, and the rest are quarters. The amount of money in the bag is
    (A) less than $150
    (B) between $150 and $300
    (C) between $301 and $450
    (D) more than $450

12. Six quarts of a 20% solution of alcohol in water are mixed with 4 quarts of a 60% solution of alcohol in water. The alcoholic strength of the mixture is
   (A) 80%   (C) 36%
   (B) 40%   (D) 72%

13. A man insures 80% of his property and pays a $2\frac{1}{2}$% premium amounting to $348. What is the total value of his property?
   (A) $17,000   (C) $18,400
   (B) $18,000   (D) $17,400

14. A clerk divided his 35-hour work week as follows: $\frac{1}{5}$ of his time was spent in sorting mail; $\frac{1}{2}$ of his time in filing letters; and $\frac{1}{7}$ of his time in reception work. The rest of his time was devoted to messenger work. The percent of time spent on messenger work by the clerk during the week was most nearly
   (A) 6%   (C) 14%
   (B) 10%   (D) 16%

15. In a school in which 40% of the enrolled students are boys, 80% of the boys are present on a certain day. If 1152 boys are present, the total school enrollment is
   (A) 1440   (C) 3600
   (B) 2880   (D) 5400

Percent Problems — Correct Answers

1.	**(D)**	6.	**(A)**	11.	**(A)**
2.	**(A)**	7.	**(A)**	12.	**(C)**
3.	**(D)**	8.	**(C)**	13.	**(D)**
4.	**(B)**	9.	**(C)**	14.	**(D)**
5.	**(C)**	10.	**(C)**	15.	**(C)**

Problem Solutions — Percents

1. $10\% = .10 = .1$

   Answer: (D) 0.1

2. $5.37\% = .0537 = \dfrac{537}{10,000}$

   Answer: (A) $\dfrac{537}{10,000}$

3. Base (number following "of") $= \frac{5}{6}$
   Percentage (number following "is") $= \frac{3}{4}$

   $\text{Rate} = \dfrac{\text{Percentage}}{\text{Base}}$
   $= \text{Percentage} \div \text{Base}$

   $\text{Rate} = \frac{3}{4} \div \frac{5}{6}$

   $= \frac{3}{4} \times \frac{6}{5}$

   $= \frac{9}{10}$

   $\frac{9}{10} = .9 = 90\%$

   Answer: (D) 90%

4. Base (number following "of") $= 24$
   Percentage (number following "is") $= 14$

   $\text{Rate} = \text{Percentage} \div \text{Base}$
   $\text{Rate} = 14 \div 24$
   $= .58\frac{1}{3}$
   $= 58\frac{1}{3}\%$

   Answer: (B) $58\frac{1}{3}\%$

5. 200% of 800 = 2.00 × 800
            = 1600

   Answer: **(C)** 1600

6. He must answer 80% of 35 correctly. Therefore, he may miss 20% of 35.
   20% of 35 = .20 × 35
              = 7

   Answer: **(A)** 7

7. Since $118.80 represents a 20% reduction, $118.80 = 80% of the regular price.

   Regular price = $\frac{\$118.80}{80\%}$
                 = $118.80 ÷ .80
                 = $148.50

   Answer: **(A)** $148.50

8. All the items in a circle graph total 100%. Add the figures given for housing, food, clothing, and taxes:

       26.2%
       28.4%
       12 %
    + 12.7%
       79.3%

   Subtract this total from 100% to find the percent for miscellaneous items:

      100.0%
    − 79.3%
       20.7%

   Answer: **(C)** 20.7%

9. Price of shuttlecocks = 24 × $.35 = $ 8.40
   Price of rackets   = 4 × $2.75 = $11.00
   Total price   = $19.40
   Discount is 30%, and 100% − 30% = 70%
   Actual cost = 70% of 19.40
              = .70 × 19.40
              = 13.58

   Answer: **(C)** $13.58

10. Subtract weight of wood after drying from original weight of wood to find amount of moisture in wood:

       10
     − 8
       2 ounces of moisture in wood

Moisture content = $\frac{2 \text{ ounces}}{10 \text{ ounces}}$ = .2 = 20%

Answer: **(C)** 20%

11. Find the number of each kind of coin:
    10% of 800 = .10 × 800 = 80 dimes
    30% of 800 = .30 × 800 = 240 nickels
    60% of 800 = .60 × 800 = 480 quarters

    Find the value of the coins:
      80 dimes = 80 × .10 = $ 8.00
    240 nickels = 240 × .05 = 12.00
    480 quarters = 480 × .25 = 120.00
                     Total $140.00

    Answer: **(A)** less than $150

12. First solution contains 20% of 6 quarts of alcohol.
    Alcohol content = .20 × 6
                   = 1.2 quarts
    Second solution contains 60% of 4 quarts of alcohol.
    Alcohol content = .60 × 4
                   = 2.4 quarts
    Mixture contains: 1.2 + 2.4 = 3.6 quarts alcohol
              6 + 4 = 10 quarts liquid

    Alcoholic strength of mixture = $\frac{3.6}{10}$ = 36%

    Answer: **(C)** 36%

13. 2½% of insured value = $348

    Insured value = $\frac{348}{2\frac{1}{2}\%}$
                  = 348 ÷ .025
                  = $13,920

    $13,920 is 80% of total value

    Total value = $\frac{\$13,920}{80\%}$
               = $13,920 ÷ .80
               = $17,400

    Answer: **(D)** $17,400

14. ⅕ × 35 = 7 hr sorting mail
    ½ × 35 = 17½ hr filing
    ⅐ × 35 = 5 hr reception
             29½ hr accounted for

$35 - 29\frac{1}{2} = 5\frac{1}{2}$ hr left for messenger work

% spent on messenger work:

$$= \frac{5\frac{1}{2}}{35}$$
$$= 5\frac{1}{2} \div 35$$
$$= \frac{11}{2} \times \frac{1}{35}$$
$$= \frac{11}{70}$$
$$= .15\frac{5}{7}$$

Answer: **(D)** $15\frac{5}{7}$ = most nearly 16%

15. 80% of the boys = 1152

$$\text{Number of boys} = \frac{1152}{80\%}$$
$$= 1152 \div .80$$
$$= 1440$$

40% of students = 1440

$$\text{Total number of students} = \frac{1440}{40\%}$$
$$= 1440 \div .40$$
$$= 3600$$

Answer: **(C)** 3600

POWERS AND ROOTS

1. The numbers that are multiplied to give a product are called the **factors** of the product.

   Example: In $2 \times 3 = 6$, 2 and 3 are factors.

2. If the factors are the same, an **exponent** may be used to indicate the number of times the factor appears.

   Example: In $3 \times 3 = 3^2$, the number 3 appears as a factor twice, as is indicated by the exponent 2.

3. When a product is written in exponential form, the number the exponent refers to is called the **base**. The product itself is called the **power**.

   Example: In 2^5, the number 2 is the base and 5 is the exponent.
   $2^5 = 2 \times 2 \times 2 \times 2 \times 2 = 32$, so 32 is the power.

4. a. If the exponent used is 2, we say that the base has been **squared**, or raised to the second power.

   Example: 6^2 is read "six squared" or "six to the second power."

   b. If the exponent used is 3, we say that the base has been **cubed**, or raised to the third power.

   Example: 5^3 is read "five cubed" or "five to the third power."

   c. If the exponent is 4, we say that the base has been raised to the fourth power. If the exponent is 5, we say the base has been raised to the fifth power, etc.

   Example: 2^8 is read "two to the eighth power."

5. A number that is the product of a number squared is called a **perfect square**.

   Example: 25 is a perfect square because $25 = 5^2$.

6. a. If a number has exactly two equal factors, each factor is called the **square root** of the number.

   Example: $9 = 3 \times 3$; therefore, 3 is the square root of 9.

   b. The symbol $\sqrt{}$ is used to indicate square root.

   Example: $\sqrt{9} = 3$ means that the square root of 9 is 3, or $3 \times 3 = 9$.

7. The square root of the most common perfect squares may be found by using the following table, or by trial and error; that is, by finding the number that, when squared, yields the given perfect square.

Number	Perfect Square	Number	Perfect Square
1	1	10	100
2	4	11	121
3	9	12	144
4	16	13	169
5	25	14	196
6	36	15	225
7	49	20	400
8	64	25	625
9	81	30	900

Example: To find $\sqrt{81}$, note that 81 is the perfect square of 9, or $9^2 = 81$. Therefore, $\sqrt{81} = 9$.

8. To find the square root of a number that is not a perfect square, use the following method:

   a. Locate the decimal point.

   b. Mark off the digits in groups of two in both directions beginning at the decimal point.

   c. Mark the decimal point for the answer just above the decimal point of the number whose square root is to be taken.

   d. Find the largest perfect square contained in the left-hand group of two.

   e. Place its square root in the answer. Subtract the perfect square from the first digit or pair of digits.

   f. Bring down the next pair.

   g. Double the partial answer.

   h. Add a trial digit to the right of the doubled partial answer. Multiply this new number by the trial digit. Place the correct new digit in the answer.

   i. Subtract the product.

   j. Repeat steps f–i as often as necessary.

You will notice that you get one digit in the answer for every group of two you marked off in the original number.

Illustration: Find the square root of 138,384.

SOLUTION:

$$
\begin{array}{r}
3 \\
\sqrt{13'83'84.} \\
3^2 = 9 \\
\hline
4\ 83
\end{array}
$$

$$
\begin{array}{r}
3\ \ 7\ \ 2. \\
\sqrt{13'83'84.} \\
3^2 = 9 \\
\hline
4\ 83 \\
7 \times 67 = 4\ 69 \\
\hline
14\ 84 \\
2 \times 742 = 14\ 84 \\
\hline
\end{array}
$$

The number must first be marked off in groups of two figures each, beginning at the decimal point, which, in the case of a whole number, is at the right. The number of figures in the root will be the same as the number of groups so obtained.

The largest square less than 13 is 9. $\sqrt{9} = 3$

Place its square root in the answer. Subtract the perfect square from the first digit or pair of digits. Bring down the next pair. To form our trial divisor, annex 0 to this root "3" (making 30) and multiply by 2.

483 ÷ 60 = 8. Multiplying the trial divisor 68 by 8, we obtain 544, which is too large. We then try multiplying 67 by 7. This is correct. Add the trial digit to the right of the doubled partial answer. Place the new digit in the answer. Subtract the product. Bring down the final group. Annex 0 to the new root 37 and multiply by 2 for the trial divisor:

$$2 \times 370 = 740$$
$$1484 \div 740 = 2$$

Place the 2 in the answer.

Answer: The square root of 138,384 is 372.

Illustration: Find the square root of 3 to the nearest hundredth.

$$
\begin{array}{r l}
 & \phantom{\sqrt{}}\;1.\ 7\ 3\ 2 \\
\text{SOLUTION:} & \sqrt{3.00'00'00} \\
1^2 = & 1 \\
20 & 2\ 00 \\
7 \times 27 = & 1\ 89 \\
340 & 11\ 00 \\
3 \times 343 = & 10\ 29 \\
3460 & 71\ 00 \\
2 \times 3462 = & 69\ 24 \\
\end{array}
$$

Answer: The square root of 3 is 1.73 to the nearest hundredth.

9.   To find the square root of a fraction, find the square root of its numerator and of its denominator.

Example: $\sqrt{\frac{4}{9}} = \dfrac{\sqrt{4}}{\sqrt{9}} = \frac{2}{3}$

10.   a.   If a number has exactly three equal factors, each factor is called the **cube root** of the number.

b.   The symbol $\sqrt[3]{}$ is used to indicate the cube root.

Example: $8 = 2 \times 2 \times 2$; therefore, $\sqrt[3]{8} = 2$

Practice Problems Involving Powers and Roots

1. The square of 10 is
   (A) 1
   (B) 2
   (C) 5
   (D) 100

2. The cube of 9 is
   (A) 3
   (B) 27
   (C) 81
   (D) 729

3. The fourth power of 2 is
   (A) 2
   (B) 4
   (C) 8
   (D) 16

4. In exponential form, the product $7 \times 7 \times 7 \times 7 \times 7$ may be written
   (A) 5^7
   (B) 7^5
   (C) 2^7
   (D) 7^2

5. The value of 3^5 is
   (A) 243
   (B) 125
   (C) 35
   (D) 15

6. The square root of 1175, to the nearest whole number, is
   (A) 32
   (B) 33
   (C) 34
   (D) 35

7. Find $\sqrt{503}$ to the nearest tenth.
   (A) 22.4
   (B) 22.5
   (C) 22.6
   (D) 22.7

8. Find $\sqrt{\frac{1}{4}}$.
   (A) 2
   (B) $\frac{1}{2}$
   (C) $\frac{1}{8}$
   (D) $\frac{1}{16}$

9. Find $\sqrt[3]{64}$.
   (A) 3
   (B) 4
   (C) 8
   (D) 32

10. The sum of 2^2 and 2^3 is
    (A) 9
    (B) 10
    (C) 12
    (D) 32

Powers and Roots Problems — Correct Answers

1. **(D)**	5. **(A)**	8. **(B)**
2. **(D)**	6. **(C)**	9. **(B)**
3. **(D)**	7. **(A)**	10. **(C)**
4. **(B)**		

Problem Solutions — Powers and Roots

1. $10^2 = 10 \times 10 = 100$

   Answer: **(D)** 100

2. $9^3 = 9 \times 9 \times 9$
   $= 81 \times 9$
   $= 729$

   Answer: **(D)** 729

3. $2^4 = 2 \times 2 \times 2 \times 2$
    $= 4 \times 2 \times 2$
    $= 8 \times 2$
    $= 16$

    Answer: **(D)** 16

4. $7 \times 7 \times 7 \times 7 \times 7 = 7^5$

    Answer: **(B)** 7^5

5. $3^5 = 3 \times 3 \times 3 \times 3 \times 3$
    $= 243$

    Answer: **(A)** 243

6.

$$\begin{array}{r} 3 \quad 4. \quad 2 \\ \sqrt{11'75.00} \end{array}$$ = 34 to the nearest whole number

$$3^2 = \quad 9$$
$$\overline{\quad 2\ 75}$$
$$4 \times 64 = \quad 2\ 56$$
$$\overline{\quad 19\ 00}$$
$$2 \times 682 = \quad 13\ 64$$
$$\overline{\quad 5\ 36}$$

Answer: **(C)** 34

7.

$$\begin{array}{r} 2 \quad 2. \quad 4 \quad 2 \\ \sqrt{5'03.00'00} \end{array}$$ = 22.4 to the nearest tenth

$$2^2 = \quad 4$$
$$\overline{\quad 1\ 03}$$
$$2 \times 42 = \quad 84$$
$$\overline{\quad 19\ 00}$$
$$4 \times 444 = \quad 17\ 76$$
$$\overline{\quad 1\ 24\ 00}$$
$$2 \times 4482 = \quad 89\ 64$$
$$\overline{\quad 34\ 36}$$

Answer: **(A)** 22.4

8. $\sqrt{\frac{1}{4}} = \dfrac{\sqrt{1}}{\sqrt{4}} = \frac{1}{2}$

    Answer: **(B)** $\frac{1}{2}$

9. Since $4 \times 4 \times 4 = 64$, $\sqrt[3]{64} = 4$

    Answer: **(B)** 4

10. $2^2 + 2^3 = 4 + 8 = 12$

    Answer: **(C)** 12

DENOMINATE NUMBERS (MEASUREMENT)

1. A **denominate number** is a number that specifies a given measurement. The unit of measure is called the **denomination**.

    Example: 7 miles, 3 quarts, and 5 grams are denominate numbers.

2. a. The English system of measurement uses such denominations as pints, ounces, pounds, and feet.

    b. The metric system of measurement uses such denominations as grams, liters, and meters.

English System of Measurement

3. To convert from one unit of measure to another, find in the Table of Measures how many units of the smaller denomination equal one unit of the larger denomination. This number is called the **conversion number**.

4. To convert from one unit of measure to a smaller unit, multiply the given number of units by the conversion number.

    Illustration: Convert 7 yards to inches.

    SOLUTION: 1 yard = 36 inches (conversion number)

    7 yards = 7 × 36 inches

    = 252 inches

    Answer: 252 in

    Illustration: Convert 2 hours 12 minutes to minutes.

    SOLUTION: 1 hour = 60 minutes (conversion number)

    2 hr 12 min = 2 hr + 12 min

    2 hr = 2 × 60 min = 120 min

    2 hr 12 min = 120 min + 12 min

    = 132 min

    Answer: 132 min

5. To convert from one unit of measure to a larger unit:

   a. Divide the given number of units by the conversion number.

   Illustration: Convert 48 inches to feet.

   SOLUTION: 1 foot = 12 inches (conversion number)

             48 in ÷ 12 = 4 ft

   Answer: 4 ft

   b. If there is a remainder it is expressed in terms of the smaller unit of measure.

   Illustration: Convert 35 ounces to pounds and ounces.

   SOLUTION: 1 pound = 16 ounces (conversion number)

$$35 \text{ oz} \div 16 = 16 \overline{)\begin{array}{r} 2 \text{ lb} \\ 35 \text{ oz} \\ \underline{32} \\ 3 \text{ oz} \end{array}}$$

$$= 2 \text{ lb } 3 \text{ oz}$$

   Answer: 2 lb 3 oz

6. To add denominate numbers, arrange them in columns by common unit, then add each column. If necessary, simplify the answer, starting with the smallest unit.

   Illustration: Add 1 yd 2 ft 8 in, 2 yd 2 ft 10 in, and 3 yd 1 ft 9 in.

   SOLUTION: 1 yd 2 ft 8 in
                   2 yd 2 ft 10 in
             + 3 yd 1 ft 9 in
               6 yd 5 ft 27 in
           = 6 yd 7 ft 3 in   (since 27 in = 2 ft 3 in)
           = 8 yd 1 ft 3 in   (since 7 ft = 2 yd 1 ft)

   Answer: 8 yd 1 ft 3 in

7. To subtract denominate numbers, arrange them in columns by common unit, then subtract each column starting with the smallest unit. If necessary, borrow to increase the number of a particular unit.

   Illustration: Subtract 2 gal 3 qt from 7 gal 1 qt.

   SOLUTION: 7 gal 1 qt =   6 gal 5 qt
             − 2 gal 3 qt = − 2 gal 3 qt
                         4 gal 2 qt
        Note that 1 gal was borrowed from 7 gal.
                 1 gal = 4 qt
        Therefore, 7 gal 1 qt = 6 gal 5 qt

   Answer: 4 gal 2 qt

8. To multiply a denominate number by a given number:

   a. If the denominate number contains only one unit, multiply the numbers and write the unit.

   Example: 3 oz × 4 = 12 oz

b. If the denominate number contains more than one unit of measurement, multiply the number of each unit by the given number and simplify the answer, if necessary.

Illustration: Multiply 4 yd 2 ft 8 in by 2.

SOLUTION:

$$
\begin{array}{r}
4 \text{ yd } 2 \text{ ft } 8 \text{ in} \\
\times \qquad\qquad 2 \\
\hline
8 \text{ yd } 4 \text{ ft } 16 \text{ in}
\end{array}
$$

= 8 yd 5 ft 4 in (since 16 in = 1 ft 4 in)
= 9 yd 2 ft 4 in (since 5 ft = 1 yd 2 ft)

Answer: 9 yd 2 ft 4 in

9. To divide a denominate number by a given number, convert all units to the smallest unit, then divide. Simplify the answer, if necessary.

Illustration: Divide 5 lb 12 oz by 4.

SOLUTION:

1 lb = 16 oz, therefore
5 lb 12 oz = 92 oz
92 oz ÷ 4 = 23 oz
= 1 lb 7 oz

Answer: 1 lb 7 oz

10. Alternate method of division:

a. Divide the number of the largest unit by the given number.

b. Convert any remainder to the next largest unit.

c. Divide the total number of that unit by the given number.

d. Again convert any remainder to the next unit and divide.

e. Repeat until no units remain.

Illustration: Divide 9 hr 21 min 40 sec by 4.

SOLUTION:

$$
\begin{array}{r}
2 \text{ hr} \quad 20 \text{ min} \quad 25 \text{ sec} \\
4 \,\overline{)\, 9 \text{ hr} \quad 21 \text{ min} \quad 40 \text{ sec}} \\
\underline{8 \text{ hr}} \qquad\qquad\qquad \\
1 \text{ hr} = 60 \text{ min} \qquad\qquad \\
\underline{81 \text{ min}} \qquad\qquad \\
80 \text{ min} \qquad\qquad \\
1 \text{ min} = \underline{60 \text{ sec}} \\
100 \text{ sec} \\
\underline{100 \text{ sec}} \\
0 \text{ sec}
\end{array}
$$

Answer: 2 hr 20 min 25 sec

Metric Measurement

11. The basic units of the metric system are the meter (m), which is used for length; the gram (g), which is used for weight; and the liter (*l*), which is used for capacity, or volume.

12. The prefixes that are used with the basic units, and their meanings, are:

Prefix	Abbreviation	Meaning
micro	**m**	one millionth of (.000001)
milli	m	one thousandth of (.001)
centi	c	one hundredth of (.01)
deci	d	one tenth of (.1)
deka	da or dk	ten times (10)
hecto	h	one hundred times (100)
kilo	k	one thousand times (1000)
mega	M	one million times (1,000,000)

13. To convert *to* a basic metric unit from a prefixed metric unit, multiply by the number indicated in the prefix.

    Example: Convert 72 millimeters to meters.

    $$72 \text{ millimeters} = 72 \times .001 \text{ meters}$$
    $$= .072 \text{ meters}$$

    Example: Convert 4 kiloliters to liters.

    $$4 \text{ kiloliters} = 4 \times 1000 \text{ liters}$$
    $$= 4000 \text{ liters}$$

14. To convert *from* a basic unit to a prefixed unit, divide by the number indicated in the prefix.

    Example: Convert 300 liters to hectoliters.

    $$300 \text{ liters} = 300 \div 100 \text{ hectoliters}$$
    $$= 3 \text{ hectoliters}$$

    Example: Convert 4.5 meters to decimeters.

    $$4.5 \text{ meters} = 4.5 \div .1 \text{ decimeters}$$
    $$= 45 \text{ decimeters}$$

15. To convert from any prefixed metric unit to another prefixed unit, first convert to a basic unit, then convert the basic unit to the desired unit.

    Illustration: Convert 420 decigrams to kilograms.

    SOLUTION: $420 \text{ dg} = 420 \times .1 \text{ g} = 42 \text{ g}$
    $42 \text{ g} = 42 \div 1000 \text{ kg} = .042 \text{ kg}$

    Answer: .042 kg

16. To add, subtract, multiply, or divide using metric measurement, first convert all units to the same unit, then perform the desired operation.

   Illustration: Subtract 1200 g from 2.5 kg.

   SOLUTION:

   $$
   \begin{array}{rcl}
   2.5\ \text{kg} &=& 2500\ \text{g} \\
   -\ 1200\ \text{g} &=& -\ 1200\ \text{g} \\
   \hline
    & & 1300\ \text{g}
   \end{array}
   $$

   Answer: 1300 g or 1.3 kg

17. To convert from a metric measure to an English measure, or the reverse:

   a. In the Table of English–Metric Conversions, find how many units of the desired measure are equal to one unit of the given measure.

   b. Multiply the given number by the number found in the table.

   Illustration: Find the number of pounds in 4 kilograms.

   SOLUTION: From the table, 1 kg = 2.2 lb.

   $$4\ \text{kg} = 4 \times 2.2\ \text{lb}$$
   $$= 8.8\ \text{lb}$$

   Answer: 8.8 lb

   Illustration: Find the number of meters in 5 yards.

   SOLUTION: 1 yd = .9 m

   $$5\ \text{yd} = 5 \times .9\ \text{m}$$
   $$= 4.5\ \text{m}$$

   Answer: 4.5 m

Temperature Measurement

18. The temperature measurement currently used in the United States is the degree Fahrenheit (°F). The metric measurement for temperature is the degree Celsius (°C), also called degree Centigrade.

19. Degrees Celsius may be converted to degrees Fahrenheit by the formula:

   $$°F = \tfrac{9}{5}°C + 32°$$

   Illustration: Water boils at 100°C. Convert this to °F.

   SOLUTION:
   $$°F = \frac{9}{\cancel{5}_{1}} \times \cancel{100}^{\,20}° + 32°$$
   $$= 180° + 32°$$
   $$= 212°$$

   Answer: 100°C = 212°F

20. Degrees Fahrenheit may be converted to degrees Celsius by the formula:

$$°C = \tfrac{5}{9}(°F - 32°)$$

In using this formula, perform the subtraction in the parentheses first, then multiply by $\tfrac{5}{9}$.

Illustration: If normal body temperature is 98.6°F, what is it on the Celsius scale?

SOLUTION:
$$°C = \tfrac{5}{9}(98.6° - 32°)$$
$$= \tfrac{5}{9} \times 66.6°$$
$$= \tfrac{333°}{9}$$
$$= 37°$$

Answer: Normal body temperature = 37°C.

Practice Problems Involving Measurement

1. A carpenter needs boards for 4 shelves, each 2'9" long. How many feet of board should he buy?
   (A) 11
   (B) $11\tfrac{1}{6}$
   (C) 13
   (D) $15\tfrac{1}{2}$

2. The number of half-pints in 19 gallons of milk is
   (A) 76
   (B) 152
   (C) 304
   (D) 608

3. The product of 8 ft 7 in multiplied by 8 is
   (A) 69 ft 6 in
   (B) 68.8 ft
   (C) $68\tfrac{2}{3}$ ft
   (D) 68 ft 2 in

4. $\tfrac{1}{3}$ of 7 yards is
   (A) 2 yd
   (B) 4 ft
   (C) $3\tfrac{1}{2}$ yd
   (D) 7 ft

5. Six gross of special drawing pencils were purchased for use in an office. If the pencils were used at the rate of 24 a week, the maximum number of weeks that the six gross of pencils would last is
   (A) 6 weeks
   (B) 12 weeks
   (C) 24 weeks
   (D) 36 weeks

6. If 7 ft 9 in is cut from a piece of wood that is 9 ft 6 in, the piece left is
   (A) 1 ft 9 in
   (B) 1 ft 10 in
   (C) 2 ft 2 in
   (D) 2 ft 5 in

7. Take 3 hours 49 minutes from 5 hours 13 minutes.
   (A) 1 hr 5 min
   (B) 1 hr 10 min
   (C) 1 hr 18 min
   (D) 1 hr 24 min

8. A piece of wood 35 feet 6 inches long was used to make 4 shelves of equal lengths. The length of each shelf was
   (A) 8.9 in
   (B) 8 ft 9 in
   (C) 8 ft $9\tfrac{1}{2}$ in
   (D) 8 ft $10\tfrac{1}{2}$ in

9. The number of yards equal to 126 inches is
   (A) 3.5
   (B) 10.5
   (C) 1260
   (D) 1512

10. If there are 231 cubic inches in one gallon, the number of cubic inches in 3 pints is closest to which one of the following?
    (A) 24
    (B) 29
    (C) 57
    (D) 87

11. The sum of 5 feet $2\tfrac{3}{4}$ inches, 8 feet $\tfrac{1}{2}$ inch, and $12\tfrac{1}{2}$ inches is
    (A) 14 ft $3\tfrac{3}{4}$ in
    (B) 14 ft $5\tfrac{3}{4}$ in
    (C) 14 ft $9\tfrac{1}{4}$ in
    (D) 15 ft $\tfrac{1}{2}$ in

12. Add 5 hr 13 min, 3 hr 49 min, and 14 min. The sum is
    (A) 8 hr 16 min
    (B) 9 hr 16 min
    (C) 9 hr 76 min
    (D) 8 hr 6 min

13. Assuming that 2.54 centimeters = 1 inch, a metal rod that measures $1\frac{1}{2}$ feet would most nearly equal which one of the following?
    (A) 380 cm   (C) 30 cm
    (B) 46 cm   (D) 18 cm

14. A micromillimeter is defined as one millionth of a millimeter. A length of 17 micromillimeters may be represented as
    (A) .00017 mm   (C) .000017 mm
    (B) .0000017 mm   (D) .00000017 mm

15. How many liters are equal to 4200 ml?
    (A) .42   (C) 420
    (B) 4.2   (D) 420,000

16. Add 26 dg, .4 kg, 5 g, and 184 cg.
    (A) 215.40 g   (C) 409.44 g
    (B) 319.34 g   (D) 849.00 g

17. Four full bottles of equal size contain a total of 1.28 liters of cleaning solution. How many milliliters are in each bottle?
    (A) 3.20   (C) 320
    (B) 5.12   (D) 512

18. How many liters of water can be held in a 5-gallon jug? (See Conversion Table.)
    (A) 19   (C) 40
    (B) 38   (D) 50

19. To the nearest degree, what is a temperature of 12°C equal to on the Fahrenheit scale?
    (A) 19°   (C) 57°
    (B) 54°   (D) 79°

20. A company requires that the temperature in its offices be kept at 68°F. What is this in °C?
    (A) 10°   (C) 20°
    (B) 15°   (D) 25°

Measurement Problems — Correct Answers

1. (A)	6. (A)	11. (A)	16. (C)
2. (C)	7. (D)	12. (B)	17. (C)
3. (C)	8. (D)	13. (B)	18. (A)
4. (D)	9. (A)	14. (C)	19. (B)
5. (D)	10. (D)	15. (B)	20. (C)

Problem Solutions — Measurement

1.   2 ft 9 in
      $\times$ 4
      8 ft 36 in = 11 ft

    Answer: **(A)** 11

2. Find the number of half-pints in 1 gallon:
        1 gal = 4 qts

    4 qts = 4 × 2 pts = 8 pts
    8 pts = 8 × 2 = 16 half-pints

    Multiply to find the number of half-pints in 19 gallons:

        19 gal = 19 × 16 half-pints
               = 304 half-pints

    Answer: **(C)** 304

3. $\begin{array}{r} 8 \text{ ft} \quad 7 \text{ in} \\ \times \qquad 8 \\ \hline 64 \text{ ft } 56 \text{ in} = 68 \text{ ft } 8 \text{ in} \end{array}$
(since 56 in = 4 ft 8 in)
$8 \text{ in} = \frac{8}{12} \text{ ft} = \frac{2}{3} \text{ ft}$
68 ft 8 in = $68\frac{2}{3}$ ft

Answer: **(C)** $68\frac{2}{3}$ ft

4. $\frac{1}{3} \times 7$ yd = $2\frac{1}{3}$ yd
$= 2$ yd 1 ft
$= 2 \times 3$ ft + 1 ft
$= 7$ ft

Answer: **(D)** 7 ft

5. Find the number of units in 6 gross:
1 gross = 144 units
6 gross = 6 × 144 units
$= 864$ units
Divide units by rate of use:
$864 \div 24 = 36$

Answer: **(D)** 36 weeks

6. $\begin{array}{r} 9 \text{ ft } 6 \text{ in} = \quad 8 \text{ ft } 18 \text{ in} \\ - 7 \text{ ft } 9 \text{ in} = -7 \text{ ft } \quad 9 \text{ in} \\ \hline 1 \text{ ft } \quad 9 \text{ in} \end{array}$

Answer: **(A)** 1 ft 9 in

7. $\begin{array}{r} 5 \text{ hours } 13 \text{ minutes} = \quad 4 \text{ hours } 73 \text{ minutes} \\ - 3 \text{ hours } 49 \text{ minutes} = -3 \text{ hours } 49 \text{ minutes} \\ \hline 1 \text{ hour } \quad 24 \text{ minutes} \end{array}$

Answer: **(D)** 1 hr 24 min

8. $\begin{array}{r} \quad 8 \text{ feet} \quad 10 \text{ inches} + \frac{2}{4} \text{ inches} = 8 \text{ ft } 10\frac{1}{2} \text{ in} \\ 4 \overline{) 35 \text{ feet} \quad 6 \text{ inches}} \\ \underline{32 \text{ feet}} \\ 3 \text{ feet} = \underline{36 \text{ inches}} \\ 42 \text{ inches} \\ \underline{40 \text{ inches}} \\ 2 \text{ inches} \end{array}$

Answer: **(D)** 8 ft $10\frac{1}{2}$ in

9. 1 yd = 36 in
$126 \div 36 = 3.5$

Answer: **(A)** 3.5

10. 1 gal = 4 qt = 8 pt
Therefore, 1 pt = 231 cubic inches ÷ 8
$= 28.875$ cubic inches
3 pts = 3 × 28.875 cubic inches
$= 86.625$ cubic inches

Answer: **(D)** 87

11. $\begin{array}{r} 5 \text{ feet} \quad 2\frac{3}{4} \text{ inches} \\ 8 \text{ feet} \quad \frac{1}{2} \text{ inches} \\ + \qquad 12\frac{1}{2} \text{ inches} \\ \hline 13 \text{ feet } 15\frac{3}{4} \text{ inches} \\ = 14 \text{ feet} \quad 3\frac{3}{4} \text{ inches} \end{array}$

Answer: **(A)** 14 feet $3\frac{3}{4}$ inches

12. $\begin{array}{r} 5 \text{ hr } 13 \text{ min} \\ 3 \text{ hr } 49 \text{ min} \\ + \qquad 14 \text{ min} \\ \hline 8 \text{ hr } 76 \text{ min} \\ = 9 \text{ hr } 16 \text{ min} \end{array}$

Answer: **(B)** 9 hr 16 min

13. 1 foot = 12 inches
$1\frac{1}{2}$ feet = $1\frac{1}{2} \times 12$ inches = 18 inches
1 inch = 2.54 cm
Therefore,
18 inches = 18 × 2.54 cm
$= 45.72$ cm

Answer: **(B)** 46 cm

14. 1 micromillimeter = .000001 mm
17 micromillimeters = 17 × .000001 mm
$= .000017$ mm

Answer: **(C)** .000017 mm

15. 4200 ml = 4200 × .001 l
$= 4.200$ l

Answer: **(B)** 4.2

16. Convert all of the units to grams:
$\begin{array}{r} 26 \text{ dg} = 26 \times .1 \text{ g} = 2.6 \text{ g} \\ .4 \text{ kg} = .4 \times 1000 \text{ g} = 400 \quad \text{g} \\ 5 \text{ g} = 5 \quad \text{g} \\ 184 \text{ cg} = 184 \times .01 \text{ g} = \underline{1.84 \text{ g}} \\ 409.44 \text{ g} \end{array}$

Answer: **(C)** 409.44 g

17. 1.28 liters $\div 4 = .32$ liters
           $.32$ liters $= .32 \div .001$ ml
                      $= 320$ ml

Answer: **(C)** 320

18. Find the number of liters in 1 gallon:

           1 qt $= .95\ l$
           1 gal $= 4$ qts
           1 gal $= 4 \times .95\ l = 3.8\ l$

Multiply to find the number of liters in 5 gallons:

           5 gal $= 5 \times 3.8\ l = 19\ l$

Answer: **(A)** 19

19. $°F = \frac{9}{5} \times 12° + 32°$
              $= \frac{108°}{5} + 32°$
              $= 21.6° + 32°$
              $= 53.6°$

Answer: **(B)** 54°

20. $°C = \frac{5}{9}(68° - 32°)$
              $= \frac{5}{9} \times \overset{4}{\underset{1}{36°}}$
              $= 20°$

Answer: **(C)** 20°

STATISTICS AND PROBABILITY

Statistics

1. The **averages** used in statistics include the **arithmetic mean**, the **median** and the **mode**.

2. a. The most commonly used average of a group of numbers is the **arithmetic mean**. It is found by adding the numbers given and then dividing this sum by the number of items being averaged.

    Illustration: Find the arithmetic mean of 2, 8, 5, 9, 6, and 12.

    SOLUTION: There are 6 numbers.

    $$\text{Arithmetic mean} = \frac{2 + 8 + 5 + 9 + 6 + 12}{6}$$
    $$= \frac{42}{6}$$
    $$= 7$$

    Answer: The arithmetic mean is 7.

    b. If a problem calls for simply the "average" or the "mean," it is referring to the arithmetic mean.

3. If a group of numbers is arranged in order, the middle number is called the **median**. If there is no single middle number (this occurs when there is an even number of items), the median is found by computing the arithmetic mean of the two middle numbers.

    Example: The median of 6, 8, 10, 12, and 14 is 10.

    Example: The median of 6, 8, 10, 12, 14, and 16 is the arithmetic mean of 10 and 12.

    $$\frac{10 + 12}{2} = \frac{22}{2} = 11.$$

4. The **mode** of a group of numbers is the number that appears most often.

    Example: The mode of 10, 5, 7, 9, 12, 5, 10, 5 and 9 is 5.

5. To obtain the average of quantities that are weighted:

    a. Set up a table listing the quantities, their respective weights, and their respective values.

    b. Multiply the value of each quantity by its respective weight.

    c. Add up these products.

    d. Add up the weights.

    e. Divide the sum of the products by the sum of the weights.

157

Illustration: Assume that the weights for the following subjects are: English 3, History 2, Mathematics 2, Foreign Languages 2, and Art 1. What would be the average of a student whose marks are: English 80, History 85, Algebra 84, Spanish 82, and Art 90?

SOLUTION:

Subject	Weight	Mark
English	3	80
History	2	85
Algebra	2	84
Spanish	2	82
Art	1	90

English	$3 \times 80 =$	240
History	$2 \times 85 =$	170
Algebra	$2 \times 84 =$	168
Spanish	$2 \times 82 =$	164
Art	$1 \times 90 =$	90
		832

Sum of the weights: $3 + 2 + 2 + 2 + 1 = 10$

$$832 \div 10 = 83.2$$

Answer: Average = 83.2

Probability

6. The study of probability deals with predicting the outcome of chance events; that is, events in which one has no control over the results.

   Examples: Tossing a coin, rolling dice, and drawing concealed objects from a bag are chance events.

7. The probability of a particular outcome is equal to the number of ways that outcome can occur, divided by the total number of possible outcomes.

   Example: In tossing a coin, there are 2 possible outcomes: heads or tails. The probability that the coin will turn up heads is $1 \div 2$ or $\frac{1}{2}$.

   Example: If a bag contains 5 balls of which 3 are red, the probability of drawing a red ball is $\frac{3}{5}$. The probability of drawing a non-red ball is $\frac{2}{5}$.

8. a. If an event is certain, its probability is 1.

   Example: If a bag contains only red balls, the probability of drawing a red ball is 1.

   b. If an event is impossible, its probability is 0.

   Example: If a bag contains only red balls, the probability of drawing a green ball is 0.

9. Probability may be expressed in fractional, decimal, or percent form.

   Example: An event having a probability of $\frac{1}{2}$ is said to be 50% probable.

10. A probability determined by random sampling of a group of items is assumed to apply to other items in that group and in other similar groups.

Illustration: A random sampling of 100 items produced in a factory shows that 7 are defective. How many items of the total production of 50,000 can be expected to be defective?

SOLUTION: The probability of an item being defective is $\frac{7}{100}$, or 7%. Of the total production, 7% can be expected to be defective.

$$7\% \times 50,000 = .07 \times 50,000 = 3500$$

Answer: 3500 items

Practice Problems Involving Statistics and Probability

1. The arithmetic mean of 73.8, 92.2, 64.7, 43.8, 56.5, and 46.4 is
   (A) 60.6   (C) 64.48
   (B) 62.9   (D) 75.48

2. The median of the numbers 8, 5, 7, 5, 9, 9, 1, 8, 10, 5, and 10 is
   (A) 5   (C) 8
   (B) 7   (D) 9

3. The mode of the numbers 16, 15, 17, 12, 15, 15, 18, 19, and 18 is
   (A) 15   (C) 17
   (B) 16   (D) 18

4. A clerk filed 73 forms on Monday, 85 forms on Tuesday, 54 on Wednesday, 92 on Thursday, and 66 on Friday. What was the average number of forms filed per day?
   (A) 60   (C) 74
   (B) 72   (D) 92

5. The grades received on a test by twenty students were: 100, 55, 75, 80, 65, 65, 85, 90, 80, 45, 40, 50, 85, 85, 85, 80, 80, 70, 65, and 60. The average of these grades is
   (A) 70   (C) 77
   (B) 72   (D) 80

6. A buyer purchased 75 six-inch rulers costing 15¢ each, 100 one-foot rulers costing 30¢ each, and 50 one-yard rulers costing 72¢ each. What was the average price per ruler?
   (A) $26\frac{1}{8}$¢   (C) 39¢
   (B) $34\frac{1}{3}$¢   (D) 42¢

7. What is the average of a student who received 90 in English, 84 in Algebra, 75 in French, and 76 in Music, if the subjects have the following weights: English 4, Algebra 3, French 3, and Music 1?
   (A) 81   (C) 82
   (B) $81\frac{1}{2}$ (D) 83

Questions 8–11 refer to the following information:

A census shows that on a certain block the number of children in each family is 3, 4, 4, 0, 1, 2, 0, 2, and 2, respectively.

8. Find the average number of children per family.
   (A) 2   (C) 3
   (B) $2\frac{1}{2}$ (D) $3\frac{1}{2}$

9. Find the median number of children.
   (A) 1   (C) 3
   (B) 2   (D) 4

10. Find the mode of the number of children.
(A) 0   (C) 2
(B) 1   (D) 4

11. What is the probability that a family chosen at random on this block will have 4 children?
(A) $\frac{4}{9}$ (C) $\frac{4}{7}$
(B) $\frac{2}{9}$ (D) $\frac{2}{1}$

12. What is the probability that an even number will come up when a single die is thrown?
(A) $\frac{1}{6}$ (C) $\frac{1}{2}$
(B) $\frac{1}{3}$ (D) 1

13. A bag contains 3 black balls, 2 yellow balls, and 4 red balls. What is the probability of drawing a black ball?
(A) $\frac{1}{2}$ (C) $\frac{2}{3}$
(B) $\frac{1}{3}$ (D) $\frac{4}{9}$

14. In a group of 1000 adults, 682 are women. What is the probability that a person chosen at random from this group will be a man?
(A) .318   (C) .5
(B) .682   (D) 1

15. In a balloon factory, a random sampling of 100 balloons showed that 3 had pinholes in them. In a sampling of 2500 balloons, how many may be expected to have pinholes?
(A) 30   (C) 100
(B) 75   (D) 750

Statistics and Probability Problems — Correct Answers

1. **(B)**   6. **(B)**   11. **(B)**
2. **(C)**   7. **(D)**   12. **(C)**
3. **(A)**   8. **(A)**   13. **(B)**
4. **(C)**   9. **(B)**   14. **(A)**
5. **(B)**   10. **(C)**   15. **(B)**

Problem Solutions — Statistics and Probability

1. Find the sum of the values:

73.8 + 92.2 + 64.7 + 43.8 + 56.5 + 46.4 = 377.4

There are 6 values.

Arithmetic mean = $\frac{377.4}{6}$ = 62.9

Answer: **(B)** 62.9

2. Arrange the numbers in order:

1, 5, 5, 5, 7, 8, 8, 9, 9, 10, 10

The middle number, or median, is 8.

Answer: **(C)** 8

3. The mode is that number appearing most frequently. The number 15 appears three times.

Answer: **(A)** 15

4. Average $= \dfrac{73 + 85 + 54 + 92 + 66}{5}$

    $= \dfrac{370}{5}$

    $= 74$

    Answer: **(C)** 74

5. Sum of the grades $= 1440$.

    $\dfrac{1440}{20} = 72$

    Answer: **(B)** 72

6. $\begin{array}{r} 75 \times 15¢ = 1125¢ \\ 100 \times 30¢ = 3000¢ \\ \underline{50} \times 72¢ = \underline{3600¢} \\ 225 \qquad 7725¢ \end{array}$

    $\dfrac{7725¢}{225} = 34\frac{1}{3}¢$

    Answer: **(B)** $34\frac{1}{3}¢$

7.
Subject	Grade	Weight
English	90	4
Algebra	84	3
French	75	3
Music	76	1

    $(90 \times 4) + (84 \times 3) + (75 \times 3) + (76 \times 1)$

    $360 + 252 + 225 + 76 = 913$

    Weight $= 4 + 3 + 3 + 1 = 11$

    $913 \div 11 = 83$ average

    Answer: **(D)** 83

8. Average $= \dfrac{3 + 4 + 4 + 0 + 1 + 2 + 0 + 2 + 2}{9}$

    $= \dfrac{18}{9}$

    $= 2$

    Answer: **(A)** 2

9. Arrange the numbers in order:

    $$0, 0, 1, 2, 2, 2, 3, 4, 4$$

    Of the 9 numbers, the fifth (middle) number is 2.

    Answer: **(B)** 2

10. The number appearing most often is 2.

    Answer: **(C)** 2

11. There are 9 families, 2 of which have 4 children. The probability is $\frac{2}{9}$.

    Answer: **(B)** $\frac{2}{9}$

12. Of the 6 possible numbers, three are even (2, 4, and 6). The probability is $\frac{3}{6}$, or $\frac{1}{2}$.

    Answer: **(C)** $\frac{1}{2}$

13. There are 9 balls in all. The probability of drawing a black ball is $\frac{3}{9}$, or $\frac{1}{3}$.

    Answer: **(B)** $\frac{1}{3}$

14. If 682 people of the 1000 are women, $1000 - 682 = 318$ are men. The probability of choosing a man is $\frac{318}{1000} = .318$.

    Answer: **(A)** .318

15. There is a probability of $\frac{3}{100} = 3\%$ that a balloon may have a pinhole.

    $$3\% \times 2500 = 75.00$$

    Answer: **(B)** 75

OPERATIONS WITH ALGEBRAIC OPERATIONS

Vocabulary

1. a. In addition, the numbers that are being added are called the **addends**. The solution to an addition problem is the **sum** or **total**.

   b. There are several ways to express an addition problem such as 10 + 2:

the sum of 10 and 2	2 more than 10
the total of 10 and 2	2 greater than 10
2 added to 10	10 increased by 2

2. a. In subtraction, the number from which something is subtracted is the **minuend**, the number being subtracted is the **subtrahend** and the answer is the **difference**.

   Example: In 25 − 22 = 3, the minuend is 25, the subtrahend is 22 and the difference is 3.

   b. A subtraction problem such as 25 − 22 may be expressed as:

25 minus 22	from 25 take 22
25 less 22	25 decreased by 22
the difference of 25 and 22	22 less than 25
subtract 22 from 25	

3. a. In multiplication, the answer is called the **product** and the numbers being multiplied are the **factors** of the product.

   b. In the multiplication $3 \cdot 5 = 15$ [which may also be written as 3(5) = 15 or (3)(5) = 15] all of the following expressions apply:

15 is the product of 3 and 5	15 is a multiple of 3
3 is a factor of 15	15 is a multiple of 5
5 is a factor of 15	

4. a. In division, the number being divided is the **dividend**, the number the dividend is divided by is the **divisor** and the answer is the **quotient**. Any number left over in the division is the **remainder**.

   Example: In 12 ÷ 2 = 6, the dividend is 12, the divisor is 2 and the quotient is 6.

   Example: In $\begin{array}{r} 7 \\ 3\,\overline{)\,22} \\ \underline{21} \\ 1 \end{array}$
   22 is the dividend
   3 is the divisor
   1 is the remainder

b. The division problem $12 \div 2$ may be expressed as:

> 12 divided by 2   2 divided into 12
> the quotient of 12 and 2

Because $12 \div 2 = 6$ with no remainder, 2 is called a **divisor** of 12, and 12 is said to be **divisible** by 2.

Properties

5. Addition is a **commutative** operation; this means that two numbers may be added in either order without changing their sum:

$$2 + 3 = 3 + 2$$
$$a + b = b + a$$

Multiplication is also commutative:

$$4 \cdot 5 = 5 \cdot 4$$
$$ab = ba$$

6. Subtraction and division problems are *not* commutative; changing the order within a subtraction or division problem may affect the answer:

$$10 - 6 \neq 6 - 10$$
$$8 \div 4 \neq 4 \div 8$$

7. Addition and multiplication are **associative**; that is, if a problem involves only addition or only multiplication, the parentheses may be changed without affecting the answer. Parentheses are grouping symbols that indicate work to be done first.

$$(5 + 6) + 7 = 5 + (6 + 7)$$
$$(2 \cdot 3) \cdot 4 = 2 \cdot (3 \cdot 4)$$
$$(a + b) + c = a + (b + c)$$
$$(ab)c = a(bc)$$

8. Subtraction and division are *not* associative. Work within parentheses *must* be performed first.

$$(8 - 5) - 2 \neq 8 - (5 - 2)$$
$$(80 \div 4) \div 2 \neq 80 \div (4 \div 2)$$

9. a. Multiplication is **distributive** over addition. If a sum is to be multiplied by a number, instead of adding first and then multiplying, each addend may be multiplied by the number and the products added.

$$5(6 + 3) = 5 \cdot 6 + 5 \cdot 3$$
$$a(b + c) = ab + ac$$

b. Multiplication is also distributive over subtraction.

$$8(10 - 6) = 8 \cdot 10 - 8 \cdot 6$$
$$a(b - c) = ab - ac$$

c. The distributive property may be used in both directions.

$$5a + 3a = (5 + 3)a = 8a$$
$$847 \cdot 94 + 847 \cdot 6 = 847(94 + 6) = 847(100) = 84{,}700$$

Signed Numbers

10. a. A **signed number** is a number with a positive (+) or negative (−) sign in front
of it. Signed numbers may be represented on a number line as follows:

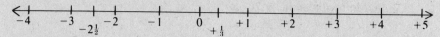

b. If a number (except zero) is written without a sign, it is assumed to be **positive**.

c. Zero is considered a signed number even though it is neither positive nor
negative.

d. The magnitude, or **absolute value**, of a signed number is the number without
its sign. The symbol used for absolute value is $|\ |$.

Examples: The absolute value of −3 is 3.
$$|-3| = 3$$
The absolute value of +6 is 6.
$$|+6| = 6$$

11. **Addition:**

a. To add two signed numbers that have the same sign, add their absolute values
and give the answer the common sign.

Examples: $(+3) + (+4) = +7$
$(-6) + (-2) = -8$

b. To add two signed numbers that have different signs, subtract their absolute
values. Give the answer the sign of the number with the *larger* absolute value.

Examples: $(-4) + (+1) = -3$
$(+5) + (-9) = -4$
$(-6) + (+7) = +1$

12. **Subtraction:**

To subtract two signed numbers, change the sign of the subtrahend. Then use the
rules for addition of signed numbers.

Examples: $(-3) - (-5) = (-3) + (+5) = +2$
$(+10) - (-6) = (+10) + (+6) = +16$
$(+8) - (+9) = (+8) + (-9) = -1$
$(-7) - (+3) = (-7) + (-3) = -10$

13. **Multiplication:**

To multiply two signed numbers, multiply their absolute values. If the signed numbers have the same sign, the answer is positive. If the signed numbers have different
signs, the answer is negative.

Examples: $(+3)(+4) = +12$
$(-5)(-2) = +10$
$(-6)(+3) = -18$
$(+8)(-1) = -8$

14. **Division:**

To divide two signed numbers, divide their absolute values. If the signed numbers have the same sign, the answer is positive. If the signed numbers have different signs, the answer is negative.

Examples: $(+20) \div (+4) = +5$
$(-18) \div (-9) = +2$
$(-14) \div (+2) = -7$
$(+15) \div (-5) = -3$

15. To evaluate algebraic expressions and formulas:

a. Substitute the given values for the letters in the expression.

b. Perform the arithmetic in the following order:

First, perform the operations within parentheses (if any);

Second, compute all powers and roots;

Third, perform all multiplications and divisions in order from left to right;

Fourth, perform all additions and subtractions in order from left to right.

Illustration: If $P = 2(L + W)$, find P when $L = 10$ and $W = 5$

SOLUTION: Substitute 10 for L and 5 for W:

$P = 2(10 + 5)$ First, add numbers in parentheses.
$= 2(15)$ Then multiply 2 by 15.
$= 30$

Answer: 30

Illustration: Evaluate $5a^2 - 2b$ if $a = 3$ and $b = 10$

SOLUTION: Substitute 3 for a and 10 for b:

$5 \cdot 3^2 - 2 \cdot 10$ First, find 3^2.
$5 \cdot 9 - 2 \cdot 10$ Next, multiply $5 \cdot 9$ and $2 \cdot 10$.
$45 - 20$ Then subtract 20 from 45.
25

Answer: 25

16. a. Algebraic expressions may contain numbers (constants) or letters (variables) or both.

b. In an algebraic expression, if several quantities are being added or subtracted, each of these quantities is called a **term**.

Example: In $4x^2 + 5y + 6$, the terms are: $4x^2$, $5y$, 6.

c. The number factor of each term is called the **coefficient**. The letter part is called the **literal factor**.

Example: In $3x^2$, 3 is the coefficient and x is the literal factor. Note that 2 is the exponent and is part of the literal factor.

d. Any variable appearing without a coefficient is assumed to have a coefficient of 1: $b = 1b$

e. Any variable appearing without an exponent is assumed to have an exponent of 1: $b = b^1$

17. a. If two or more terms have identical literal factors, they are called **like terms**.

   Example: $3a$, $6a$ and a are like terms
   $2x^4$ and $5x^2$ are *not* like terms

   b. Terms may be added (or subtracted) only if they are like terms. Add (or subtract) the coefficients and repeat the literal factor. This is called **combining like terms**.

   Examples:
   $$3d + 2d = 5d$$
   $$6xy + (-4)xy = 2xy$$
   $$10z^3 + 5z^3 - 8z^3 = 7z^3$$

   c. In most algebraic expressions it is easier to consider the operation that separates terms to be addition only, and the $+$ or $-$ sign immediately preceding each term to be the sign of the coefficient of that term.

Polynomials

18. An expression containing a single term is called a **monomial**. An expression containing more than one term is called a **polynomial**. Special polynomials are **binomials** (two terms) and **trinomials** (three terms).

19. To add (or subtract) two polynomials, add (or subtract) the coefficients of the like terms and repeat the literal factors. The unlike terms may *not* be combined.

   Examples: Add
   $$\begin{array}{r} 4x^2 - 3x + 2 \\ 2x^2 - 7x - 5 \\ \hline 6x^2 - 10x - 3 \end{array}$$

   Subtract
   $$\begin{array}{r} 7a - 2b + 4c \\ 9a + 6b - 2c \\ \hline -2a - 8b + 6c \end{array}$$
   (Recall that in subtraction the sign of the subtrahend is changed and the rules of addition are used.)

20. To multiply two monomials, multiply their coefficients and add the exponents of like variables.

   Examples:
   $$2x^5 \cdot 3x^4 = 6x^9$$
   $$y^4 \cdot y^{10} = y^{14}$$
   $$9b^3 \cdot 2b = 18b^4 \quad \text{(Note that } 2b = 2b^1\text{)}$$
   $$(-4a^2b^3)(-3a^{11}b^8) = +12a^{13}b^{11}$$

21. To multiply a polynomial by a monomial, use the distributive property and multiply each term of the polynomial by the monomial.

   Examples: $3(2x + 4y) = 6x + 12y$
   $y^2(5y - 3y^5) = 5y^3 - 3y^7$

22. To multiply a polynomial by a polynomial, multiply each term of the first polynomial by each term of the second polynomial, then add any like terms in the answer.

   Examples:
   $$(x + 3)(x + 4) = x^2 + 4x + 3x + 12$$
   $$= x^2 + 7x + 12$$
   $$(a - 1)(b + 5) = ab + 5a - 1b - 5$$
   $$(y + 4)(y^2 + 2y - 3) = y^3 + 2y^2 - 3y + 4y^2 + 8y - 12$$
   $$= y^3 + 6y^2 + 5y - 12$$

23. To divide two monomials, divide their coefficients and subtract the exponents of like variables.

    Examples: $\dfrac{12a^5}{3a^2} = 4a^3$

    $\dfrac{ac^7}{ac^5} = c^2$ (Note that $\dfrac{a}{a} = 1$)

    $\dfrac{-6b^{10}c^7}{+2bc^2} = -3b^9c^5$

24. To divide a polynomial by a monomial, divide each term of the polynomial by the monomial.

    Examples: $\dfrac{15a^2 - 12a}{3} = 5a^2 - 4a$

    $(12x^3 - 8x^2 + 20x) \div 4x = 3x^2 - 2x + 5$

Simplifying Algebraic Expressions

25. Algebraic expressions containing parentheses can be simplified by using the following rules:

    a. If a positive (+) sign is immediately before the parentheses, the parentheses may simply be omitted.

    Example: $3x + (2y + z) = 3x + 2y + z$

    b. If a negative (−) sign immediately precedes parentheses, the sign of each term within the parentheses must be changed. The parentheses may then be omitted.

    Example: $4 - (2x - y + z) = 4 - 2x + y - z$

    c. If a number or letter is indicated as a multiplier immediately before parentheses, the distributive property is used to multiply each term inside the parentheses by the multiplier.

    Example: $a - 3(b + c) = a - 3b - 3c$

    d. After removing parentheses, combine like terms.

    Example: $5z + 2(3z - 4) = 5z + 6z - 8$
    $= 11z - 8$

Factoring

26. To **factor** an expression means to find those quantities whose product is the original expression.

27. **Common factors:**

    If all of the terms of a polynomial have a common factor, the distributive property may be used.

    Examples: $ax + ay = a(x + y)$
    $12d - 8f = 4(3d - 2f)$
    $x^3 + 2x^2 - 4x = x(x^2 + 2x - 4)$

28. **Difference of two squares:**

A binomial which is the difference of two squares has as its factors two binomials, one the sum of the square roots, the other the difference of the square roots.

Examples: $\quad x^2 - 9 = (x + 3)(x - 3)$
$$25 - y^2 = (5 + y)(5 - y)$$

29. **Trinomials:**

a. Quadratic trinomials are of the form: $ax^2 + bx + c$, where a, b and c are constants and $a \neq 0$. Some — but not all — quadratic trinomials can be factored into two binomials, each the sum of an x term and a numerical term.

b. When $a = 1$, the trinomial is written $x^2 + bx + c$. Each binomial factor will be the sum of x and a number. The product of the numbers is c; their sum is b.

Illustration: Factor $x^2 + 7x + 12$

SOLUTION: The product of the numerical parts of the factors must be 12. Pairs of numbers whose product is 12 are:

$$1 \text{ and } 12$$
$$2 \text{ and } 6$$
$$3 \text{ and } 4$$

Of these pairs, the only one whose sum is 7 is 3 and 4. Therefore, the factors are $(x + 3)$ and $(x + 4)$.

Answer: $x^2 + 7x + 12 = (x + 3)(x + 4)$

Illustration: Factor $y^2 + 5y - 6$

SOLUTION: Pairs of numbers whose product is -6 are:

$$-1 \text{ and } +6$$
$$+1 \text{ and } -6$$
$$+2 \text{ and } -3$$
$$-2 \text{ and } +3$$

The pair whose sum is $+5$ is -1 and $+6$. Therefore, the factors are $(y - 1)$ and $(y + 6)$.

Answer: $y^2 + 5y - 6 = (y - 1)(y + 6)$

Illustration: Factor $z^2 - 11z + 10$

SOLUTION: The numbers whose product is positive are either both positive or both negative. In this case the sum of the numbers is negative, so consider only the negative pairs. The pairs of negative numbers whose product is $+10$ are:

$$-1 \text{ and } -10$$
$$-2 \text{ and } -5$$

The pair with -11 as its sum is -1 and -10. Therefore the factors are $(z - 1)$ and $(z - 10)$.

Answer: $z^2 - 11z + 10 = (z - 1)(z - 10)$

c. When $a \neq 1$ in the trinomial $ax^2 + bx + c$, the product of the x terms in the binomial factors must be ax^2, the product of the number terms must be c, and when the binomials are multiplied their product must be $ax^2 + bx + c$.

While there will be more than one possible pair of factors in which the product of the number terms is c, the correct pair is the only one whose product is the original trinomial.

Illustration: Factor $3x^2 + 10x + 8$

SOLUTION: The possible pairs of factors to be considered are:

$$(3x + 1)(x + 8)$$
$$(3x + 8)(x + 1)$$
$$(3x + 2)(x + 4)$$
$$(3x + 4)(x + 2)$$

In each case the product of the x terms is $3x^2$ and the product of the number terms is 8. Since the middle term is positive, any negative possibilities are ignored. Multiplying each pair of factors gives:

$$(3x + 1)(x + 8) = 3x^2 + 24x + 1x + 8$$
$$= 3x^2 + 25x + 8$$
$$(3x + 8)(x + 1) = 3x^2 + 3x + 8x + 8$$
$$= 3x^2 + 11x + 8$$
$$(3x + 2)(x + 4) = 3x^2 + 12x + 2x + 8$$
$$= 3x^2 + 14x + 8$$
$$(3x + 4)(x + 2) = 3x^2 + 6x + 4x + 8$$
$$= 3x^2 + 10x + 8$$

Therefore, $3x^2 + 10x + 8$ may be factored as $(3x + 4)(x + 2)$.

30. An expression may require more than one type of factoring before it is factored completely. To factor *completely*:

a. Use the distributive property to remove the highest common factor from each term.

b. If possible, factor the resulting polynomial as the difference of two squares or as a quadratic trinomial.

Examples:
$$3x^2 - 48 = 3(x^2 - 16)$$
$$= 3(x + 4)(x - 4)$$
$$2ay^2 + 12ay - 14a = 2a(y^2 + 6y - 7)$$
$$= 2a(y + 7)(y - 1)$$

Radicals

31. The symbol $\sqrt{x}$ means the positive square root of x. The $\sqrt{}$ is called the **radical sign**, and x is called the **radicand**. The symbol $-\sqrt{x}$ means the negative square root of x.

32. Many radicals may be simplified by using the principle $\sqrt{ab} = \sqrt{a} \cdot \sqrt{b}$

Examples:
$$\sqrt{100} = \sqrt{25}\sqrt{4} = 5 \cdot 2 = 10$$
$$\sqrt{18} = \sqrt{9}\sqrt{2} = 3\sqrt{2}$$
$$\sqrt{75} = \sqrt{25}\sqrt{3} = 5\sqrt{3}$$

Note that the factors chosen must include at least one perfect square.

33. a. Radicals with the same radicands may be added or subtracted as like terms.

   Examples: $3\sqrt{5} + 4\sqrt{5} = 7\sqrt{5}$
   $10\sqrt{2} - 6\sqrt{2} = 4\sqrt{2}$

   b. Radicals with different radicands may be combined only if they can be simplified to have like radicands.

   Example: $\sqrt{50} + \sqrt{32} - 2\sqrt{2} + \sqrt{3} = \sqrt{25}\sqrt{2} + \sqrt{16}\sqrt{2} - 2\sqrt{2} + \sqrt{3}$
   $= 5\sqrt{2} + 4\sqrt{2} - 2\sqrt{2} + \sqrt{3}$
   $= 7\sqrt{2} + \sqrt{3}$

34. To multiply radicals, first multiply the coefficients. Then multiply the radicands.

   Example: $2\sqrt{3} \cdot 4\sqrt{5} = 8\sqrt{15}$

35. To divide radicals, first divide the coefficients. Then divide the radicands.

   Example: $\dfrac{14\sqrt{20}}{2\sqrt{2}} = 7\sqrt{10}$

Summary of Kinds of Numbers

36. The numbers that have been used in this section are called **real numbers** and may be grouped into special categories.

   a. The **natural** numbers, or counting numbers, are:

   $$1, 2, 3, 4, 5, 6, 7, 8, 9, 10, 11, 12, \ldots$$

   b. A natural number (other than 1) is a **prime** number if it can be exactly divided only by itself and 1. If a natural number has other divisors it is a **composite** number. The numbers 2, 3, 5, 7, and 11 are prime numbers, while 4, 6, 8, 9 and 12 are composites.

   c. The **whole** numbers consist of 0 and the natural numbers:

   $$0, 1, 2, 3, \ldots$$

   d. The **integers** consist of the natural numbers, the negatives of the natural numbers, and zero:

   $$\ldots -3, -2, -1, 0, 1, 2, 3, 4, \ldots$$

   Even integers are exactly divisible by 2:

   $$\ldots -6, -4, -2, 0, 2, 4, 6, 8, \ldots$$

   Odd integers are not divisible by 2:

   $$\ldots -5, -3, -1, 1, 3, 5, 7, 9, \ldots$$

   e. The **rational** numbers are numbers that can be expressed as the quotient of two integers (excluding division by 0). Rational numbers include integers, fractions, terminating decimals (such as 1.5 or .293) and repeating decimals (such as .333 . . . or .74867676767 . . .).

   f. The **irrational** numbers cannot be expressed as the quotient of two integers, but can be written as non-terminating, non-repeating decimals. The numbers $\sqrt{2}$ and π are irrational.

Practice Problems

1. The value of $2(-3) - |-4|$ is
   (A) -10 (C) 2
   (B) -2 (D) 10

2. The value of $3a^2 + 2a - 1$ when $a = -1$ is
   (A) -3 (C) 3
   (B) 0 (D) 6

3. If $2x^4$ is multiplied by $7x^3$ the product is
   (A) $9x^7$ (C) $14x^7$
   (B) $9x^{12}$ (D) $14x^{12}$

4. The expression $3(x - 4) - (3x - 5) + 2(x + 6)$ is equivalent to
   (A) $2x - 15$ (C) $2x + 5$
   (B) $2x + 23$ (D) $-2x - 15$

5. The product of $(x + 5)$ and $(x + 5)$ is
   (A) $2x + 10$ (C) $x^2 + 10x + 25$
   (B) $x^2 + 25$ (D) $x^2 + 10$

6. The quotient of $(4x^3 - 2x^2) \div (x^2)$ is
   (A) $4x^3 - 1$ (C) $4x^5 - 2x^4$
   (B) $4x - 2x^2$ (D) $4x - 2$

7. The expression $(+3x^4)^2$ is equal to
   (A) $6x^8$ (C) $9x^8$
   (B) $6x^6$ (D) $9x^6$

8. If $3x - 1$ is multiplied by $2x$, the product is
   (A) $4x$ (C) $6x^2 - 1$
   (B) $5x^2$ (D) $6x^2 - 2x$

9. One factor of the trinomial $x^2 - 3x - 18$ is
   (A) $x - 9$ (C) $x - 3$
   (B) $x - 6$ (D) $x + 9$

10. The sum of $\sqrt{18}$ and $\sqrt{72}$ is
    (A) $18\sqrt{2}$ (C) $3\sqrt{10}$
    (B) $9\sqrt{2}$ (D) 40

Practice Problems — Correct Answers

1. **(A)**   5. **(C)**   8. **(D)**
2. **(B)**   6. **(D)**   9. **(B)**
3. **(C)**   7. **(C)**   10. **(B)**
4. **(C)**

Problem Solutions

1.
$$2(-3) - |-4| = -6 - 4$$
$$= -10$$

Recall that $|-4|$ means the *absolute value* of -4, which is 4.

Answer: **(A)** -10

2. If $a = -1$,
$$3a^2 + 2a - 1 = 3(-1)^2 + 2(-1) - 1$$
$$= 3(+1) + 2(-1) - 1$$
$$= 3 - 2 - 1$$
$$= 0$$

Answer: **(B)** 0

3. $(2x^4)(7x^3) = 14x^7$ To multiply monomials, multiply coefficients and add exponents of like variables.

Answer: **(C)** $14x^7$

4. $3(x - 4) - (3x - 5) + 2(x + 6)$
$= 3x - 12 - 3x + 5 + 2x + 12$
$= 2x + 5$

Answer: **(C)** $2x + 5$

5. $(x + 5)(x + 5) = x^2 + 5x + 5x + 25$
$= x^2 + 10x + 25$

Answer: **(C)** $x^2 + 10x + 25$

6. $(4x^3 - 2x^2) \div x^2 = 4x^3 \div x^2 - 2x^2 \div x^2$
$= 4x - 2$

Answer: **(D)** $4x - 2$

7. $(+3x^4)^2 = (+3x^4)(+3x^4)$
$= 9x^8$

Answer: **(C)** $9x^8$

8. $2x(3x - 1) = 2x \cdot 3x - 2x \cdot 1$
$= 6x^2 - 2x$

Answer: **(D)** $6x^2 - 2x$

9. Factor $x^2 - 3x - 18$ by finding two numbers whose product is -18 and whose sum is -3. Pairs of numbers whose product is -18 are:

-1 and $+18$
$+1$ and -18
-9 and $+2$
$+9$ and -2
-6 and $+3$
$+6$ and -3

Of these pairs, the one whose sum is -3 is -6 and $+3$. Therefore, the factors of $x^2 - 3x - 18$ are $(x - 6)$ and $(x + 3)$.

Answer: **(B)** $x - 6$

10. $\sqrt{18} + \sqrt{72} = \sqrt{9}\sqrt{2} + \sqrt{36}\sqrt{2}$
$= 3\sqrt{2} + 6\sqrt{2}$
$= 9\sqrt{2}$

Answer: **(B)** $9\sqrt{2}$

EQUATIONS, INEQUALITIES AND PROBLEMS IN ALGEBRA

Equations

1. a. An **equation** states that two quantities are equal.

   b. The solution to an equation is a number which can be substituted for the letter, or **variable**, to give a true statement.

   Example: In the equation $x + 7 = 10$,
   if 5 is substituted for x, the equation becomes $5 + 7 = 10$, which is false. If 3 is substituted for x, the equation becomes $3 + 7 = 10$, which is true. Therefore, $x = 3$ is a solution for the equation $x + 7 = 10$.

   c. To **solve an equation** means to find all solutions for the variables.

2. a. An equation has been solved when it is transformed or rearranged so that a variable is isolated on one side of the equal sign and a number is on the other side.

   b. There are two basic principles which are used to transform equations:

   I) The same quantity may be added to, or subtracted from, both sides of an equation.

   Example: To solve the equation $x - 3 = 2$, add 3 to both sides:

   $$\begin{array}{rcr} x - 3 &=& 2 \\ +3 & & +3 \\ \hline x &=& 5 \end{array}$$

   Adding 3 isolates x on one side and leaves a number on the other side. The solution to the equation is $x = 5$.

   Example: To solve the equation $y + 4 = 10$, subtract 4 from both sides (adding -4 to both sides will have the same effect):

   $$\begin{array}{rcr} y + 4 &=& 10 \\ -4 & & -4 \\ \hline y &=& 6 \end{array}$$

   The variable has been isolated on one side of the equation. The solution is $y = 6$.

173

II) Both sides of an equation may be multiplied by, or divided by, the same quantity.

Example: To solve $2a = 12$, divide both sides by 2:

$$\frac{2a}{2} = \frac{12}{2}$$
$$a = 6$$

Example: To solve $\frac{b}{5} = 10$, multiply both sides by 5:

$$5 \cdot \frac{b}{5} = 10 \cdot 5$$
$$b = 50$$

3. To solve equations containing more than one operation:

   a. First eliminate any number that is being added to or subtracted from the variable.

   b. Then eliminate any number that is multiplying or dividing the variable.

   Illustration: Solve

$3x - 6 =$	9		
$+ 6$	$+6$		Adding 6 eliminates -6.
$3x \quad =$	15		
$\frac{3x}{3} \quad =$	$\frac{15}{3}$		Dividing by 3 eliminates the 3 which is multiplying the x.
$x \quad =$	5		The solution to the original equation is $x = 5$.

4. A variable term may be added to, or subtracted from, both sides of an equation. This is necessary when the variable appears on both sides of the original equation.

   Illustration: Solve

$6y + 9 =$	$2y + 1$	Eliminate the y term from the right side by subtracting $2y$ from both sides.
$-2y$	$-2y$	
$4y + 9 =$	$+ 1$	
$- 9$	$- 9$	Eliminate 9 from the left side by subtracting 9 from both sides.
$4y \quad =$	$- 8$	
$\frac{4y}{4} \quad =$	$\frac{-8}{4}$	Divide both sides by 4 to eliminate the multiplication by 4 and isolate the y.
$y \quad =$	-2	

5. It may be necessary to first **simplify** the expression on each side of an equation by removing parentheses or combining like terms.

   Illustration: Solve

$5z - 3(z - 2) =$	8	
$5z - 3z + 6 =$	8	Remove parentheses first.
$2z + 6 =$	8	Combine like terms.
$- 6$	-6	Subtract 6 from both sides.
$\frac{2z}{2} \quad =$	$\frac{2}{2}$	Divide by 2 to isolate the z.
$z \quad =$	1	

6. To check the solution to any equation, replace the variable with the solution in the original equation, perform the indicated operations, and determine whether a true statement results.

Example: Earlier it was found that x = 5 is the solution for the equation 3x − 6 = 9. To check, substitute 5 for x in the equation:

$$3 \cdot 5 - 6 = 9 \qquad \text{Perform the operations on the left side.}$$
$$15 - 6 = 9$$
$$9 = 9 \qquad \text{A true statement results; therefore the solution is correct.}$$

Solving Problems

7. Many types of problems can be solved by using algebra. To solve a problem:

   a. Read it carefully. Determine what information is given and what information is unknown and must be found.

   b. Represent the *unknown* quantity with a letter.

   c. Write an equation that expresses the relationship given in the problem.

   d. Solve the equation.

Example: If 7 is added to twice a number, the result is 23. Find the number.

SOLUTION: Let x = the unknown number. Then write the equation:

$$7 + 2x = 23$$
$$\underline{-7 \qquad\qquad -7}$$
$$\frac{2x}{2} = \frac{16}{2}$$
$$x = 8$$

Answer: 8

Example: There are 6 more women than men in a group of 26 people. How many women are there?

SOLUTION: Let m = the number of men. Then, m + 6 = the number of women.

$$(m + 6) + m = 26$$
$$m + 6 + m = 26 \qquad \text{Remove parentheses.}$$
$$2m + 6 = 26 \qquad \text{Combine like terms.}$$
$$\underline{\qquad -6 \qquad -6}$$
$$\frac{2m}{2} = \frac{20}{2}$$
$$m = 10$$
$$m + 6 = 16$$

Answer: There are 16 women.

Example: John is 3 years older than Mary. If the sum of their ages is 39, how old is Mary?

SOLUTION: Let m = Mary's age. Then, m + 3 = John's age. The sum of their ages is 39.

$$m + (m + 3) = 39$$
$$m + m + 3 = 39$$
$$2m + 3 = 39$$
$$\underline{\quad -3 \quad -3}$$
$$\frac{2m}{2} = \frac{36}{2}$$
$$m = 18$$

Answer: Mary is 18 years old.

Consecutive Integer Problems

8. a. **Consecutive integers** are integers that follow one another.

   Example: 7, 8, 9, and 10 are consecutive integers.
   −5, −4, −3, −2 and −1 are consecutive integers.

   b. Consecutive integers may be represented in algebra as:

   $$x, x + 1, x + 2, x + 3, \ldots$$

   Example: Find three consecutive integers whose sum is 39.

   SOLUTION: Let x = first consecutive integer. Then, x + 1 = second consecutive integer and x + 2 = third consecutive integer.

   $$x + (x + 1) + (x + 2) = 39$$
   $$x + x + 1 + x + 2 = 39$$
   $$3x + 3 = 39$$
   $$\underline{\quad -3 \quad -3}$$
   $$\frac{3x}{3} = \frac{36}{3}$$
   $$x = 12$$

   Answer: The integers are 12, 13 and 14.

9. Consecutive even and consecutive odd integers are both represented as x, x + 2, x + 4, x + 6, . . .

   If x is even, then x + 2, x + 4, x + 6, . . . will all be even.
   If x is odd, then x + 2, x + 4, x + 6, . . . will all be odd.

   Example: Find four consecutive odd integers such that the sum of the largest and twice the smallest is 21.

   SOLUTION: Let x, x + 2, x + 4, and x + 6 be the four consecutive odd integers. Here, x is the smallest and x + 6 is the largest. The largest integer plus twice the smallest is 21.

   $$x + 6 + 2x = 21$$
   $$3x + 6 = 21$$
   $$\underline{\quad -6 \quad -6}$$
   $$\frac{3x}{3} = \frac{15}{3}$$
   $$x = 5$$

   Answer: The integers are 5, 7, 9, and 11.

Motion Problems

10. **Motion problems** are based on the following relationship:

$$\textbf{Rate} \cdot \textbf{Time} = \textbf{Distance}$$

Rate is usually given in miles per hour. Time is usually given in hours and distance is given in miles.

Example: A man traveled 225 miles in 5 hours. How fast was he traveling (what was his rate)?

SOLUTION: Let r = rate

$$\text{rate} \cdot \text{time} = \text{distance}$$
$$r \cdot 5 = 225$$
$$\frac{5r}{5} = \frac{225}{5}$$
$$r = 45 \text{ miles per hour}$$

Example: John and Henry start at the same time from cities 180 miles apart and travel toward each other. John travels at 40 miles per hour and Henry travels at 50 miles per hour. In how many hours will they meet?

SOLUTION: Let h = number of hours. Then, $40h$ = distance traveled by John, and $50h$ = distance traveled by Henry. The total distance is 180 miles.

$$40h + 50h = 180$$
$$\frac{90h}{90} = \frac{180}{90}$$
$$h = 2 \text{ hours}$$

Answer: They will meet in 2 hours.

Perimeter Problems

11. To solve a perimeter problem, express each side of the figure algebraically. The **perimeter** of the figure is equal to the sum of all of the sides.

Example: A rectangle has four sides. One side is the length and the side next to it is the width. The opposite sides of a rectangle are equal. In a particular rectangle, the length is one less than twice the width. If the perimeter is 16, find the length and the width.

SOLUTION:

Let w = width

Then $2w - 1$ = length

The sum of the four sides is 16.

$$w + (2w - 1) + w + (2w - 1) = 16$$
$$w + 2w - 1 + w + 2w - 1 = 16$$
$$6w - 2 = 16$$
$$\underline{+2 \quad +2}$$
$$\frac{6w}{6} = \frac{18}{6}$$
$$w = 3$$
$$2w - 1 = 2(3) - 1 = 5$$

Answer: The width is 3 and the length is 5.

Ratio and Proportion Problems

12. a. A ratio is the quotient of two numbers. The ratio of 2 to 5 may be expressed $2 \div 5$, $\frac{2}{5}$, 2 is to 5, 2:5, or algebraically as $2x:5x$.

The numbers in a ratio are called the terms of the ratio.

Example: Two numbers are in the ratio 3:4. Their sum is 35. Find the numbers.

SOLUTION:

Let $3x$ = the first number
$4x$ = the second number

Note that $\frac{3x}{4x} = \frac{3}{4} = 3:4$

The sum of the numbers is 35.

$$3x + 4x = 35$$
$$\frac{7x}{7} = \frac{35}{7}$$
$$x = 5$$
$$3x = 15$$
$$4x = 20$$

Answer: The numbers are 15 and 20.

b. A ratio involving more than two numbers may also be expressed algebraically. The ratio 2:3:7 is equal to $2x:3x:7x$. The individual quantities in the ratio are $2x$, $3x$, and $7x$.

13. a. A **proportion** states that two ratios are equal.

b. In the proportion a:b = c:d (which may also be written $\frac{a}{b} = \frac{c}{d}$), the inner terms, b and c, are called the **means**; the outer terms, a and d, are called the **extremes**.

Example: In 3:6 = 5:10, the means are 6 and 5; the extremes are 3 and 10.

c. In any proportion, the product of the means equals the product of the extremes. In a:b = c:d, bc = ad.

Example: In 3:6 = 5:10, or $\frac{3}{6} = \frac{5}{10}$, $6 \cdot 5 = 3 \cdot 10$.

d. In many problems, the quantities involved are in proportion. If three quantities are given in a problem and the fourth quantity is unknown, determine whether the quantities should form a proportion. The proportion will be the equation for the problem.

Example: A tree that is 20 feet tall casts a shadow 12 feet long. At the same time, a pole casts a shadow 3 feet long. How tall is the pole?

SOLUTION: Let p = height of pole. The heights of objects and their shadows are in proportion.

$$\frac{\text{tree}}{\text{tree's shadow}} = \frac{\text{pole}}{\text{pole's shadow}}$$

$$\frac{20}{12} = \frac{p}{3}$$

12p = 60   The product of the means equals the product of the extremes.

$$\frac{12p}{12} = \frac{60}{12}$$

$$p = 5$$

Answer: The pole is 5 feet tall.

Example: The scale on a map is 3 cm = 500 km. If two cities appear 15 cm apart on the map, how far apart are they actually?

SOLUTION: Let d = actual distance. The quantities on maps and scale drawings are in proportion with the quantities they represent.

$$\frac{\text{first map distance}}{\text{first actual distance}} = \frac{\text{second map distance}}{\text{second actual distance}}$$

$$\frac{3\text{ cm}}{500\text{ km}} = \frac{15\text{ cm}}{d\text{ km}}$$

3d = 7500   The product of the means equals the product of the extremes.

$$\frac{3d}{3} = \frac{7500}{3}$$

$$d = 2500$$

Answer: The cities are 2500 km apart.

Percent Problems

14. **Percent** problems may be solved algebraically by translating the relationship in the problem into an equation. The word "of" means multiplication, and "is" means equal to.

Example: 45% of what number is 27?

SOLUTION: Let n = the unknown number. 45% of n is 27.

$.45n = 27$ Change the % to a decimal (45% = .45)

$45n = 2700$ Multiplying both sides by 100 eliminates the decimal.

$$\frac{45n}{45} = \frac{2700}{45}$$

$$n = 60$$

Example: Mr. Jones receives a salary raise from $15,000 to $16,200. Find the percent of increase.

SOLUTION: Let p = percent. The increase is 16,200 − 15,000 = 1,200. What percent of 15,000 is 1,200?

$$p \cdot 15,000 = 1,200$$

$$\frac{15000p}{15000} = \frac{1200}{15000}$$

$$p = .08$$

$$p = 8\%$$

15. **Interest** is the price paid for the use of money in loans, savings and investments. Interest problems are solved using the formula $I = \mathbf{prt}$, where:

$$I = \text{interest}$$
$$p = \text{principal (amount of money bearing interest)}$$
$$r = \text{rate of interest, in \%}$$
$$t = \text{time, in years}$$

Example: How long must $2000 be invested at 6% to earn $240 in interest?

SOLUTION:
$$\text{Let } t = \text{time}$$
$$I = \$240$$
$$p = \$2000$$
$$r = 6\% \text{ or } .06$$

$$240 = 2000(.06)t$$
$$\frac{240}{120} = \frac{120t}{120}$$
$$2 = t$$

Answer: The $2000 must be invested for 2 years.

16. a. A **discount** is a percent that is deducted from a marked price. The marked price is considered to be 100% of itself.

Example: If an item is discounted 20%, its selling price is 100% − 20%, or 80%, of its marked price.

Example: A radio is tagged with a sale price of $42.50, which is 15% off the regular price. What is the regular price?

SOLUTION: Let r = regular price. The sale price is 100% − 15%, or 85%, of the regular price. 85% of r = $42.50

$$.85r = \$42.50$$
$$\frac{85r}{85} = \frac{4250}{85} \quad \text{Multiply by 100 to eliminate the decimals.}$$
$$r = 50$$

Answer: The regular price was $50.

b. If two discounts are given in a problem, an intermediate price is computed by taking the first discount on the marked price. The second discount is then computed on the intermediate price.

Example: An appliance company gives a 15% discount for purchases made during a sale, and an additional 5% discount if payment is made in cash. What will the price of a $800 refrigerator be if both discounts are taken?

SOLUTION: First discount: 100% − 15% = 85%

After the first discount, the refrigerator will cost:
$$85\% \text{ of } \$800 = .85(\$800)$$
$$= \$680$$

The intermediate price is $680.

Second discount: 100% − 5% = 95%.

After the second discount, the refrigerator will cost:
$$95\% \text{ of } \$680 = .95(\$680)$$
$$= \$646$$

Answer: The final price will be $646.

17. a. **Profit** is the amount of money added to the dealer's cost of an item to find the selling price. The cost price is considered 100% of itself.

Example: If the profit is 20% of the cost, the selling price must be 100% + 20%, or 120% of the cost.

Example: A furniture dealer sells a sofa at $870, which represents a 45% profit over the cost. What was the cost to the dealer?

SOLUTION: Let c = cost price. 100% + 45% = 145%. The selling price is 145% of the cost.

$$145\% \text{ of } c = \$870$$
$$1.45c = 870$$
$$\frac{145c}{145} = \frac{87000}{145}$$
$$c = 600$$

Answer: The sofa cost the dealer $600.

b. If an article is sold at a **loss**, the amount of the loss is deducted from the cost price to find the selling price.

Example: An article that is sold at a 25% loss has a selling price of 100% − 25%, or 75%, of the cost price.

Example: Mr. Charles bought a car for $8000. After a while he sold it to Mr. David at a 30% loss. What did Mr. David pay for the car?

SOLUTION: The car was sold for 100% − 30%, or 70%, of its cost price.
$$70\% \text{ of } \$8000 = .70(\$8000)$$
$$= \$5600$$

Answer: Mr. David paid $5600 for the car.

18. **Tax** is computed by finding a percent of a base amount.

Example: A homeowner pays $2500 in school taxes. What is the assessed value of his property if school taxes are 3.2% of the assessed value?

SOLUTION: Let v = assessed value.
$$3.2\% \text{ of } v = 2500$$
$$.032v = 2500$$
$$\frac{32v}{32} = \frac{2500000}{32} \quad \text{(Multiply by 1000 to eliminate decimals)}$$
$$v = 78125$$

Answer: The value of the property is $78,125.

Inequalities

19. a. The = symbol indicates the relationship between two equal quantities. The symbols used to indicate other relationships between two quantities are:

    $\neq$ not equal to
    $>$ greater than
    $<$ less than
    $\geq$ greater than or equal to
    $\leq$ less than or equal to

    b. A number is **greater** than any number appearing to its left on the number line. A number is **less** than any number appearing to its right on the number line.

    Examples:

    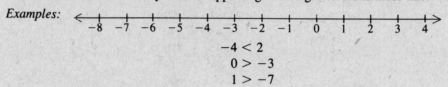

    $$-4 < 2$$
    $$0 > -3$$
    $$1 > -7$$

20. a. An **inequality** states that one quantity is greater than, or less than, another quantity.

    b. Inequalities are solved in the same way as equations, except that in multiplying or dividing both sides of an inequality by a negative quantity, the inequality symbol is reversed.

    Example: Solve for x:

    $$3x - 4 > 11$$

    $\underline{+4 \quad\quad +4}$ Add 4 to both sides.

    $\dfrac{3x}{3} > \dfrac{15}{3}$ Divide both sides by 3. Since 3 is positive, the inequality symbol remains the same.

    $$x > 5$$

    The solution $x > 5$ means that all numbers greater than 5 are solutions to the inequality.

    Example: Solve for y:

    $$2y + 3 > 7y - 2$$

    $\underline{-7y \quad\quad -7y}$ Subtract 7y from both sides.

    $-5y + 3 > -2$

    $\underline{\quad -3 \quad\quad -3}$ Subtract 3 from both sides.

    $-5y > -5$ Divide both sides by -5. When dividing

    $y < 1$ both sides by a negative number, reverse the inequality symbol.

Quadratic Equations

21. a. A **quadratic equation** is an equation in which the variable has 2 as its greatest exponent. Quadratic equations may be put into the form $ax^2 + bx + c = 0$, where a, b and c are constants and $a \neq 0$.

b. The solution of quadratic equations is based on the principle that if the product of two quantities is zero, at least one of those quantities must be zero.

   If one side of a quadratic equation is zero and the other side can be written as the product of two factors, each of those factors may be set equal to zero and the resulting equations solved.

Example: Solve $x^2 - 7x + 10 = 0$

The factors of the trinomial are	$(x - 2)(x - 5) = 0$
Set each factor equal to zero:	$x - 2 = 0$; $x - 5 = 0$
Solve each equation:	$x = 2$ $x = 5$

The solutions of $x^2 - 7x + 10 = 0$ are 2 and 5.

Example: Solve $x^2 - 5 = 4$

$$\frac{\begin{array}{rr} & -4 \quad -4 \end{array}}{x^2 - 9 = \quad 0}$$ Add -4 to both sides to obtain 0 on the right side.

$(x + 3)(x - 3) = 0$ Factor $x^2 - 9$.

$x + 3 = 0$ | $x - 3 = 0$ Set each factor equal to zero.

$\dfrac{-3 \quad -3}{x \quad = -3}$ | $\dfrac{+3 \quad +3}{x \quad = 3}$ Solve each equation.

The solutions of $x^2 - 5 = 4$ are 3 and -3.

Example: Solve $3z^2 - 12z = 0$

$3z(z - 4) = 0$ Factor $3z^2 - 12z$.

$\dfrac{3z}{3} = \dfrac{0}{3}$ | $z - 4 = 0$ Set each factor equal to zero.

  | $\dfrac{+4 \quad +4}{z \quad = 4}$ Solve each equation.

$z = 0$ |

The solutions of $3z^2 - 12z = 0$ are 0 and 4.

Practice Problems

1. If $6x - (2x + 6) = x + 3$, then $x =$
   (A) -3 (C) 1
   (B) -1 (D) 3

2. If $y^2 - 5y - 6 = 0$, then $y =$
   (A) 6 or -1 (C) -2 or 3
   (B) -6 or 1   (D) 2 or -3

3. Solve for z: $8z + 5 - 10z > -3$
   (A) $z > 4$ (C) $z < 4$
   (B) $z > -4$ (D) $z < -4$

4. If $2x^3 + 5x = 4x^3 - 2x^3 + 10$, then $x =$
   (A) -2 (C) 1
   (B) -1 (D) 2

5. One number is three times another number. If their difference is 30, the smaller number is
   (A) 5   (C) 15
   (B) 10   (D) 20

6. The perimeter of the figure below is 41. The length of the longest side is
   (A) 10   (C) 12
   (B) 11   (D) 13

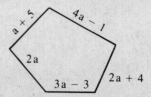

7. The sum of four consecutive even integers is 12. The smallest of the integers is
   (A) −2
   (C) 2
   (B) 0
   (D) 4

8. An estate was divided among three heirs, A, B and C, in the ratio 2:3:4. If the total estate was $22,500, what was the smallest inheritance?
   (A) $1000
   (C) $2500
   (B) $1250
   (D) $5000

9. A dealer buys a TV set for $550 and wishes to sell it at a 20% profit. What should his selling price be?
   (A) $570
   (C) $660
   (B) $600
   (D) $672

10. Michael earns $50 for 8 hours of work. At the same rate of pay, how much will he earn for 28 hours of work?
    (A) $150
    (C) $186
    (B) $175
    (D) $232

11. Mrs. Smith wishes to purchase a freezer with a list price of $500. If she waits for a "15% off" sale and receives an additional discount of 2% for paying cash, how much will she save?
    (A) $75.50
    (C) $85.00
    (B) $83.50
    (D) $150.00

12. A photograph is 8″ wide and 10″ long. If it is enlarged so that the new length is 25″, the new width will be
    (A) $18\frac{1}{2}$″
    (C) 24″
    (B) 20″
    (D) $31\frac{1}{4}$″

13. Jean sells cosmetics, earning a 12% commission on all sales. How much will she need in sales to earn $300 in commission?
    (A) $1800
    (C) $3600
    (B) $2500
    (D) $4000

14. Mr. Taylor leaves home at 8 AM, traveling at 45 miles per hour. Mrs. Taylor follows him, leaving home at 10 AM and traveling at 55 miles per hour. How long will it take Mrs. Taylor to catch up with Mr. Taylor?
    (A) 7 hours
    (C) 9 hours
    (B) 8 hours
    (D) 10 hours

15. Sam buys a jacket marked $85. He pays $90.95 including sales tax. What percent sales tax does he pay?
    (A) 4%
    (C) 6%
    (B) 5%
    (D) 7%

Practice Problems — Correct Answers

1.	**(D)**	6.	**(B)**	11.	**(B)**
2.	**(A)**	7.	**(B)**	12.	**(B)**
3.	**(C)**	8.	**(D)**	13.	**(B)**
4.	**(D)**	9.	**(C)**	14.	**(C)**
5.	**(C)**	10.	**(B)**	15.	**(D)**

Problem Solutions

1. $6x - (2x + 6) = x + 3$

    $6x - 2x - 6 = x + 3$ Remove parentheses first.

    $4x - 6 = x + 3$ Combine the like terms on the left side.

    $\underline{-x \qquad\qquad -x}$ Eliminate the x term from the right side.

    $3x - 6 = 3$

    $\underline{+6 \qquad\quad +6}$ Eliminate the number term from the left side.

    $\dfrac{3x}{3} = \dfrac{9}{3}$ Divide both sides by 3 to isolate x.

    $x = 3$

    Answer: **(D)**   3

2. $y^2 - 5y - 6 = 0$

    $(y - 6)(y + 1) = 0$ Factor the trinomial side of the quadratic equation.

    $y - 6 = 0 \quad | \quad y + 1 = 0$ Set each factor equal to zero.

    $\underline{+6 \qquad +6} \; | \; \underline{-1 \qquad -1}$ Solve each equation.

    $y = 6 \quad | \quad y = -1$

    Answer: **(A)**   6 or -1

3. $8z + 5 - 10z > -3$

    $-2z + 5 > -3$ Combine the like terms on the left side.

    $\underline{-5 \qquad -5}$

    $-2z > -8$ Divide both sides by -2 and reverse the inequality

    $z < 4$ symbol.

    Answer: **(C)** $z < 4$

4. $2x^3 + 5x = 4x^3 - 2x^3 + 10$

    $2x^3 + 5x = 2x^3 + 10$ Combine the like terms on the right side.

    $\underline{-2x^3 \qquad\quad -2x^3}$ Subtracting $2x^3$ from both sides leaves a

    $\dfrac{5x}{5} = \dfrac{10}{5}$ simple equation.

    $x = 2$

    Answer: **(D)**   2

5. Let n = the smaller number. Then 3n = the larger number. The difference of the numbers is 30.

    $$3n - n = 30$$
    $$\frac{2n}{2} = \frac{30}{2}$$
    $$n = 15$$

    Answer: **(C)**   15

6. The perimeter is equal to the sum of the sides.

$$a + 5 + 4a - 1 + 2a + 4 + 3a - 3 + 2a = 41$$

$$12a + 5 = 41 \qquad \text{Combine like terms.}$$

$$\frac{-5}{} \quad \frac{-5}{}$$

$$\frac{12a}{12} = \frac{36}{12}$$

$$a = 3$$

The sides are:
$$a + 5 = 3 + 5 = 8$$
$$4a - 1 = 4 \cdot 3 - 1 = 11$$
$$2a + 4 = 2 \cdot 3 + 4 = 10$$
$$3a - 3 = 3 \cdot 3 - 3 = 6$$
$$2a = 2 \cdot 3 = 6$$

The longest side is 11.

Answer: **(B)** 11

7. Let x, $x + 2$, $x + 4$ and $x + 6$ represent the four consecutive even integers. The sum of the integers is 12.

$$x + x + 2 + x + 4 + x + 6 = 12$$
$$4x + 12 = 12$$
$$\frac{-12}{} \quad \frac{-12}{}$$
$$\frac{4x}{4} = \frac{0}{4}$$
$$x = 0$$
$$x + 2 = 2$$
$$x + 4 = 4$$
$$x + 6 = 6$$

The smallest integer is 0.

Answer: **(B)** 0

8. Let $2x$, $3x$ and $4x$ represent the shares of the inheritance. The total estate was $22,500.

$$2x + 3x + 4x = 22500$$
$$\frac{9x}{9} = \frac{22500}{9}$$
$$x = 2500$$
$$2x = 2 \cdot 2500 = 5000$$
$$3x = 3 \cdot 2500 = 7500$$
$$4x = 4 \cdot 2500 = 10,000$$

The smallest inheritance was $2x$, or $5000.

Answer: **(D)** $5000

9. His selling price will be (100% + 20%) of his cost price.

$$120\% \text{ of } \$550 = 1.20(\$550)$$
$$= \$660$$

Answer: **(C)** $660

10. The amount earned is proportional to the number of hours worked.

Let m = unknown pay

$$\frac{m}{28} = \frac{50}{8}$$

$8m = 28 \cdot 50$ The product of the means is equal to the product of the extremes.

$$\frac{8m}{8} = \frac{1400}{8}$$

$$m = 175$$

Answer: **(B)** $175

11. The selling price after the 15% discount is 85% of list.

selling price $= .85(500)$
$= 425$

The selling price after the additional 2% discount is 98% of 425.

new selling price $= .98(425)$
$= 416.50$

The original price was $500. Mrs. Smith buys at $416.50. She saves
$500 - $416.50 = $83.50

Answer: **(B)** $83.50

12. The old dimensions and the new dimensions are in proportion. Let w = new width.

$$\frac{\text{new width}}{\text{old width}} = \frac{\text{new length}}{\text{old length}}$$

$$\frac{w}{8} = \frac{25}{10}$$

$$10w = 200$$

$$w = 20$$

Answer: **(B)** 20″

13. Let s = needed sales. 12% of sales will be $300.

$$\frac{.12s}{.12} = \frac{300}{.12}$$ Divide by .12, or first multiply by 100 to clear the decimal, then divide by 12.

$$s = 2500$$

Answer: **(B)** $2500

14. Let h = the number of hours needed by Mrs. Taylor. Mr. Taylor started two hours earlier; therefore, he travels h + 2 hours. Mrs. Taylor's distance is 55h. Mr. Taylor's distance is 45(h + 2). When Mrs. Taylor catches up with Mr. Taylor, they will have traveled equal distances.

$$
\begin{aligned}
55h &= 45(h + 2) \\
55h &= 45h + 90 \\
-45h &= -45h \\
\hline
10h &= 90 \\
h &= 9
\end{aligned}
$$

Answer: **(C)** 9 hours

15. The amount of tax is $90.95 − $85 = $5.95. Find the percent $5.95 is of $85. Let p = percent.

$$\frac{p \cdot 85}{85} = \frac{5.95}{85}$$
$$p = .07 = 7\%$$

Answer: **(D)** 7%

GEOMETRY

Angles

1. a. An **angle** is the figure formed by two lines meeting at a point.

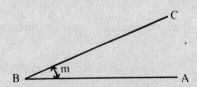

   b. The point B is the **vertex** of the angle and the lines BA and BC are the **sides** of the angle.

2. There are three common ways of naming an angle:

   a. By a small letter or figure written within the angle, as ∡ m.

   b. By the capital letter at its vertex, as ∡ B.

   c. By three capital letters, the middle letter being the vertex letter, as ∡ ABC.

3. a. When two straight lines intersect (cut each other), four angles are formed. If these four angles are equal, each angle is a **right angle** and contains 90°. The symbol ⌐ is used to indicate a right angle.

Example:

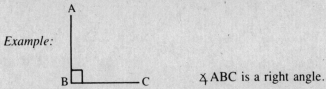

   ∡ ABC is a right angle.

   b. An angle less than a right angle is an **acute angle**.

   c. If the two sides of an angle extend in opposite directions forming a straight line, the angle is a **straight angle** and contains 180°.

   d. An angle greater than a right angle (90°) and less than a straight angle (180°) is an **obtuse angle**.

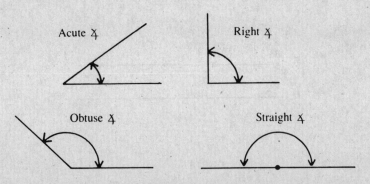

4. a. Two angles are **complementary** if their sum is 90°. To find the complement of an angle, subtract the given number of degrees from 90°.

    Example: The complement of 60° = 90° − 60° = 30°.

    b. Two angles are **supplementary** if their sum is 180°. To find the supplement of an angle, subtract the given number of degrees from 180°.

    Example: The supplement of 60° = 180° − 60° = 120°.

5. When two straight lines intersect, any pair of opposite angles are called **vertical angles** and are equal.

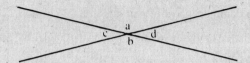

       ∡a and ∡b are vertical angles
       ∡a = ∡b
       ∡c and ∡d are vertical angles
       ∡c = ∡d

6. Two lines are **perpendicular** to each other if they meet to form a right angle. The symbol ⊥ is used to indicate that the lines are perpendicular.

    Example:

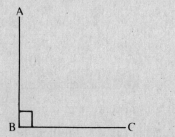

∡ABC is a right angle.
Therefore, AB ⊥ BC.

7. a. Lines that do not meet no matter how far they are extended are called **parallel lines**. The symbol ‖ is used to indicate that two lines are parallel.

    Example: AB ‖ CD

b. A line that intersects parallel lines is called a **transversal**. The pairs of angles formed have special names and relationships.

Example:

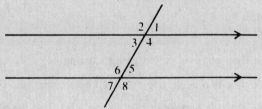

alternate interior angles:

$$\angle 3 = \angle 5$$
$$\angle 4 = \angle 6$$

corresponding angles:

$$\angle 1 = \angle 5$$
$$\angle 2 = \angle 6$$
$$\angle 3 = \angle 7$$
$$\angle 4 = \angle 8$$

Several pairs of angles, such as $\angle 1$ and $\angle 2$, are supplementary. Several pairs, such as $\angle 6$ and $\angle 8$, are vertical angles and are therefore equal.

Triangles

8. A triangle is a closed, three-sided figure. The following figures are triangles.

  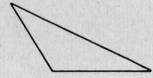

9. a. The sum of the three angles of a triangle is 180°.

  b. To find an angle of a triangle given the other two angles, add the given angles and subtract their sum from 180°.

Illustration: Two angles of a triangle are 60° and 40°. Find the third angle.

SOLUTION: $60° + 40° = 100°$
$\qquad\qquad\qquad 180° - 100° = 80°$

Answer: The third angle is 80°.

10. a. A triangle with two equal sides is called an **isosceles triangle**.

  b. In an isosceles triangle, the angles opposite the equal sides are also equal.

Example:

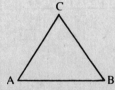

If AC = BC, then $\angle A = \angle B$

11. a. A triangle with all three sides equal is called an **equilateral triangle**.

   b. Each angle of an equilateral triangle is 60°.

12. a. A triangle with a right angle is called a **right triangle**.

   b. In a right triangle, the two acute angles are complementary.

   c. In a right triangle, the side opposite the right angle is called the **hypotenuse** and is the longest side. The other two sides are called **legs**.

Example:

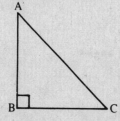

In right triangle ABC, AC is the hypotenuse. AB and BC are the legs.

13. The **Pythagorean Theorem** states that in a right triangle, the square of the hypotenuse equals the sum of the squares of the legs.

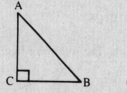

$$(AC)^2 + (BC)^2 = (AB)^2$$

Illustration: Find the hypotenuse (h) in a right triangle that has legs 6 and 8.

SOLUTION:

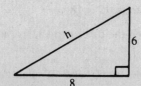

$$6^2 + 8^2 = h^2$$
$$36 + 64 = h^2$$
$$100 = h^2$$
$$\sqrt{100} = h$$
$$10 = h$$

Illustration: One leg of a right triangle is 5. The hypotenuse is 13. Find the other leg.

SOLUTION: Let the unknown leg be represented by x.

$$5^2 + x^2 = 13^2$$
$$25 + x^2 = 169$$
$$\underline{-25 \qquad\qquad -25}$$
$$x^2 = 144$$
$$x = \sqrt{144}$$
$$x = 12$$

Answer: The other leg is 12.

14. a. In a right triangle with equal legs (an isosceles right triangle), each acute angle is equal to 45°. There are special relationships between the legs and the hypotenuse:

$$\text{each leg} = \tfrac{1}{2}(\text{hypotenuse})\sqrt{2}$$
$$\text{hypotenuse} = (\text{leg})\sqrt{2}$$

$$AC = BC = \tfrac{1}{2}(AB)\sqrt{2}$$
$$AB = (AC)\sqrt{2} = (BC)\sqrt{2}$$

Example: In isosceles right triangle RST,

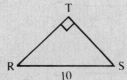

$$RT = \tfrac{1}{2}(10)\sqrt{2}$$
$$= 5\sqrt{2}$$
$$ST = RT = 5\sqrt{2}$$

b   In a right triangle with acute angles of 30° and 60°, the leg opposite the 30° angle is one-half the hypotenuse. The leg opposite the 60° angle is one-half the hypotenuse multiplied by $\sqrt{3}$.

Example:

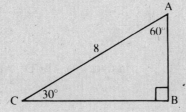

$$AB = \tfrac{1}{2}(8) = 4$$
$$BC = \tfrac{1}{2}(8)\sqrt{3} = 4\sqrt{3}$$

Quadrilaterals

15. a. A **quadrilateral** is a closed, four-sided figure in two dimensions. Common quadrilaterals are the **parallelogram**, **rectangle**, and **square**.

b. The sum of the four angles of a quadrilateral is 360°.

16. a. A **parallelogram** is a quadrilateral in which both pairs of opposite sides are parallel.

b. Opposite sides of a parallelogram are equal.

c. Opposite angles of a parallelogram are equal.

Example:

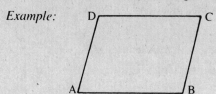

In parallelogram ABCD,
AB ∥ CD, AB = CD, ∡A = ∡C
AD ∥ BC, AD = BC, ∡B = ∡D

17. a. A **rhombus** is a parallelogram that has all sides equal.

b. A **rectangle** is a parallelogram that has all right angles.

c. A **square** is a rectangle that has all sides equal. A square is also a rhombus.

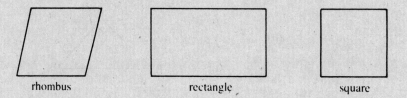

18. A **trapezoid** is a quadrilateral with one and only one pair of opposite sides parallel.

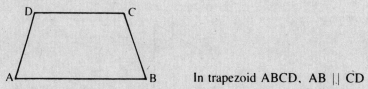

In trapezoid ABCD, AB ∥ CD

Circles

19. A **circle** is a closed plane curve, all points of which are equidistant from a point within called the center.

20. a. A **complete circle** contains 360°.

b. A **semi-circle** contains 180°.

21. a. A **chord** is a line segment connecting any two points on the circle.

b. A **radius** of a circle is a line segment connecting the center with any point on the circle.

c. A **diameter** is a chord passing through the center of the circle.

d. A **secant** is a chord extended in either one or both directions.

e. A **tangent** is a line touching a circle at one point and only one.

f. The **circumference** is the curved line bounding the circle.

g. An **arc** of a circle is any part of the circumference.

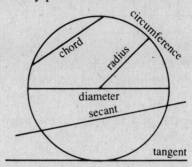

22. a. A **central angle**, as ∢AOB in the figure below, is an angle whose vertex is the center of the circle and whose sides are radii. A central angle is equal in degrees to (or has the same number of degrees as) its intercepted arc.

b. An **inscribed angle**, as ∢MNP, is an angle whose vertex is on the circle and whose sides are chords. An inscribed angle is equal in degrees to one-half its intercepted arc. ∢MNP equals one-half the degrees in arc MP.

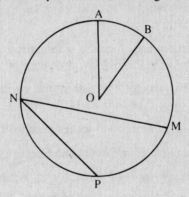

Perimeter

23. The **perimeter** of a two-dimensional figure is the distance around the figure.

Example: The perimeter of the figure below is 9 + 8 + 4 + 3 + 5 = 29

24. a. The perimeter of a triangle is found by adding all of its sides.

Example: If the sides of a triangle are 4, 5 and 7, its perimeter is 4 + 5 + 7 = 16.

b. If the perimeter and two sides of a triangle are given, the third side is found by adding the two given sides and subtracting this sum from the perimeter.

Illustration: Two sides of a triangle are 12 and 15. The perimeter is 37. Find the other side.

SOLUTION: $12 + 15 = 27$
$37 - 27 = 10$

Answer: The third side is 10.

25.   The perimeter of a rectangle equals twice the sum of the length and the width. The length is any side; the width is the side next to the length. The formula is: $P = 2(l + w)$.

Example: The perimeter of a rectangle whose length is 7 feet and width is 3 feet equals $2 \times 10 = 20$ ft.

26.   The perimeter of a square equals one side multiplied by 4. The formula is: $P = 4s$.

Example: The perimeter of a square one side of which is 5 feet equals 4×5 feet $= 20$ feet.

27.   a.   The **circumference** of a circle is equal to the product of the diameter multiplied by π. The formula is $C = \pi d$.

b.   The number π (''pi'') is approximately equal to $\frac{22}{7}$, or 3.14 (3.1416 for greater accuracy). The problem will state which value to use; otherwise, express the answer in terms of ''pi,'' π.

Example: The circumference of a circle whose diameter is 4 inches $= 4\pi$ inches; or, if it is stated that $\pi = \frac{22}{7}$, then the circumference $= 4 \times \frac{22}{7} = \frac{88}{7} = 12\frac{4}{7}$ inches.

c.   Since the diameter is twice the radius, the circumference equals twice the radius multiplied by π. The formula is $C = 2\pi r$.

Example: If the radius of a circle is 3 inches, then the circumference $= 6\pi$ inches.

d.   The diameter of a circle equals the circumference divided by π.

Example: If the circumference of a circle is 11 inches, then, assuming $\pi = \frac{22}{7}$,

$$\text{diameter} = 11 \div \frac{22}{7} \text{ inches}$$
$$= \overset{1}{\cancel{11}} \times \frac{7}{\underset{2}{\cancel{22}}} \text{ inches}$$
$$= \tfrac{7}{2} \text{ inches, or } 3\tfrac{1}{2} \text{ inches}$$

Area

28.   a.   In a figure of two dimensions, the total space within the figure is called the **area**.

b.   Area is expressed in square denominations, such as **square inches**, **square centimeters** and **square miles**.

c.   In computing area, all dimensions must be in the same denomination.

29.   The area of a square is equal to the square of the length of any side. The formula is $A = s^2$.

Example: The area of a square one side of which is 6 inches is $6 \times 6 = 36$ square inches.

30. a. The area of a rectangle equals the product of the length multiplied by the width. The formula is $A = l \times w$.

Example: If the length of a rectangle is 6 feet and its width is 4 feet, then the area is $6 \times 4 = 24$ square feet.

  b. If given the area of a rectangle and one dimension, you can find the other dimension by dividing the area by the given dimension.

Example: If the area of a rectangle is 48 square feet and one dimension is 4 feet, then the other dimension is $48 \div 4 = 12$ feet.

31. a. The altitude, or **height**, of a parallelogram is a line drawn from a vertex perpendicular to the opposite side, or **base**.

Example:
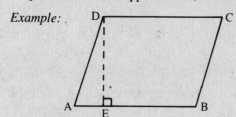

DE is the height
AB is the base

  b. The area of a parallelogram is equal to the product of its base and its height. The formula is $A = b \times h$.

Example: If the base of a parallelogram is 10 centimeters and its height is 5 centimeters, its area is $10 \times 5 = 50$ square centimeters.

  c. To find the base or the height of a parallelogram given one of these dimensions and given the area, divide the area by the given dimension.

Example: If the area of a parallelogram is 40 square inches and its height is 8 inches, its base is $40 \div 8 = 5$ inches.

32. a. The altitude, or height, of a triangle is a line drawn from a vertex perpendicular to the opposite side, called the base.

  b. The area of a triangle is equal to one-half the product of the base and the height. The formula is $A = \frac{1}{2}b \times h$.

Example: The area of a triangle that has a height of 5 inches and a base of 4 inches is $\frac{1}{2} \times 5 \times 4 = \frac{1}{2} \times 20 = 10$ square inches.

  c. In a right triangle, one leg may be considered the height and the other leg the base. Therefore, the area of a right triangle is equal to one-half the product of the legs.

Example: The legs of a right triangle are 3 and 4. Its area is $\frac{1}{2} \times 3 \times 4 = 6$ square units.

33. The area of a rhombus is equal to one-half the product of its diagonals. The formula is: $A = \frac{1}{2} \cdot d_1 \cdot d_2$.

Example: If the diagonals of a rhombus are 4 and 6,

$$\text{Area} = \frac{1}{2} \cdot 4 \cdot 6$$
$$= 12$$

34. The area of a trapezoid is equal to one-half the product of the height and the sum of the bases.

$$\text{Area} = \tfrac{1}{2}\text{h}(\text{base}_1 + \text{base}_2)$$

Example: The area of trapezoid ABCD $= \tfrac{1}{2} \cdot 4 \cdot (5 + 10)$
$$= 2 \cdot 15$$
$$= 30$$

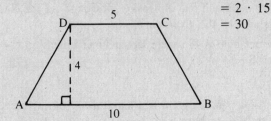

35. a. The area of a circle is equal to the radius squared multiplied by π. The formula is $A = \pi r^2$.

Example: If the radius of a circle is 6 inches, then the area $= 36\pi$ square inches.

b. To find the radius of a circle given the area, divide the area by π and find the square root of the quotient.

Example: To find the radius of a circle of area 100π:

$$\frac{100\pi}{\pi} = 100$$

$$\sqrt{100} = 10 = \text{radius}$$

36. Some figures are composed of several geometric shapes. To find the area of such figures, it is necessary to find the area of each of their parts.

Illustration: Find the area of the figure below:

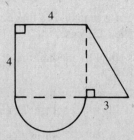

SOLUTION: The figure is composed of three parts: a square of side 4, a semi-circle of diameter 4 (the lower side of the square), and a right triangle with legs 3 and 4 (the right side of the square).

$$\text{Area of square} = 4^2 = 16$$

$$\text{Area of triangle} = \tfrac{1}{2} \times 3 \times 4 = 6$$

$$\text{Area of semi-circle is } \tfrac{1}{2} \text{ area of circle} = \tfrac{1}{2}\pi r^2$$

$$\text{Radius} = \tfrac{1}{2} \times 4 = 2$$

$$\text{Area} = \tfrac{1}{2}\pi r^2$$

$$= \tfrac{1}{2}\pi 2^2 = 2\pi$$

$$\text{Total area} = 16 + 6 + 2\pi = 22 + 2\pi$$

Three-Dimensional Figures

37. a. In a three dimensional figure, the total space contained within the figure is called the **volume** and is expressed in cubic denominations.

    b. The total outside surface is called the **surface area** and it is expressed in square denominations.

    c. In computing volume and surface area, all dimensions must be expressed in the same denomination.

38. a. A rectangular solid is a figure of three dimensions having six rectangular faces meeting each other at right angles. The three dimensions are **length**, **width**, and **height**. The figure below is a rectangular solid; "l" is the length, "w" is the width, and "h" is the height.

    b. The volume of a rectangular solid is the product of the length, width, and height; $V = l \times w \times h$.

    Example: The volume of a rectangular solid whose length is 6 ft, width 3 ft, and height 4 ft is $6 \times 3 \times 4 = 72$ cubic ft.

39. a. A **cube** is a rectangular solid whose edges are equal. The figure below is a cube; the length, width, and height are all equal to "e."

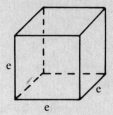

    b. The volume of a cube is equal to the edge cubed; $v = e^3$.

    Example: The volume of a cube whose height is 6 inches equals $6^3 = 6 \times 6 \times 6 = 216$ cubic inches.

    c. The surface area of a cube is equal to the area of any side multiplied by 6.

    Example: The surface area of a cube whose length is 5 inches $= 5^2 \times 6 = 25 \times 6 = 150$ square inches.

40. The volume of a circular cylinder is equal to the product of π, the radius squared, and the height.

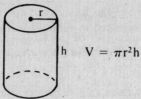

$$V = \pi r^2 h$$

Example: A circular cylinder has a radius of 7 inches and a height of $\frac{1}{2}$ inch. Using $\pi = \frac{22}{7}$, its volume is:

$$\frac{22}{7} \times 7 \times 7 \times \frac{1}{2} = 77 \text{ cubic inches}$$

41. The volume of a sphere is equal to $\frac{4}{3}$ the product of π and the radius cubed.

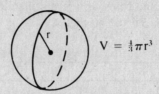

$$V = \frac{4}{3}\pi r^3$$

Example: If the radius of a sphere is 3 cm, its volume in terms of π is:

$$\frac{4}{3} \times \pi \times 3 \times 3 \times 3 = 36\pi \text{ cubic centimeters}$$

42. The volume of a cone is given by the formula $V = \frac{1}{3}\pi r^2 h$, where r is the radius and h is the height.

Example: In the cone shown below, if h = 9 cm, r = 10 cm and π = 3.14, then the volume is:

$$\frac{1}{3} \times 3.14 \times 10 \times 10 \times 9 \text{ cm}^3 = 3.14 \times 300 \text{ cm}^3$$
$$= 942 \text{ cm}^3$$

43. The volume of a pyramid is given by the formula $V = \frac{1}{3}Bh$, where B is the area of the base and h is the height.

Example: In the pyramid shown below, the height is 10 inches and the side of the base is 3 inches. Since the base is a square,

$$B = 3^2 = 9 \text{ square inches}$$
$$V = \frac{1}{3} \times 9 \times 10 = 30 \text{ cubic inches}$$

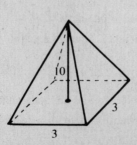

Summary of Geometric Formulas

Perimeter

Any 2-dimensional figure	P = sum of all the sides
Rectangle	$P = 2(l + w)$
Square	$P = 4s$
Circle	Circumference $= 2\pi r = \pi d$

Area

Square	$A = s^2$
Rectangle	$A = l \cdot w$
Parallelogram	$A = b \cdot h$
Triangle	$A = \frac{1}{2} \cdot b \cdot h$
Right triangle	$A = \frac{1}{2} \cdot leg_1 \cdot leg_2$
Rhombus	$A = \frac{1}{2} \cdot d_1 \cdot d_2$
Trapezoid	$A = \frac{1}{2} \cdot h(b_1 + b_2)$
Circle	$A = \pi r^2$

Volume

Rectangular solid	$V = l \cdot w \cdot h$
Cube	$V = e^3$
Circular cylinder	$V = \pi r^2 h$
Sphere	$V = \frac{4}{3}\pi r^3$
Cone	$V = \frac{1}{3}\pi r^2 h$
Pyramid	$V = \frac{1}{3} \cdot B \cdot h$ (B = area of base)

Practice Problems Involving Geometry

1. If the perimeter of a rectangle is 68 yards and the width is 48 feet, the length is
   (A) 10 yards (C) 20 feet
   (B) 18 yards (D) 56 feet

2. The total length of fencing needed to enclose a rectangular area 46 feet by 34 feet is
   (A) 26 yards 1 foot (C) 52 yards 2 feet
   (B) $26\frac{2}{3}$ yards (D) $53\frac{1}{3}$ yards

3. An umbrella 50″ long can lie on the bottom of a trunk whose length and width are, respectively
   (A) 36″, 30″ (C) 42″, 36″
   (B) 42″, 24″ (D) 39″, 30″

4. A road runs 1200 ft. from A to B, and then makes a right angle going to C, a distance of 500 ft. A new road is being built directly from A to C. How much shorter will the new road be?
   (A) 400 ft. (C) 850 ft.
   (B) 609 ft. (D) 1300 ft.

5. A certain triangle has sides that are, respectively, 6 inches, 8 inches, and 10 inches long. A rectangle equal in area to that of the triangle has a width of 3 inches. The perimeter of the rectangle, expressed in inches, is
   (A) 11 (C) 22
   (B) 16 (D) 24

6. If AB || DE, ∡C = 50° and ∡1 = 60°, then ∡A =
   (A) 30°
   (B) 60°
   (C) 70°
   (D) 50°

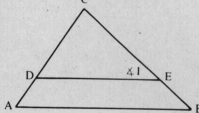

7. A rectangular bin 4 feet long, 3 feet wide, and 2 feet high is solidly packed with bricks whose dimensions are 8 inches, 4 inches, and 2 inches. The number of bricks in the bin is
   (A) 54 (C) 1296
   (B) 648 (D) none of these

8. If the cost of digging a trench is $2.12 a cubic yard, what would be the cost of digging a trench 2 yards by 5 yards by 4 yards?
   (A) $21.20 (C) $64.00
   (B) $40.00 (D) $84.80

9. A piece of wire is shaped to enclose a square, whose area is 121 square inches. It is then re-shaped to enclose a rectangle whose length is 13 inches. The area of the rectangle, in square inches, is
   (A) 64 (C) 117
   (B) 96 (D) 144

10. The area of a 2-foot-wide walk around a garden that is 30 feet long and 20 feet wide is
    (A) 104 sq. ft. (C) 680 sq. ft.
    (B) 216 sq. ft. (D) 704 sq. ft.

11. The area of a circle is 49π. Find its circumference, in terms of π.
    (A) 14π (C) 49π
    (B) 28π (D) 98π

12. In two hours, the minute hand of a clock rotates through an angle of
    (A) 90° (C) 360°
    (B) 180° (D) 720°

13. A box is 12 inches in width, 16 inches in length, and 6 inches in height. How many square inches of paper would be required to cover it on all sides?
    (A) 192 (C) 720
    (B) 360 (D) 1440

14. If the volume of a cube is 64 cubic inches, the sum of its edges is
    (A) 48 inches   (C) 16 inches
    (B) 32 inches   (D) 24 inches

15. The diameter of a conical pile of cement is 30 feet and its height is 14 feet. If $\frac{3}{4}$ cubic yard of cement weighs 1 ton, the number of tons of cement in the cone to the nearest ton is
    (Volume of a cone $= \frac{1}{3}\pi r^2 h$; use $\pi = \frac{22}{7}$)
    (A) 92   (C) 489
    (B) 163   (D) 652

Geometry Problems — Correct Answers

1. **(B)**	6. **(C)**	11. **(A)**
2. **(D)**	7. **(B)**	12. **(D)**
3. **(C)**	8. **(D)**	13. **(C)**
4. **(A)**	9. **(C)**	14. **(A)**
5. **(C)**	10. **(B)**	15. **(B)**

Problem Solutions — Geometry

1. Perimeter $= 2(l + w)$. Let the length be x yards.

    Each width $= 48$ ft
    $\qquad\qquad\quad = 16$ yd
    $2(x + 16) = 68$
    $2x + 32 = 68$
    $\underline{\quad\; -32 \quad\; -32}$
    $\dfrac{2x}{2} = \dfrac{36}{2}$
    $\qquad x = 18$

    Answer: **(B)** 18 yards

2.   Perimeter $= 2(l + w)$
    $\qquad\qquad\quad = 2(46 + 34)$ feet
    $\qquad\qquad\quad = 2 \times 80$ feet
    $\qquad\qquad\quad = 160$ feet
    160 feet $= 160 \div 3$ yards $= 53\frac{1}{3}$ yards

    Answer: **(D)** $53\frac{1}{3}$ yards

3. The umbrella would be the hypotenuse of a right triangle whose legs are the dimensions of the trunk. According to the Pythagorean Theorem, in any right triangle the square of the hypotenuse equals the sum of the squares of the legs. Therefore, the sum of the dimensions squared must at least equal the length of the umbrella squared: $(50)^2 = 2500$.

    The only set of dimensions that fills this condition is (C):

    $(42)^2 + (36)^2 = 1764 + 1296$
    $\qquad\qquad\qquad\quad\; = 3060$

    Answer: **(C)** 42", 36"

4. The new road is the hypotenuse of a right triangle whose legs are the old road.

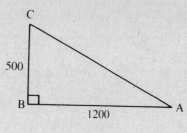

$$(AC)^2 = 500^2 + 1200^2$$
$$= 250000 + 1440000$$
$$= 1690000$$
$$AC = \sqrt{1690000}$$
$$= \sqrt{169} \cdot \sqrt{10000}$$
$$= 13 \cdot 100$$
$$= 1300$$

Old road = 500 ft + 1200 ft
= 1700 ft
New road = 1300 ft
Difference = 400 ft

Answer: **(A)** 400 feet

5. Since $6^2 + 8^2 = 10^2$, or $36 + 64 = 100$, the triangle is a right triangle. Its area is $\frac{1}{2} \times 6 \times 8 =$ 24 sq. in. (area of a triangle $= \frac{1}{2} \cdot b \cdot h$). Therefore, the area of the rectangle is also 24 square inches. If the width of the rectangle is 3 inches, the length is $24 \div 3 = 8$ inches. Then, the perimeter of the rectangle is $2(3 + 8) = 2 \times 11 = 22$ inches.

Answer: **(C)** 22

6. $\angle B$ and $\angle 1$ are corresponding angles formed by the parallel lines AB and DE and the transversal BC. Therefore, $\angle 1 = \angle B = 60°$.

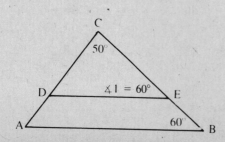

The sum of the angles of a triangle is 180°.
$$\angle A + \angle B + \angle C = 180°$$
$$\angle A + 60° + 50° = 180°$$
$$\angle A + 110° = 180°$$
$$\underline{-110° \quad -110°}$$
$$\angle A = 70°$$

Answer: **(C)** 70°

7. Convert the dimensions of the bin to inches:

4 feet = 48 inches
3 feet = 36 inches
2 feet = 24 inches

Volume of bin = $48 \times 36 \times 24$ cubic inches
= 41,472 cubic inches

Volume of each brick = $8 \times 4 \times 2$ cubic inches
= 64 cubic inches

$41472 \div 64 = 648$ bricks

Answer: **(B)** 648

8. The trench contains:
$$2 \text{ yd} \times 5 \text{ yd} \times 4 \text{ yd} = 40 \text{ cubic yards}$$
$$40 \times \$2.12 = \$84.80$$

Answer: **(D)** $84.80

9. If the area of the square is 121 square inches, each side is $\sqrt{121} = 11$ inches and the perimeter is $4 \times 11 = 44$ inches. The perimeter of the rectangle is then 44 inches. If the two lengths are each 13 inches, their total is 26 inches. $44 - 26 = 18$ inches remain for the two widths. Therefore, each width is equal to $18 \div 2 = 9$ inches.

The area of a rectangle with length 13 inches and width 9 inches is $13 \times 9 = 117$ square inches.

Answer: **(C)** 117

10.

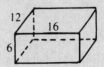

The walk consists of:

a) 2 rectangles of length 30 ft and width 2 ft.
Area of each = 2 × 30 = 60 sq ft
Area of both = 120 sq ft

b) 2 rectangles of length 20 ft and width 2 ft.
Area of each = 2 × 20 = 40 sq ft
Area of both = 80 sq ft

c) 4 squares, each having a side of 2 ft.
Area of each square = 2^2 = 4 sq ft
Area of 4 squares = 16 sq ft

Total area of walk = 120 + 80 + 16
= 216 sq ft

Alternatively, you may solve this problem by finding the area of the garden and the area of the garden plus the walk, then subtracting to find the area of the walk alone:

Area of garden = 20 × 30 = 600 sq ft

Area of garden + walk:
(20 + 2 + 2) × (30 + 2 + 2) = 24 × 34
= 816 sq ft

Area of walk alone:
816 − 600 = 216 sq ft

Answer: **(B)** 216 sq ft

11. Area of a circle = πr^2. If the area is 49π, the radius is $\sqrt{49}$ = 7.

Circumference = $2\pi r$
= 2 × π × 7
= 14π

Answer: **(A)** 14π

12. In one hour, the minute hand rotates through 360°. In two hours it rotates through 2 × 360° = 720°.

Answer: **(D)** 720°

13.

Area of top = 12 × 16 = 192 sq in.
Area of bottom = 12 × 16 = 192 sq in.
Area of front = 6 × 16 = 96 sq in.
Area of back = 6 × 16 = 96 sq in.
Area of right side = 6 × 12 = 72 sq in.
Area of left side = 6 × 12 = 72 sq in.

Total surface area:
192 + 192 + 96 + 96 + 72 + 72 = 720 sq in.

Answer: **(C)** 720

14. For a cube, V = e^3. If the volume is 64 cubic inches, each edge is $\sqrt[3]{64}$ = 4 inches.
A cube has 12 edges. If each edge is 4 inches, the sum of the edges is 4 × 12 = 48 inches.

Answer: **(A)** 48 inches

15. If diameter = 30, radius = 15.

$$V = \frac{1}{3} \times \frac{22}{7} \times 15 \times 15 \times 14$$

= 3300 cubic feet

27 cubic feet = 1 cubic yard
3300 cu ft ÷ 27 cu ft = $122\frac{2}{9}$ cu yd
$122\frac{2}{9} \div \frac{3}{4} = \frac{1100}{9} \times \frac{4}{3} = \frac{4400}{27}$
= 163 tons to the nearest ton

Answer: **(B)** 163

PRACTICE WITH MATHEMATICAL PROBLEMS

DIRECTIONS: Solve each of the following problems, using available space on the page for your scratch work. Mark the letter of the correct answer on your answer sheet.

You may refer to the following data in solving the problems.

Triangle:

The angles of a triangle added together equal 180°.
The angle BDC is a right angle; therefore,

   (I) the area of triangle ABC $= \dfrac{AC \times BD}{2}$

   (II) $AB^2 = AD^2 + DB^2$

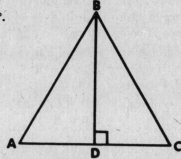

Circle:

There are 360° of arc in a circle.
The area of a circle of radius r $= \pi r^2$
The circumference of a circle $= 2\pi r$
A straight angle has 180°.

Symbol references:

|| is parallel to
$\leqq$ is less than or equal to
$\geqq$ is greater than or equal to
$\angle$ angle

> is greater than
< is less than
$\perp$ is perpendicular to
$\triangle$ triangle

Notes: The diagrams which accompany problems should provide data helpful in working out the solutions. These diagrams are not necessarily drawn precisely to scale. Unless otherwise stated, all figures lie in the same plane. All numbers are real numbers.

1. If a circle of radius 10 inches has its radius decreased 3 inches, what percent is its area decreased?

   (A) 9
   (B) 49
   (C) 51
   (D) 70
   (E) 91

2. If a hat cost $4.20 after a 40% discount, what was its original price?

   (A) $2.52
   (B) $4.60
   (C) $5.33
   (D) $7.00
   (E) $10.50

3. If r = 5x, how many tenths of r does ½ of x equal?

   (A) 1
   (B) 2
   (C) 3
   (D) 4
   (E) 5

4. If ⅜ of a bucket can be filled in 1 minute, how many minutes will it take to fill the rest of the bucket?

   (A) ⁴⁄₇
   (B) ⁴⁄₃
   (C) 1
   (D) ¾
   (E) ⅞

5. In a right triangle, the ratio of the legs is 1:2. If the area of the triangle is 25 square units, what is the length of the hypotenuse?

   (A) $\sqrt{5}$
   (B) $5\sqrt{3}$
   (C) $10\sqrt{3}$
   (D) $5\sqrt{5}$
   (E) $25\sqrt{5}$

6. The total length of fencing needed to enclose a rectangular area 46 feet by 34 feet is

   (A) 26 yards 1 foot
   (B) 26⅔ yards
   (C) 52 yards 2 feet
   (D) 53⅓ yards
   (E) 37⅔ yards

7. QOR is a quadrant of a circle. PS = 6 and PT = 8. What is the length of arc QR?

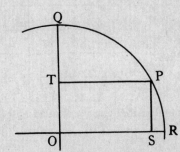

   (A) 10π
   (B) 5π
   (C) 20π
   (D) 24
   (E) It cannot be determined from the information given.

8. If (p,q) φ (r,s) = (ps-qr, qs) then (−1,3) φ (3,−2) =

(A) (−7,−6)
(B) (−7,6)
(C) (7,−6)
(D) (11,−6)
(E) (−11, −6)

9. In the figure, line PQ is parallel to line RS, angle y = 60° and angle Z = 130°. How many degrees are there in angle x?

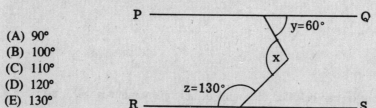

(A) 90°
(B) 100°
(C) 110°
(D) 120°
(E) 130°

10. A circle is inscribed in a given square and another circle is circumscribed about the same square. What is the ratio of the area of the inscribed circle to the circumscribed circle?

(A) 1 : 4
(B) 3 : 4
(C) 2 : 3
(D) 4 : 9
(E) 1 : 2

11. In the series, 3, 7, 12, 18, 25———the 9th term is

(A) 88
(B) 63
(C) 50
(D) 86
(E) 75

12. In the graph below, the axes and the origin are not shown. If point P has coordinates (3, 7), what are the coordinates of point Q?

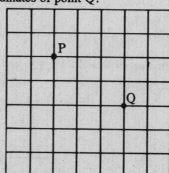

(A) (5,6)
(B) (1,10)
(C) (6,9)
(D) (6,5)
(E) (5,10)

13. A prime number is a number that can be divided only by itself and one. Which is *not* a prime number?

(A) 23
(B) 37

(C) 87
(D) 53
(E) 101

14. If p and q are positive numbers, the fraction $\dfrac{p}{q}$ will have a value less than 3 if

(A) pq < 3
(B) p < q
(C) q < 3
(D) p < 3q
(E) 3p < q

15. Three quarts of water are added to 5 quarts of a 20% solution of sulphuric acid. What percent of the resulting solution is pure sulphuric acid?

(A) 23
(B) 17
(C) 12½
(D) 33⅓
(E) 50

16. What is the value of rs in the equation 43rs + 17 = 77rs?

(A) ½
(B) −½
(C) 2
(D) −2
(E) 43/60

17. If p > q and r < 0, which of the following are true?

  I. pr < qr
 II. p + r > q + r
III. p − r < q − r

(A) I only
(B) II only
(C) I and III only
(D) I and II only
(E) I, II and III

18. PQRS is a square and PTS is an equilateral traingle. How many degrees are there in angle TRS?

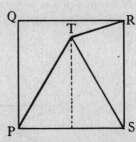

(A) 60
(B) 75
(C) 80
(D) 50
(E) Cannot be determined from the information given.

19. Six tractors can plow a field in 8 hours if they all work together. How many hours will it take 4 tractors to do the job?

(A) 9
(B) 10
(C) 11
(D) 12
(E) 14

20. Which is the *least* of the following numbers?

(A) $\frac{1}{5}$

(B) $\sqrt{5}$

(C) $\frac{1}{\sqrt{5}}$

(D) $\frac{\sqrt{5}}{5}$

(E) $\frac{1}{5\sqrt{5}}$

21. The area of the right triangle is 24 square inches. The ratio of its legs is 2 : 3. Find the number of inches in the hypotenuse of the triangle.

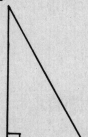

(A) $2\sqrt{13}$
(B) $\sqrt{26}$
(C) $4\sqrt{13}$
(D) $\sqrt{13}$
(E) $\sqrt{104}$

22. A rectangular block of metal weighs 3 ounces. How many pounds will a similar block of the same metal weigh if the edges are twice as large?

(A) $\frac{3}{8}$
(B) $\frac{3}{4}$
(C) $1\frac{1}{2}$
(D) 3
(E) 24

23. In the figure below, M and N are mid-points of the sides PR and PQ, respectively, of △PQR. What is the ratio of the area of △MNS to that of △PQR?

(A) 1 : 4
(B) 2 : 5
(C) 1 : 8
(D) 2 : 9
(E) 1 : 12

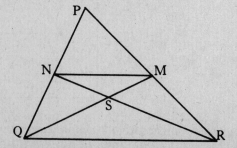

24. Nine playing cards from the same deck are placed as shown in the figure below to form a large rectangle of area 180 sq. in. How many inches are there in the perimeter of this large rectangle?

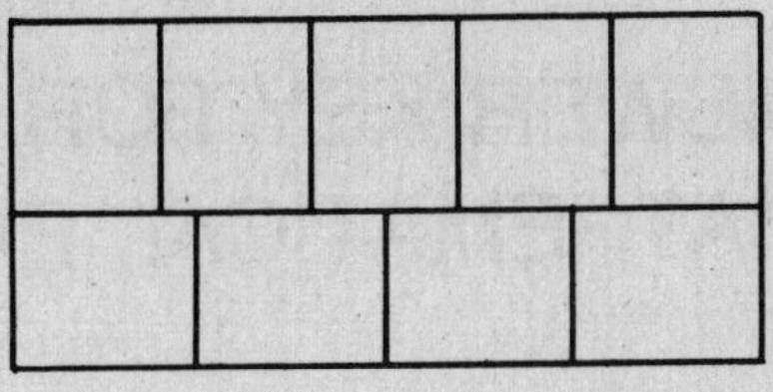

(A) 29
(B) 58
(C) 64
(D) 116
(E) 210

25. If an apple weighs $\frac{4}{5}$ of its weight plus $\frac{4}{5}$ of an ounce, what is its weight in ounces?

(A) $3\frac{1}{2}$
(B) $1\frac{3}{5}$
(C) 4
(D) $4\frac{4}{5}$
(E) 5

ANSWER KEY FOR PRACTICE MATHEMATICAL PROBLEMS

1. C	6. D	11. B	16. A	21. E
2. D	7. B	12. D	17. D	22. C
3. A	8. A	13. C	18. B	23. E
4. B	9. C	14. D	19. D	24. B
5. D	10. E	15. C	20. E	25. C

EXPLANATORY ANSWERS FOR PRACTICE MATHEMATICAL PROBLEMS

1. **(C)** Area of outer circle $= 100\pi$
   Area of inner circle $= 49\pi$
   Decrease in area $= 51\pi$

   % decrease $= \dfrac{51\pi}{100\pi} = 51\%$

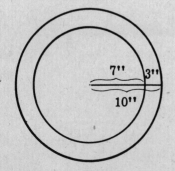

2. **(D)** Let x $=$ original price.
   Then .60x $=$ \$ 4.20
   or   6x $=$ \$42.00
   x $=$ \$ 7.00

3. **(A)** r $= 5$ x
   Divide both sides by 10

   $\dfrac{r}{10} = \dfrac{5}{10}$ x

   or $\dfrac{1}{10}$ r $= \dfrac{1}{2}$x

   Hence, 1 is the answer.

4. **(B)** Let x $=$ no. of minutes to fill $\frac{4}{7}$ of bucket.

   Then $\dfrac{\frac{3}{7}}{1} = \dfrac{\frac{4}{7}}{x}$ or $\dfrac{3}{1} = \dfrac{4}{x}$

   $3x = 4 \qquad x = \dfrac{4}{3}$

5. **(D)**

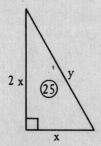

   $\frac{1}{2} \cdot x \cdot 2x = 25$
   $x^2 = 25$
   $x = 5$
   $2x = 10$
   $y^2 = 5^2 + 10^2$
   $y^2 = 25 + 100$
   $y^2 = 125$
   $\quad = \sqrt{125} = \sqrt{25 - 5}$
   $\quad = 5\sqrt{5}$

6. **(D)** The perimeter of a 46' × 34' rectangle is 160 feet, which equals $53\frac{1}{3}$ yards.

212

7. **(B)** Draw OP. Then in right triangle OPS,

$$OP^2 = PS^2 + OS^2 = 6^2 + 8^2 = 10^2$$

$$OP = 10$$

Then $QR = \frac{1}{4} \cdot 2\pi r = \frac{1}{4} \cdot 2\pi \cdot 10 = 5\pi$

8. **(A)** $(-1,3) \; \phi \; (3,-2) = [(-1)(-2) - 3 \cdot 3, 3(-2)]$
$$= (2-9, -6)$$
$$= (-7, -6)$$

9. **(C)** Through Point K, draw KM parallel to PQ and RS. Then

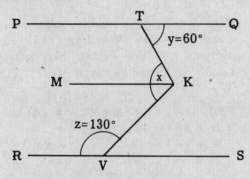

$$\angle x = \angle MKV + \angle MKT$$
$$\angle MKV = \angle KVS = 180 - 130 = 50°$$
$$\angle MKT = \angle QTK = 60°$$
Then $\angle x = 60° + 50° = 110°$

10. **(E)** Let r = radius of inscribed circle and s = radius of circumscribed circle. Then in right triangle OPQ, $PQ = OQ = r$ and $s = OP = r\sqrt{2}$

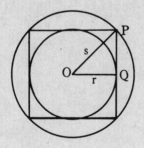

Area of inscribed circle $= \pi r^2$

Area of circumscribed circle $= \pi s^2$
$$= \pi(r\sqrt{2})^2 = 2\pi r^2$$

Ratio $= \dfrac{\pi r^2}{2\pi r^2} = 1 : 2$

11. **(B)** 3, 7, 12, 18, 25,
Differences are 4, 5, 6, 7, 8, ... etc.
Thus, series progresses as follows: 3, 7, 12, 18, 25, 33, 42, 52, 63

12. **(D)** The abscissa of Q is 3 more than that of P. The ordinate of Q is 2 less than that of P. Hence, coordinates of Q are $(3 + 3, 7 - 2)$ $= (6, 5)$

13. **(C)** $87 = 3 \times 29$
Thus, 87 is not a prime number. 23, 37, 53 and 101 have no other factors and are, therefore, prime.
Hence, 87.

14. **(D)** $\dfrac{p}{q} < 3$
Multiply both sides by q (positive).
$p < 3q$

15. **(C)**

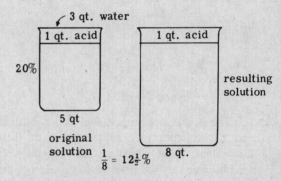

$\frac{1}{8} = 12\frac{1}{2}\%$

16. **(A)** $43rs + 17 = 77rs$
Subtract 43rs from both sides.
$17 = 34rs$
$rs = \frac{17}{34} = \frac{1}{2}$

17. **(D)**   I. If $p > q$ and $r < o$, multiplying both sides by r reverses the inequality: $pr < qr$
  II. Also $p + r > q + r$
  III. However, subtracting r from both sides leaves inequality in same sense. Hence, I and II, only.

18. **(B)** $\angle TSP = 60°$
Since $PSR = 90°$, $\angle TSR = 90 - 60 = 30°$
Since $TS = PS = SR$, $\angle RTS = \angle TRS$
Thus, $\angle TRS - \frac{1}{2}(180° - 30°) = \frac{1}{2}(150°) = 75°$

19. **(D)** This is an inverse proportion.

$$\frac{6}{4} = \frac{x}{8}$$

$$4x = 48$$
$$x = 12$$

20. **(E)**
   (A) $\frac{1}{5} = .2$
   (B) $\sqrt{5} = 2.2 +$
   (C) $\frac{1}{\sqrt{5}} = \frac{\sqrt{5}}{5} = \frac{2.2}{5} = .4 +$
   (C) and (D) are same
   (E) $\frac{1}{5\sqrt{5}} = \frac{1}{5\sqrt{5}} \cdot \frac{\sqrt{5}}{\sqrt{5}} = \frac{\sqrt{5}}{25} = \frac{2.2}{25}$
   $= .09$ approx.

   Hence, $\frac{1}{5\sqrt{5}}$ is least value.

21. **(E)** Let legs be 2x and 3x
   Then $(2x)^2 + (3x)^2 = $ hypot.^{2}
   But $\frac{1}{2} \cdot 2x \cdot 3x = 24$
   $3x^2 = 24$
   $x^2 = 8$
   $x = \sqrt{8}$
   Thus, $(2\sqrt{8})^2 + (3\sqrt{8})^2 = $ hypot.^{2}
   $32 + 72 = $ hypot.$^2 = 104$
   hypot. $= \sqrt{104}$

22. **(C)** The weights are proportional to the volumes and the volumes vary as the cubes of their dimensions. If the edges are doubled, the volume becomes $2^3 = 8$ times as large. Hence, the weight $= 8 \times 3 = 24$ ounces $= 1\frac{1}{2}$ lbs.

23. **(E)** MN $- \frac{1}{2}$QR and MN is parallel with QR. Since $\triangle$MNS $\sim \triangle$QSR, it follows that the altitude from S to MN $= \frac{1}{2}$ the altitude from S to QR. Hence, the altitude from S to NM $= \frac{1}{3}$ of $\frac{1}{2}$ the altitude from P to QR, or $\frac{1}{6}$ of this altitude (h).
   Thus, $\triangle$NMS $= \frac{1}{2} \cdot$ MN $\cdot$ alt. from S to MN
   $= \frac{1}{2}(\frac{1}{2}QR)(\frac{1}{6}h)$
   $= \frac{1}{2}(\frac{1}{12}QR \cdot h) = \frac{1}{12}(\frac{1}{2} \cdot QR \cdot h)$
   But $\frac{1}{2} \cdot QR \cdot h = \triangle$PQR
   Hence, $\triangle$MNS $= \frac{1}{12} \cdot \triangle$PQR
   Ratio is 1 : 12

24. **(B)** Let L = length of each card and W = width of each card. Then 5W = length of large rectangle and L + W = width of large rectangle. (Length of large rectangle = 4L.) (Thus, 5W = 4L)
   $5W(L + W) = 180$, also $9LW = 180$
   $5LW + 5W^2 = 180$ or $LW = 20$
   $LW + W^2 = 36$
   $20 + W^2 = 36$
   $W^2 = 16$
   $W = 4$ and $L = 5$
   Thus, perimeter $= 2[5W + (L + W)] = 2[20 + 9] = 58$

25. **(C)** Let x = weight in ounces of the apple.
   Then $x = \frac{4}{5}x + \frac{4}{5}$
   $5x = 4x + 4$
   $x = 4$

QUANTITATIVE COMPARISONS

DIRECTIONS: For each of the following questions, two quantities are given—one in Column A, the other in Column B. Compare the two quantities and mark your answer sheet as follows:

(A) if the quantity in Column A is greater
(B) if the quantity in Column B is greater
(C) if the quantities are equal
(D) if the relationship cannot be determined from the information given.

NECESSARY INFORMATION:

• In each question, information concerning one or both of the quantities to be compared is centered above the entries in the two columns.

• A symbol that appears in any column represents the same thing in Column A as it does in Column B.

• All numbers used are real numbers; letters such as x, y, and t stand for real numbers.

• Assume that the position of points, angles, regions and so forth are in the order shown and that all figures lie in a plane unless otherwise indicated.

• Figures are not necessarily drawn to scale.

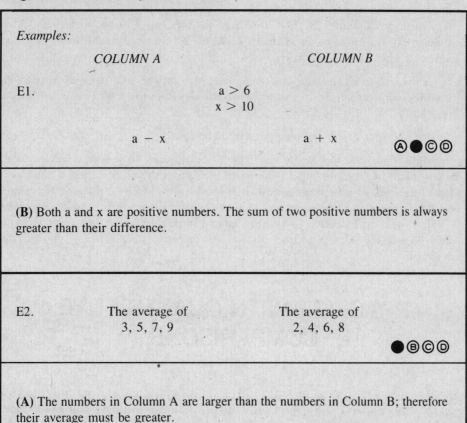

Examples:

COLUMN A	COLUMN B

E1.

$$a > 6$$
$$x > 10$$

| $a - x$ | $a + x$ | Ⓐ ● Ⓒ Ⓓ |

(B) Both a and x are positive numbers. The sum of two positive numbers is always greater than their difference.

E2.

| The average of 3, 5, 7, 9 | The average of 2, 4, 6, 8 | ● Ⓑ Ⓒ Ⓓ |

(A) The numbers in Column A are larger than the numbers in Column B; therefore their average must be greater.

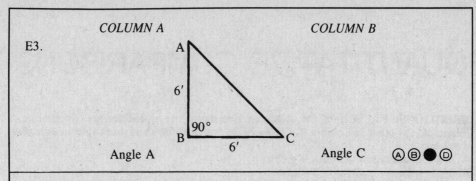

COLUMN A	COLUMN B

E3.

Angle A   Angle C   Ⓐ Ⓑ ● Ⓓ

(C) △ ABC is a right isosceles △. The fact that ABC is a right △ is irrelevant. Since ∠ A is opposite a side that is equal in length to the side opposite ∠ C, ∠ A must be equal to ∠ C.

These Quantitative Comparison questions require a special type of mental flexibility. They require you to translate two quantities into similar terms so that they may be readily compared. The mental gymnastics involved are somewhat akin to those required in solving verbal analogies.

To answer quantitative comparison questions you must, of course, be thoroughly at ease with the mathematical concepts involved. Furthermore, you must keep an open mind to the possibility of unusual answers. While quantitative comparisons are not meant to be trick questions, they offer more opportunities for wrong answers than do routine mathematical questions. A few caveats:

• Any quantity multiplied by 0 = 0. Watch out for 0 as a factor in Column A or Column B. The value of an unknown could be 0. Always try substituting 0 for an unknown when making your comparison.

• When two negative numbers are multiplied, the answer is a positive number. In making your comparisons, consider the possibility that the unknown is a negative number.

• Unless otherwise stated, two unknowns could be equal.

Simplification is the real key to quantitative comparisons, so you must be alert to all the possibilities for simplifying a statement. Calculations should be kept to a minimum. Most of the questions can be answered on the basis of inspection and logical reasoning. Feel free to cancel or to rewrite terms so as to compare the simplest possible quantities. If you do find it necessary to perform computations, you need not carry them to completion if the answer to the comparison becomes clear midway through the calculation.

PRACTICE WITH QUANTITATIVE COMPARISONS

DIRECTIONS: For each of the following questions, two quantities are given—one in Column A, the other in Column B. Compare the two quantities and mark your answer sheet as follows:
(A) if the quantity in Column A is greater
(B) if the quantity in Column B is greater

(C) if the quantities are equal

(D) if the relationship cannot be determined from the information given.

NECESSARY INFORMATION:

- In each question, information concerning one or both of the quantities to be compared is centered above the entries in the two columns.

- A symbol that appears in any column represents the same thing in Column A as it does in Column B.

- All numbers used are real numbers; letters such as x, y, and t stand for real numbers.

- Assume that the position of points, angles, regions and so forth are in the order shown and that all figures lie in a plane unless otherwise indicated.

- Figures are not necessarily drawn to scale.

	COLUMN A	COLUMN B
1.	The average of 18, 20, 22, 24, 26	The average of 19, 21, 23, 25
2.	$8 + 14(8 - 6)$	$14 + 8(8 - 6)$
3.	6% of 30	The number 30 is 6% of
4.	$(\frac{1}{5})^3$	$(\frac{1}{5})^2$
5.	2^2	$\sqrt[3]{64}$
6.	$8 - 6 \times 2 + 7$	$9 + 12 \div 4 - 6$

7. The ratio of boys to girls in a math class is 3:1

Ratio of girls to the entire class	1:3

COLUMN A	COLUMN B

8.

A sport jacket priced
$48 after a 20% discount

Original price of the
sport jacket

$60

---

9. (Base 2 Number) 10101

(Base 3 Number) 121

---

10. A package of meat weighing
1.8 lbs. (unit price 92.6¢
per lb.)

A package of meat weighing
2.3 lbs. (unit price 67.5¢
per lb.)

11.
$$\begin{cases} x - y = -6 \\ x + y = -2 \end{cases}$$

x

y

12.
$$(x - 6)(x + 4) = 0$$

The smallest root of
the equation

The negative of the
greatest root of the
equation

13.
$$x/4 = y^2$$

x

y

14.
$$x = -1$$

$3x^2 - 2x + 4$

$2x^3 + x^2 + 4$

15.
$$6 > y > -2$$

$y/4$

$4/y$

COLUMN A	COLUMN B

16.
$$\begin{cases} x < 0 \\ y < 0 \end{cases}$$

x + y   x − y

17.
$$A * B = A^2 + B$$
Substitute the following
values of A * B into
the equation.

$\frac{1}{3} * \frac{1}{2}$ $\frac{1}{2} * \frac{1}{3}$

---

18.   t < 0

t^3 t^2

---

19. The sum of the   The product of the
factors of: factors of:
$$x^2 + 5x + 6 = 0$$ $$x^2 - x - 6 = 0$$

---

20.   a/b = c/d

a + b   c + d

21.

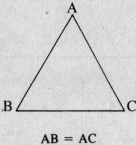

AB = AC
∠A < ∠B

BC   AB

COLUMN A   **COLUMN B**

22.

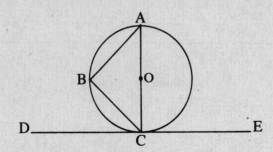

AC is a diameter of circle 0

DE is tangent to circle 0

∠ACE   ∠ABC

23.

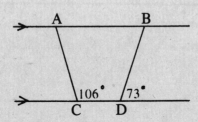

AC   BD

24.

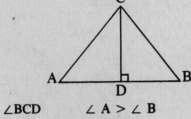

∠BCD   ∠ A > ∠ B   ∠ACD

COLUMN A   COLUMN B

25.

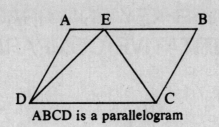

ABCD is a parallelogram

Areas of   Area of △DEC
△AED + △EBC

ANSWER KEY FOR PRACTICE QUANTITATIVE COMPARISONS

1. C	6. B	11. B	16. B	21. B
2. A	7. B	12. A	17. A	22. C
3. B	8. C	13. D	18. B	23. B
4. B	9. A	14. A	19. A	24. A
5. C	10. A	15. D	20. D	25. C

EXPLANATORY ANSWERS FOR PRACTICE QUANTITATIVE COMPARISONS

1. **(C)**
The average of Column A is 22
The average of Column B is 22
∴ Column A = Column B

2. **(A)**

$8 + 14 (8 - 6)$	$14 + 8 (8 - 6)$
$8 + 14 (2)$	$14 + 8 (2)$
$8 + 28$	$14 + 16$
36	30

∴ Column A > Column B

3. **(B)**

$6\% = .06$	$\frac{6}{100} = 30x$
$.06 (30) = 1.80$	
1.8	$6x = 3000$
	$x = 500$

∴ Column B > Column A

4. **(B)**
$(\frac{1}{5})^3 = \frac{1}{125}$ $(\frac{1}{5})^2 = \frac{1}{25}$
∴ Column B > Column A

5. **(C)**
$2^2 = 4$ $\sqrt[3]{64} = 4$
∴ Column A = Column B

6. **(B)**

$8 - 6 \times 2 + 7$	$9 + 12 \div 4 - 6$
$8 - 12 + 7$	$9 + 3 - 6$
3	6

∴ Column B > Column A

7. **(B)**
The ratio of girls to entire class is 1:4
The ratio 1:3 > the ratio 1:4
∴ Column B > Column A

8. **(C)**
Let x = the original price
$x - 20\%$ of $x = 48$
$x - \frac{1}{5}x = 48$
$\frac{4}{5}x = 48$
$x = 60$
∴ Column A = Column B

9. **(A)**

16	8	4	2	1		9	3	1
1	0	1	0	1		1	2	1

$16 + 0 + 4 + 0 + 1$ $9 + 6 + 1$
21   16
∴ Column A > Column B

10. **(A)**

.926	.675
× 1.8	× 2.3
7408	2025
926	1350
$1.6668 = \$1.67$	$1.5525 = \$1.55$

∴ Column A > Column B

11. **(B)**

$$x - y = -6 \qquad \text{Substituting } x = -4$$
$$x + y = -2 \qquad x - y = -6$$
$$2x = -8 \qquad -4 - y = -6$$
$$x = -4 \qquad -y = -2$$
$$y = 2$$

∴ Column B > Column A

12. **(A)**

$$(x - 6)(x + 4) = 0$$
$$\qquad\qquad x + 4 = 0$$
$$x - 6 = 0 \qquad x = -4$$
$$x = 6$$

-6 = the negative of greatest root

-4 = smallest root

$-4 > -6$

∴ Column A > Column B

13. **(D)**

There is insufficient information to determine the values of x and y. Hence, it cannot be determined which variable is greater.

14. **(A)**

$$3x^2 - 2x + 4 \qquad 2(-1)^3 + (-1)^2 + 4$$
$$3(-1)^2 - 2(-1) + 4 \qquad 2(-1) + 1 + 4$$
$$3(1) + 2 + 4 \qquad -2 + 1 + 4$$
$$9 \qquad\qquad 3$$

∴ Column A > Column B

15. **(D)**

Y could equal $\{5, 4, 3, 2, 1, 0, -1\}$

There is insufficient information to determine the value of Column A or Column B.

16. **(B)**

Since x and y are both less than zero, then x and y are both negative. It is also known that two negatives subtracted is greater than the same two negatives added.

∴ Column B > Column A

17. **(A)**

If $A * B = A^2 + B$

then $\frac{1}{3} * \frac{1}{2} = (\frac{1}{3})^2 + \frac{1}{2}$, and $\frac{1}{2} * \frac{1}{3} = (\frac{1}{2})^2 + \frac{1}{3}$

$$\frac{1}{9} + \frac{1}{2} \qquad\qquad \frac{1}{4} + \frac{1}{3}$$
$$\frac{2}{18} + \frac{9}{18} \qquad\qquad \frac{3}{12} + \frac{4}{12}$$
$$\frac{11}{18} \qquad\qquad\qquad \frac{7}{12}$$
$$\frac{22}{36} \qquad\qquad\qquad \frac{21}{36}$$

∴ Column A > Column B

18. **(B)**

Since t is less than zero, then t is negative. A negative squared is greater than a negative cubed.

∴ Column B > Column A

19. **(A)**

$$x^2 + 5x + 6 = 0 \qquad x^2 - x - 6 = 0$$
$$(x + 3)(x + 2) = 0 \qquad (x - 3)(x + 2) = 0$$
$$x = -3 \qquad\qquad x = 3$$
$$x = -2 \qquad\qquad x = -2$$

Their sum $= -5$ \qquad Their product $= -6$

∴ Column A > Column B

20. **(D)**

There is insufficient information to determine the values of the four variables.

21. **(B)**

Since AB = AC

then $\angle B = \angle C$ (an isosceles $\triangle$)

since $\angle A < \angle B$

then $\angle A < \angle C$ (substitution)

∴ BC < AB (the greater side lies opposite the greater $\angle$)

∴ Column B > Column A

22. **(C)**

A diameter forms a perpendicular when drawn to a tangent, therefore, $\angle ACE = 90°$. Also, a triangle inscribed in a semi-circle is a right triangle, therefore $\angle ABC = 90°$.

∴ Column A = Column B

23. **(B)**

The shortest line that can be drawn between two parallel lines is a perpendicular line. A transversal increases in size when the angle it makes with one of the parallels gets further away from 90°.

$106° - 90° = 16°$

$90° - 73° = 17°$

∴ BD > AC

∴ Column B > Column A

24. **(A)**

Since $\angle CDB = \angle CDA = 90°$ (given) then $\angle A + \angle ACD = \angle B + \angle BCD = 90°$ (the acute angles of a right triangle equal 90°) and since $\angle A > \angle B$ (given) then $\angle ACD < \angle BCD$ (equals minus unequals are unequal in reverse order)

∴ Column A > Column B

25. **(C)**

A triangle inscribed in a parallelogram is equal in area to one-half the area of the parallelogram. Since $\triangle DEC$ is equal in area to $\frac{1}{2}$ the area of parallelogram ABCD, then triangles ADE and EBC equal the other half of the parallelogram.

∴ Column A = Column B

ANSWER SHEET FOR MODEL EXAMINATION II

Completely blacken the answer space of your choice. Mark only one answer for each question. Erase stray marks.

SECTION I
VERBAL

1 Ⓐ Ⓑ Ⓒ Ⓓ Ⓔ	12 Ⓐ Ⓑ Ⓒ Ⓓ Ⓔ	23 Ⓐ Ⓑ Ⓒ Ⓓ Ⓔ	34 Ⓐ Ⓑ Ⓒ Ⓓ Ⓔ	45 Ⓐ Ⓑ Ⓒ Ⓓ Ⓔ	56 Ⓐ Ⓑ Ⓒ Ⓓ Ⓔ
2 Ⓐ Ⓑ Ⓒ Ⓓ Ⓔ	13 Ⓐ Ⓑ Ⓒ Ⓓ Ⓔ	24 Ⓐ Ⓑ Ⓒ Ⓓ Ⓔ	35 Ⓐ Ⓑ Ⓒ Ⓓ Ⓔ	46 Ⓐ Ⓑ Ⓒ Ⓓ Ⓔ	57 Ⓐ Ⓑ Ⓒ Ⓓ Ⓔ
3 Ⓐ Ⓑ Ⓒ Ⓓ Ⓔ	14 Ⓐ Ⓑ Ⓒ Ⓓ Ⓔ	25 Ⓐ Ⓑ Ⓒ Ⓓ Ⓔ	36 Ⓐ Ⓑ Ⓒ Ⓓ Ⓔ	47 Ⓐ Ⓑ Ⓒ Ⓓ Ⓔ	58 Ⓐ Ⓑ Ⓒ Ⓓ Ⓔ
4 Ⓐ Ⓑ Ⓒ Ⓓ Ⓔ	15 Ⓐ Ⓑ Ⓒ Ⓓ Ⓔ	26 Ⓐ Ⓑ Ⓒ Ⓓ Ⓔ	37 Ⓐ Ⓑ Ⓒ Ⓓ Ⓔ	48 Ⓐ Ⓑ Ⓒ Ⓓ Ⓔ	59 Ⓐ Ⓑ Ⓒ Ⓓ Ⓔ
5 Ⓐ Ⓑ Ⓒ Ⓓ Ⓔ	16 Ⓐ Ⓑ Ⓒ Ⓓ Ⓔ	27 Ⓐ Ⓑ Ⓒ Ⓓ Ⓔ	38 Ⓐ Ⓑ Ⓒ Ⓓ Ⓔ	49 Ⓐ Ⓑ Ⓒ Ⓓ Ⓔ	60 Ⓐ Ⓑ Ⓒ Ⓓ Ⓔ
6 Ⓐ Ⓑ Ⓒ Ⓓ Ⓔ	17 Ⓐ Ⓑ Ⓒ Ⓓ Ⓔ	28 Ⓐ Ⓑ Ⓒ Ⓓ Ⓔ	39 Ⓐ Ⓑ Ⓒ Ⓓ Ⓔ	50 Ⓐ Ⓑ Ⓒ Ⓓ Ⓔ	61 Ⓐ Ⓑ Ⓒ Ⓓ Ⓔ
7 Ⓐ Ⓑ Ⓒ Ⓓ Ⓔ	18 Ⓐ Ⓑ Ⓒ Ⓓ Ⓔ	29 Ⓐ Ⓑ Ⓒ Ⓓ Ⓔ	40 Ⓐ Ⓑ Ⓒ Ⓓ Ⓔ	51 Ⓐ Ⓑ Ⓒ Ⓓ Ⓔ	62 Ⓐ Ⓑ Ⓒ Ⓓ Ⓔ
8 Ⓐ Ⓑ Ⓒ Ⓓ Ⓔ	19 Ⓐ Ⓑ Ⓒ Ⓓ Ⓔ	30 Ⓐ Ⓑ Ⓒ Ⓓ Ⓔ	41 Ⓐ Ⓑ Ⓒ Ⓓ Ⓔ	52 Ⓐ Ⓑ Ⓒ Ⓓ Ⓔ	63 Ⓐ Ⓑ Ⓒ Ⓓ Ⓔ
9 Ⓐ Ⓑ Ⓒ Ⓓ Ⓔ	20 Ⓐ Ⓑ Ⓒ Ⓓ Ⓔ	31 Ⓐ Ⓑ Ⓒ Ⓓ Ⓔ	42 Ⓐ Ⓑ Ⓒ Ⓓ Ⓔ	53 Ⓐ Ⓑ Ⓒ Ⓓ Ⓔ	64 Ⓐ Ⓑ Ⓒ Ⓓ Ⓔ
10 Ⓐ Ⓑ Ⓒ Ⓓ Ⓔ	21 Ⓐ Ⓑ Ⓒ Ⓓ Ⓔ	32 Ⓐ Ⓑ Ⓒ Ⓓ Ⓔ	43 Ⓐ Ⓑ Ⓒ Ⓓ Ⓔ	54 Ⓐ Ⓑ Ⓒ Ⓓ Ⓔ	65 Ⓐ Ⓑ Ⓒ Ⓓ Ⓔ
11 Ⓐ Ⓑ Ⓒ Ⓓ Ⓔ	22 Ⓐ Ⓑ Ⓒ Ⓓ Ⓔ	33 Ⓐ Ⓑ Ⓒ Ⓓ Ⓔ	44 Ⓐ Ⓑ Ⓒ Ⓓ Ⓔ	55 Ⓐ Ⓑ Ⓒ Ⓓ Ⓔ	

SECTION II
MATHEMATICAL

1 Ⓐ Ⓑ Ⓒ Ⓓ Ⓔ	10 Ⓐ Ⓑ Ⓒ Ⓓ Ⓔ	19 Ⓐ Ⓑ Ⓒ Ⓓ	27 Ⓐ Ⓑ Ⓒ Ⓓ	35 Ⓐ Ⓑ Ⓒ Ⓓ Ⓔ	43 Ⓐ Ⓑ Ⓒ Ⓓ Ⓔ
2 Ⓐ Ⓑ Ⓒ Ⓓ Ⓔ	11 Ⓐ Ⓑ Ⓒ Ⓓ Ⓔ	20 Ⓐ Ⓑ Ⓒ Ⓓ	28 Ⓐ Ⓑ Ⓒ Ⓓ	36 Ⓐ Ⓑ Ⓒ Ⓓ Ⓔ	44 Ⓐ Ⓑ Ⓒ Ⓓ Ⓔ
3 Ⓐ Ⓑ Ⓒ Ⓓ Ⓔ	12 Ⓐ Ⓑ Ⓒ Ⓓ Ⓔ	21 Ⓐ Ⓑ Ⓒ Ⓓ	29 Ⓐ Ⓑ Ⓒ Ⓓ	37 Ⓐ Ⓑ Ⓒ Ⓓ Ⓔ	45 Ⓐ Ⓑ Ⓒ Ⓓ Ⓔ
4 Ⓐ Ⓑ Ⓒ Ⓓ Ⓔ	13 Ⓐ Ⓑ Ⓒ Ⓓ Ⓔ	22 Ⓐ Ⓑ Ⓒ Ⓓ	30 Ⓐ Ⓑ Ⓒ Ⓓ	38 Ⓐ Ⓑ Ⓒ Ⓓ Ⓔ	46 Ⓐ Ⓑ Ⓒ Ⓓ Ⓔ
5 Ⓐ Ⓑ Ⓒ Ⓓ Ⓔ	14 Ⓐ Ⓑ Ⓒ Ⓓ Ⓔ	23 Ⓐ Ⓑ Ⓒ Ⓓ	31 Ⓐ Ⓑ Ⓒ Ⓓ	39 Ⓐ Ⓑ Ⓒ Ⓓ Ⓔ	47 Ⓐ Ⓑ Ⓒ Ⓓ Ⓔ
6 Ⓐ Ⓑ Ⓒ Ⓓ Ⓔ	15 Ⓐ Ⓑ Ⓒ Ⓓ Ⓔ	24 Ⓐ Ⓑ Ⓒ Ⓓ	32 Ⓐ Ⓑ Ⓒ Ⓓ	40 Ⓐ Ⓑ Ⓒ Ⓓ Ⓔ	48 Ⓐ Ⓑ Ⓒ Ⓓ Ⓔ
7 Ⓐ Ⓑ Ⓒ Ⓓ Ⓔ	16 Ⓐ Ⓑ Ⓒ Ⓓ	25 Ⓐ Ⓑ Ⓒ Ⓓ	33 Ⓐ Ⓑ Ⓒ Ⓓ Ⓔ	41 Ⓐ Ⓑ Ⓒ Ⓓ Ⓔ	49 Ⓐ Ⓑ Ⓒ Ⓓ Ⓔ
8 Ⓐ Ⓑ Ⓒ Ⓓ Ⓔ	17 Ⓐ Ⓑ Ⓒ Ⓓ	26 Ⓐ Ⓑ Ⓒ Ⓓ	34 Ⓐ Ⓑ Ⓒ Ⓓ Ⓔ	42 Ⓐ Ⓑ Ⓒ Ⓓ Ⓔ	50 Ⓐ Ⓑ Ⓒ Ⓓ Ⓔ
9 Ⓐ Ⓑ Ⓒ Ⓓ Ⓔ	18 Ⓐ Ⓑ Ⓒ Ⓓ				

SCORE SHEET

Raw Scores

ANTONYMS	___ – ___ ÷ 4 = ___
SENTENCE COMPLETIONS	___ – ___ ÷ 4 = ___
VERBAL ANALOGIES	___ – ___ ÷ 4 = ___
READING COMPREHENSION	___ – ___ ÷ 4 = ___

Total Verbal Score ___

MATHEMATICAL PROBLEMS   ___ – ___ ÷ 4 = ___

Note: Do not forget to add together the two sets of problems that come before and after "Quantitative Comparisons."

QUANTITATIVE COMPARISONS   ___ – ___ ÷ 3 = ___

Total Mathematical Score ___

Percents

ANTONYMS ___ (score) ÷ 20 = ___ × 100 = ___%
SENTENCE COMPLETIONS ___ (score) ÷ 10 = ___ × 100 = ___%
VERBAL ANALOGIES ___ (score) ÷ 15 = ___ × 100 = ___%
READING COMPREHENSION ___ (score) ÷ 20 = ___ × 100 = ___%
MATHEMATICAL PROBLEMS ___ (score) ÷ 33 = ___ × 100 = ___%
QUANTITATIVE COMPARISONS ___ (score) ÷ 17 = ___ × 100 = ___%
TOTAL VERBAL ___ (total verbal score) ÷ 65 = ___ × 100 = ___%
TOTAL MATH ___ (total math score) ÷ 50 = ___ × 100 = ___%

PROGRESS CHART

	Exam I	Exam II
ANTONYMS	%	%
SENTENCE COMPLETIONS	%	%
VERBAL ANALOGIES	%	%
READING COMPREHENSION	%	%
MATHEMATICAL PROBLEMS	%	%
QUANTITATIVE COMPARISONS	%	%

MODEL EXAMINATION II

Section I
Time—50 minutes; 65 questions

DIRECTIONS: For each question, mark the letter preceding the word or phrase that is opposite or most nearly opposite in meaning to the capitalized word. Where more than one option appears to be correct, choose the *best* opposite.

Example:

ABOVE

(A) near
(B) around
(C) touching
(D) below
(E) next to

1. CONSEQUENCE

  (A) truth
  (B) plan
  (C) cause
  (D) retaliation
  (E) verdict

2. TANGIBLE

  (A) required
  (B) explainable
  (C) presentable
  (D) illegal
  (E) untouchable

3. VACUOUS

  (A) brilliant
  (B) dirty
  (C) plausible
  (D) equine
  (E) peaceful

4. INFLAMMABLE

  (A) soaked
  (B) fireproof
  (C) on fire
  (D) flammable
  (E) burned out

5. SURCHARGE

  (A) commence
  (B) receipt
  (C) bill
  (D) discount
  (E) copy

6. LETHARGIC

  (A) silky
  (B) limpid
  (C) equestrian
  (D) vigorous
  (E) metallic

7. AXIS

  (A) saw
  (B) ally
  (C) orbit
  (D) enemy
  (E) edge

8. SUPERCILIOUS

  (A) humble
  (B) superior
  (C) hairy
  (D) silent
  (E) heathen

9. WINCE

  (A) scream
  (B) smile
  (C) receive
  (D) command
  (E) reach out

10. PACIFY

(A) change
(B) assault
(C) tremble
(D) conceal
(E) exhibit

11. FECUND

(A) sinister
(B) pure
(C) young
(D) barren
(E) beneficial

12. INCARCERATE

(A) remit
(B) extinguish
(C) decline
(D) feign
(E) release

13. COMPENDIOUS

(A) inexpensive
(B) ideal
(C) overwhelming
(D) evil
(E) fearful

14. TEMERITY

(A) verve
(B) beginning
(C) humility
(D) strength
(E) celerity

15. TRACTABLE

(A) retarded
(B) brilliant
(C) airborne
(D) abnormal
(E) stubborn

16. BENIGN

(A) cavernous
(B) relevant
(C) tumorous
(D) malevolent
(E) precarious

17. DULCET

(A) musical
(B) optimistic
(C) stringless
(D) acerb
(E) pessimistic

18. TURBID

(A) tranquil
(B) limp
(C) pious
(D) arabian
(E) dry

19. MOPPET

(A) vacuum cleaner
(B) large dog
(C) marionette
(D) stuffed animal
(E) adult

20. SOPORIFIC

(A) pain-killing
(B) narcotic
(C) healthy
(D) awakening
(E) drying

DIRECTIONS: Each of the following questions consists of an incomplete sentence followed by five words or pairs of words. Choose that word or pair of words which, when substituted for the blank space or spaces, *best* completes the meaning of the sentence and mark the letter of your choice on your answer sheet.

Example:

It is wise to get a written _____ of the costs of labor and materials before _____ someone to do the work.

(A) account . . hiring
(B) promise . . condemning
(C) estimate . . commissioning
(D) invoice . . seeking
(E) compilation . . urging

 Ⓐ Ⓑ ● Ⓓ Ⓔ

21. Politicians are not the only ones who have made _____; being human, we have all blundered at some time in our lives.

    (A) explanations
    (B) arguments
    (C) errors
    (D) excuses
    (E) amendments

22. Because of his _____ nature, he often acts purely on impulse.

    (A) stoic
    (B) reflective
    (C) passionate
    (D) wistful
    (E) studious

23. To promote the production and use of domestic products, the _____ were limited and _____ forbidden.

    (A) supplies .. hoarding
    (B) costs .. profits
    (C) exports .. imports
    (D) quantities .. advertising
    (E) selections .. competition

24. The spirit of science is always trying to lead men to the study of _____ and away from the spinning of fanciful theories out of their own minds.

    (A) tradition
    (B) order
    (C) legalities
    (D) literature
    (E) philosophy

25. Both good and bad tastes exist in the world of art, and arguments about taste are _____.

    (A) necessary
    (B) exciting
    (C) childish
    (D) meaningful
    (E) educated

26. The fame of the author does not _____ the quality of his works. We must avoid equating success with infallibility.

    (A) prejudice
    (B) assure

(C) dignify
(D) extol
(E) magnify

27. The mechanisms that develop hatred in man are most potent, since there is more _____ than _____ in the world.

    (A) apathy .. evil
    (B) tolerance .. prejudice
    (C) joy .. rapture
    (D) love .. hatred
    (E) strife .. tranquility

28. It is not the similarity in instruments which produces harmony in music, but an insubstantiality of each one; all instruments of the orchestra must be _____ when separate, and each must be _____ by association with the others.

    (A) self-sufficient .. unaffected
    (B) sensuous .. hidden
    (C) colorless .. artistic
    (D) unique .. vitalized
    (E) wearisome .. stately

29. Mining is often called the _____ industry, since it neither creates nor replenishes what it takes.

    (A) robber
    (B) ecology
    (C) natural
    (D) evil
    (E) unscientific

30. Spores are a form of life that remain _____ until environmental conditions exist in which they can become _____.

    (A) inactive .. vibrant
    (B) hidden .. dangerous
    (C) suppressed .. visible
    (D) controlled .. rampant
    (E) harmless .. compulsive

DIRECTIONS: Each of the following questions consists of a capitalized pair of words followed by five pairs of words lettered A to E. The capitalized words bear some meaningful relationship to each other. Choose the lettered pair of words whose relationship is most similar to that expressed by the capitalized pair and mark its letter on your answer sheet.

Example:

RAIN : DROP ::

(A) snow : ice
(B) drop : flake
(C) zero : cold
(D) ice : cold
(E) snow : flake

---

31. ISLAND : OCEAN ::

(A) hill : stream
(B) forest : valley
(C) oasis : desert
(D) tree : field
(E) flower : seed

32. MATHEMATICS : NUMEROLOGY ::

(A) biology : botany
(B) psychology : physiology
(C) anatomy : medicine
(D) astronomy : astrology
(E) philosophy : science

33. DISLIKABLE : ABHORRENT ::

(A) trustworthy : helpful
(B) ominous : loving
(C) silly : young
(D) tender : hard
(E) difficult : arduous

34. RETINUE : MONARCH ::

(A) cortege : escort
(B) princess : queen
(C) return : throne
(D) second : first
(E) moon : earth

35. MINARET : MOSQUE ::

(A) Christian : Moslem
(B) steeple : church
(C) dainty : grotesque
(D) modern : classic
(E) Romanesque : Gothic

36. WHEAT : CHAFF ::

(A) wine : dregs
(B) bread : roll
(C) laughter : raillery
(D) oat : oatmeal
(E) crop : corn

37. DRAMA : DIRECTOR ::

(A) class : principal
(B) movie : scenario
(C) actor : playwright
(D) tragedy : Sophocles
(E) magazine : editor

38. AFFLUENT : LUCK ::

(A) charitable : stinginess
(B) greedy : cruelty
(C) free-flowing : barrier
(D) impoverished : laziness
(E) fluent : hesitance

39. PICCOLO : BASSOON ::

(A) orchestra : band
(B) concert : opera
(C) trumpet : trombone
(D) sweet : sour
(E) violin : bass

40. PLEASED : THRILLED ::

(A) tipsy : drunken
(B) sensible : lively
(C) intelligent : dumb
(D) liberal : tolerant
(E) generous : cheerful

41. ELLIPSE : CURVE ::

(A) stutter : speech
(B) triangle : base
(C) revolution : distance
(D) square : polygon
(E) circumference : ball

42. SUGAR : SACCHARIN ::

(A) candy : cake
(B) hog : lard
(C) cane : stalk
(D) spice : pepper
(E) butter : margarine

43. REQUEST : DEMAND ::

(A) reply : respond
(B) regard : reject
(C) inquire : require
(D) wish : crave
(E) seek : hide

44. WATER : FAUCET ::

(A) fuel : throttle
(B) H_2O : O
(C) kitchen : sink
(D) steam : solid
(E) leak : plumber

45. MONEY : GREED ::

(A) finance : creed
(B) property : desire
(C) dollar sign : capitalism
(D) food : voracity
(E) work : slavery

DIRECTIONS: Below each of the following passages, you will find five questions or incomplete statements about the passage. Each statement or question is followed by five response options. Read the passage carefully. On the basis of what was stated or implied in the passage, select the option which *best* completes each statement or answers each question. You may refer to the passage as often as necessary. Mark the letter of your choice on your answer sheet.

The United States is the most energy hungry country in the world. Our economy is based upon manufacturing processes which consume a great deal of fuel. Our lifestyle involves frequent travel, commitment to personal comfort obtained by maintaining constant indoor temperature all year around and extensive use of powered gadgets for pleasure and for convenience.

At one time the United States was able to satisfy its own energy needs with the help of its extensive coal resources and its own oil supply. However, the demand for energy has expanded so rapidly that our ability to meet our own needs has been outstripped. In addition, recent realization of the health hazards inherent in the air pollution created by burning coal has resulted in greater demand for cleaner-burning oil. And so, we have turned to foreign sources to supply that oil. In the past few decades, the bulk of our imported oil has come from the Persian Gulf area. There oil is found in abundance and, with the assistance of American technology, production has been able to keep up with world demand.

While the governments of the Persian Gulf countries were stable and unambitious, all went well for us. However, with awakening national awareness and a sudden realization that the world was dependent upon them, the oil-rich nations have begun to take advantage of their power. These countries have discovered that they can raise their prices to exorbitant heights and that they can bend the policies of other nations to their will by withholding oil from the world market. The political situation around the world has become one of tyranny by the oil-rich nations.

To attempt to counter this situation, the President of the United States has urged austerity in American behavior. A national speed limit has been set at 55 mph to conserve gasoline. Public buildings are required to maintain winter temperatures at 65° F. and summer temperatures at 75° F. Rationing has been proposed and alternate means for obtaining the required energy are being explored.

Even in the midst of occasional shortages and long gasoline lines and while the President is encouraging modification of energy demands, one of the Republican Presidential candidates insists that the United States is an "energy rich" nation that does not need to conserve gasoline or fuel oil. This position is very comforting to those citizens who prefer not to alter their lifestyles for the sake of energy conservation. On the other hand, this disdain of the need for conservation is most frightening to persons who fear that true shortages and resource depletion will rapidly result if consumption goes on unchecked.

The candidate claims that the state of Alaska alone "has more oil than Saudi Arabia" and suggests that these reserves of oil are not tapped because they are located in wilderness preserves where oil exploration is forbidden by statute. He feels that all of America's energy problems would be quickly solved if the oil companies were permitted and encouraged to go in and just "bring out the oil."

As may be expected, there are many who receive

these pronouncements with skepticism. These people would like to have more concrete evidence of the existence of these oil reserves and of the feasibility of actually obtaining and transporting the oil for our own use. They ask for facts and figures and documentation.

The candidate maintains that all of his contentions can be proven and cites formulas prepared by "experts." However, he reserves the right to keep confidential the identities of his "experts." The formula by which he has determined that there is more oil in Alaska than in Saudi Arabia is as follows: double the "potential" reserves in Alaska and compare them with the "proven" reserves in Saudi Arabia. Since "there are more potential oil reserves" in Alaska than "proven" reserves in Saudi Arabia the formula proves, without a doubt, that America has no fuel shortage now and no prospect for shortage for many generations to come.

46. The attitude of the candidate would be likely to encourage

(A) research into energy efficient automobile engines
(B) careful placement of land mines
(C) proponents of the use of coal to generate cheap electricity
(D) anti-nuclear agitators
(E) traffic fatalities

47. In order to accept the contention that there is more oil in Alaska than in Saudi Arabia, we must

(A) trust the government
(B) insist upon the identity of the "expert"
(C) drill for oil at selected Alaskan sites to see if the potential reserves really exist
(D) believe the formula
(E) believe that Saudi Arabia has only as much oil as it says it has

48. If it is true that there is far more oil in Alaska than was hitherto believed, which of the following is most likely to occur *first?*

(A) The price of oil will go up.
(B) The price of oil will go down.
(C) Supplies of oil will increase markedly.
(D) There will be a fuel shortage.
(E) Supplies will go up and the price will come down.

49. As part of his legislative program, we would expect the candidate to promise to

(A) repeal all anti-pollution restrictions on industry
(B) press for reversal of "forever wild" legislation
(C) increase the tariff on imported oil
(D) accelerate development of "alternative sources" of energy
(E) change the national speed limit

50. If we were not so dependent upon their oil, the Persian Gulf nations would probably

I. lose much of their political power
II. join the Russian bloc
III. lower their prices
IV. face an energy crisis

(A) I and II
(B) III and IV
(C) I and III
(D) II and IV
(E) I, II and III

A vast health checkup is now being conducted in the western Swedish province of Varmland with the use of an automated apparatus for high-speed multiple-blood analyses. Developed by two brothers, the apparatus can process more than 4,000 blood samples a day, subjecting each to 10 or more tests. Automation has cut the cost of the analyses by about 90 percent.

The results so far have been astonishing, for (10) hundreds of Swedes have learned that they have silent symptoms of disorders that neither they nor their physicians were aware of. Among them are iron-deficiency anemia, hypercholesterolemia, hypertension and even diabetes.

The automated blood analysis apparatus was developed by Dr. Gunnar Jungner, 49-year-old associate professor of clinical chemistry at Goteborg University, and his brother, Ingmar, 39, the physician in charge of the central chemical laboratory of Stockholm's Hospital for Infectious Diseases. (20)

The idea was conceived when Dr. Gunnar Jungner was working as a clinical chemist in northern Sweden and was asked by local physicians to devise a way of performing multiple analyses on a single blood sample. The design was ready in 1961.

Consisting of calorimeters, pumps and other com-

Model Examination II   /   233

ponents, many of them American-made, the Jungner apparatus was set up here in Stockholm. Samples from Varmland Province are drawn into the auto-
(30) mated system at 90-second intervals. The findings clatter forth in the form of numbers printed by an automatic typewriter.

The Jungners predict that advance knowledge about a person's potential ailments made possible by the chemical screening process will result in consid-erable savings in hospital and other medical costs. Thus, they point out, the blood analyses will actually turn out to cost nothing.

In the beginning, the automated blood analyses
(40) ran into considerable opposition from some physi-cians who had no faith in machines and saw no need for so many tests. Some laboratory technicians who saw their jobs threatened also protested. But the opposition is said to be waning.

51. Automation is viewed by the writer with

(A) animosity
(B) indecision
(C) remorse
(D) favor
(E) indifference

52. The results of the use of the Jungner apparatus indicate that

(A) a person may become aware of an ailment not previously detected
(B) blood diseases can be cured very easily
(C) diabetes does not respond to the apparatus
(D) practically all Swedish physicians have welcomed the invention
(E) only one analysis may be made at a time

53. All of the following statements about automated blood analysis are true *except:*

(A) the analysis is recorded in a permanent form
(B) the idea for the apparatus involved an inter-national effort
(C) the system has met opposition from physi-cians and technicians
(D) the machine is more efficient than other types of analysis
(E) the process is a means to save on hospital costs

54. The main purpose of the passage is to

(A) predict the future of medical care
(B) describe a health check-up system
(C) show how Sweden has superior health care
(D) warn about the dangers of undetected dis-ease
(E) describe in detail the workings of a new machine

55. The prediction process that the Jungners use is essentially

(A) biological
(B) physiological
(C) chemical
(D) anatomical
(E) biophysical

A Polish proverb claims that fish, to taste right, should swim three times—in water, in butter and in wine. The early efforts of the basic scientists in the food industry were directed at improving the prepara-tion, preservation, and distribution of safe and nu-tritious food. Our memories of certain foodstuffs eaten during the Second World War suggest that, although these might have been safe and nutritious, they certainly did not taste right nor were they particularly appetizing in appearance or smell. This neglect of the sensory appeal of foods is happily becoming a thing of the past. Indeed, the University of California considered the subject of sufficient importance to warrant the setting-up of a course in the analysis of foods by sensory methods. The book, *Principles of Sensory Evaluation of Food,* grew out of this course. The authors hope that it will be useful to food technologists in industry and also to others engaged in research into the problem of sensory evaluation of foods.

The scope of the book is well illustrated by the chapter headings: "The Sense of Taste"; "Olfac-tion"; "Visual, Auditory, Tactile, and Other Senses"; and "Factors Influencing Sensory Mea-surements." There are further chapters on panel testing, difference and directional difference tests, quantity-quality evaluation, consumer studies, statis-tical procedures (including design of experiments), and physical and chemical tests. An attempt has clearly been made to collect every possible piece of information which might be useful, more than one thousand five hundred references being quoted. As a result, the book seems at first sight to be an exhaustive and critically useful review of the literature. This it certainly is, but this is by no means its only achievement, for there are many suggestions for further lines of research, and the discursive passages are crisply provocative of new ideas and new ways of looking at established findings.

Of particular interest is the weight given to the psychological aspects of perception, both objectively and subjectively. The relation between stimuli and perception is well covered, and includes a valuable discussion of the uses and disadvantages of the Weber fraction in the evaluation of differences. It is interesting to find that in spite of many attempts to separate and define the modalities of taste, nothing better has been achieved than the familiar classification into sweet, sour, salty and bitter. Nor is there as yet any clear-cut evidence of the physiological nature of the taste stimulus. With regard to smell, systems of classification are of little value because of the extraordinary sensitivity of the nose and because the response to the stimulus is so subjective. The authors suggest that a classification based on the size, shape and electronic status of the molecule involved merits further investigation, as does the theoretical proposition that weak physical binding of the stimulant molecule to the receptor site is a necessary part of the mechanism of stimulation.

Apart from taste and smell, there are many other components of perception of the sensations from food in the mouth. The basic modalities of pain, cold, warmth and touch, together with vibration sense, discrimination and localization may all play a part, as, of course, does auditory reception of bone-conducted vibratory stimuli from the teeth when eating crisp or crunchy foods. In this connection the authors rightly point out that this type of stimulus requires much more investigation, suggesting that a start might be made by using subjects afflicted with various forms of deafness. It is, of course, well known that extraneous noise may alter discrimination, and the attention of the authors is directed to the work of Prof. H. J. Eysenck on the "stimulus hunger" of extroverts and the "stimulus avoidance" of introverts. (It is perhaps unfair to speculate, not that the authors do, that certain breakfast cereals rely on sound volume to drown any deficiencies in flavor, or that the noisier types are mainly eaten by extroverts.)

56. The reviewer uses a Polish proverb at the beginning of the article in order to

(A) introduce, in an interesting manner, the discussion of food
(B) show the connection between food and nationality
(C) indicate that there are various ways to prepare food
(D) bring out the difference between American and Polish cooking
(E) impress upon the reader the food value of fish

57. The reviewer's appraisal of *Principles of Sensory Evaluation of Food* is one of

(A) mixed feelings
(B) indifference
(C) derogation
(D) high praise
(E) faint praise

58. The Weber fraction was originated by

(A) Max Weber (1881–1961), American painter.
(B) Ernest Heinrich Weber (1795–1878), German physiologist
(C) Baron Karl Maria Friedrich Ernest von Weber (1786–1826), German composer
(D) Max Weber (1864–1920), German political economist and sociologist
(E) George Weber (1808–1888), German historian

59. The writer of the article does *not* express the view, either directly or by implication, that

(A) more sharply defined classifications of taste are needed than those which are used at present
(B) more research should be done regarding the molecular constituency of food
(C) food values are objectively determined by an expert "smeller"
(D) psychological considerations would play an important part in food evaluation
(E) temperature is an important factor in the appraisal of food

60. The chapter headings listed at the beginning of the second paragraph make no specific reference to the sense of

(A) smell
(B) sight
(C) touch

(D) muscular movement
(E) hearing

There is also a confused notion in the minds of many persons, that the gathering of the property of the poor into the hands of the rich does no ultimate harm, since, in whosesoever hands it may be, it must be spent at last, and thus, they think, return to the poor again. This fallacy has been again and again exposed; but granting the plea true, the same apol- ogy may, of course, be made for blackmail, or any other form of robbery. It might be (though practi-
(10) cally it never is) as advantageous for the nation that the robber should have the spending of the money he extorts, as that the person robbed should have spent it. But this is no excuse for the theft. If I were to put a turnpike on the road where it passes my own gate, and endeavor to exact a shilling from every passenger, the public would soon do away with my gate, without listening to any pleas on my part that it was as advantageous to them, in the end, that I should spend their shillings, as that they themselves
(20) should. But if, instead of outfacing them with a turnpike, I can only persuade them to come in and buy stones, or old iron, or any other useless thing, out of my ground, I may rob them to the same extent, and be, moreover, thanked as a public bene- factor and promoter of commercial prosperity. And this main question for the poor of England—for the poor of all countries—is wholly omitted in every treatise on the subject of wealth. Even by the labour- ers themselves, the operation of capital is regarded
(30) only in its effect on their immediate interests, never in the far more terrific power of its appointment of the kind and the object of labour. It matters little, ultimately, how much a labourer is paid for making anything; but it matters fearfully what the thing is, which he is compelled to make. If his labour is so ordered as to produce food, and fresh air, and fresh water, no matter that his wages are low;—the food and the fresh air and water will be at last there, and he will at last get them. But if he is paid to destroy
(40) food and fresh air, or to produce iron bars instead of them,—the food and air will finally *not* be there, and he will *not* get them, to his great and final inconvenience. So that, conclusively, in political as in household economy, the great question is, not so much what money you have in your pocket, as what you will buy with it and do with it.

61. We may infer that the writer lived in the

(A) 1960s in America
(B) Victorian Age in England
(C) 18th century in France
(D) Periclean Age in Greece
(E) Renaissance in Italy

62. It can be inferred that the author favors

(A) capitalism
(B) totalitarianism
(C) socialism
(D) anarchism
(E) theocracy

63. The passage implies that

(A) "a stitch in time saves nine"
(B) "it is better late than never"
(C) "he who steals my purse steals trash"
(D) "none but the brave deserve the fair"
(E) "there are two sides to every story"

64. It can be inferred that in regard to the accumula- tion of wealth the author

(A) equates the rich with the thief
(B) indicates that there is no truly honest businessman
(C) condones some dishonesty in business dealings
(D) believes destruction of property is good because it creates consumer demand
(E) says that the robber is a benefactor

65. The passage does not indicate that

(A) stealing is sometimes pardonable
(B) there are legal ways to rob the public
(C) the poor are being abused
(D) a worker's wages are of little concern to the nation-at-large
(E) the kind of products purchased is of general importance

END OF SECTION I

IF YOU COMPLETE THIS SECTION BEFORE TIME IS UP, CHECK OVER YOUR WORK.

Section II
Time—50 minutes; 50 questions

DIRECTIONS: Solve each of the following problems, using available space on the page for your scratch work. Mark the letter of the correct answer on your answer sheet.

You may refer to the following data in solving the problems.

Triangle:

The angles of a triangle added together equal 180°.
The angle BDC is a right angle; therefore,

(I) the area of triangle ABC = $\dfrac{AC \times BD}{2}$

(II) $AB^2 = AD^2 + DB^2$

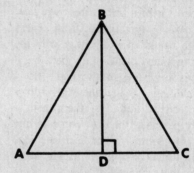

Circle:

There are 360° of arc in a circle.
The area of a circle of radius $r = \pi r^2$
The circumference of a circle $= 2\pi r$
A straight angle has 180°.

Symbol references:

‖ is parallel to
$\leqq$ is less than or equal to
$\geqq$ is greater than or equal to
∠ angle

\> is greater than
< is less than
⊥ is perpendicular to
△ triangle

Notes: The diagrams which accompany problems should provide data helpful in working out the solutions. These diagrams are not necessarily drawn precisely to scale. Unless otherwise stated, all figures lie in the same plane. All numbers are real numbers.

1. Which of the following fractions is more than $\frac{3}{4}$?

(A) $\frac{35}{71}$
(B) $\frac{13}{20}$
(C) $\frac{71}{101}$
(D) $\frac{19}{24}$
(E) $\frac{15}{20}$

2. If $820 + R + S - 610 = 342$, and if $R = 2S$, then $S =$

(A) 44
(B) 48
(C) 132
(D) 184
(E) 192

236

3. What is the cost, in dollars, to carpet a room x yards long and y yards wide, if the carpet costs two dollars per square foot?

(A) xy
(B) 2xy
(C) 3xy
(D) 6xy
(E) 18xy

4. If $7M = 3M - 20$, then $M + 7 =$

(A) 0
(B) 2
(C) 5
(D) 12
(E) 17

5. In circle O below, AB is a diameter, angle BOD contains 15° and angle EOA contains 85°. Find the number of degrees in angle ECA.

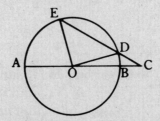

(A) 15
(B) 35
(C) 50
(D) 70
(E) 85

6. The diagonal of a rectangle is 10. The area of the rectangle

(A) must be 24
(B) must be 48
(C) must be 50
(D) must be 100
(E) cannot be determined from the data given

7. In triangle PQR in the figure below, angle P is greater than angle Q and the bisectors of angle P and angle Q meet in S. Then

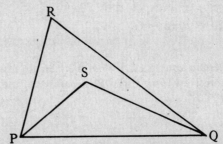

(A) SQ > SP
(B) SQ = SP
(C) SQ < SP
(D) SQ ≥ SP
(E) no conclusion concerning the relative lengths of SQ and SP can be drawn from the data given

8. The coordinates of vertices X and Y of an equilateral triangle XYZ are $(-4, 0)$ and $(4, 0)$, respectively. The coordinates of Z may be

(A) $(0, 2\sqrt{3})$
(B) $(0, 4\sqrt{3})$
(C) $(4, 4\sqrt{3})$
(D) $(0, 4)$
(E) $(4\sqrt{3}, 0)$

9. In the accompanying figure, ACB is a straight angle and DC is perpendicular to CE. If the number of degrees in angle ACD is represented by x, the number of degrees in angle BCE is represented by

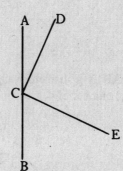

(A) $90 - x$
(B) $x - 90$
(C) $90 + x$
(D) $180 - x$
(E) $45 + x$

10. What is the smallest positive number which, when it is divided by 3, 4, or 5, will leave a remainder of 2?

(A) 22
(B) 42
(C) 62
(D) 122
(E) 182

11. A taxi charges 20 cents for the first quarter of a mile and 5 cents for each additional quarter of a mile. The charge, in cents, for a trip of d miles is

(A) $20 + 5d$
(B) $20 + 5 (4d - 1)$
(C) $20 + 20d$
(D) $20 + 4 (d - 1)$
(E) $20 + 20 (d - 1)$

12. In a certain army post, 30% of the men are from New York State, and 10% of these are from New York City. What percent of the men in the post are from New York City?

(A) 3
(B) .3
(C) .03
(D) 13
(E) 20

13. From 9 A.M. to 2 P.M., the temperature rose at a constant rate from $-14°F$ to $+36°F$. What was the temperature at noon?

   (A) $-4°$
   (B) $+6°$
   (C) $+16°$
   (D) $+26°$
   (E) $+31°$

14. There are just two ways in which 5 may be expressed as the sum of two different positive (non-zero) integers; namely, $5 = 4 + 1 = 3 + 2$. In how many ways may 9 be expressed as the sum of two different positive (non-zero) integers?

   (A) 3
   (B) 4
   (C) 5
   (D) 6
   (E) 7

15. A board 7 feet 9 inches long is divided into three equal parts. What is the length of each part?

   (A) 2 ft. 7 in.
   (B) 2 ft. $6\frac{1}{3}$ in.
   (C) 2 ft. $8\frac{1}{3}$ in.
   (D) 2 ft. 8 in.
   (E) 2 ft. 9 in.

DIRECTIONS: For each of the following questions, two quantities are given—one in Column A, the other in Column B. Compare the two quantities and mark your answer sheet as follows:
(A) if the quantity in Column A is greater
(B) if the quantity in Column B is greater
(C) if the quantities are equal
(D) if the relationship cannot be determined from the information given.

NECESSARY INFORMATION:
• In each question, information concerning one or both of the quantities to be compared is centered above the entries in the two columns.

• A symbol that appears in any column represents the same thing in Column A as it does in Column B.

• All numbers used are real numbers; letters such as x, y, and t stand for real numbers.

• Assume that the position of points, angles, regions and so forth are in the order shown and that all figures lie in a plane unless otherwise indicated.

• Figures are not necessarily drawn to scale.

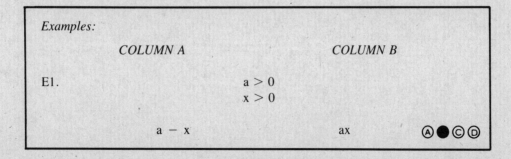

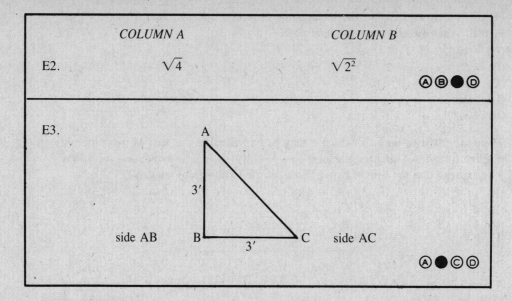

	COLUMN A	COLUMN B
E2.	$\sqrt{4}$	$\sqrt{2^2}$

Ⓐ Ⓑ ● Ⓓ

E3.

side AB   side AC

Ⓐ ● Ⓒ Ⓓ

16.

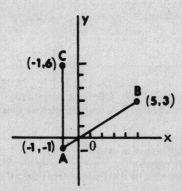

The length of $\overline{AB}$ The length of $\overline{AC}$

17.

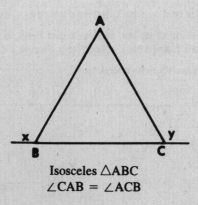

Isosceles △ABC
∠CAB = ∠ACB

∠x   ∠y

COLUMN A   COLUMN B

18.

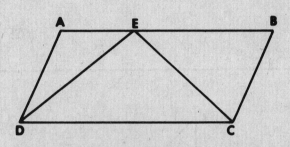

Parallelogram ABCD
E a point on AB

Area of △DEC   Area of △AED
                                + Area △EBC

---

19.   x = −1

x³ + x² − x + 1   x² − x² + x − 1

---

20.   The edge of a cube   The edge of a cube whose
           whose volume is 27   total surface area is 54

---

21. $\dfrac{\frac{1}{2} + \frac{1}{3}}{\frac{2}{3}}$ $\dfrac{\frac{2}{3}}{\frac{1}{2} + \frac{1}{3}}$

---

22.   x radius of a given circle

           Area of a circle   Area of a circle
           radius = x³   radius = 3x

---

23. $[(-\tfrac{1}{2})^2]^3$ $[(-\tfrac{1}{2})^3]^2$

	COLUMN A	COLUMN B
24.	$(\frac{1}{4})^{-2}$	4^2

25.	.02	$\sqrt{.02}$

26.

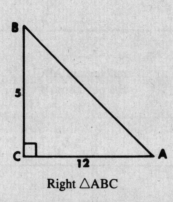

Right △ABC

$(AB)^2$ $(AC)^2 + 5CB$

27.   Area of circle with   Area of equilateral
         radius 7   triangle with side 14

28.

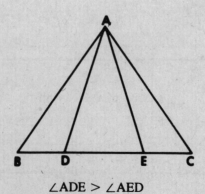

∠ADE > ∠AED

∠B   ∠C

COLUMN A   COLUMN B

29.

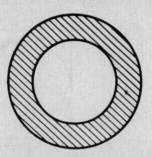

Radius of large circle = 10
Radius of small circle = 7

Area of shaded portion   Area of small circle

30.

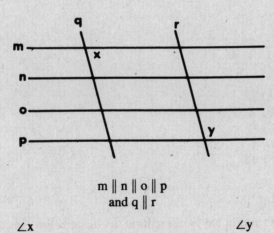

m ∥ n ∥ o ∥ p
and q ∥ r

∠x   ∠y

31.   a < 0 < b

a²   b/2

32.   t < 0 < r

t²   r

DIRECTIONS: Solve each of the following problems, using available space on the page for your scratch work. Mark the letter of the correct answer on your answer sheet.

33. In the figure below, the largest possible circle is cut out of a square piece of tin. The area of the remaining piece of tin is approximately (in square inches)

(A) .75
(B) 3.14
(C) .14
(D) .86
(E) 1.0

34. Which of the following is equal to 3.14×10^6?

(A) 314
(B) 3,140
(C) 31,400
(D) 314,000
(E) 3,140,000

35. $\dfrac{36}{29 - \dfrac{4}{0.2}} =$

(A) $\frac{4}{3}$
(B) 2
(C) 4
(D) $\frac{3}{4}$
(E) 18

36. In terms of the square units in the figure below, what is the area of the semicircle?

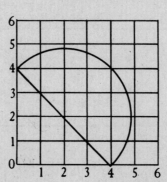

(A) 32π
(B) 16π
(C) 8π
(D) 4π
(E) 2π

37. The sum of three consecutive odd numbers is always divisible by

   I. 2   II. 3   III. 5   IV. 6

   (A) only I
   (B) only II
   (C) only I and II
   (D) only I and III
   (E) only II and IV

38. In the diagram, triangle ABC is inscribed in a circle and CD is tangent to the circle. If angle BCD is 40° how many degrees are there in angle A?

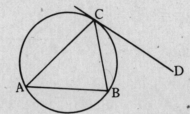

   (A) 20
   (B) 30
   (C) 40
   (D) 50
   (E) 60

39. If a discount of 20% off the marked price of a suit saves a man $15, how much did he pay for the suit?

   (A) $35
   (B) $60
   (C) $75
   (D) $150
   (E) $300

40. The ice compartment in a refrigerator is 8 inches deep, 5 inches high, and 4 inches wide. How many ice cubes will it hold, if each cube is 2 inches on a side?

   (A) 16
   (B) 20
   (C) 40
   (D) 80
   (E) 160

41. Find the last number in the series: 8 , 4 , 12 , 6 , 18 , 9 , ?

   (A) 19
   (B) 20
   (C) 22
   (D) 24
   (E) 27

42. A 15-gallon mixture of 20% alcohol has 5 gallons of water added to it. The strength of the mixture, as a percent, is near

   (A) 15
   (B) $13\frac{1}{3}$
   (C) $16\frac{2}{3}$
   (D) $12\frac{1}{2}$
   (E) 20

43. In the figure below, QXRS is a parallelogram and P is any point on side QS. What is the ratio of the area of triangle PXR to the area of QXRS?

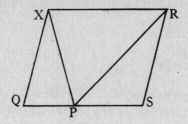

(A) 1 : 4
(B) 1 : 3
(C) 2 : 3
(D) 3 : 4
(E) 1 : 2

44. If x (p + 1) = M, then p =

(A) M − 1

(B) M

(C) $\dfrac{M - 1}{x}$

(D) M − x − 1

(E) $\dfrac{M}{x} - 1$

45. If T tons of snow fall in 1 second, how many tons fall in M minutes?

(A) 60 MT

(B) MT + 60

(C) MT

(D) $\dfrac{60M}{T}$

(E) $\dfrac{MT}{60}$

46. If $\dfrac{P}{Q} = \dfrac{4}{5}$ what is the value of 2P + Q?

(A) 14
(B) 13
(C) −1
(D) 3
(E) cannot be determined from the information given

47. The figure shows one square inside another and a rectangle of diagonal T. The best approximation to the value of T, in inches, is given by which of the following inequalities?

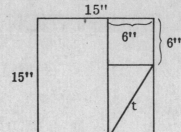

(A) $6 < T < 9$
(B) $11 < T < 12$
(C) $12 < T < 13$
(D) $9 < T < 11$
(E) $10 < T < 11$

48. A boy takes a 25-question test and answers all questions. His percent score is obtained by giving him 4 points for each correct answer, and then subtracting 1 point for each wrong answer. If he obtains a score of 70%, how many questions did he answer correctly?

(A) 17
(B) 18
(C) 19
(D) 20
(E) 21

49. A pulley having a 9 inch diameter is belted to a pulley having a 6 inch diameter, as shown in the figure. If the large pulley runs at 120 rpm, how fast does the small pulley run, in revolutions per minute?

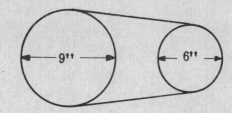

(A) 80
(B) 100
(C) 160
(D) 180
(E) 240

50. In the figure below, the side of the large square is 14. The four smaller squares are formed by joining the mid-points of opposite sides. Find the value of Y.

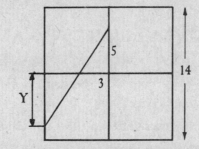

(A) 5
(B) 6
(C) $6\frac{2}{3}$
(D) $6\frac{5}{8}$
(E) 6.8

END OF EXAMINATION

IF YOU FINISH BEFORE TIME IS CALLED, CHECK OVER YOUR WORK ON SECTION II. DO NOT RETURN TO SECTION I.

MODEL EXAMINATION II—ANSWER KEY

Section I

1. C	14. C	27. E	40. A	53. B
2. E	15. E	28. D	41. D	54. B
3. A	16. D	29. A	42. E	55. C
4. B	17. D	30. A	43. D	56. A
5. D	18. A	31. C	44. A	57. D
6. D	19. E	32. D	45. D	58. B
7. E	20. D	33. E	46. D	59. C
8. A	21. C	34. E	47. D	60. D
9. E	22. C	35. B	48. A	61. B
10. B	23. C	36. A	49. B	62. C
11. D	24. B	37. E	50. C	63. E
12. E	25. C	38. D	51. D	64. A
13. C	26. B	39. E	52. A	65. A

Section II

1. D	11. B	21. A	31. D	41. E
2. A	12. A	22. D	32. D	42. A
3. E	13. C	23. C	33. D	43. E
4. B	14. B	24. C	34. E	44. E
5. B	15. A	25. B	35. C	45. A
6. E	16. A	26. C	36. D	46. E
7. A	17. D	27. A	37. B	47. E
8. B	18. C	28. D	38. C	48. C
9. A	19. A	29. A	39. B	49. D
10. C	20. C	30. D	40. A	50. C

EXPLANATORY ANSWERS

Section I

1. **(C)** CAUSE. CONSEQUENCE means effect.

2. **(E)** UNTOUCHABLE. TANGIBLE means real or capable of being touched.

3. **(A)** BRILLIANT means very bright or intelligent. VACUOUS means stupid.

4. **(B)** FIREPROOF. INFLAMMABLE means easily inflamed; in other words, subject to easy ignition and rapid combustion. Hence, inflammable is a synonym for flammable. The "in" in this instance is *not* a negative prefix, but is part of the word inflame.

248

5. **(D)** A DISCOUNT is a deduction from the regular cost of an item. A SURCHARGE is an additional tax or cost added to the regular price of the item.

6. **(D)** VIGOROUS means energetic. LETHARGIC means sluggish.

7. **(E)** EDGE. An AXIS is a central line about which a body rotates. The motions of the earth are to rotate on its axis and to travel about the sun following its orbit. These are separate motions, but they are not opposite, hence (C) is incorrect. During World War II, the Fascist alliance was called the "Axis" while the opposing forces were called the "Allies." This was terminology specific to a situation and does not represent a true antonym, thus (B) is incorrect.

8. **(A)** HUMBLE means meek and modest. SUPERCILIOUS means haughty and proud.

9. **(E)** REACH OUT. WINCE means shrink back.

10. **(B)** ASSAULT means violent attack. PACIFY means attempt to restore calm.

11. **(D)** BARREN means not productive. FECUND means fertile and prolific.

12. **(E)** RELEASE. INCARCERATE means to confine.

13. **(C)** OVERWHELMING means crushingly large. COMPENDIOUS means concise. The noun compendium refers to a brief summary or digest of a large comprehensive subject.

14. **(C)** HUMILITY means humbleness. TEMERITY means nerve or boldness.

15. **(E)** STUBBORN means obstinate. TRACTABLE means obedient or easily led.

16. **(D)** MALEVOLENT means bearing vicious ill will. BENIGN means gentle or harmless.

17. **(D)** ACERB means sour. DULCET means sweet.

18. **(A)** TRANQUIL means calm. TURBID means agitated.

19. **(E)** ADULT. MOPPET means child.

20. **(D)** AWAKENING. SOPORIFIC means causing one to fall asleep.

21. **(C)** The word that is needed must be a synonym for blunder (a stupid or gross mistake). That word is ERROR.

22. **(C)** One who acts purely on impulse is most likely to have a PASSIONATE (emotional or intense) nature.

23. **(C)** Limiting EXPORTS of domestic products will create a larger supply for home consumption. Forbidding IMPORTS of foreign products will force consumers to buy the domestic products.

24. **(B)** The completion needed is a word which is opposite in meaning to "the spinning of fanciful theories." Of the choices given, the study of ORDER best fulfills this requirement.

25. **(C)** Taste is a matter of individual preference, and personal preference in the world of art is a private concern with no effect on the world at large. Therefore, arguments about taste are CHILDISH (foolish and nonproductive).

26. **(B)** The second sentence provides the clue to the meaning of the first. If success does not mean infallibility (certainty), then the fame of an author does not ASSURE the quality of his work.

27. **(E)** The completion here demands words that are opposites. In addition, the first blank requires a word that would promote hatred. Only STRIFE, meaning conflict, and TRANQUILITY, meaning peace, fulfill these requirements and complete the meaning of the sentence.

28. **(D)** If it is not similarity (likeness) in instruments that produces harmony, then each instrument must be UNIQUE (different) when separate. Yet the insubstantiality (frailty) of each one is VITALIZED (given vigor or life) by its association with the others.

29. **(A)** Since mining does not create (bring into being) or replenish (replace) what it takes, it may be called a ROBBER industry. With these characteristics, mining might also be considered to be evil, but ROBBER is the most specific completion. It is the adjective which best describes an industry that does not replenish what it takes.

30. **(A)** The sense of the sentence calls for two words which are opposites and which can both be applied to life forms. Spores are the tiny particles in certain plants which act as seeds in the production of new plants. These spores remain dormant or INACTIVE until the proper conditions exist to render them vigorous or

VIBRANT, thus creating a new generation of plants.

31. **(C)** An OASIS is surrounded by DESERT; an ISLAND is surrounded by OCEAN. This is a variation of the *part to whole* relationship.

32. **(D)** ASTRONOMY is the science of celestial bodies, while ASTROLOGY is the occult (mysterious or supernatural) study of celestial bodies; MATHEMATICS is the science of numbers, while NUMEROLOGY is the occult science of numbers. The relationship is one of *association*.

33. **(E)** An ARDUOUS task is an extremely DIFFICULT one; an ABHORRENT task is extremely DISLIKABLE. The relationship is one of *degree*.

34. **(E)** The MOON is a satellite of the EARTH, attending upon and revolving about the earth; a RETINUE is that body of retainers (servants) which is constantly attendant upon a MONARCH or other person of rank. This is an *association* relationship.

35. **(B)** A STEEPLE is a tower rising over a CHURCH; a MINARET is the tower attached to a MOSQUE. The relationship is that of *part to whole*.

36. **(A)** The DREGS are the worthless residue at the bottom of a WINE barrel; the CHAFF is the worthless part of the GRAIN, which is left over after threshing. The relationship is that of *whole to part*.

37. **(E)** The EDITOR is responsible for the production of a MAGAZINE; the DIRECTOR is responsible for the production of a DRAMA. The relationship is one of *function*.

38. **(D)** A person is likely to become IMPOVERISHED because of LAZINESS; a person is likely to become AFFLUENT because of LUCK. This is an *effect and cause* relationship.

39. **(E)** A VIOLIN is a stringed instrument, smaller and more high pitched than a BASS; a PICCOLO is a woodwind instrument, smaller and more high pitched than a BASSOON. The relationship is one of *degree*.

40. **(A)** To be DRUNKEN is to be extremely TIPSY; to be THRILLED is to be extremely PLEASED. The relationship is one of *degree*.

41. **(D)** A SQUARE is a POLYGON (a closed plane figure bounded by straight lines); an ELLIPSE is a closed plane CURVE. The relationship is one of *definition*.

42. **(E)** MARGARINE is a man-made BUTTER substitute; SACCHARIN is a man-made SUGAR substitute. The relationship is one of *association*.

43. **(D)** To CRAVE is to WISH or desire very strongly; to DEMAND is to REQUEST very strongly. The relationship is one of *degree*.

44. **(A)** A THROTTLE controls the flow of FUEL; a FAUCET controls the flow of WATER. The relationship is one of *function*.

45. **(D)** VORACITY is an insatiable desire for FOOD; GREED is an insatiable desire for MONEY. The relationship is one of *association*.

46. **(D)** The attitude of the candidate would be likely to encourage anti-nuclear agitators. Those people who oppose further development of nuclear power for the production of energy fear the danger of radiation from leaks and worry about the problems of disposal of nuclear waste. If the attitude of the candidate were to prevail, the belief in the need for new sources of energy would dissipate and the anti-nuclear agitators might prevail as well.

47. **(D)** Regardless of what is known of "proven" reserves in Saudi Arabia or what is proven about "potential" reserves in Alaska, one must, in addition, believe in the validity of the formula in order to accept the contention that there is *more* oil in Alaska than in Saudi Arabia.

48. **(A)** Even if it is true that there is a vast supply of oil beneath Alaska, this oil is not instantly available. Locating the oil, establishing drilling facilities and arranging for transportation involve a great deal of time and expense. During the long period of development of the Alaskan resources, the foreign suppliers would most assuredly raise their prices. Pass-along of development costs would assure that prices would not go down, even with self-sufficiency. Increase in oil supplies would be a later development.

49. **(B)** Since the candidate contends that the oil reserves are located in wilderness preserves where exploration is prohibited by statute, the

first energy program he would present to Congress would have to press for reversal of this restrictive legislation.

50. **(C)** If we were not so dependent upon their oil, the Persian Gulf nations would lower their prices to achieve competitive status with domestic oil producers and alternative fuels. The political power of the Gulf countries is based upon other nations' dependency upon their oil supplies. Were this dependency to disappear, the power of the Gulf countries would also disappear.

51. **(D)** The author deals at great length with the advantages of automated blood analysis. He cites both the cost benefits and the health benefits. In the final paragraph he briefly mentions the opposition, but shows no sympathy with it.

52. **(A)** See the second paragraph.

53. **(B)** Some of the components of the machine were made in America, but the idea was strictly a Swedish one, specifically that of the Jungner brothers.

54. **(B)** As announced in the first sentence, the passage deals with the health check-up system being implemented in Sweden. The passage deals with the system of initial screening through multiple-blood analyses made possible by high-speed automated equipment.

55. **(C)** The Jungners are chemists. Theirs is a chemical screening process. (See line 35.)

56. **(A)** This is the only sensible choice. The passage does not deal with the differences betweeen the foods of different nations nor does it deal with various ways of preparing food nor with the food value of fish.

57. **(D)** The reviewer praises the book's scope, the exhaustiveness of its material and the intelligence of its innovative suggestions.

58. **(B)** Since the Weber fraction deals with the relationships between stimuli and perception it must certainly have been originated by and named after a physiologist.

59. **(C)** Not only is this view not expressed, but it is made quite clear that the senses serve to enhance the appeal of food but certainly not to determine its food value. On the contrary, some of the

foods which may have the greatest sensory appeal may be the least nutritious.

60. **(D)** Muscular movement is not a sense, so cannot be subsumed under "Other." "Olfaction" is smell, "Visual" refers to sight, "Tactile" refers to touch, and "Auditory" refers to hearing.

61. **(B)** The reference is to England; the spelling of "labourer" is the English spelling; a shilling is an English monetary unit.

62. **(C)** The church is never mentioned in this passage, nor are forms of government as such. The author is quite clearly anticapitalist in his sneering remark of lines 20 to 25. On the other hand, the author seems to be arguing for the fair and equal distribution of the necessities and niceties of life and seems quite unconcerned with the need for wealth, so socialism would be his ideal.

63. **(E)** The suggestion in lines 20 to 25 shows how the same act is open to various interpretations.

64. **(A)** The analogy which the author makes is that of the rich man with the robber. The passage does not discuss the honesty of businessmen nor does it condone any dishonesty. Further, the passage points out the fallacy in the thinking that destruction of property is good because it creates consumer demand. The discussion of robber as benefactor is a facetious one.

65. **(A)** The passage states quite definitely, ". . . this is no excuse for the theft." On the other hand, it implies that selling useless objects is a legal way to rob the poor and that the nation-at-large does not care about the poor.

SECTION II

1. **(D)** $\frac{3}{4} = .75$

   $\frac{35}{71}$ is slightly less than $\frac{35}{70} = .5$

   $\frac{13}{20} = \frac{13 \times 5}{20 \times 5} = \frac{65}{100} = .65$

   $\frac{71}{101}$ is very close to $\frac{7}{10}$ or .7

$$\frac{15}{20} = \frac{15 \times 5}{20 \times 5} = \frac{75}{100} = .75$$

which equals $\frac{3}{4}$

$$\frac{19}{24} = \begin{array}{r} .79 \text{ which is more than } \frac{3}{4} \\ 24\overline{)19.00} \\ \underline{168} \\ 220 \\ \underline{216} \end{array}$$

2. **(A)**
$$820 + R + S - 610 = 342$$
$$R + S + 210 = 342$$
$$R + S = 132$$
If $R = 2S$, then $2S + S = 132$
$$3S = 132$$
$$S = 44$$

3. **(E)**

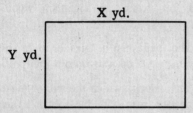

X yd.

Y yd.

Area = xy sq. yd.
= 9 xy sq. ft.
9 xy · 2 = 18 xy

4. **(B)**
$$7M = 3M - 20$$
$$4M = -20$$
$$M = -5$$
$$M + 7 = -5 + 7 = 2$$

5. **(B)** Arc EA = 85° and arc BD = 15°, since a central angle is measured by its arc; then

angle ECA = $\frac{1}{2}$(AE − BD)
= $\frac{1}{2}$(85 − 15)
= $\frac{1}{2}$ · 70
= 35°

6. **(E)** If we know only the hypotenuse of a right triangle, we cannot determine its legs. Hence, the area of the rectangle cannot be determined from the data given.

7. **(A)** If angle P > angle Q, then $\frac{1}{2}$ angle P > $\frac{1}{2}$ angle Q; then angle SPQ > angle SQP. Since the larger side lies opposite the larger angle, it follows that SQ > SP.

8. **(B)** Since Z is equidistant from X and Y, it must lie on the Y-axis. Then △OZY is a

30° − 60° − 90° triangle with YZ = 8
Hence OZ = $\frac{8}{2}\sqrt{3}$ = $4\sqrt{3}$
Coordinates of Z are $(0, 4\sqrt{3})$

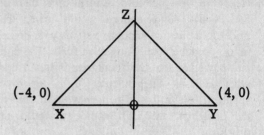

9. **(A)** Since ACB is a straight angle and angle DCE is a right angle, then angle ACD and angle BCE are complementary. Hence BCE= 90 − x.

10. **(C)** The smallest, positive number divisible by 3, 4, or 5 is 3 · 4 · 5 = 60. Hence the desired number is

60 + 2 = 62

11. **(B)** Since there are 4d quarter miles in d miles, the charge = 20 + 5 (4d − 1)

12. **(A)** Assume that there are 100 men on the post; then 30 are from New York State and $\frac{1}{10}$ × 30 = 3 are from New York City.
$\frac{3}{100}$ = 3%

13. **(C)** Rise in temp. = 36 − (− 14) = 36 + 14 = 50° $\frac{50}{5}$ = 10° (hourly rise)

Hence, at noon, temp. = −14 + 3(10) = −14 + 30 = +16°

14. **(B)** 9 = 8 + 1 = 7 + 2 = 6 + 3 = 5 + 4
Thus, 4 ways

15. **(A)** $\frac{7 \text{ ft. } 9 \text{ in.}}{3} = \frac{6 \text{ ft. } 21 \text{ in.}}{3}$ = 2 ft. 7 in.

16. **(A)**
$$\overline{AB} = \sqrt{(\Delta x)^2 + (\Delta y)^2}$$
$$= \sqrt{36 + 16}$$
$$= \sqrt{52}$$
$$\overline{AC} = \sqrt{(\Delta x)^2 + (\Delta y)^2}$$
$$= \sqrt{(0)^2 + (7)^2}$$
$$= \sqrt{49}$$

∴ Column A > Column B

17. **(D)** The value of ∠x or ∠y cannot be determined unless the measure of at least one angle is known.

18. **(C)**
A triangle inscribed in a parallelogram is equal in area to one-half the parallelogram. Therefore the area of $\triangle DEC$ equals the combined areas of $\triangle ADE$ and $\triangle EBC$.

19. **(A)**
$x^3 + x^2 - x + 1 =$
$$(-1)^3 + (-1)^2 - (-1) + 1$$
$$= -1 + 1 + 1 + 1$$
$$= 2$$
$x^3 - x^2 + x - 1 =$
$$(-1)^3 - (-1)^2 + (-1) - 1$$
$$= -1 - 1 - 1 - 1$$
$$= -4$$

$\therefore$ Column A > Column B

20. **(C)**
$$e^3 = 27 \qquad 6e^2 = 54$$
$$e = 3 \qquad e^2 = 9$$
$$e = 3$$

$\therefore$ Column A = Column B

21. **(A)**

$$\frac{\frac{1}{2} + \frac{1}{3}}{\frac{2}{3}} = \frac{\frac{3+2}{6}}{\frac{2}{3}}$$

$$= \frac{\frac{5}{6}}{\frac{2}{3}}$$

$$= \frac{\frac{15}{12}}{1} \text{ (multiplying numerator and denominator by } \tfrac{3}{2})$$

$$= \frac{15}{12}$$

$$\frac{\frac{2}{3}}{\frac{1}{2} + \frac{1}{3}} = \frac{\frac{2}{3}}{\frac{3+2}{6}}$$

$$= \frac{\frac{2}{3}}{\frac{5}{6}}$$

$$= \frac{\frac{12}{15}}{1} \text{ (multiplying numerator and denominator by } \tfrac{6}{5})$$

$$= \frac{12}{15}$$
$$\frac{15}{12} > \frac{12}{15}$$

$\therefore$ Column A > Column B

22. **(D)**
We cannot determine the areas of the circles unless the value of x is known.

23. **(C)**
$$[(-\tfrac{1}{2})^2]^3 = (\tfrac{1}{4})^3 \qquad [(-\tfrac{1}{2})^3]^2 = (-\tfrac{1}{8})^2$$
$$= \tfrac{1}{64} \qquad\qquad\qquad = \tfrac{1}{64}$$

$\therefore$ Column A = Column B

24. **(C)**

$$(\tfrac{1}{4})^{-2} = \frac{1}{(\tfrac{1}{4})^2} \qquad 4^2 = 16$$

$$= \frac{1}{\tfrac{1}{16}}$$

$$= 16$$

$\therefore$ Column A = Column B

25. **(B)**
$$.02 = \sqrt{.0004}$$
$$\therefore \sqrt{.02} > \sqrt{.0004}$$

$\therefore$ Column B > Column A

26. **(C)**
By the Pythagorean Theorem
$$(AB)^2 = (AC)^2 + (BC)^2$$
However,
$$(BC)^2 = 5^2 = 25$$
and
$$5CB = 5 \cdot 5 = 25$$
$$\therefore (BC)^2 = 5CB$$
$$\therefore (AB)^2 = (AC)^2 + 5CB$$
(substituting 5CB for $(BC)^2$ in the Pythagorean Theorem)

$\therefore$ Column A = Column B

27. **(A)**
Area of circle $= \pi r^2$
$$= \pi (7)^2$$
$$= 49\pi$$

Area of equilateral triangle $= \dfrac{8^2}{4}\sqrt{3}$

$$= \frac{(14)^2}{4}\sqrt{3}$$

$$= \frac{196}{4}\sqrt{3}$$

$$= 49\sqrt{3}$$

$$49\pi > 49\sqrt{3}$$

$\therefore$ Column A > Column B

28. **(D)**
Not enough information is given to determine the values of the angles.

29. **(A)**

$$\begin{pmatrix} \text{Area of} \\ \text{shaded} \\ \text{portion} \end{pmatrix} = \begin{pmatrix} \text{Area of} \\ \text{larger} \\ \text{circle} \end{pmatrix} - \begin{pmatrix} \text{Area of} \\ \text{smaller} \\ \text{circle} \end{pmatrix}$$

$$= \pi(10^2) - \pi(7^2)$$
$$= 100\pi - 49\pi$$
$$= 51\pi$$

$$\begin{pmatrix} \text{Area of} \\ \text{smaller} \\ \text{circle} \end{pmatrix} = \pi r^2$$

$$= \pi(7^2)$$
$$= 49\pi$$

$$51\pi > 49\pi$$

$$\therefore \text{ Column A} > \text{Column B}$$

30. **(D)**

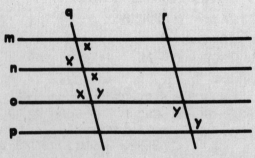

All that can be determined is that x and y are supplementary.

31. **(D)**
There is insufficient information to determine an answer.

32. **(D)**
There is insufficient information to determine an answer.

33. **(D)** Area of Square $= 2^2 = 4$
Area of Circle $= \pi \cdot 1^2 = \pi$
Difference $= 4 - \pi = 4 - 3.14 = .86$

34. **(E)** $3.14 \times 10^6 = 3.14 \times 1,000,000$
$$= 3,140,000$$

35. **(C)** $\dfrac{36}{29 - \dfrac{4}{0.2}} = \dfrac{36}{29 - 20} = \dfrac{36}{9} = 4$

36. **(D)** Diameter $= 4\sqrt{2}$, since it is the hypotenuse of a right isosceles $\triangle$ of leg 4
Then the radius $= 2\sqrt{2}$
Area of semicircle $= \frac{1}{2} \times \pi (2\sqrt{2})^2$
$$= \frac{1}{2} \times \pi \cdot 8 = 4\pi$$

37. **(B)** Consecutive odd numbers may be represented as $2n + 1$
$$2n + 3$$
$$\underline{2n + 5}$$
$$\text{Sum} = 6n + 9$$
Always divisible by 3. Thus, only II.

38. **(C)** Angle BCD is formed by tangent and chord and is equal to one-half arc BC. Angle A is inscribed angle and also equal to one-half of arc BC.
Hence angle A = angle BCD = 40°

39. **(B)** Let x = amount of marked price.
Then $\frac{1}{5}x = 15$
$$x = 75$$
$$75 - 15 = \$60$$

40. **(A)** Since the ice cubes are 2 inches on an edge, there can be only 2 layers of 8 cubes each or a total of 16 cubes.

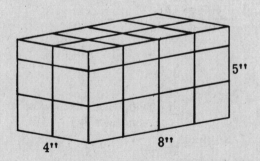

41. **(E)** There is a double recurring pattern here as indicated: Multiply by .5; then multiply by 3. Hence, the last term is 27.

42. **(A)** The new solution is $\frac{3}{20}$ pure alcohol or 15%.

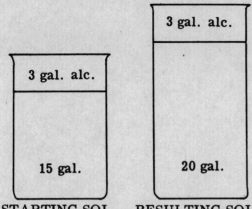

STARTING SOL.   RESULTING SOL.

43. **(E)** Area of ▱ = XR × altitude from P to XR.

Area of $\triangle$XPR = $\frac{1}{2}$ XR × altitude from P to XR.

Hence, ratio of area of $\triangle$ to ▱ = 1:2

44. **(E)** x(p + 1) = M Divide both sides by x.

$$p + 1 = \frac{M}{x}$$

$$\text{or } p = \frac{M}{x} - 1$$

45. **(A)** $\dfrac{T}{1} = \dfrac{x}{60M}$

x = 60 MT

46. **(E)** If $\dfrac{P}{Q} = \dfrac{4}{5}$

Then 5P = 4Q

However, there is no way of determining from this the value of 2P + Q.

47. **(E)** The right triangle of which T is hypotenuse has legs which are obviously 6 inches and 9 inches.

Hence, $T^2 = 6^2 + 9^2$
$T^2 = 36 + 81 = 117$
$T = \sqrt{117}$
or 10 < T < 11

48. **(C)** Let x = number of questions correct.
25 − x = number of questions wrong.

Then 4x − 1(25 − x) = 70
$\qquad$ 4x − 25 + x = 70
$\qquad\qquad\qquad$ 5x = 95
$\qquad\qquad\qquad\quad$ x = 19

49. **(D)** This is an inverse proportion; that is:

$$\frac{9}{6} = \frac{x}{120}$$

6x = 1080
x = 180

50. **(C)** The similar triangles in the configuration produce the proportion

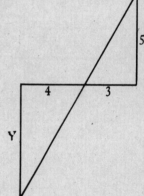

$$\frac{3}{5} = \frac{4}{Y}$$

3Y = 20
Y = $6\frac{2}{3}$

ANSWER SHEET FOR MODEL EXAMINATION III

Completely blacken the answer space of your choice. Mark only one answer for each question. Erase stray marks.

SECTION I
VERBAL

1 Ⓐ Ⓑ Ⓒ Ⓓ Ⓔ	12 Ⓐ Ⓑ Ⓒ Ⓓ Ⓔ	23 Ⓐ Ⓑ Ⓒ Ⓓ Ⓔ	34 Ⓐ Ⓑ Ⓒ Ⓓ Ⓔ	45 Ⓐ Ⓑ Ⓒ Ⓓ Ⓔ	56 Ⓐ Ⓑ Ⓒ Ⓓ Ⓔ
2 Ⓐ Ⓑ Ⓒ Ⓓ Ⓔ	13 Ⓐ Ⓑ Ⓒ Ⓓ Ⓔ	24 Ⓐ Ⓑ Ⓒ Ⓓ Ⓔ	35 Ⓐ Ⓑ Ⓒ Ⓓ Ⓔ	46 Ⓐ Ⓑ Ⓒ Ⓓ Ⓔ	57 Ⓐ Ⓑ Ⓒ Ⓓ Ⓔ
3 Ⓐ Ⓑ Ⓒ Ⓓ Ⓔ	14 Ⓐ Ⓑ Ⓒ Ⓓ Ⓔ	25 Ⓐ Ⓑ Ⓒ Ⓓ Ⓔ	36 Ⓐ Ⓑ Ⓒ Ⓓ Ⓔ	47 Ⓐ Ⓑ Ⓒ Ⓓ Ⓔ	58 Ⓐ Ⓑ Ⓒ Ⓓ Ⓔ
4 Ⓐ Ⓑ Ⓒ Ⓓ Ⓔ	15 Ⓐ Ⓑ Ⓒ Ⓓ Ⓔ	26 Ⓐ Ⓑ Ⓒ Ⓓ Ⓔ	37 Ⓐ Ⓑ Ⓒ Ⓓ Ⓔ	48 Ⓐ Ⓑ Ⓒ Ⓓ Ⓔ	59 Ⓐ Ⓑ Ⓒ Ⓓ Ⓔ
5 Ⓐ Ⓑ Ⓒ Ⓓ Ⓔ	16 Ⓐ Ⓑ Ⓒ Ⓓ Ⓔ	27 Ⓐ Ⓑ Ⓒ Ⓓ Ⓔ	38 Ⓐ Ⓑ Ⓒ Ⓓ Ⓔ	49 Ⓐ Ⓑ Ⓒ Ⓓ Ⓔ	60 Ⓐ Ⓑ Ⓒ Ⓓ Ⓔ
6 Ⓐ Ⓑ Ⓒ Ⓓ Ⓔ	17 Ⓐ Ⓑ Ⓒ Ⓓ Ⓔ	28 Ⓐ Ⓑ Ⓒ Ⓓ Ⓔ	39 Ⓐ Ⓑ Ⓒ Ⓓ Ⓔ	50 Ⓐ Ⓑ Ⓒ Ⓓ Ⓔ	61 Ⓐ Ⓑ Ⓒ Ⓓ Ⓔ
7 Ⓐ Ⓑ Ⓒ Ⓓ Ⓔ	18 Ⓐ Ⓑ Ⓒ Ⓓ Ⓔ	29 Ⓐ Ⓑ Ⓒ Ⓓ Ⓔ	40 Ⓐ Ⓑ Ⓒ Ⓓ Ⓔ	51 Ⓐ Ⓑ Ⓒ Ⓓ Ⓔ	62 Ⓐ Ⓑ Ⓒ Ⓓ Ⓔ
8 Ⓐ Ⓑ Ⓒ Ⓓ Ⓔ	19 Ⓐ Ⓑ Ⓒ Ⓓ Ⓔ	30 Ⓐ Ⓑ Ⓒ Ⓓ Ⓔ	41 Ⓐ Ⓑ Ⓒ Ⓓ Ⓔ	52 Ⓐ Ⓑ Ⓒ Ⓓ Ⓔ	63 Ⓐ Ⓑ Ⓒ Ⓓ Ⓔ
9 Ⓐ Ⓑ Ⓒ Ⓓ Ⓔ	20 Ⓐ Ⓑ Ⓒ Ⓓ Ⓔ	31 Ⓐ Ⓑ Ⓒ Ⓓ Ⓔ	42 Ⓐ Ⓑ Ⓒ Ⓓ Ⓔ	53 Ⓐ Ⓑ Ⓒ Ⓓ Ⓔ	64 Ⓐ Ⓑ Ⓒ Ⓓ Ⓔ
10 Ⓐ Ⓑ Ⓒ Ⓓ Ⓔ	21 Ⓐ Ⓑ Ⓒ Ⓓ Ⓔ	32 Ⓐ Ⓑ Ⓒ Ⓓ Ⓔ	43 Ⓐ Ⓑ Ⓒ Ⓓ Ⓔ	54 Ⓐ Ⓑ Ⓒ Ⓓ Ⓔ	65 Ⓐ Ⓑ Ⓒ Ⓓ Ⓔ
11 Ⓐ Ⓑ Ⓒ Ⓓ Ⓔ	22 Ⓐ Ⓑ Ⓒ Ⓓ Ⓔ	33 Ⓐ Ⓑ Ⓒ Ⓓ Ⓔ	44 Ⓐ Ⓑ Ⓒ Ⓓ Ⓔ	55 Ⓐ Ⓑ Ⓒ Ⓓ Ⓔ	

SECTION II
MATHEMATICAL

1 Ⓐ Ⓑ Ⓒ Ⓓ Ⓔ	10 Ⓐ Ⓑ Ⓒ Ⓓ Ⓔ	19 Ⓐ Ⓑ Ⓒ Ⓓ	27 Ⓐ Ⓑ Ⓒ Ⓓ	35 Ⓐ Ⓑ Ⓒ Ⓓ Ⓔ	43 Ⓐ Ⓑ Ⓒ Ⓓ Ⓔ
2 Ⓐ Ⓑ Ⓒ Ⓓ Ⓔ	11 Ⓐ Ⓑ Ⓒ Ⓓ Ⓔ	20 Ⓐ Ⓑ Ⓒ Ⓓ	28 Ⓐ Ⓑ Ⓒ Ⓓ	36 Ⓐ Ⓑ Ⓒ Ⓓ Ⓔ	44 Ⓐ Ⓑ Ⓒ Ⓓ Ⓔ
3 Ⓐ Ⓑ Ⓒ Ⓓ Ⓔ	12 Ⓐ Ⓑ Ⓒ Ⓓ Ⓔ	21 Ⓐ Ⓑ Ⓒ Ⓓ	29 Ⓐ Ⓑ Ⓒ Ⓓ	37 Ⓐ Ⓑ Ⓒ Ⓓ Ⓔ	45 Ⓐ Ⓑ Ⓒ Ⓓ Ⓔ
4 Ⓐ Ⓑ Ⓒ Ⓓ Ⓔ	13 Ⓐ Ⓑ Ⓒ Ⓓ Ⓔ	22 Ⓐ Ⓑ Ⓒ Ⓓ	30 Ⓐ Ⓑ Ⓒ Ⓓ	38 Ⓐ Ⓑ Ⓒ Ⓓ Ⓔ	46 Ⓐ Ⓑ Ⓒ Ⓓ Ⓔ
5 Ⓐ Ⓑ Ⓒ Ⓓ Ⓔ	14 Ⓐ Ⓑ Ⓒ Ⓓ Ⓔ	23 Ⓐ Ⓑ Ⓒ Ⓓ	31 Ⓐ Ⓑ Ⓒ Ⓓ	39 Ⓐ Ⓑ Ⓒ Ⓓ Ⓔ	47 Ⓐ Ⓑ Ⓒ Ⓓ Ⓔ
6 Ⓐ Ⓑ Ⓒ Ⓓ Ⓔ	15 Ⓐ Ⓑ Ⓒ Ⓓ Ⓔ	24 Ⓐ Ⓑ Ⓒ Ⓓ	32 Ⓐ Ⓑ Ⓒ Ⓓ	40 Ⓐ Ⓑ Ⓒ Ⓓ Ⓔ	48 Ⓐ Ⓑ Ⓒ Ⓓ Ⓔ
7 Ⓐ Ⓑ Ⓒ Ⓓ Ⓔ	16 Ⓐ Ⓑ Ⓒ Ⓓ	25 Ⓐ Ⓑ Ⓒ Ⓓ	33 Ⓐ Ⓑ Ⓒ Ⓓ Ⓔ	41 Ⓐ Ⓑ Ⓒ Ⓓ Ⓔ	49 Ⓐ Ⓑ Ⓒ Ⓓ Ⓔ
8 Ⓐ Ⓑ Ⓒ Ⓓ Ⓔ	17 Ⓐ Ⓑ Ⓒ Ⓓ	26 Ⓐ Ⓑ Ⓒ Ⓓ	34 Ⓐ Ⓑ Ⓒ Ⓓ Ⓔ	42 Ⓐ Ⓑ Ⓒ Ⓓ Ⓔ	50 Ⓐ Ⓑ Ⓒ Ⓓ Ⓔ
9 Ⓐ Ⓑ Ⓒ Ⓓ Ⓔ	18 Ⓐ Ⓑ Ⓒ Ⓓ				

SCORE SHEET

Raw Scores

ANTONYMS ___ — ___ ÷ 4 = ___
SENTENCE COMPLETIONS ___ — ___ ÷ 4 = ___
VERBAL ANALOGIES ___ — ___ ÷ 4 = ___
READING COMPREHENSION ___ — ___ ÷ 4 = ___

Total Verbal Score ___

MATHEMATICAL PROBLEMS ___ — ___ ÷ 4 = ___

Note: Do not forget to add together the two sets of problems that come before and after "Quantitative Comparisons."

QUANTITATIVE COMPARISONS ___ — ___ ÷ 3 = ___

Total Mathematical Score ___

Percents

ANTONYMS ___ (score) ÷ 20 = ___ × 100 = ___%
SENTENCE COMPLETIONS ___ (score) ÷ 10 = ___ × 100 = ___%
VERBAL ANALOGIES ___ (score) ÷ 15 = ___ × 100 = ___%
READING COMPREHENSION ___ (score) ÷ 20 = ___ × 100 = ___%
MATHEMATICAL PROBLEMS ___ (score) ÷ 33 = ___ × 100 = ___%
QUANTITATIVE COMPARISONS ___ (score) ÷ 17 = ___ × 100 = ___%
TOTAL VERBAL ___ (total verbal score) ÷ 65 = ___ × 100 = ___%
TOTAL MATH ___ (total math score) ÷ 50 = ___ × 100 = ___%

PROGRESS CHART

	Exam I	Exam II	Exam III
ANTONYMS	%	%	%
SENTENCE COMPLETIONS	%	%	%
VERBAL ANALOGIES	%	%	%
READING COMPREHENSION	%	%	%
MATHEMATICAL PROBLEMS	%	%	%
QUANTITATIVE COMPARISONS	%	%	%

MODEL EXAMINATION III

Section I
Time—50 minutes; 65 questions

DIRECTIONS: For each question, mark the letter preceding the word or phrase that is opposite or most nearly opposite in meaning to the capitalized word. Where more than one option appears to be correct, choose the *best* opposite.

Example:

BRAVE

(A) sensible
(B) sensitive
(C) cowardly
(D) strong
(E) weak

1. MUTINY

   (A) exchange
   (B) excess
   (C) valor
   (D) hesitation
   (E) obedience

2. ASSAIL

   (A) pretend
   (B) conceal
   (C) divide
   (D) commend
   (E) despise

3. OBSCURE

   (A) disclose
   (B) dishonor
   (C) discover

(D) disavow
(E) disable

4. TENACITY

   (A) vacillation
   (B) inspiration
   (C) retaliation
   (D) equalization
   (E) purification

5. SLOVENLY

   (A) youthful
   (B) intelligent
   (C) swift
   (D) popular
   (E) tidy

6. EXORBITANT

   (A) axiomatic
   (B) astral
   (C) reasonable
   (D) disobedient
   (E) obedient

7. ANTECEDENT

   (A) agreement
   (B) opposition
   (C) prerequisite
   (D) preventative
   (E) subsequent

8. CAPTIVATE

   (A) alienate
   (B) stipulate
   (C) stimulate
   (D) indicate
   (E) palliate

9. COMPLIANCE

(A) profanity
(B) strictness
(C) approval
(D) freedom
(E) rebellion

10. INTELLIGIBLE

(A) dull
(B) unclear
(C) faulty
(D) unteachable
(E) pathetic

11. CONSENSUS

(A) poll
(B) disharmony
(C) conference
(D) attitude
(E) miscount

12. SAVANT

(A) diplomat
(B) master
(C) moron
(D) miser
(E) spendthrift

13. LIMPID

(A) stiff
(B) strong
(C) vivid
(D) translucent
(E) muddy

14. ASSUAGE

(A) cleanse
(B) sway
(C) aggravate
(D) bless
(E) advance

15. NEFARIOUS

(A) grotesque
(B) virtuous
(C) jovial
(D) pious
(E) ugly

16. SANGUINARY

(A) holy
(B) bitter
(C) grainy
(D) pale
(E) kind

17. OSCILLATORY

(A) suborbital
(B) hugging
(C) stationary
(D) angry
(E) agreeable

18. SECRETE

(A) surprise
(B) smell
(C) immigrate
(D) lavish
(E) display

19. CONSCRIPT

(A) typewrite
(B) volunteer
(C) scribble
(D) duplicate
(E) rebut

20. TURGID

(A) dry
(B) simple
(C) pious
(D) muddy
(E) tranquil

DIRECTIONS: Each of the following questions consists of an incomplete sentence followed by five words or pairs of words. Choose that word or pair of words which, when substituted for the blank space or spaces, *best* completes the meaning of the sentence and mark the letter of your choice on your answer sheet.

Example:

Although he has a reputation for _____, his manner on that occasion was so _____ that everyone felt perfectly at ease.

(A) friendliness . . reluctant
(B) aloofness . . gracious
(C) flightiness . . malign
(D) fabrication . . plausible
(E) fawning . . hostile

Ⓐ ● Ⓒ Ⓓ Ⓔ

---

21. Human knowledge is an outgrowth of _____ experience, and even a genius can only create on the basis of his _____.

    (A) actual . . studies
    (B) past . . heritage
    (C) understandable . . experiments
    (D) intellectual . . dexterity
    (E) religious . . superiority

22. The _____ mob roamed through the streets of the city, shouting their _____ of law and order.

    (A) influential . . fear
    (B) indifferent . . horror
    (C) disciplined . . disrespect
    (D) hysterical . . hatred
    (E) extraneous . . support

23. Errors in existing theories are discovered, and the theories are either _____ or _____.

    (A) improved . . obeyed
    (B) removed . . followed
    (C) altered . . discarded
    (D) explained . . excused
    (E) accepted . . rejected

24. In observing the _____ society of the ant, the scientist can learn much about the more _____ society of man.

(A) hostile . . evil
(B) elementary . . complicated
(C) plain . . homogeneous
(D) unadorned . . unsophisticated
(E) significant . . natural

25. Hope springs eternal, and a man who has been _____ all his life will still come to the conclusion that he is _____.

    (A) happy . . sad
    (B) wrong . . right
    (C) healthy . . strong
    (D) good . . evil
    (E) imprisoned . . guilty

26. The desire for peace should not be equated with _____, for _____ peace can be maintained only by brave men.

    (A) cowardice . . lasting
    (B) bravery . . stable
    (C) intelligence . . ignoble
    (D) pacification . . transitory
    (E) neutrality . . apathetic

27. Government often seems to regard money as the route to social salvation: a _____ for all the troubles of humanity.

    (A) provocation
    (B) standard
    (C) panacea
    (D) nucleus
    (E) resource

28. By using a flood control reservoir for _____ before the threat of a flood, the ability of the reservoir to control the flood is _____.

    (A) control . . impeded
    (B) storage . . lessened
    (C) recreation . . improved
    (D) emergencies . . weakened
    (E) evaporation . . reduced

29. The racial problem is of such _____ that it makes going to the moon seem _____.

    (A) complexity . . helpful
    (B) certainty . . problematic
    (C) magnitude . . child's play
    (D) docility . . effortless
    (E) distinctness . . necessary

30. To be _____ a theatrical setting must resemble
_____.

    (A) believable .. home
    (B) effective .. reality
    (C) reasonable .. beauty
    (D) respectable .. ideas
    (E) noticeable .. nature

**DIRECTIONS: Each of the following questions consists
of a capitalized pair of words followed by five pairs of
words lettered A to E. The capitalized words bear some
meaningful relationship to each other. Choose the lettered pair of words whose relationship is most similar
to that expressed by the capitalized pair and mark its
letter on your answer sheet.**

Example:

PIG : PORK ::

    (A) steer : beef
    (B) ranch : cattle
    (C) cow : steer
    (D) pony : horse
    (E) steer : cow

---

31. ARGUMENT : DEBATE ::

    (A) philosophy : psychology
    (B) challenge : opponent
    (C) violence : peace
    (D) individual : group
    (E) fight : contest

32. LETTUCE : LEAF ::

    (A) potato : eye
    (B) rose : thorn
    (C) onion : bulb
    (D) grass : stem
    (E) grape : vine

33. SODIUM : SALT ::

    (A) soda : solution
    (B) molecule : atom
    (C) oxygen : water

    (D) chemistry : biochemistry
    (E) analysis : synthesis

34. DAM : WATER ::

    (A) over : under
    (B) embargo : trade
    (C) curse : H_2O
    (D) beaver : fish
    (E) river : stream

35. CALIBER : RIFLE ::

    (A) reputation : blast
    (B) compass : bore
    (C) army : navy
    (D) gauge : rails
    (E) cavalry : infantry

36. CHOP : MINCE ::

    (A) fry : bake
    (B) meat : cake
    (C) axe : mallet
    (D) Washington : Lincoln
    (E) stir : beat

37. PECCADILLO : CRIME ::

    (A) district attorney : criminal
    (B) hesitate : procrastinate
    (C) armadillo : bone
    (D) bushel : peck
    (E) sheriff : jail

38. WOOD : PAPER ::

    (A) iron : steel
    (B) chair : wall
    (C) cut : clip
    (D) fireplace : lighter
    (E) forest : fire

39. CONCRETE : ADOBE ::

    (A) brick : building
    (B) paper : papyrus
    (C) American : Mexican
    (D) pour : spill
    (E) contractor : purchaser

40. PUBLICATION : LIBEL ::

    (A) newspaper : editorial
    (B) radio : television

(C) information : liability
(D) journalism : attack
(E) speech : slander

41. CANAL : PANAMA ::

(A) water : country
(B) ships : commerce
(C) chord : circle
(D) locks : waterway
(E) country : continent

42. ALLEVIATE : AGGRAVATE ::

(A) joke : worry
(B) elevate : agree
(C) level : grade
(D) plastic : rigid
(E) alluvial : gravelly

43. BEHAVIOR : IMPROPRIETY ::

(A) honesty : morality
(B) freedom : servitude
(C) response : stimulus
(D) word : malapropism
(E) grammar : usage

44. ELM : TREE ::

(A) dollar : dime
(B) currency : dime
(C) map : leaves
(D) oak : maple
(E) dollar : money

45. DOCTOR : DISEASE ::

(A) miser : money
(B) illness : prescription
(C) sheriff : crime
(D) theft : punishment
(E) intern : hospital

DIRECTIONS: Below each of the following passages, you will find five questions or incomplete statements about the passage. Each statement or question is followed by five response options. Read the passage carefully. On the basis of what was stated or implied in the passage, select the option which *best* completes each statement or answers each question. You may refer to the passage as often as necessary. Mark the letter of your choice on your answer sheet.

The future of the American project to drill a hole through the mantle of the Earth now seems in doubt. Recently, the Committee on Science and Astronautics of the U. S. House of Representatives jibbed at approving the new estimate of 28 million dollars for the cost of completing the Mohole. It remains to be seen whether the corresponding Senate committee will take the same view, but the prospects are not encouraging. For even if the Senate should consider that present costs are justifiable, the difference between the House and the Senate would somehow have to be reconciled before work could go ahead. Nobody will be surprised that those most closely associated with the Mohole project have been cast down by this latest twist in the long tortuous history of this project.

Two separate questions arise. The wisdom of the House Committee's decision is, for example, open to question, chiefly because the Mohole project is now so far advanced. A technique for drilling deep holes in the ocean floor has been developed, and orders for the drilling barges have been placed. By canceling now, Congress will save only a portion of the total cost of the Mohole. It is capricious, to say the least of it, for the politicians to pull hard on the pursestrings at this late stage. It would have been much more to the point if they had taken a hard skeptical look at the project four years ago, for there was then good reason for believing that the drilling program was being pushed ahead too quickly and with too little preliminary study. A more deliberate program might have been easier to contain within the bounds of a public budget, and might have been more rewarding as well. But Congress cannot put the clock back to the beginning by a crude cancellation.

The second issue is even more alarming. Hitherto, Congress has not exercised to any important extent its constitutional right to arbitrate on the fine details of scientific programs financed by public money. It is true that plans for building—and siting—big particle accelerators have usually been examined in detail by Congressional committees, and the National Institutes of Health have occasionally been showered with more money than they could usefully spend. But the great public agencies have usually been allowed to manage their own affairs within the framework of a budget agreed by Congress. Though the details of the program of the National Science Foundation have been examined by Congress in the process of accounting for the spending of public money, Congress has usually trusted the judgment of its scientific public servants on the disposition of these funds. On the face of it, the Mohole decision looks like a departure from this practice. It could be a dangerous precedent.

46. According to the passage, the Mohole project has had a difficult history due to

(A) debate among scientists as to its advisability
(B) difficulty in developing appropriate drilling instruments
(C) adverse publicity from the National Science Foundation
(D) problems in obtaining financial support for the project
(E) early failures of the project to produce worthwhile scientific information

47. The attitude of the author toward the lawmakers is one of

(A) irony
(B) chagrin
(C) distaste
(D) approval
(E) humor

48. It can be inferred from the passage that the Mohole project

(A) will continue to be funded at the rate of 28 million dollars per year
(B) is a pet project of the Committee on Science and Astronautics
(C) is favored more in the Senate than in the House of Representatives
(D) is an international effort to gain scientific knowledge about the earth
(E) has been handled with indecisiveness by Congress

49. The main purpose of the passage is to

(A) describe how one may obtain funds for scientific projects
(B) show how Congress has failed in its ability to find scientific projects to support
(C) create public sympathy for a project that is vital to national security
(D) describe the difficulties a particular project is having in obtaining funds
(E) show the reasons for greater scientific exploration of the earth

50. The author believes that in regard to scientific projects Congress should

(A) have a special committee to evaluate all projects
(B) support only those that are directly related to national survival
(C) trust the judgment of its scientific advisors
(D) divide money equally among each deserving project
(E) provide greater information to the public

One of the most despicable developments of the 1970's has been the large-scale taking of hostages for political purposes. Ordinary citizens are completely powerless against the fury of fanatical terrorists who seize and hold hostages without consideration for human life, that of their hostages or their own.

There is seldom warning as to when or where hostage-taking terrorists will strike. In the past decade they have skyjacked and diverted airplanes, (10) intercepted moving trains, overtaken dormitories of sleeping athletes and stormed foreign embassies. In all cases, the innocent victims have been frightened and threatened and have had their plans disrupted. In many cases there has been physical injury and often death as well. The psychological damage to surviving victims cannot be measured. Many never fully recover their equanimity. Nightmares, uncontrollable fears and inability to function as independent members of society plague many victims for the rest of (20) their lives.

Hostage-takers are almost always political, nationalistic or religious fanatics. They are most often members of "third-world" groups. They represent the nationalist spirit of newly formed nations, the new-found power of once-subservient populations, the radical influence of new political ideals in people just beginning to realize self-government.

The captors tend to make multiple demands of those who attempt to secure freedom for the (30) captives. Among these demands we usually see a demand for a large sum of money, request for safe passage and immunity from prosecution for themselves, insistence upon release of political and/or criminal prisoners in a target country, and the requirement that those whom they consider to be their enemies be delivered into their hands.

The "home governments" of the hostages are faced with a real dilemma. First and foremost they must safeguard the lives of the captives, yet, to give (40)

in to the demands of terrorists is to encourage other terrorists. If one group succeeds in satisfying its demands by the taking of hostages, other groups will soon follow their example. Furthermore, to release legitimate prisoners is simply to provide more manpower for the terrorist ranks. And, to deliver unto the terrorists their "enemies" is morally repugnant to civilized governments. Compounding the unwillingness to "exchange" prisoners or to encourage
(50) hostage-taking is a basic mistrust of the terrorists. How can one trust the word of a group which is so unscrupulous as to take innocent hostages in the first place? How can one believe that if their demands are met, the terrorists will then release the hostages unharmed?

Yet, the hostages must be freed and future hostage-taking discouraged. Resolution of the hostage problem is one of the most pressing tasks for government today.

51. The purpose of this passage is to

(A) describe a dilemma
(B) propose a solution
(C) explain preventative measures
(D) clarify terrorist psychology
(E) secure the release of hostages

52. Terrorists are described as "unscrupulous" because they

(A) lie
(B) steal
(C) do not worry about their own safety
(D) commit immoral acts
(E) make extravagent demands

53. The term "third-world groups" used in line 24 refers to

(A) non-Christians
(B) minorities
(C) members of groups which have recently forged their own identity
(D) Moslems
(E) inhabitants of outer space

54. Of the following demands often made by terrorists, which are the most difficult with which to comply?

I. release of political prisoners
II. release of criminal prisoners
III. delivery to the terrorists those whom they consider to be their enemies

(A) I only
(B) III only
(C) I and III
(D) I and II
(E) I, II and III

55. The mood of the author is

(A) resigned
(B) frustrated
(C) pessimistic
(D) optimistic
(E) angry

Hong Kong's size and association with Britain, and its position in relation to its neighbors in the Pacific, particularly China, determine the course of conduct it has to pursue. Hong Kong is no more than a molecule in the great substance of China. It was part of the large province of Kwantung, which came under Chinese sovereignty about 200 B.C., in the period of the Han Dynasty. In size, China exceeds 3¾ million square miles, and it has a population estimated to be greater than 700 million. Its very immensity has contributed to its survival over a great period of time. Without probing into the origins of its remarkable civilization, we can mark that it has a continuous history of more than 4,000 years. And, through the centuries, it has always been able to defend itself in depth, trading space for time.

In this setting Hong Kong is minute. Its area is a mere 398 square miles, about one two-hundredth part of the province of which it was previously part, Kwantung. Fortunately, however, we cannot dispose of Hong Kong as simply as this. There are components in its complex and unique existence which affect its character and, out of all physical proportion, increase its significance.

Amongst these, the most potent are its people, their impressive achievements in partnership with British administration and enterprise, and the rule of law which protects personal freedom in the British tradition.

What is Hong Kong, and what is it trying to do? In 1841 Britain acquired outright, by treaty, the Island of Hong Kong to use as a base for trade with China, and, in 1860, the Kowloon Peninsula, lying immediately to the north, to complete the perimeter of the superb harbor, which has determined Hong Kong's history and character. In 1898 Britain leased for 99 years a hinterland on the mainland of China to a depth of less than 25 miles, much of it very hilly. Hong Kong prospered as a center of trade with China, expanding steadily until it fell to the Japanese in 1941. Although the rigors of a severe occupation set everything back, the Liberation in 1945 was the herald of an immediate and spectacular recovery in trade. People poured into the Colony, and this flow became a flood during 1949–50, when the Chinese National Government met defeat at the hands of the Communists. Three-quarters of a million people entered the Colony at that stage, bringing the total population to $2\frac{1}{8}$ millions. Today the population is more than $3\frac{3}{4}$ millions.

Very soon two things affected commercial expansion. First, the Chinese Government restricted Hong Kong's exports to China because she feared unsettled internal conditions, mounting inflation and a weakness in her exchange position. Secondly, during the Korean War, the United Nations imposed an embargo on imports into China, the main source of Hong Kong's livelihood. This was a crisis for Hong Kong; its China trade went overnight, and, by this time, it had over one million refugees on its hands. But something dramatic happened. Simply stated, it was this: Hong Kong switched from trading to manufacture. It did it so quickly that few people, even in Hong Kong, were aware at the time of what exactly was happening, and the rest of the world was not quickly convinced of Hong Kong's transformation into a center of manufacturing. Its limited industry began to expand rapidly and, although more slowly, to diversify, and it owed not a little to the immigrants from Shanghai, who brought their capital, their experience and expertise with them. Today Hong Kong must be unique amongst so-called developing countries in the dependence of its economy on industrialization. No less than 40 percent of the labor force is engaged in the manufacturing industries; and of the products from these Hong Kong exports 90 percent, and it does this despite the fact that its industry is exposed to the full competition of the industrially mature nations. The variety of its goods now ranges widely from the products of shipbuilding and ship-breaking, through textiles and plastics, to air-conditioners, transistor radios and cameras.

More than 70 percent of its exports are either manufactured or partly manufactured in Hong Kong, and the value of its domestic exports in 1964 was about 750 million dollars. In recent years these figures have been increasing at about 15 percent a year. America is the largest market, taking 25 percent of the value of Hong Kong's exports; then follows the United Kingdom, Malaysia, West Germany, Japan, Canada and Australia; but all countries come within the scope of its marketing.

56. The article gives the impression that
    (A) English rule constituted an important factor in Hong Kong's economy
    (B) refugees from China were a liability to the financial status of Hong Kong
    (C) Hong Kong has taken a developmental course comparable to that of the new African nations
    (D) British forces used their military might imperialistically to acquire Hong Kong
    (E) there is a serious dearth of skilled workers in Hong Kong

57. The economic stability of Hong Kong is mostly attributable to
    (A) its shipbuilding activity
    (B) businessmen and workers from Shanghai who settled in Hong Kong
    (C) its political separation from China
    (D) its exports to China
    (E) a change in the area of business concentration

58. Hong Kong's population is about _____ that of China.
    (A) 1/50
    (B) 1/100
    (C) 1/200
    (D) 1/500
    (E) 1/1000

59. The author states or implies that
    (A) the United States imports more goods from Hong Kong than all the other nations combined
    (B) about three-quarters of Hong Kong's exports are raw materials
    (C) Malaysia, Canada, and West Germany provide excellent markets for Hong Kong goods
    (D) approximately one-half of the Hong Kong workers are involved with manufacturing
    (E) the United Nations has consistently cooperated to improve the economy of Hong Kong

60. Hong Kong first came under Chinese rule approximately

    (A) a century ago
    (B) eight centuries ago
    (C) fourteen centuries ago
    (D) twenty-one centuries ago
    (E) forty centuries ago

It is a measure of how far the Keynesian revolution has proceeded that the central thesis of "The General Theory" now sounds rather commonplace. Until it appeared, economists, in the classical (or non-socialist) tradition, had assumed that the economy, if left to itself, would find its equilibrium at full employment. Increases or decreases in wages and in interest rates would occur as necessary to bring about this pleasant result. If men were unem-
(10) ployed, their wages would fall in relation to prices. With lower wages and wider margins, it would be profitable to employ those from whose toil an adequate return could not previously have been made. It followed that steps to keep wages at artificially high levels, such as might result from the ill-considered efforts of unions, would cause unemployment. Such efforts were deemed to be the principal cause of unemployment.

Movements in interest rates played a complemen-
(20) tary role by insuring that all income would ultimately be spent. Thus, were people to decide for some reason to increase their savings, the interest rates on the now more abundant supply of loanable funds would fall. This, in turn, would lead to increased investment. The added outlays for investment goods would offset the diminished outlays by the more frugal consumers. In this fashion, changes in consumer spending or in investment decisions were kept from causing any change in total spending that
(30) would lead to unemployment.

Keynes argued that neither wage movements nor changes in the rate of interest had, necessarily, any such agreeable effect. He focused attention on the total of purchasing power in the economy—what freshmen are now taught to call aggregate demand. Wage reductions might not increase employment; in conjunction with other changes, they might merely reduce this aggregate demand. And he held that interest was not the price that was paid to people to
(40) save but the price they got for exchanging holdings of cash, or its equivalent, their normal preference in assets, for less liquid forms of investment. And it

was difficult to reduce interest beyond a certain level. Accordingly, if people sought to save more, this wouldn't necessarily mean lower interest rates and a resulting increase in investment. Instead, the total demand for goods might fall, along with employment and also investment, until savings were brought back into line with investment by the pressure of hardship which had reduced saving in favor (50) of consumption. The economy would find its equilibrium not at full employment but with an unspecified amount of unemployment.

Out of this diagnosis came the remedy. It was to bring aggregate demand back up to the level where all willing workers were employed, and this could be accomplished by supplementing private expenditure with public expenditure. This should be the policy wherever intentions to save exceed intentions to invest. Since public spending would not perform this (60) offsetting role if there were compensating taxation (which is a form of saving), the public spending should be financed by borrowing—by incurring a deficit. So far as Keynes can be condensed into a few paragraphs, this is it. "The General Theory" is more difficult. There are nearly 400 pages, some of them of fascinating obscurity.

61. According to the passage, "The General Theory" holds to which of the following beliefs?

    I. Government intervention is necessary to curtail unemployment.
    II. Public spending should be financed by borrowing.
    III. Steps to increase wages might create unemployment.

    (A) I only
    (B) II only
    (C) I and II only
    (D) II and III only
    (E) I, II, and III

62. The writer's attitude toward the Keynesian economic philosophy seems to be

    (A) antagonistic
    (B) questioning
    (C) accepting
    (D) mocking
    (E) bombastic

63. It is undeniable that Keynes would

(A) favor the full employment of only those who wished to be employed
(B) favor full employment at the cost of forcing unwilling workers to work
(C) oppose government spending in conjunction with private spending
(D) oppose a government deficit
(E) force people to work

64. The main purpose of the passage is to

(A) describe a theory that provides for government spending as a means of economic control
(B) show how traditional economists fail to provide for full employment
(C) criticize an economic theory that provides workers with a less than adequate return on their investment
(D) show ways economists have failed to account for variations in consumer spending
(E) analyze the role interest rates play in reducing aggregate demand

65. The following statements are not in correct chronological order. Place them in the correct order.

I. A rise in investment would follow.
II. The rate of interest would fluctuate so that people would eventually spend what they had earned.
III. There was assurance, therefore, that fluctuations in investment and/or purchasing would not throw workers out of jobs.
IV. Accordingly, as a person decided to save more, the rate of interest on loans would decrease.

(A) IV, III, I, II
(B) II, IV, I, III
(C) III, I, IV, II
(D) I, IV, III, II
(E) IV, III, II, I

END OF SECTION 1

IF YOU COMPLETE THIS SECTION BEFORE TIME IS UP, CHECK OVER YOUR WORK.

Section II
Time—50 minutes; 50 questions

DIRECTIONS: Solve each of the following problems, using available space on the page for your scratch work. Mark the letter of the correct answer on your answer sheet.
You may refer to the following data in solving the problems.

Triangle:

The angles of a triangle added together equal 180°.
The angle BDC is a right angle; therefore,

(I) the area of triangle ABC $= \dfrac{AC \times BD}{2}$

(II) $AB^2 = AD^2 + DB^2$

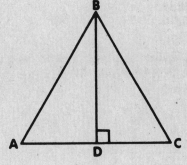

Circle:

There are 360° of arc in a circle.
The area of a circle of radius r $= \pi r^2$
The circumference of a circle $= 2\pi r$
A straight angle has 180°.

Symbol references:

|| is parallel to
$\leqq$ is less than or equal to
$\geqq$ is greater than or equal to
$\angle$ angle

$>$ is greater than
$<$ is less than
$\perp$ is perpendicular to
$\triangle$ triangle

Notes: The diagrams which accompany problems should provide data helpful in working out the solutions. These diagrams are not necessarily drawn precisely to scale. Unless otherwise stated, all figures lie in the same plane. All numbers are real numbers.

1. Which one of these quantities is the smallest?

   (A) $\frac{4}{5}$
   (B) $\frac{7}{9}$
   (C) .76
   (D) $\frac{5}{7}$
   (E) $\frac{9}{11}$

2. A girl earns twice as much in December as in each of the other months. What part of her entire year's earnings does she earn in December?

   (A) $\frac{2}{11}$
   (B) $\frac{2}{13}$
   (C) $\frac{3}{14}$
   (D) $\frac{1}{6}$
   (E) $\frac{1}{7}$

269

3. If $x = -1$, then $3x^3 + 2x^2 + x + 1 =$

(A) -1
(B) 1
(C) -5
(D) 5
(E) 2

4. How many twelfths of a pound are equal to $83\frac{1}{3}\%$ of a pound?

(A) 5
(B) 10
(C) 12
(D) 14
(E) 16

5. An equilateral triangle 3 inches on a side is cut up into smaller equilateral triangles one inch on a side. What is the greatest number of such triangles that can be formed?

(A) 3
(B) 6
(C) 9
(D) 12
(E) 15

6. If $\dfrac{a}{b} = \dfrac{3}{5}$, then $15a =$

(A) 3b
(B) 5b
(C) 6b
(D) 9b
(E) 15b

7. A square 5 units on a side has one vertex at the point $(1, 1)$. Which one of the following points *cannot* be diagonally opposite a vertex?

(A) $(6, 6)$
(B) $(-4, 6)$
(C) $(-4, -4)$
(D) $(6, -4)$
(E) $(4, -6)$

8. Five equal squares are placed side by side to make a single rectangle whose perimeter is 372 inches. Find the number of square inches in the area of one of these squares.

(A) 72
(B) 324
(C) 900
(D) 961
(E) 984

9. Which is the smallest of the following numbers?

(A) $\sqrt{3}$

(B) $\dfrac{1}{\sqrt{3}}$

(C) $\dfrac{\sqrt{3}}{3}$

(D) $\frac{1}{3}$

(E) $\dfrac{1}{3\sqrt{3}}$

10. In the figure, what percent of the area of rectangle PQRS is shaded?

(A) 20
(B) 25
(C) 30
(D) $33\frac{1}{3}$
(E) 40

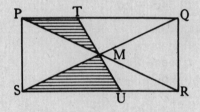

11. $\frac{1}{3}$ of an audience consists of boys and $\frac{1}{3}$ of it consists of girls. What percent of the audience consists of children?

(A) $66\frac{2}{3}$
(B) 50
(C) $37\frac{1}{2}$
(D) 40
(E) $33\frac{1}{3}$

12. One wheel has a diameter of 30 inches and a second wheel has a diameter of 20 inches. The first wheel travels a certain distance in 240 revolutions. In how many revolutions does the second wheel travel the same distance?

(A) 120
(B) 160
(C) 360
(D) 420
(E) 480

13. If x and y are two different real numbers and rx = ry, then r =

(A) 0
(B) 1

(C) $\dfrac{x}{y}$

(D) $\dfrac{y}{x}$

(E) x − y

14. If $\dfrac{m}{n} = \dfrac{5}{6}$, then what is $3m + 2n$?

(A) 0
(B) 2
(C) 7
(D) 10
(E) cannot be determined from the information given.

15. If $x > 1$, which of the following increase(s) as x increase(s)?

1. $x - \dfrac{1}{x}$

II. $\dfrac{1}{x^2 - x}$

III. $4x^3 - 2x^2$

(A) only I
(B) only II
(C) only III
(D) only I and III
(E) I, II, and III

DIRECTIONS: For each of the following questions, two quantities are given—one in Column A, the other in Column B. Compare the two quantities and mark your answer sheet as follows:
(A) if the quantity in Column A is greater
(B) if the quantity in Column B is greater
(C) if the two quantities are equal
(D) if the relationship cannot be determined from the information given.

NECESSARY INFORMATION:
• In each question, information concerning one or both of the quantities to be compared is centered above the entries in the two columns.

• A symbol that appears in any column represents the same thing in Column A as it does in Column B.

• All numbers used are real numbers; letters such as x, y, and t stand for real numbers.

• Assume that the position of points, angles, regions and so forth are in the order shown and that all figures lie in a plane unless otherwise indicated.

• Figures are not necessarily drawn to scale.

Examples:

	COLUMN A	COLUMN B
E1.	$a < 0$ $x < 0$	
	$a + x$	ax

Ⓐ ● Ⓒ Ⓓ

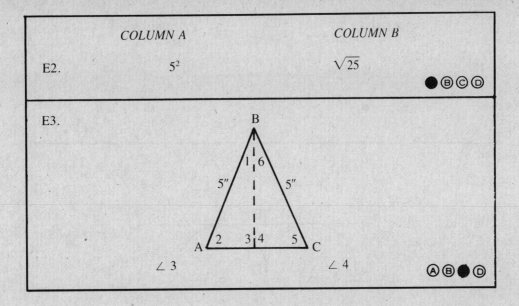

	COLUMN A	COLUMN B
E2.	5^2	$\sqrt{25}$

● Ⓑ Ⓒ Ⓓ

E3.

∠ 3   ∠ 4

Ⓐ Ⓑ ● Ⓓ

16.   6% of 42   7% of 36

---

17. $x = -2$

$3x^2 + 2x - 1$ $x^3 + 2x^2 + 1$

18.

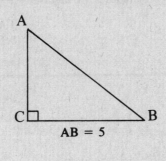

AB = 5

AC   BC

---

19. $(\tfrac{1}{2})^{-2}$ $(\tfrac{1}{2})^{-3}$

---

20. $16 \div 4 + 8 \times 2 - 8$ $3 \times 4 + 10 \div 5 - 3$

COLUMN A   COLUMN B

21.
$$\frac{a}{a + b} = \frac{c}{c + d}$$

cb   ad

22.

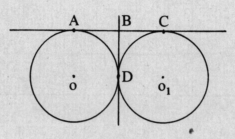

AC is tangent to circles Q and
O_1
BD is a common tangent

AB   BC

23.   A radio priced $47.25
             includes a 5% mark-up

$44.89   The original price
                            before mark-up

24.
$$\begin{cases} a - b = -1 \\ -b - a = -3 \end{cases}$$

b   a

25.   25% of the 300
             girls in our school
             have blond hair

The ratio of girls with   1:3
blond hair to those
without blond hair

COLUMN A   COLUMN B

26.

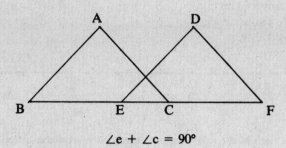

$$\angle e + \angle c = 90°$$

$\angle b + \angle a + \angle d + \angle f$ 270°

---

27. $(36)^{\frac{1}{2}}$ $(\frac{1}{36})^{-\frac{1}{2}}$

28.

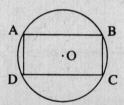

**ABCD is a parallelogram
inscribed in circle 0**

$\angle A + \angle C$ $\angle B + \angle D$

---

29. $2x^2 + 9x - 18 = 0$

The sum of the roots   The product of the roots

---

30. $A * B = A^2 + B^{-2}$
Substitute the following values
of A * B into the equation.

6 * 8   8 * 6

---

31.   .01 divided by .1   .01 times .1

COLUMN A	*COLUMN B*
32. The number of sections a circle can be divided into by 4 chords	10

_____

DIRECTIONS: Solve each of the following problems, using available space on the page for your scratch work. Mark the letter of the correct answer on your answer sheet.

33. In the figure, PQRS is a parallelogram, and ST = TV = VR. What is the ratio of the area of triangle SPT to the area of the parallelogram?

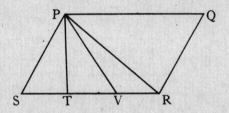

(A) $\frac{1}{6}$
(B) $\frac{1}{5}$
(C) $\frac{1}{3}$
(D) $\frac{2}{7}$
(E) cannot be determined from the information given

34. One angle of a triangle is 82°. The other two angles are in the ratio 2:5. Find the number of degrees in the smallest angle of the triangle.

(A) 14
(B) 25
(C) 28
(D) 38
(E) 82

35. If a boy can mow a lawn in t minutes, what part can he do in 15 minutes?

(A) t − 15

(B) $\frac{t}{15}$

(C) 15t

(D) 15 − t

(E) $\frac{15}{t}$

36. A typist uses lengthwise a sheet of paper 9 inches by 12 inches. She leaves a 1-inch margin on each side and a 1½-inch margin on top and bottom. What fractional part of the page is used for typing?

    (A) $\frac{21}{22}$
    (B) $\frac{7}{12}$
    (C) $\frac{5}{8}$
    (D) $\frac{3}{4}$
    (E) $\frac{5}{12}$

37. It takes a boy 9 seconds to run a distance of 132 feet. What is his speed in miles per hour?

    (A) 8
    (B) 9
    (C) 10
    (D) 11
    (E) 12

38. A rectangular sign is cut down by 10% of its height and 30% of its width. What percent of the original area remains?

    (A) 30
    (B) 37
    (C) 57
    (D) 70
    (E) 63

39. How many of the numbers between 100 and 300 begin or end with 2?

    (A) 20
    (B) 40
    (C) 180
    (D) 100
    (E) 110

40. If Mary knows that y is an integer greater than 2 and less than 7, and John knows that y is an integer greater than 5 and less than 10, then Mary and John may correctly conclude that

    (A) y can be exactly determined
    (B) y may be either of 2 values
    (C) y may be any of 3 values
    (D) y may be any of 4 values
    (E) there is no value of y satisfying these conditions

41. The area of a square is $49x^2$. What is the length of a diagonal of the square?

    (A) $7x$
    (B) $7x\sqrt{2}$
    (C) $14x$
    (D) $7x^2$
    (E) $\dfrac{7x}{\sqrt{2}}$

42. In the figure, MNOP is a square of area 1, Q is the mid-point of MN, and R is the mid-point of NO. What is the ratio of the area of triangle PQR to the area of the square?

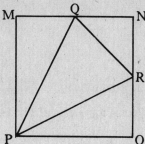

(A) $\frac{1}{4}$

(B) $\frac{1}{3}$

(C) $\frac{7}{16}$

(D) $\frac{3}{8}$

(E) $\frac{1}{2}$

43. If a rectangle is 4 feet by 12 feet, how many two-inch tiles would have to be put around the outside edge to completely frame the rectangle?

(A) 32

(B) 36

(C) 192

(D) 196

(E) 200

44. One-tenth is what part of three-fourths?

(A) $\frac{40}{3}$

(B) $\frac{3}{40}$

(C) $\frac{15}{2}$

(D) $\frac{1}{8}$

(E) $\frac{2}{15}$

45. The area of square PQRS is 49. What are the coordinates of Q?

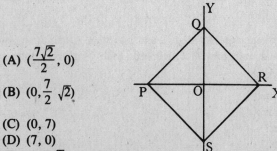

(A) $(\frac{7\sqrt{2}}{2}, 0)$

(B) $(0, \frac{7}{2}\sqrt{2})$

(C) $(0, 7)$

(D) $(7, 0)$

(E) $(0, 7\sqrt{2})$

46. Village A has a population of 6,800, which is decreasing at a rate of 120 per year. Village B has a population of 4,200, which is increasing at a rate of 80 per year. In how many years will the population of the two villages be equal?

(A) 9

(B) 11

(C) 13

(D) 14

(E) 16

47. The average of 8 numbers is 6; the average of 6 other numbers is 8. What is the average of all 14 numbers?

(A) 6
(B) $6\frac{6}{7}$
(C) 7
(D) $7\frac{2}{7}$
(E) $8\frac{1}{7}$

48. If x is between 0 and 1, which of the following increases as x increases?

I. $1 - x^2$
II. $x - 1$
III. $\frac{1}{x^2}$

(A) I and II
(B) II and III
(C) I and III
(D) II only
(E) I only

49. In the formula $T = \frac{2\sqrt{L}}{g}$, g is a constant.

By what number must L be multiplied so that T will be multiplied by 3?

(A) 3
(B) 6
(C) 9
(D) 12
(E) $\sqrt{3}$

50. Three circles are tangent externally to each other and have radii of 2 inches, 3 inches, and 4 inches respectively. How many inches are in the perimeter of the triangle formed by joining the centers of the three circles?

(A) 9
(B) 12
(C) 15
(D) 18
(E) 21

END OF EXAMINATION

IF YOU FINISH BEFORE TIME IS CALLED, CHECK OVER YOUR WORK ON SECTION II. DO NOT RETURN TO SECTION I.

MODEL EXAMINATION III—ANSWER KEY

Section I

1. E	14. C	27. C	40. E	53. C
2. D	15. B	28. B	41. C	54. E
3. A	16. E	29. C	42. D	55. B
4. A	17. C	30. B	43. D	56. A
5. E	18. E	31. E	44. A	57. E
6. C	19. B	32. C	45. C	58. C
7. E	20. B	33. C	46. D	59. C
8. A	21. B	34. B	47. B	60. D
9. E	22. D	35. D	48. E	61. C
10. B	23. C	36. E	49. D	62. C
11. B	24. B	37. B	50. C	63. A
12. C	25. B	38. A	51. A	64. A
13. E	26. A	39. B	52. D	65. B

Section II

1. D	11. B	21. C	31. A	41. B
2. B	12. C	22. C	32. A	42. D
3. A	13. A	23. B	33. A	43. D
4. B	14. E	24. A	34. C	44. E
5. C	15. D	25. C	35. E	45. B
6. D	16. C	26. C	36. B	46. C
7. E	17. A	27. C	37. C	47. B
8. D	18. D	28. C	38. E	48. D
9. E	19. B	29. A	39. E	49. C
10. B	20. A	30. B	40. A	50. D

EXPLANATORY ANSWERS

SECTION I

1. **(E)** OBEDIENCE. MUTINY means rebellion.

2. **(D)** COMMEND means to praise. ASSAIL means to attack with words or blows.

3. **(A)** DISCLOSE means to reveal or show. OBSCURE means to conceal or hide.

4. **(A)** VACILLATION means hesitancy or irresolution. TENACITY means persistence.

5. **(E)** TIDY. SLOVENLY means untidy.

6. **(C)** REASONABLE. EXORBITANT means excessive or unreasonable.

7. **(E)** SUBSEQUENT means following. ANTECEDENT means preceding.

8. **(A)** ALIENATE means to make unfriendly or to estrange. CAPTIVATE means to attract or to charm.

9. **(E)** REBELLION means defiance of established authority. COMPLIANCE means yielding to the desires of others.

10. **(B)** UNCLEAR. INTELLIGIBLE means easily understood.

11. **(B)** DISHARMONY means lack of agreement. CONSENSUS means general agreement or unanimity.

12. **(C)** A MORON is a very dull person. A SAVANT is a very wise person, one with a great deal of knowledge in a specialized field.

13. **(E)** MUDDY. LIMPID means clear.

14. **(C)** AGGRAVATE means to intensify. ASSUAGE means to ease or to relieve.

15. **(B)** VIRTUOUS means righteous. NEFARIOUS means evil.

16. **(E)** KIND means friendly or loving. SANGUINARY means murderous or bloodthirsty. Pale, (D), is the opposite of *sanguine*, meaning ruddy. Bitter, (B), is the opposite of *sanguine*, meaning cheerful.

17. **(C)** STATIONARY means immobile. OSCILLATORY means fluctuating or swinging.

18. **(E)** DISPLAY means to show. SECRETE means to hide.

19. **(B)** VOLUNTEER. A CONSCRIPT is a draftee.

20. **(B)** SIMPLE means plain and unadorned. TURGID means pompous or inflated.

21. **(B)** The second half of the sentence is intended to serve as a complement to or example of the opening argument. The only completion that establishes this relationship between the clauses in the sentence are PAST experience and HERITAGE, which are synonymous.

22. **(D)** The word "mob" has a negative connotation and requires an adjective which is also negative. HYSTERICAL (emotional and unmanageable) best meets this requirement. The emotion that a shouting mob is most likely to show is HATRED of law and order.

23. **(C)** When errors are discovered in existing theories, those theories must either be ALTERED (changed) in the light of the new information or they must be DISCARDED altogether, if the new information renders the old theories false.

24. **(B)** The sentence compares two different societies and therefore requires completions that are both parallel and opposite. ELEMENTARY (simple) and COMPLICATED (intricate) best meet these requirements.

25. **(B)** The second half of the sentence is offered as proof of the first half. Because man always lives with hope, one who has been consistently WRONG can still conclude that with each succeeding decision he will prove to be RIGHT.

26. **(A)** The first blank requires a word which connotes an attitude opposite to that held by brave men. Such an attitude is COWARDICE or fear. A peace which is maintained is LASTING.

27. **(C)** If money is regarded as the route to social salvation, it is by definition regarded as a PANACEA (cure-all) for all the troubles of mankind.

28. **(B)** If a flood control reservoir is used for STORAGE of water, its ability to control a flood is LESSENED because the stored water cuts down on the amount of flood water the reservoir can accommodate.

29. **(C)** This sentence presents two problems which are being compared in terms of the ease of their solution. The only choices which fulfill the requirements of such a comparison are MAGNITUDE and CHILD'S PLAY.

30. **(B)** A theatrical setting serves to create a mood or a feeling of being in another time or place. If the setting is to be EFFECTIVE (to make the desired impression on the audience), it must have some semblance of REALITY.

31. **(E)** An ARGUMENT is an emotional DEBATE; a FIGHT is an emotional CONTEST. The relationship is one of *degree*.

32. **(C)** The BULB is an edible part of an ONION; the LEAF is an edible part of the LETTUCE. The relationship is one of *function*.

33. **(C)** OXYGEN is a constituent element of WATER; SODIUM is a constituent element of SALT. The relationship is that of *part to whole*.

34. **(B)** An EMBARGO obstructs the flow of TRADE; a DAM obstructs the flow of WATER. The relationship is one of *function*.

35. **(D)** GAUGE is a standard of measurement for RAILS; CALIBER is a standard of measurement for RIFLES. The relationship is one of *function*.

36. **(E)** To BEAT is to STIR vigorously; to MINCE is to CHOP vigorously. The relationship is one of *degree*.

37. **(B)** To HESITATE is to pause briefly, while to PROCRASTINATE is to extend the delay; a PECCADILLO is a small offense, while a CRIME is a major offense. The relationship is one of *degree*.

38. **(A)** PAPER is made from WOOD; STEEL is made from IRON. The relationship is a version of *part to whole*.

39. **(B)** PAPYRUS is a primitive writing material, precursor to PAPER; ADOBE is a primitive building material, still used but largely supplanted by CONCRETE. The relationship is one of *sequence*.

40. **(E)** SLANDER is defamation in SPEECH; LIBEL is defamation in writing or PUBLICATION. The relationship is one of *association*.

41. **(C)** A CHORD cuts through a CIRCLE; the CANAL cuts through PANAMA. The relationship is one of *function*.

42. **(D)** PLASTIC (pliable) is the opposite of RIGID (stiff); ALLEVIATE (lessen) is the opposite of AGGRAVATE (intensify). The relationship is that of *antonyms*.

43. **(D)** A MALAPROPISM is incorrect use of a WORD; IMPROPRIETY is incorrect BEHAVIOR. The relationship is that of *whole to part*.

44. **(A)** A DOLLAR is a kind of MONEY; an ELM is a kind of TREE. The relationship is that of *part to whole*.

45. **(C)** The role of a SHERIFF is to eliminate CRIME; the role of a DOCTOR is to eliminate DISEASE. The relationship is one of *function*.

46. **(D)** Undoubtedly the Mohole project has had a long, tortuous history for a number of reasons. The question, however, asks, "According to the passage . . ." The passage deals with money problems.

47. **(B)** Chagrin means disappointment. The author does seem to be disappointed with the lawmakers' handling of the whole question.

48. **(E)** None of the other choices can be inferred from the passage. Congress' changing of its mind about continuing with the project is a clear sign of indecisiveness.

49. **(D)** While some of the other options might be secondary aims of the passage, its main purpose, as is stated at the outset, is to describe the financial problems of the American project to drill a hole through the mantle of the Earth.

50. **(C)** The author states that the decision on the Mohole project is a departure from Congress' usual practice of trusting the judgment of its scientific advisors. Since he then expresses the opinion that this departure "could be a dangerous precedent," he clearly feels that Congress should revert to accepting the advice of the scientists on scientific matters.

51. **(A)** The main and, really, the only purpose of this passage is to describe the various factors working in a hostage situation and the problems faced by those who try to solve it.

52. **(D)** An unscrupulous person has no conscience or principles. The terrorists may or may not lie and steal; they do make extravagant demands. Most serious, though, is the manner in which they treat their fellow man. All aspects of their behavior may be included in the general statement, "they commit immoral acts."

53. **(C)** The term "third world" is used to apply to the emerging nations, especially those of Africa, Asia, the South Pacific and the Caribbean, to majority groups which are beginning to gain power, such as the black South Africans, and to ethnic groups which are seeking to establish an identity—the Palestinians, for instance.

54. **(E)** All these demands made by terrorists are equally difficult for governments to accede to. The less frequent demands for money or for free television time to broadcast grievances are much easier to deal with.

55. **(B)** More than anything else, the author is frustrated by the dilemma posed in a typical hostage situation.

56. **(A)** When the third paragraph speaks of the "impressive achievements in partnership with British administration and enterprise . . ." it certainly implies that the English rule has had an effect on the Hong Kong economy.

57. **(E)** At a time when its China trade had come to a sudden halt, Hong Kong achieved economic stability by abruptly changing its business concentration from trading to manufacturing. The consumer goods which Hong Kong manufactures have an extensive international market. The immigrants from Shanghai contributed to the diversity of the products manufactured, but they cannot be assigned the major credit for the economic stability.

58. **(C)** The population of mainland China is over 700,000,000. The population of Hong Kong is over 3,750,000. Since 1/200 of 700,000,000 is 3,500,000, 1/200 is the closest expressed ratio.

59. **(C)** Malaysia, Canada and West Germany are mentioned as being among Hong Kong's best markets. The United States imports about 25% of Hong Kong's manufactured goods, a substantial proportion, but not more than all other countries combined. Approximately 40% of the labor force is involved in manufacturing.

60. **(D)** Hong Kong came under Chinese sovereignty about 200 B.C., which was twenty-one centuries ago.

61. **(C)** Statements I and II may be found in lines 54 to 58 and in lines 62 to 64. Statement III, that steps to increase wages might lead to unemployment, (see lines 14 to 17) is attributed to pre-Keynesian or classical economists. Since the theories are placed in opposition, this is clearly not a belief of "The General Theory."

62. **(C)** The passage is strictly factual, not antagonistic, questioning, mocking, nor bombastic. The first sentence does set an accepting tone.

63. **(A)** Since Keynes' remedy for unemployment was to bring aggregate demand back up to the level where all *willing* workers were employed, it is quite clear that he would not insist that all the able-bodied must work.

64. **(A)** This does seem to be the purpose of the passage. The writer brings traditional economics into the passage mainly to make clear the unique features of the Keynesian theory, not for the purpose of criticizing classical economics. The passage is a general exposition of some of the major features of "The General Theory" with a simplified description of the means for government manipulation of the economy.

65. **(B)** A careful reading of the seond paragraph of the passage provides an adequate basis for putting these statements of traditional economic belief into order.

SECTION II

1. **(D)** $\frac{4}{5} = .8$

$$\frac{7}{9} = 9\overline{)7.00} = .78$$

$$\frac{5}{7} = 7\overline{)5.00} = .71$$

$$\frac{9}{11} = 11\overline{)9.00} = .82$$

Thus $\frac{5}{7}$ is the smallest quantity.

2. **(B)** Let $x =$ amount earned each month
$2x =$ amount earned in December
Then $11x + 2x = 13x$ (entire earnings)
$$\frac{2x}{13x} = \frac{2}{13}$$

3. **(A)** $3x^3 + 2x^2 + x + 1$
$= 3(-1)^3 + 2(-1)^2 + (-1) + 1$
$= 3(-1) + 2(1) - 1 + 1$
$= -3 + 2 + 0$
$= -1$

4. **(B)** $\frac{x}{12} = \frac{83\frac{1}{3}}{100} = \frac{250}{300}$

or $\frac{x}{12} = \frac{25}{30} = \frac{5}{6}$

$6x = 60$
$x = 10$

5. **(C)** Since the ratio of the sides is $3:1$, the ratio of the areas is $9:1$.

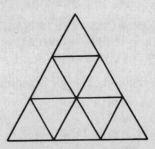

The subdivision into 9 △ is shown

6. **(D)** $\frac{a}{b} = \frac{3}{5}$

$5a = 3b$

Multiply both sides by 3.
$15a = 9b$

7. **(E)** The opposite vertices may be any of the number pairs $(1 \pm 5, 1 \pm 5)$ or $(6, 6)$, $(-4, -4)$, $(-4, 6)$, $(6, -4)$.

Thus $(4, -6)$ is not possible.

8. **(D)**

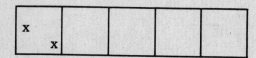

Perimeter of rectangle $= x + 5x + x + 5x$
Thus $12x = 372$
$x = 31$
Area of square $= 31^2 = 961$

9. **(E)** $\sqrt{3} = 1.73$ (approx.)

$\frac{1}{\sqrt{3}} = \frac{\sqrt{3}}{3} = \frac{1.73}{3} = .57$

$\frac{\sqrt{3}}{3} = \frac{1.73}{3} = .57$

$\frac{1}{3} = .3333 \ldots \ldots$

$\frac{1}{3\sqrt{3}} = \frac{\sqrt{3}}{3 \cdot 3} = \frac{\sqrt{3}}{9} = \frac{1.73}{9} = .19$

Thus the smallest is $\frac{1}{3\sqrt{3}}$

10. **(B)**

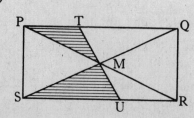

Since $\triangle TQM \cong \triangle SMU$, it follows that the shaded area $= \triangle PTM + \triangle TQM = \triangle PMQ$. But $=PMQ = \frac{1}{2} \triangle PQS = \frac{1}{4} PQRS$. $\frac{1}{4} = 25\%$

11. **(B)** Let $x =$ number of people in audience

then $\frac{1}{6}x =$ no. of boys
$\frac{1}{3}x =$ no. of girls
$\frac{1}{6}x + \frac{1}{3}x = \frac{1}{6}x + \frac{2}{6}x = \frac{3}{6}x =$
$\frac{1}{2}x =$ no. of children
$\frac{1}{2} = 50\%$

12. **(C)** The number of revolutions is inversely proportional to size of wheel.

Thus $\frac{30}{20} = \frac{n}{240}$

Where $n =$ no. of revolutions for 2nd wheel.
$2n = 720$
$n = 360$

13. **(A)** r cannot equal any number other than zero, for, if we divided by r, x would equal y. Since $x \neq y$, it follows that $r = 0$.

14. **(E)** $\frac{m}{n} = \frac{5}{6}$

$6m - 5n$
$6m - 5n = 0$

However, it is not possible to determine from this the value of $3m + 2n$.

15. **(D)** I. As x increases, $\frac{1}{x}$ decreases and

$x - \frac{1}{x}$ increases.

II. $\frac{1}{x^2 - x} = \frac{1}{x(x - 1)}$

As x increases, both x and $(x - 1)$ increase, and $\frac{1}{x(x - 1)}$ decreases.

III. $4x^3 - 2x^2 = 2x^2(2x - 1)$. As x increases, both $2x^2$ and $(2x - 1)$ increase, and their product increases. Therefore, I and III increase.

16. **(C)**

$6\% = .06$	$7\% = .07$
$.06(42) = 2.52$	$.07(36) = 2.52$

$\therefore$ Column A $=$ Column B

17. **(A)**

$3x^2 + 2x - 1$	$x^3 + 2x^2 + 1$
$3(-2)^2 + 2(-2) - 1$	$(-2)^3 + 2(-2)^2 + 1$
$3(4) - 4 - 1$	$-8 + 8 + 1$
$12 - 4 - 1$	$+ 1$
7	

$\therefore$ Column A $>$ Column B

18. **(D)** The relationship between column A and column B cannot be determined from the information given.

19. **(B)**

$(\frac{1}{2})^{-2}$ $\qquad$ $(\frac{1}{2})^{-3}$

$1/(\frac{1}{2})^2$ $\qquad$ $1/(\frac{1}{2})^3$

$1/\frac{1}{4} = 4$ $\qquad$ $1/\frac{1}{8} = 8$

$\therefore$ Column B > Column A

20. **(A)**

$16 \div 4 + 8 \times 2 - 8$ $\qquad$ $3 \times 4 + 10 \div 5 - 3$

$\qquad 4 + 16 - 8$ $\qquad\qquad 12 + 2 - 3$

$\qquad\qquad 20 - 8$ $\qquad\qquad\qquad 14 - 3$

$\qquad\qquad\quad 12$ $\qquad\qquad\qquad\quad 11$

$\therefore$ Column A > Column B

21. **(C)**

In a proportion the product of the means equals the product of the extremes.

If $a/a + b = c/c + d$

then $c(a + b) = a(c + d)$

and $ac + cb = ac + ad$

$\qquad cb = ad$ (subtraction)

$\therefore$ Column A = Column B

22. **(C)**

Tangents to a circle from an external point are equal.

$\qquad AB = BD$

and $BC = BD$

$\qquad AB = BC$ (substitution)

$\therefore$ Column A = Column B

23. **(B)**

Original Price + Original Price (mark-up) = Selling Price

$\qquad$ Let x = original price

then $x + .05(x) = \$47.25$

$\qquad\quad 1.05x = \$47.25$

$\qquad\qquad\quad x = \$45$

$\$45 > \$44.89$

$\therefore$ Column B > Column A

24. **(A)**

$\quad a - b = -1$ $\qquad\qquad a - b = -1$

$\underline{-a - b = -3}$ $\qquad\qquad a - (2) = -1$

$\quad -2b = -4$ $\qquad\qquad\qquad a = 1$

$\qquad b = 2$

$\therefore$ Column A > Column B

25. **(C)**

$.25(300) = 75$ (girls with blond hair)

$300 - 75 = 225$ (girls without blond hair)

$\qquad 75/225 = \frac{1}{3}$

$\therefore$ Column A = Column B

26. **(C)**

The sum of the angles of a triangle equal 180°.

$\qquad\qquad \angle a + \angle b + \angle c = 180°$

$\qquad$ and $\angle d + \angle e + \angle f = 180°$

$\therefore \ \angle a + \angle b + \angle c + \angle d + \angle e + \angle f = 360°$

$\qquad$ also $\ \angle e + \angle c = 90°$

$\angle b + \angle a + \angle d + \angle f = 270°$ (subtraction)

$\qquad \therefore$ Column A = Column B

27. **(C)**

$(36)^{1/2}$ $\qquad\qquad (\frac{1}{36})^{-1/2}$

$\sqrt{36}$ $\qquad\qquad\quad 1/\sqrt{\frac{1}{36}}$

6 $\qquad\qquad\qquad 1/\frac{1}{6} = 6$

$\therefore$ Column A = Column B

28. **(C)** A parallelogram inscribed in a circle is a rectangle. Therefore, all angles equal 90°.

$\qquad$ Hence, $\angle A + \angle C = \angle B + \angle D$

$\qquad \therefore$ Column A = Column B

29. **(A)**

$\quad 2x^2 + 9x - 18 = 0$

$(2x - 3)(x + 6) = 0$

$2x - 3 = 0 \qquad x + 6 = 0$

$\quad 2x = 3 \qquad\qquad x = -6$

$\quad\ x = \frac{3}{2}$

$\therefore$ The sum of the roots $= -6 + 1\frac{1}{2} = -4\frac{1}{2}$ and the product of the roots $= \frac{3}{2}(-6) = -9$

$\qquad\qquad -4\frac{1}{2} > -9$

$\qquad \therefore$ Column A > Column B

30. **(B)**

$\qquad$ If $A * B = A^2 + B^{-2}$

then $6 * 8 = 6^2 + \frac{1}{8}^2$ and $8 * 6 = 8^2 + \frac{1}{6}^2$

$\qquad\qquad = 36 + \frac{1}{64}$ $\qquad\qquad = 64 + \frac{1}{36}$

$\qquad\qquad = 36\frac{1}{64}$ $\qquad\qquad\quad = 64\frac{1}{36}$

$\qquad\qquad 64\frac{1}{36} > 36\frac{1}{64}$

$\qquad \therefore$ Column B > Column A

31. **(A)**

$.01 \div .1 = .1 \qquad\qquad .01(.1) = .001$

$\qquad\qquad .1 > .001$

$\qquad \therefore$ Column A > Column B

32. **(A)**

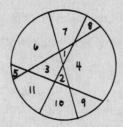

A circle can be divided into 11 sections by four chords.

$$11 > 10$$
$$\therefore \text{ Column A} > \text{Column B}$$

33. **(A)** $\triangle SPT = \frac{1}{3}\triangle PSR$ since they have common altitude and the base $ST = \frac{1}{3}SR$.

But $\triangle PSR = \frac{1}{2} \boxed{P}\ PQRS$.

Hence $\triangle SPT = \frac{1}{3} \cdot \frac{1}{2} \boxed{P} = \frac{1}{6} \boxed{P}$

34. **(C)** Let the other two angles be 2x and 5x.
Thus, $2x + 5x + 82 = 180$
$$7x = 98$$
$$x = 14$$
$$2x = 28$$
$$5x = 70$$
Smallest angle $= 28°$

35. **(E)** His rate is $\frac{1}{t}$ of the lawn per minute.

Hence, in 15 minutes, he will do

$$15 \cdot \frac{1}{t} = \frac{15}{t} \text{ of the lawn}$$

36. **(B)** Typing space is $12 - 3 = 9$ inches long and $9 - 2 = 7$ inches wide. Part used =

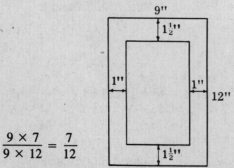

$$\frac{9 \times 7}{9 \times 12} = \frac{7}{12}$$

37. **(C)** 132 ft. $= \frac{132}{5280} = \frac{1}{40}$ mile
9 seconds $= \frac{9}{3600} = \frac{1}{400}$ hour
$\frac{1}{40}$ mile in $\frac{1}{400}$ hour =
1 mile in $\frac{1}{10}$ hour =
10 miles in 1 hour =
10 mph

38. **(E)** Let the original sign be 10 by 10.

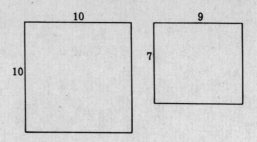

Then the new sign is 9 by 7

$$\frac{63}{100} = 63\%$$

39. **(E)** All the numbers from 200 to 299 begin with 2. There are 100 of these. Then all numbers like 102, 112, ———, 192 end with 2.
There are ten of these.
Hence, there are 110 such numbers.

40. **(A)** If $2 < y < 7$ and $5 < y < 10$, then $5 < y < 7$ (intersection of 2 sets). Since y is an integer, it must be 6.

41. **(B)** If the area is $49x^2$, the side of the square is 7x. Therefore, the diagonal of the square must be the hypotenuse of a right isosceles triangle of leg 7x.

$$\text{Hence diagonal} = 7x\sqrt{2}$$

42. **(D)** Since $MP = 1$ and $MQ = \frac{1}{2}$, the area of $\triangle PMQ =$ area of $\triangle POR = \frac{1}{2} \cdot 1 \cdot \frac{1}{2} = \frac{1}{4}$

The area of $\triangle QNR = \frac{1}{2} \cdot \frac{1}{2} \cdot \frac{1}{2} = \frac{1}{8}$
Area of $\triangle PQR = 1 - 2(\frac{1}{4}) - \frac{1}{8} = 1 - \frac{5}{8} = \frac{3}{8}$

43. **(D)** 72 tiles along each length. 24 tiles along each width. $2 \times 96 = 192$ tiles along perimeter. But 4 more are needed for the corners of the frame.

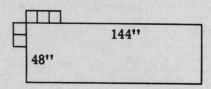

Hence, 196 tiles are needed.

44. **(E)** $\frac{1}{10} = x \cdot \frac{3}{4} = \frac{3x}{4}$

Cross-multiplying, we obtain
$$30x = 4$$
$$x = \tfrac{2}{15}$$

45. **(B)** Since QR = 7, and QOR is a right, isoceles triangle, OQ = $\frac{7}{\sqrt{2}} = \frac{7\sqrt{2}}{2}$

Hence, coordinates of Q are $(0, \frac{7}{2}\sqrt{2})$

46. **(C)** Let x = no. of years for 2 populations to be equal

Then 6,800 − 120x = 4,200 + 80x

$\qquad$ 2,600 = 200x

$\qquad\qquad$ x = 13

47. **(B)** 8 × 6 = 48

$\qquad$ 6 × 8 = 48 (sum of all 14 numbers)

Average = $\frac{96}{14} = 6\frac{6}{7}$

48. **(D)**

  I. As x increases, $(1 - x^2)$ decreases.

  II. As x increases, $(x - 1)$ increases.

  III. As x increases, $\frac{1}{x^2}$ decreases.

Hence, II only increases.

49. **(C)** $T = 2\pi\sqrt{\dfrac{L}{g}}$

In order for T to be tripled, L must be multiplied by 9, since the square root of this factor will be 3.

50. **(D)** The line of center of two tangent circles passes through the point of tangency.

Hence, perimeter of $\triangle$ = (2 + 3) + (3 + 4) + (4 + 2) = 5 + 7 + 6 = 18

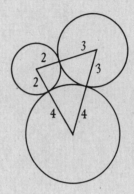

ANSWER SHEET FOR MODEL EXAMINATION IV

Completely blacken the answer space of your choice. Mark only one answer for each question. Erase stray marks.

SECTION I
VERBAL

1 Ⓐ Ⓑ Ⓒ Ⓓ Ⓔ	12 Ⓐ Ⓑ Ⓒ Ⓓ Ⓔ	23 Ⓐ Ⓑ Ⓒ Ⓓ Ⓔ	34 Ⓐ Ⓑ Ⓒ Ⓓ Ⓔ	45 Ⓐ Ⓑ Ⓒ Ⓓ Ⓔ	56 Ⓐ Ⓑ Ⓒ Ⓓ Ⓔ
2 Ⓐ Ⓑ Ⓒ Ⓓ Ⓔ	13 Ⓐ Ⓑ Ⓒ Ⓓ Ⓔ	24 Ⓐ Ⓑ Ⓒ Ⓓ Ⓔ	35 Ⓐ Ⓑ Ⓒ Ⓓ Ⓔ	46 Ⓐ Ⓑ Ⓒ Ⓓ Ⓔ	57 Ⓐ Ⓑ Ⓒ Ⓓ Ⓔ
3 Ⓐ Ⓑ Ⓒ Ⓓ Ⓔ	14 Ⓐ Ⓑ Ⓒ Ⓓ Ⓔ	25 Ⓐ Ⓑ Ⓒ Ⓓ Ⓔ	36 Ⓐ Ⓑ Ⓒ Ⓓ Ⓔ	47 Ⓐ Ⓑ Ⓒ Ⓓ Ⓔ	58 Ⓐ Ⓑ Ⓒ Ⓓ Ⓔ
4 Ⓐ Ⓑ Ⓒ Ⓓ Ⓔ	15 Ⓐ Ⓑ Ⓒ Ⓓ Ⓔ	26 Ⓐ Ⓑ Ⓒ Ⓓ Ⓔ	37 Ⓐ Ⓑ Ⓒ Ⓓ Ⓔ	48 Ⓐ Ⓑ Ⓒ Ⓓ Ⓔ	59 Ⓐ Ⓑ Ⓒ Ⓓ Ⓔ
5 Ⓐ Ⓑ Ⓒ Ⓓ Ⓔ	16 Ⓐ Ⓑ Ⓒ Ⓓ Ⓔ	27 Ⓐ Ⓑ Ⓒ Ⓓ Ⓔ	38 Ⓐ Ⓑ Ⓒ Ⓓ Ⓔ	49 Ⓐ Ⓑ Ⓒ Ⓓ Ⓔ	60 Ⓐ Ⓑ Ⓒ Ⓓ Ⓔ
6 Ⓐ Ⓑ Ⓒ Ⓓ Ⓔ	17 Ⓐ Ⓑ Ⓒ Ⓓ Ⓔ	28 Ⓐ Ⓑ Ⓒ Ⓓ Ⓔ	39 Ⓐ Ⓑ Ⓒ Ⓓ Ⓔ	50 Ⓐ Ⓑ Ⓒ Ⓓ Ⓔ	61 Ⓐ Ⓑ Ⓒ Ⓓ Ⓔ
7 Ⓐ Ⓑ Ⓒ Ⓓ Ⓔ	18 Ⓐ Ⓑ Ⓒ Ⓓ Ⓔ	29 Ⓐ Ⓑ Ⓒ Ⓓ Ⓔ	40 Ⓐ Ⓑ Ⓒ Ⓓ Ⓔ	51 Ⓐ Ⓑ Ⓒ Ⓓ Ⓔ	62 Ⓐ Ⓑ Ⓒ Ⓓ Ⓔ
8 Ⓐ Ⓑ Ⓒ Ⓓ Ⓔ	19 Ⓐ Ⓑ Ⓒ Ⓓ Ⓔ	30 Ⓐ Ⓑ Ⓒ Ⓓ Ⓔ	41 Ⓐ Ⓑ Ⓒ Ⓓ Ⓔ	52 Ⓐ Ⓑ Ⓒ Ⓓ Ⓔ	63 Ⓐ Ⓑ Ⓒ Ⓓ Ⓔ
9 Ⓐ Ⓑ Ⓒ Ⓓ Ⓔ	20 Ⓐ Ⓑ Ⓒ Ⓓ Ⓔ	31 Ⓐ Ⓑ Ⓒ Ⓓ Ⓔ	42 Ⓐ Ⓑ Ⓒ Ⓓ Ⓔ	53 Ⓐ Ⓑ Ⓒ Ⓓ Ⓔ	64 Ⓐ Ⓑ Ⓒ Ⓓ Ⓔ
10 Ⓐ Ⓑ Ⓒ Ⓓ Ⓔ	21 Ⓐ Ⓑ Ⓒ Ⓓ Ⓔ	32 Ⓐ Ⓑ Ⓒ Ⓓ Ⓔ	43 Ⓐ Ⓑ Ⓒ Ⓓ Ⓔ	54 Ⓐ Ⓑ Ⓒ Ⓓ Ⓔ	65 Ⓐ Ⓑ Ⓒ Ⓓ Ⓔ
11 Ⓐ Ⓑ Ⓒ Ⓓ Ⓔ	22 Ⓐ Ⓑ Ⓒ Ⓓ Ⓔ	33 Ⓐ Ⓑ Ⓒ Ⓓ Ⓔ	44 Ⓐ Ⓑ Ⓒ Ⓓ Ⓔ	55 Ⓐ Ⓑ Ⓒ Ⓓ Ⓔ	

SECTION II
MATHEMATICAL

1 Ⓐ Ⓑ Ⓒ Ⓓ Ⓔ	10 Ⓐ Ⓑ Ⓒ Ⓓ Ⓔ	19 Ⓐ Ⓑ Ⓒ Ⓓ	27 Ⓐ Ⓑ Ⓒ Ⓓ	35 Ⓐ Ⓑ Ⓒ Ⓓ Ⓔ	43 Ⓐ Ⓑ Ⓒ Ⓓ Ⓔ
2 Ⓐ Ⓑ Ⓒ Ⓓ Ⓔ	11 Ⓐ Ⓑ Ⓒ Ⓓ Ⓔ	20 Ⓐ Ⓑ Ⓒ Ⓓ	28 Ⓐ Ⓑ Ⓒ Ⓓ	36 Ⓐ Ⓑ Ⓒ Ⓓ Ⓔ	44 Ⓐ Ⓑ Ⓒ Ⓓ Ⓔ
3 Ⓐ Ⓑ Ⓒ Ⓓ Ⓔ	12 Ⓐ Ⓑ Ⓒ Ⓓ Ⓔ	21 Ⓐ Ⓑ Ⓒ Ⓓ	29 Ⓐ Ⓑ Ⓒ Ⓓ	37 Ⓐ Ⓑ Ⓒ Ⓓ Ⓔ	45 Ⓐ Ⓑ Ⓒ Ⓓ Ⓔ
4 Ⓐ Ⓑ Ⓒ Ⓓ Ⓔ	13 Ⓐ Ⓑ Ⓒ Ⓓ Ⓔ	22 Ⓐ Ⓑ Ⓒ Ⓓ	30 Ⓐ Ⓑ Ⓒ Ⓓ	38 Ⓐ Ⓑ Ⓒ Ⓓ Ⓔ	46 Ⓐ Ⓑ Ⓒ Ⓓ Ⓔ
5 Ⓐ Ⓑ Ⓒ Ⓓ Ⓔ	14 Ⓐ Ⓑ Ⓒ Ⓓ Ⓔ	23 Ⓐ Ⓑ Ⓒ Ⓓ	31 Ⓐ Ⓑ Ⓒ Ⓓ	39 Ⓐ Ⓑ Ⓒ Ⓓ Ⓔ	47 Ⓐ Ⓑ Ⓒ Ⓓ Ⓔ
6 Ⓐ Ⓑ Ⓒ Ⓓ Ⓔ	15 Ⓐ Ⓑ Ⓒ Ⓓ Ⓔ	24 Ⓐ Ⓑ Ⓒ Ⓓ	32 Ⓐ Ⓑ Ⓒ Ⓓ	40 Ⓐ Ⓑ Ⓒ Ⓓ Ⓔ	48 Ⓐ Ⓑ Ⓒ Ⓓ Ⓔ
7 Ⓐ Ⓑ Ⓒ Ⓓ Ⓔ	16 Ⓐ Ⓑ Ⓒ Ⓓ	25 Ⓐ Ⓑ Ⓒ Ⓓ	33 Ⓐ Ⓑ Ⓒ Ⓓ Ⓔ	41 Ⓐ Ⓑ Ⓒ Ⓓ Ⓔ	49 Ⓐ Ⓑ Ⓒ Ⓓ Ⓔ
8 Ⓐ Ⓑ Ⓒ Ⓓ Ⓔ	17 Ⓐ Ⓑ Ⓒ Ⓓ	26 Ⓐ Ⓑ Ⓒ Ⓓ	34 Ⓐ Ⓑ Ⓒ Ⓓ Ⓔ	42 Ⓐ Ⓑ Ⓒ Ⓓ Ⓔ	50 Ⓐ Ⓑ Ⓒ Ⓓ Ⓔ
9 Ⓐ Ⓑ Ⓒ Ⓓ Ⓔ	18 Ⓐ Ⓑ Ⓒ Ⓓ				

SCORE SHEET

Raw Scores

ANTONYMS	___ – ___ ÷ 4 = ___
SENTENCE COMPLETIONS	___ – ___ ÷ 4 = ___
VERBAL ANALOGIES	___ – ___ ÷ 4 = ___
READING COMPREHENSION	___ – ___ ÷ 4 = ___

Total Verbal Score   ___

MATHEMATICAL PROBLEMS   ___ – ___ ÷ 4 = ___

Note: Do not forget to add together the two sets of problems that come before and after "Quantitative Comparisons."

QUANTITATIVE COMPARISONS   ___ – ___ ÷ 3 = ___

Total Mathematical Score   ___

Percents

ANTONYMS	___ (score) ÷ 20 = ___ × 100 = ___%
SENTENCE COMPLETIONS	___ (score) ÷ 10 = ___ × 100 = ___%
VERBAL ANALOGIES	___ (score) ÷ 15 = ___ × 100 = ___%
READING COMPREHENSION	___ (score) ÷ 20 = ___ × 100 = ___%
MATHEMATICAL PROBLEMS	___ (score) ÷ 33 = ___ × 100 = ___%
QUANTITATIVE COMPARISONS	___ (score) ÷ 17 = ___ × 100 = ___%
TOTAL VERBAL	___ (total verbal score) ÷ 65 = ___ × 100 = ___%
TOTAL MATH	___ (total math score) ÷ 50 = ___ × 100 = ___%

PROGRESS CHART

	Exam I	Exam II	Exam III	Exam IV
ANTONYMS	%	%	%	%
SENTENCE COMPLETIONS	%	%	%	%
VERBAL ANALOGIES	%	%	%	%
READING COMPREHENSION	%	%	%	%
MATHEMATICAL PROBLEMS	%	%	%	%
QUANTITATIVE COMPARISONS	%	%	%	%

MODEL EXAMINATION IV

Section I
Time—50 minutes; 65 questions

DIRECTIONS: For each question, mark the letter preceding the word or phrase that is opposite or most nearly opposite in meaning to the capitalized word. Where more than one option appears to be correct, choose the *best* opposite.

Example:

DAY

(A) morning
(B) week
(C) noon
(D) month
(E) night

---

1. TEPID

    (A) milky
    (B) clean
    (C) exuberant
    (D) firm
    (E) dirty

2. OBTUSE

    (A) sensitive
    (B) slim
    (C) ill-mannered
    (D) active
    (E) angular

3. PATINA

    (A) language
    (B) dome
    (C) bun
    (D) passion
    (E) core

4. ENDORSE

    (A) allot
    (B) invest
    (C) elect
    (D) denounce
    (E) amplify

5. FUSE

    (A) obey
    (B) regulate
    (C) sever
    (D) negate
    (E) de-electrify

6. EMBELLISH

    (A) simplify
    (B) overeat
    (C) reinforce
    (D) abstain
    (E) signify

7. PROHIBITION

    (A) period of drunkenness
    (B) amendment
    (C) illegality
    (D) pretense
    (E) endorsement

8. EXTRANEOUS

    (A) immigrant
    (B) emigrant
    (C) familiar
    (D) irregular
    (E) inherent

9. ANHYDROUS

(A) snakelike
(B) headless
(C) reconstituted
(D) mixed
(E) healthy

10. MISANTHROPY

(A) love of women
(B) love of animals
(C) love of plants
(D) love of mankind
(E) love of study

11. INSOUCIANCE

(A) guilt
(B) malice
(C) appropriateness
(D) intensity
(E) end

12. HIATUS

(A) continuum
(B) large stove
(C) perennial plant
(D) nocturnal animal
(E) tiny worm

13. COGNIZANT

(A) afraid
(B) ignorant
(C) capable
(D) optimistic
(E) ungrammatical

14. TORSION

(A) compressing
(B) sliding
(C) stretching
(D) spinning
(E) straightening

15. INGENUOUS

(A) quick
(B) mischievous
(C) homely
(D) plotting
(E) stupid

16. APPOSITE

(A) irrelevant
(B) same
(C) contrary
(D) spontaneous
(E) tricky

17. INTRANSIGENT

(A) resident
(B) reconcilable
(C) foreign
(D) travel agent
(E) corroborative

18. CAVEAT

(A) deception
(B) seizure
(C) hollow
(D) string-tie
(E) invitation

19. DIURNALLY

(A) twice a year
(B) every other year
(C) every night
(D) twice a night
(E) every other month

20. OFFICIOUS

(A) unimportant
(B) impolite
(C) unofficial
(D) improper
(E) unassuming

DIRECTIONS: Each of the following questions consists of an incomplete sentence followed by five words or pairs of words. Choose that word or pair of words which, when substituted for the blank space or spaces, *best* completes the meaning of the sentence and mark the letter of your choice on your answer sheet.

Example:

A police officer's _____ job is to prevent crime.

(A) primary
(B) only
(C) ostentatious
(D) ostensible
(E) sacred

● Ⓑ Ⓒ Ⓓ Ⓔ

21. He pretended to be nonchalant but his movements betrayed signs of _____ .

(A) greed
(B) weariness
(C) tension
(D) boredom
(E) evil

22. Unethical landowners used to _____ gold in old mines to _____ naïve speculators who would pay high prices for nearly worthless land.

(A) hide .. escape
(B) find .. repay
(C) discover .. anger
(D) loot .. confuse
(E) imbed .. entice

23. The image of a farm as a _____ unit is _____, for rural and urban areas have become interdependent.

(A) manageable .. unrealistic
(B) profitable .. confusing
(C) self-sufficient .. fading
(D) productive .. common
(E) conservative .. accurate

24. His boundless energy and initiative have led him to his most _____ victories and also his most _____ errors.

(A) substantial .. profitable
(B) unusual .. unexplainable
(C) practical .. common
(D) unwarranted .. understandable
(E) noble .. tragic

25. The writer's style showed both the _____ and _____ of those he imitated.

(A) talent .. wealth
(B) strengths .. flaws
(C) intelligence .. bravery
(D) humor .. experience
(E) education .. understanding

26. The management is providing all needed building facilities to help the scientists _____ their research project.

(A) magnify
(B) retard
(C) relinquish
(D) implement
(E) terminate

27. We can easily forgo a _____ we have never had, but once obtained it often is looked upon as being _____.

(A) requirement .. unusual
(B) gift .. useless
(C) luxury .. essential
(D) bonus .. unearned
(E) necessity .. important

28. Knowledge gained from books without the benefit of practical experience is usually not as profitable in everyday work as the opposite, _____ without _____.

(A) culture .. manners
(B) experiments .. science
(C) experience .. scholarship
(D) learning .. knowing
(E) reality .. education

29. Utility is not _____, for the usefulness of an object changes with time and place.

(A) planned
(B) practical
(C) permanent
(D) understandable
(E) important

30. Science is now warring openly against art, and _____ against _____.

(A) technology .. poetry
(B) scientists .. writers
(C) machines .. progress
(D) corporations .. ecology
(E) experts .. amateurs

DIRECTIONS: Each of the following questions consists of a capitalized pair of words followed by five pairs of words lettered A to E. The capitalized words bear some meaningful relationship to each other. Choose the lettered pair of words whose relationship is most similar to that expressed by the capitalized pair and mark its letter on your answer sheet.

Example:

SURGEON : SCALPEL ::

(A) nurse : white
(B) hospital : silence
(C) carpenter : house
(D) butcher : cleaver
(E) butcher : meat

Ⓐ Ⓑ Ⓒ ● Ⓔ

31. JAIL : CRIME ::

(A) judge : criminal
(B) freedom : bird
(C) prison : thief
(D) cemetery : death
(E) victim : intruder

32. DESCRIPTION : CHARACTERIZATION ::

(A) novel : narration
(B) biographer : author
(C) artist : writer

(D) composition : argumentation
(E) picture : portrait

33. MUMBLE : TALK ::

(A) orate : speak
(B) scrawl : write
(C) bumble : buzz
(D) yell : shout
(E) mumbo : jumbo

34. HYBRID : THOROUGHBRED ::

(A) steel : iron
(B) fruit : tree
(C) stallion : mare
(D) highbrow : lowbrow
(E) superficiality : thoroughness

35. FRAGILE : CRACK ::

(A) potent : enervate
(B) irreducible : reduce
(C) frangible : strengthen
(D) odorous : spray
(E) pliable : bend

36. FULLBACK : FIELD ::

(A) halfback : infield
(B) baseball : stadium
(C) boxer : ring
(D) medal : winner
(E) helmet : pad

37. HYDRO : WATER ::

(A) helio : sun
(B) Reno : divorce
(C) canto : score
(D) hydrophobia : dog
(E) Hires : root beer

38. PEACH : BEET ::

(A) grape : apple
(B) potato : tomato
(C) currant : raspberry
(D) banana : pumpkin
(E) cherry : radish

39. SMILE : AMUSEMENT ::

(A) yell : game
(B) guffaw : laughter

(C) yawn : ennui

(D) wink : blink

(E) cry : havoc

40. MINK : LION ::

(A) chicken : wolf

(B) tiger : zebra

(C) farm : zoo

(D) lady : gentleman

(E) timidity : daring

41. DREDGE : SILT ::

(A) tug : gravel

(B) train : plane

(C) scoop : ice cream

(D) distance : sequence

(E) drudge : sludge

42. PLANTS : COAL ::

(A) water : fish

(B) air : gas

(C) animals : oil

(D) rocks : heat

(E) alcohol : burn

43. DOOR : PORTAL ::

(A) opening : closing

(B) doorway : living room

(C) house : ship

(D) knob : key

(E) porch : portico

44. DUNE : SAND ::

(A) hill : beach

(B) wind : grain

(C) salt : air

(D) glazier : glass

(E) glacier : snow

45. LAWYER : CLIENT ::

(A) student : pupil

(B) mechanic : automobile

(C) doctor : patient

(D) stenographer : letters

(E) accountant : books

DIRECTIONS: Below each of the following passages, you will find five questions or incomplete statements about the passage. Each statement or question is followed by five response options. Read the passage carefully. On the basis of what was stated or implied in the passage, select the option which *best* completes each statement or answers each question. You may refer to the passage as often as necessary. Mark the letter of your choice on your answer sheet.

Back in 1892, when Baron Pierre deCoubertin re-created the Olympics, the purpose of the games was to create friendly competition among athletes and nations. The Olympic arena was to be the showcase for the strongest, fleetest, most graceful of every nation.

Unfortunately, deCoubertin's dream has been subverted by increasing politicization of the games. Adolph Hitler began this trend in 1936. The 1936 games were held in Berlin, Germany, and American (10) black athlete, Jesse Owens, won four gold medals. Departing from the tradition by which the leader of the host nation congratulates gold medalists, Hitler refused to shake hands with a black man.

In 1968, the medal ceremony was again used as a political vehicle. This time three black Americans who had won medals in a track and field event displayed the black power sign as they stood on the stand to receive their medals.

The Olympic Committee, itself, has perpetuated (20) the politicization of the games with its ongoing debate over which Chinese delegation—the People's Republic of China (Red China) or the Nationalist Republic of China (Taiwan)—should represent the Chinese people.

The bleakest of all years in modern Olympic history was 1972. First, committees of predominantly Communist judges handed down blatantly biased rulings in boxing matches, gymnastic competitions and basketball games. Then, far worse, a (30) group of Palestinian terrorists attacked the Israeli quarters, took hostages and held siege. Eleven innocent Israeli athletes were killed.

In light of this history, it is difficult to understand the public outcry against politicization by boycott of the 1980 games. The purpose of the 1980 boycott is to protest the invasion in late December 1979 of Afghanistan by the U.S.S.R. The locale of the 1980 Olympics in Moscow, and the presence there of international press, dignitaries and athletes is a pow- (40) erful propaganda opportunity for the Russians. Russia can show its own people how popular and important it is; the world can be shown the brightest aspects of life in the U.S.S.R. Boycott of the Olympics by a large portion of the free world would seriously damage the propaganda value of the games.

A show of solidarity by the governments and athletes of the ''free world'' might demonstrate to (50) the Russians that conquest and domination of weaker countries will no longer be tolerated. The Olympics might, in an oblique way, turn out to be the instrument of peace and freedom for small nations.

If this were to happen, the Olympic games might have come full circle, back to one of its original roles. In ancient Greece, the Olympics were an extremely important event. In Olympic years, wars were suspended so that athletes of all city-states might prepare for and participate in the games and (60) the citizens of all city-states might be spectators. Wars thus suspended were sometimes never resumed. Furthermore, athletes were sometimes designated as surrogate warriors. A contest settled in the peaceful athletic arena served to settle disputes in the political arena as well. The nation of the athletic victor was the victorious nation, and the war was over.

46. Baron deCoubertin hoped that the Olympic Games would

(A) serve as a political battleground
(B) prove which government is best
(C) serve as a substitute for war
(D) offer recognition to artists
(E) allow for peaceful competition

47. The ''free world'' mentioned in line 49 refers to

(A) the ''third world''
(B) all nations which are independent
(C) non-Communist countries
(D) countries in which Olympic athletes are not paid
(E) countries which do not participate in the Olympics

48. Politicization (line 8) of the games refers to

(A) sending of separate Democratic and Republican teams
(B) use of the games for a political purpose
(C) the manner of selection of Olympic officials
(D) cheating
(E) the method by which the site of the Olympics is chosen

49. Jesse Owens was

(A) a political pawn
(B) politically motivated
(C) an Olympic judge
(D) a black liberationist
(E) in no way connected with political events

50. A successful boycott of the 1980 Olympics would show

I. that the free world is opposed to the Olympics
II. that the free world opposes politicization of the Olympics
III. that the free world opposes invasion of one country by another
IV. that athletics are unimportant

(A) II only
(B) III only
(C) I and III
(D) I, III and IV
(E) I, II, III and IV

In discussing human competence in a world of change, I want to make it crystal-clear that I am not ready to accept all the changes that are being pressed on us. I am not at all prepared to suggest that we must blindly find new competences in order to adjust to all the changes or in order to make ourselves inconspicuous in the modern habitat. Let me be specific. I see no reason in the world why modern man should develop any competence whatsoever to pay high rents in order to be permitted to live in buildings with walls that act as soundtracks rather than sound absorbers. Nor do I believe that this problem can or should be overcome by developing such novel engineering competences as ''acoustical perfume''—artificial noise to drown out next-door noises. When I don't wish to be a silent partner to the bedroom conversation of the neighbors, I am not at all satisfied by having the sound effects of a waterfall, the chirping of crickets, or incidental music superimposed on the disturbance, just to cover up the incompetence or greed of modern builders.

The other day I found myself wandering through the desolate destruction of Pennsylvania Station in New York, thoroughly incompetent in my efforts to find a ticket office. Instead I found a large poster which said that ''your new station'' was being built and that this was the reason for my temporary inconvenience. Nonsense! my station was not being built at all. My station is being destroyed, and I do not need the new competence of an advertising copy writer or a public relations consultant to obscure the facts. The competence that was needed—and which I and great numbers of like-minded contemporaries lacked—was the competence to prevent an undesirable change. In plain language—the competence to stop the organized vandalism which, in the name of progress and change, is tearing down good buildings to put up flimsy ones; is dynamiting fine landmarks to replace them with structures that can be ripped down again twenty years later without a tear.

When the packaging industry finds it increasingly easy to design containers that make reduced contents appear to be an enlarged value at a steeper price, the change does not call for the competence of a consumer psychologist to make the defrauded customer feel happy. The change calls simply for a tough public prosecutor.

Lest I be mistaken for a political or even a sentimental reactionary who wants to halt progress and change, let me add another example of modern life the improvement of which may call for radical public action rather than for any new competence. Commuter rail transportation has fallen into decline in many parts of the country. Persons dependent on it find themselves frustrated and inconvenienced. In reply to their plight, they are given explanations such as the economic difficulties facing the railroad. Explanations, however, are no substitute for remedies. The competence required here is not technological or mechanical. After all, it would be difficult to persuade any sane citizen that a technology able to dispatch men into space and return them on schedule is mechanically incapable of transporting commuters from the suburbs to the cities in comfort, in safety, and on time.

The competence lacking here is one of general intelligence of the kind that is willing to shed doctrinaire myths when they stand in the way of the facts of modern life. To make millions of commuters suffer (and I use this example only because it is readily familiar, not because it is unique today) merely because the doctrine of free, competitive enterprise must be upheld, even after competition has disappeared as a vital ingredient, is an example of ludicrous mental incompetence. So is the tendency to worry whether a public takeover of a public necessity that is no longer being adequately maintained by private enterprise constitutes socialism or merely the protection of citizens' interests.

We ought to place the stress of competence in such a fashion that we can use it to mold, control, and—in extreme instances—even to block change rather than merely to adjust or submit to it.

—by Fred M. Hechinger (reprinted with permission)

51. The attitude of the writer is

   (A) sardonic and uncompromising
   (B) critical and constructive
   (C) petulant and forbidding
   (D) maudlin and merciful
   (E) reflective and questioning

52. A ''doctrinaire myth'' (next to last paragraph) may be defined as a belief based on the false premises of

   (A) a deluded lexicographer
   (B) a public relations man
   (C) an insincere politician
   (D) a quack
   (E) an impractical theorist

53. In the article, the author urges us

   (A) to fight against unethical political deals
   (B) to disregard the claims of the advertiser
   (C) to be opposed to many of the changes going on in our society today
   (D) not to rent a luxury apartment
   (E) to avoid becoming a commuter

54. The passage in no way states or implies that

   (A) much construction today is inferior to what it was in other years
   (B) the razing of Pennsylvania Station was justifiable
   (C) consumers are often deceived
   (D) some engineering devices are not worth the trouble spent in contriving them
   (E) space scientists have made great progress

55. You would expect the author to say that

(A) there is no reason for the United States to send nuclear-powered submarines to Japanese ports
(B) a great deal of confusion reigns in credit card circles
(C) a truly fundamental need in our society is honesty of thought and attitude
(D) the damage done to our language by the structural linguists is not altogether irreparable
(E) the world's population seems now to be increasing out of all proportion to the world's ability to provide food and education

Of all the areas of learning the most important is the development of attitudes. Emotional reactions as well as logical thought processes affect the behavior of most people.

"The burnt child fears the fire" is one instance; another is the rise of despots like Hitler. Both these examples also point up the fact that attitudes stem from experience. In the one case the experience was direct and impressive; in the other it was indirect and cumulative. The Nazis were indoctrinated largely by the speeches they heard and the books they read.

The classroom teacher in the elementary school is in a strategic position to influence attitudes. This is true partly because children acquire attitudes from those adults whose word they respect.

Another reason it is true is that pupils often delve somewhat deeply into a subject in school that has only been touched upon at home or has possibly never occurred to them before. To a child who had previously acquired little knowledge of Mexico, his teacher's method of handling such a unit would greatly affect his attitude toward Mexicans.

The media through which the teacher can develop wholesome attitudes are innumerable. Social studies (with special reference to races, creeds and nationalities), science matters of health and safety, the very atmosphere of the classroom—these are a few of the fertile fields for the inculcation of proper emotional reactions.

However, when children come to school with undesirable attitudes, it is unwise for the teacher to attempt to change their feelings by cajoling or scolding them. She can achieve the proper effect by helping them obtain constructive experiences.

To illustrate, first-grade pupils afraid of policemen will probably alter their attitudes after a classroom chat with the neighborhood officer in which he explains how he protects them. In the same way, a class of older children can develop attitudes through discussion, research, outside reading and all-day trips.

Finally, a teacher must constantly evaluate her own attitudes, because her influence can be deleterious if she has personal prejudices. This is especially true in respect to controversial issues and questions on which children should be encouraged to reach their own decisions as a result of objective analysis of all the facts.

56. The central idea conveyed in the above passage is that

(A) attitudes affect our actions
(B) teachers play a significant role in developing or changing pupils' attitudes
(C) attitudes can be changed by some classroom experiences
(D) by their attitudes, teachers inadvertently affect pupils' attitudes
(E) the elementary school is a more effective milieu for developing wholesome attitudes than high school or college

57. The author implies that

(A) the teacher should guide all discussions by revealing her own attitude
(B) the elementary school is frequently the first place a child comes into contact with a variety of attitudes
(C) people usually act on the basis of reasoning rather than on emotion
(D) children's attitudes often come from those of other children
(E) schools should offer the student opportunities for travel so that he can come into contact with people he would not otherwise meet

58. A statement *not* made or implied in the passage is that

(A) attitudes can be based on the learning of falsehoods
(B) a child can develop in the classroom an attitude about the importance of brushing his teeth

(C) attitudes cannot easily be changed by re-wards and lectures

(D) the attitudes of elementary school-aged children are influenced primarily by the way they were treated as infants

(E) worthwhile attitudes may be developed in practically every subject area

59. The passage specifically states that

(A) direct experiences are more valuable than indirect ones

(B) whatever attitudes a child learns in school have already been introduced at home

(C) teachers should always conceal their own attitudes

(D) teachers can sometimes have an unwhole-some influence on children

(E) most children fear policemen

60. Changing young children's attitudes can best be achieved by

(A) threats of punishment

(B) lectures and demonstrations

(C) developing programs in which they have positive experiences

(D) reading interesting books

(E) field trips

The standardized educational or psychological tests that are widely used to aid in selecting, classify-ing, assigning, or promoting students, employees, and military personnel have been the target of recent attacks in books, magazines, the daily press, and even in Congress. The target is wrong, for in attack-ing the tests critics divert attention from the fault that lies with ill-informed or incompetent users. The tests themselves are merely tools, with characteristics that can be measured with reasonable precision under specified conditions. Whether the results will be valuable, meaningless, or even misleading depends partly upon the tool itself but largely upon the user.

All informed predictions of future performance are based upon some knowledge of relevant past perfor-mance: school grades, research productivity, sales records, batting averages, or whatever is appropriate. How well the predictions will be validated by later performance depends upon the amount, reliability, and appropriateness of the information used and on the skill and wisdom with which it is interpreted. Anyone who keeps careful score knows that the information available is always incomplete and that the predictions are always subject to error.

Standardized tests should be considered in this context. They provide a quick, objective method of getting some kinds of information about what a person has learned, the skills he has developed, or the kind of person he is. The information so obtained has, qualitatively, the same advantages and short-comings as other kinds of information. Whether to use tests, other kinds of information, or both in a particular situation depends, therefore, upon the em-pirical evidence concerning comparative validity, and upon such factors as cost and availability.

In general, the tests work most effectively when the traits or qualities to be measured can be most precisely defined (for example, ability to do well in a particular course or training program) and least effec-tively when what is to be measured or predicted cannot be well defined (for example, personality or creativity). Properly used, they provide a rapid means of getting comparable information about many people. Sometimes they identify students whose high potential has not been previously recognized. But there are many things they do not do. For example, they do not compensate for gross social inequality, and thus do not tell how able an under-privileged youngster might have been had he grown up under more favorable circumstances.

Professionals in the business and the conscientious publishers know the limitations as well as the values. They write these things into test manuals and in critiques of available tests. But they have no jurisdic-tion over users; an educational test can be adminis-tered by almost anyone, whether he knows how to interpret it or not. Nor can the difficulty be con-trolled by limiting sales to qualified users; some attempts to do so have been countered by restraint-of-trade suits.

In the long run it may be possible to establish better controls or to require high qualifications. But in the meantime, unhappily, the demonstrated value of these tests under many circumstances has given them a popularity that has led to considerable mis-use. Also unhappily, justifiable criticism of the mis-use now threatens to hamper proper use. Business and government can probably look after themselves. But school guidance and selection programs are being attacked for using a valuable tool, because some of the users are unskilled.

—by Watson Davis, Sc.D., Director of Science Service
(reprinted with permission)

61. The essence of this article on educational tests is:

   (A) These tests do not test adequately what they set out to test.
   (B) Don't blame the test—blame the user.
   (C) When a student is nervous or ill, the test results are inaccurate.
   (D) Publishers of tests are without conscience.
   (E) Educators are gradually losing confidence in the value of the tests

62. Tests like the College Entrance Scholastic Aptitude Test are, it would seem to the author,

   (A) generally unreliable
   (B) generally reliable
   (C) meaningless
   (D) misleading
   (E) neither good nor bad

63. The selection implies that, more often, the value of an educational test rests with

   (A) the interpretation of results
   (B) the test itself
   (C) the testee
   (D) emotional considerations
   (E) the directions

64. According to the passage, the validity of a test requires most of all

   (A) cooperation on the part of the person tested
   (B) sufficient preparation on the part of the applicant
   (C) clearcut directions
   (D) one answer—and only one—for each question
   (E) specificity regarding what is to be tested

65. The author fears that criticism of the tests will lead to

   (A) restraint of trade
   (B) restraint-of-trade suits
   (C) gross social inequality
   (D) "throwing out the baby with the bath water"
   (E) uncontrolled popularity

END OF SECTION I

IF YOU COMPLETE THIS SECTION BEFORE TIME IS UP, CHECK OVER YOUR WORK.

DIRECTIONS: Solve each of the following problems, using available space on the page for your scratch work. Mark the letter of the correct answer on your answer sheet.
   You may refer to the following data in solving the problems.

Triangle:

The angles of a triangle added together equal 180°.
The angle BDC is a right angle; therefore,

   (I) the area of triangle ABC $= \dfrac{AC \times BD}{2}$

   (II) $AB^2 = AD^2 + DB^2$

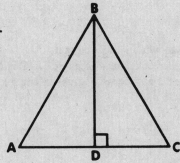

Circle:

There are 360° of arc in a circle.
The area of a circle of radius r $= \pi r^2$
The circumference of a circle $= 2\pi r$
A straight angle has 180°.

Symbol references:

$\parallel$ is parallel to	$>$ is greater than
$\leqq$ is less than or equal to	$<$ is less than
$\geqq$ is greater than or equal to	$\perp$ is perpendicular to
$\angle$ angle	$\triangle$ triangle

Notes: The diagrams which accompany problems should provide data helpful in working out the solutions. These diagrams are not necessarily drawn precisely to scale. Unless otherwise stated, all figures lie in the same plane. All numbers are real numbers.

1. What is 40% of $\frac{10}{7}$?

   (A) $\frac{2}{7}$
   (B) $\frac{4}{7}$
   (C) $\frac{10}{28}$
   (D) $\frac{1}{28}$
   (E) $\frac{28}{10}$

2. A prime number is one which is divisible only by itself and 1. Which of the following are prime numbers?

 I. 17
 II. 27
 III. 51
 IV. 59

(A) I only
(B) I and II only
(C) I, III, and IV only
(D) I and IV only
(E) III and IV only

3. As shown in the diagram, AB is a straight line and angle BOC = 20°. If the number of degrees in angle DOC is 6 more than the number of degrees in angle x, find the number of degrees in angle x.

(A) 77
(B) 75
(C) 78
(D) $22\frac{6}{7}$
(E) 87

4. As shown in the figure, a cylindrical oil tank is $\frac{1}{3}$ full. If 3 more gallons are added, the tank will be half-full. What is the capacity, in gallons, of the tank?

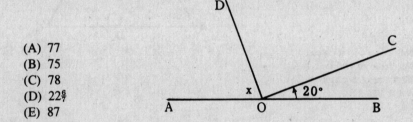

(A) 15
(B) 16
(C) 17
(D) 18
(E) 19

5. A boy receives grades of 91, 88, 86, and 78 in four of his major subjects. What must he receive in his fifth major subject in order to average 85?

(A) 86
(B) 85
(C) 84
(D) 83
(E) 82

6. If a steel bar is 0.39 feet long, its length in *inches* is

(A) less than 4
(B) between 4 and $4\frac{1}{2}$
(C) between $4\frac{1}{2}$ and 5
(D) between 5 and 6
(E) more than 6

7. In the figure, PS is perpendicular to QR. If PQ = PR = 26 and PS = 24, then QR =

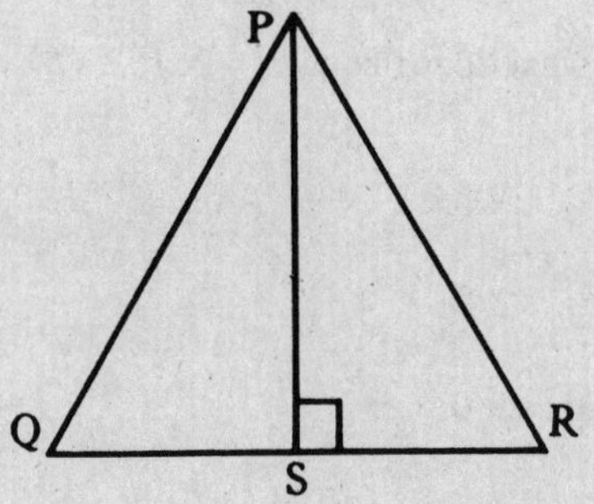

(A) 14
(B) 16
(C) 18
(D) 20
(E) 22

8. If x = 0, for what value of y is the following equation valid?
$5x^3 + 7x^2 - (4y + 13)x - 7y + 15 = 0$

(A) $-2\frac{1}{7}$
(B) 0
(C) $+2\frac{1}{7}$
(D) $\frac{15}{11}$
(E) $3\frac{1}{7}$

9. A man buys some shirts and ties. The shirts cost \$7 each and the ties cost \$3 each. If the man spends exactly \$81 and buys the maximum number of shirts possible under these conditions, what is the ratio of shirts to ties?

(A) 5:3
(B) 4:3
(C) 5:2
(D) 4:1
(E) 3:2

10. If a man walks $\frac{2}{5}$ mile in 5 minutes, what is his average rate of walking in miles per hour?

(A) 4
(B) $4\frac{1}{2}$
(C) $4\frac{4}{5}$
(D) $5\frac{1}{5}$
(E) $5\frac{3}{4}$

11. One end of a dam has the shape of a trapezoid with the dimensions indicated. What is the dam's area in square feet?

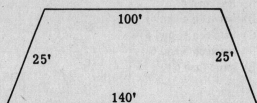

(A) 1000
(B) 1200
(C) 1500
(D) 1800
(E) cannot be determined from the information given

12. If $1 + \dfrac{1}{t} = \dfrac{t + 1}{t}$, what does t equal?

(A) +2 only
(B) +2 or −2 only
(C) +2 or −1 only
(D) −2 or +1 only
(E) t is any number except 0.

13. Point A is 3 inches from line b as shown in the diagram. In the plane that contains point A and line b, what is the total number of points which are 6 inches from A and also 1 inch from b?

(A) 0
(B) 1
(C) 2
(D) 3
(E) 4

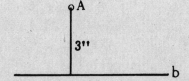

14. If R and S are different integers, both divisible by 5, then which of the following is *not necessarily* true?

(A) R − S is divisible by 5
(B) RS is divisible by 25
(C) R + S is divisible by 5
(D) $R^2 + S^2$ is divisible by 5
(E) R + S is divisible by 10

15. If a triangle of base 7 is equal in area to a circle of radius 7, what is the altitude of the triangle?

(A) 8π
(B) 10π
(C) 12π
(D) 14π
(E) cannot be determined from the information given

DIRECTIONS: For each of the following questions, two quantities are given—one in Column A, the other in Column B. Compare the two quantities and mark your answer sheet as follows:

(A) if the quantity in Column A is greater
(B) if the quantity in Column B is greater
(C) if the two quantities are equal
(D) if the relationship cannot be determined from the information given.

NECESSARY INFORMATION:

• In each question, information concerning one or both of the quantities to be compared is centered above the entries in the two columns.

• A symbol that appears in any column represents the same thing in Column A as it does in Column B.

• All numbers used are real numbers; letters such as x, y and t stand for real numbers.

• Assume that the position of points, angles, regions and so forth are in the order shown and that all figures lie in a plane unless otherwise indicated.

• Figures are not necessarily drawn to scale.

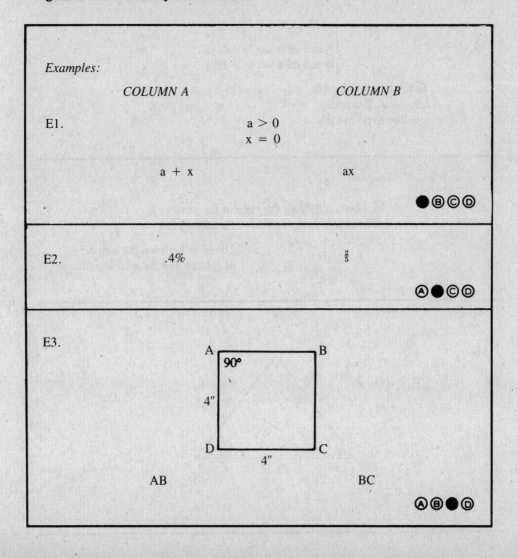

	COLUMN A	**COLUMN B**

16. $\dfrac{3/7}{5/14}$ $\qquad\qquad$ $\dfrac{5/14}{3/7}$

---

17. Difference between $\dfrac{3}{8}$ and $\dfrac{9}{8}$ $\qquad\qquad$ .5

---

18. $\dfrac{3}{5}\%$ $\qquad\qquad$ .06

---

19. $\begin{cases} \text{A can do a job in 4 days} \\ \text{B can do a job in 3 days} \end{cases}$

The number of days it takes A & B working together to do the job $\qquad\qquad$ 2 days

---

20. In a certain college the ratio of the number of freshmen to the number of seniors is 3:1

1:3 $\qquad\qquad$ The ratio between the number of seniors and the total enrollment

---

21.

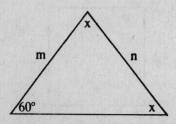

m $\qquad\qquad$ n

COLUMN A	COLUMN B

22.
$$\begin{cases} a + b = x \\ a - b = y \end{cases}$$

x · y

---

23.   (3x − 4)(2x + 3) = 0

The least root of the equation · The product of the roots of the equation

---

24.   4 + 6(−1) ÷ 3 · −1 + 1(−6) ÷ −2

25.

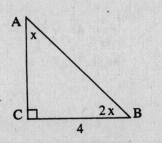

5   ·   4   ·   AB

---

26. $\sqrt[3]{125}$ · $(25)^{\frac{1}{2}}$

---

27.   (x − y)° · (x + y)°

28.

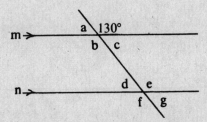

Angles b + g · Angles a + c + d

COLUMN A   **COLUMN B**

29.
$$\begin{cases} x = -1 \\ y = 1 \end{cases}$$

$xy + 2x - y$ $xy - 2x + y$

30.

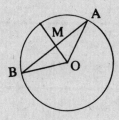

Chord AB = 6 in.
OM ⊥ AB
Radius OB = 5 in.

2(AM)   OM + AO

---

31.   During a store sale a $43.50 radio can
                be purchased at a 15% discount

The selling price of the $36
radio with the discount

---

32.   75% of ½   50% of ¾

DIRECTIONS: Solve each of the following problems, using available space on the page for your scratch work. Mark the letter of the correct answer on your answer sheet.

33. If the following numbers are arranged in order from the smallest to the largest, what will be their correct order?

   I. $\dfrac{9}{13}$

   II. $\dfrac{13}{9}$

   III. 70%

   IV. $\dfrac{1}{.70}$

   (A) II, I, III, IV
   (B) III, II, I, IV
   (C) III, IV, I, II
   (D) II, IV, III, I
   (E) I, III, IV, II

34. The coordinates of the vertices of quadrilateral PQRS are P(0, 0), Q(9, 0), R(10, 3) and S(1, 3) respectively. The area of PQRS is

   (A) $9\sqrt{10}$
   (B) $\frac{9}{2}\sqrt{10}$
   (C) $\frac{27}{2}$
   (D) 27
   (E) not determinable from the information given

35. In the circle shown, AB is a diameter. If secant AP = 8 and tangent CP = 4, find the numbers of units in the diameter of the circle.

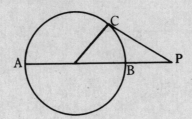

   (A) 6
   (B) $6\frac{1}{2}$
   (C) 8
   (D) $3\sqrt{2}$
   (E) cannot be determined from the information given

36. A certain type of siding for a house costs $10.50 per square yard. What does it cost for the siding for a wall 4 yards wide and 60 feet long?

   (A) $800
   (B) $840
   (C) $2520
   (D) $3240
   (E) $5040

37. A circle whose radius is 7 has its center at the origin. Which of the following points are outside the circle?

   I. (4, 4)
  II. (5, 5)
 III. (4, 5)
 IV. (4, 6)

(A) I and II only
(B) II and III only
(C) II, III, and IV only
(D) II and IV only
(E) III and IV only

38. A merchant sells a radio for $80, thereby making a profit of 25% of the cost. What is the ratio of cost to selling price?

(A) $\frac{4}{5}$
(B) $\frac{3}{4}$
(C) $\frac{5}{6}$
(D) $\frac{2}{3}$
(E) $\frac{3}{5}$

39. How many degrees between the hands of a clock at 3:40?

(A) 150°
(B) 140°
(C) 130°
(D) 125°
(E) 120°

40. Two fences in a field meet at 120°. A cow is tethered at their intersection with a 15 foot rope, as shown in the figure. Over how many square feet may the cow graze?

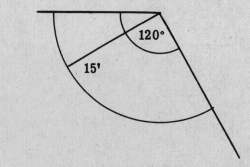

(A) 50π
(B) 75π
(C) 80π
(D) 85π
(E) 90π

41. If $\frac{17}{10} y = 0.51$, then y =

(A) 3
(B) 1.3
(C) 1.2
(D) .3
(E) .03

42. A junior class of 50 girls and 70 boys sponsored à dance. If 40% of the girls and 50% of the boys attended the dance, approximately what percent attended?

(A) 40
(B) 42
(C) 44
(D) 46
(E) 48

43. In the figure below, r, s, and t are straight lines meeting at point P, with angles formed as indicated; then y =

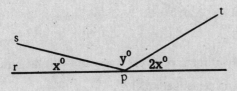

(A) 30°
(B) 120°
(C) 3x
(D) 180 − x
(E) 180 − 3x

44. $\frac{18}{33} = \frac{\sqrt{36}}{\sqrt{?}}$

(A) 11
(B) 121
(C) 66
(D) 144
(E) 1089

45. If we write all the whole numbers from 200 to 400, how many of these contain the digit 7 once and only once?

(A) 32
(B) 34
(C) 35
(D) 36
(E) 38

46. $(r + s)^2 - r^2 - s^2 = (?)$

(A) 2rs
(B) rs
(C) rs²
(D) 0
(E) 2r² + 2s²

47. In the figure, angle S is obtuse, PR = 9, PS = 6 and Q is any point on RS. Which of the following inequalities expresses possible values of the length of PQ?

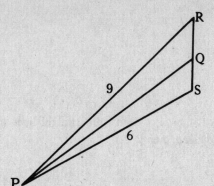

(A) $9 \geq PQ \geq 6$
(B) $9 \geq 6 \geq PQ$
(C) $6 \geq PQ \geq 9$
(D) $PQ \geq 9 \geq 6$
(E) $9 \leq PQ \leq 6$

48. If a man buys several articles for K cents per dozen and sells them for $\dfrac{K}{8}$ cents per article, what is his profit, in cents, per article?

(A) $\dfrac{K}{48}$

(B) $\dfrac{K}{12}$

(C) $\dfrac{3K}{4}$

(D) $\dfrac{K}{18}$

(E) $\dfrac{K}{24}$

49. If all P are S and no S are Q, it necessarily follows that

(A) all Q are S
(B) all Q are P
(C) no P are Q
(D) no S are P
(E) some Q are P

50. The average of four numbers is 45. If one of the numbers is increased by 6, the average will remain unchanged if each of the other three numbers is reduced by

(A) 1
(B) 2
(C) $\frac{3}{4}$
(D) 4
(E) $\frac{4}{3}$

END OF EXAMINATION

IF YOU FINISH BEFORE TIME IS CALLED, CHECK OVER YOUR WORK ON SECTION
II. DO NOT RETURN TO SECTION I.

MODEL EXAMINATION IV—ANSWER KEY

Section I

1. C	14. E	27. C	40. B	53. C
2. A	15. D	28. C	41. C	54. B
3. E	16. A	29. C	42. C	55. C
4. D	17. B	30. A	43. E	56. B
5. C	18. E	31. D	44. E	57. B
6. A	19. C	32. E	45. C	58. D
7. E	20. E	33. B	46. E	59. D
8. E	21. C	34. A	47. C	60. C
9. C	22. E	35. E	48. B	61. B
10. D	23. C	36. C	49. A	62. B
11. D	24. E	37. A	50. B	63. A
12. A	25. B	38. E	51. B	64. E
13. B	26. D	39. C	52. E	65. D

Section II

1. B	11. D	21. C	31. A	41. D
2. D	12. E	22. D	32. C	42. D
3. A	13. E	23. A	33. E	43. E
4. D	14. E	24. C	34. D	44. B
5. E	15. D	25. B	35. A	45. D
6. C	16. A	26. C	36. B	46. A
7. D	17. A	27. C	37. D	47. A
8. C	18. B	28. A	38. A	48. E
9. E	19. B	29. B	39. C	49. C
10. C	20. A	30. B	40. B	50. B

EXPLANATORY ANSWERS

SECTION I

1. **(C)** EXUBERANT means enthusiastic or extreme in degree. TEPID means unenthusiastic or lukewarm.

2. **(A)** SENSITIVE. OBTUSE means insensitive, blunt or dull.

3. **(E)** The CORE is the central part of a mass. PATINA is the surface film of metals.

4. **(D)** DENOUNCE means to criticize or to proclaim to be evil. ENDORSE means to approve.

5. **(C)** SEVER means to divide or to separate. FUSE means to blend.

6. **(A)** SIMPLIFY means to reduce to basics. EMBELLISH means to add ornamental details.

7. **(E)** ENDORSEMENT means approving. PROHIBITION means forbidding.

8. **(E)** INHERENT means basic and intrinsic to the nature of something. EXTRANEOUS means inessential, extrinsic or irrelevant.

9. **(C)** RECONSTITUTED means reformed. As the antonym of anhydrous, reconstituted means reformed by the addition of water which was previously removed. ANHYDROUS means lacking water or dehydrated.

10. **(D)** LOVE OF MANKIND. MISANTHROPY means hatred of mankind. The Greek prefix "mis" means hatred. The Greek word "anthropos" means man.

11. **(D)** INTENSITY means straining to an intense degree. INSOUCIANCE means lighthearted lack of concern.

12. **(A)** A CONTINUUM is an uninterrupted sequence. A HIATUS is a lapse in continuity.

13. **(B)** IGNORANT means unaware or uninformed. COGNIZANT means aware or knowing.

14. **(E)** STRAIGHTENING. TORSION means twisting. At first glance it might appear that (C), stretching, is also a correct answer, but twisting and stretching are not necessarily incompatible, hence (E), straightening, is the *best* answer.

15. **(D)** PLOTTING means conspiring and scheming. INGENUOUS means straightforward and innocent.

16. **(A)** IRRELEVANT. APPOSITE means relevant.

17. **(B)** RECONCILABLE means adjustable. INTRANSIGENT means uncompromising or irreconcilable.

18. **(E)** An INVITATION is a solicitation to or welcome of certain participation. A CAVEAT is a warning, especially a warning not to engage in certain behavior.

19. **(C)** EVERY NIGHT or nocturnally. DIURNALLY means daily, occurring by day every day.

20. **(E)** UNASSUMING means modest and reticent. OFFICIOUS means meddlesome or interfering where uninvited.

21. **(C)** The sense of this sentence requires a word that is opposite in meaning to nonchalant (indifferent). TENSION (meaning strain) is the only word that has this relationship to nonchalant.

22. **(E)** That the landowners are described as unethical (immoral) indicates that they would attempt to deceive the naive speculators. This would best be accomplished by IMBEDDING gold in worthless mines in order to ENTICE (tempt or lure) the speculators to pay inflated prices.

23. **(C)** The relationship established by this sentence is cause and effect. Since the effect is given as interdependence of rural and urban areas, the most reasonable cause would be a FADING of the image of the farm as a SELF-SUFFICIENT unit.

24. **(E)** The tone of the sentence establishes the need for words like "boundless" which indicate extremes. Of the choices offered, NOBLE and TRAGIC best fulfill this requirement.

25. **(B)** Since the sentence is about one writer's style, "those he imitated" must also be writers. The words needed to complete the thought therefore must be opposites which apply to even the best writers. STRENGTHS and FLAWS (weaknesses) best satisfy this requirement.

26. **(D)** The word "help" indicates the need for a positive word to complete this sentence. Therefore, you need consider only choices (A) and (D). Of these two, IMPLEMENT (meaning put into action) is a better choice than magnify (meaning to make larger).

27. **(C)** The words required to complete the thought must be opposites. A LUXURY is something we can easily do without, but once we have had that luxury for awhile we can no longer do without it and it becomes a necessity (an ESSENTIAL).

28. **(C)** The sentence mentions "knowledge gained without experience" and then asks for the opposite condition, which must be EXPERIENCE without SCHOLARSHIP.

29. **(C)** If the usefulness of an object changes, then that usefulness is by definition not PERMANENT.

30. **(A)** This sentence sets up an analogy in which science (systemization of knowledge in general)

is related to art (the production of that which is beautiful) in the same way that TECHNOLOGY (a particular branch of knowledge) is related to POETRY (a particular art form). At first glance (B) might be considered correct, but all writers are not involved in the production of art; therefore, (A) is the better choice.

31. **(D)** DEATH generally leads one to the CEMETERY; CRIME generally leads one to JAIL. The relationship is one of *effect and cause*.

32. **(E)** A PORTRAIT (picture of a person) is a kind of PICTURE; a CHARACTERIZATION (description of a person) is a kind of DESCRIPTION. The relationship is that of *whole to part*.

33. **(B)** To SCRAWL is to WRITE carelessly and illegibly; to MUMBLE is to TALK carelessly and unintelligibly. The relationship is that of *part to whole*.

34. **(A)** STEEL is an alloy (mixture of a number of elements) of IRON, which is a pure element; a HYBRID is a plant or animal of mixed origin, while a THOROUGHBRED is of pure stock. The relationship is one of *association*.

35. **(E)** A PLIABLE (flexible) object is easy to BEND; a FRAGILE (delicate) object is likely to CRACK. The relationship is one of *function*.

36. **(C)** A BOXER plies his trade in the RING: a FULLBACK plays football on a FIELD. The relationship is one of *function*.

37. **(A)** HELIO is the Greek word for SUN; HYDRO is the Greek word for WATER. Both are used as combining forms in English. The relationship is one of *definition*.

38. **(E)** A CHERRY is a fruit which grows on a tree, while a RADISH is a root vegetable; a PEACH is a fruit which grows on a tree, while a BEET is a root vegetable which grows in the earth. The relationship is based on *location*.

39. **(C)** A YAWN is a sign of ENNUI (boredom); a SMILE is a sign of AMUSEMENT. The relationship is one of *association*.

40. **(B)** A TIGER and a ZEBRA are both striped animals; the MINK and the LION are both animals of a single color. The relationship is based upon a similar *characteristic*.

41. **(C)** One uses a SCOOP to get ICE CREAM from a container; one uses a DREDGE to get SILT from the river bottom. The relationship is one of *function*.

42. **(C)** OIL is a fossil fuel, a hydrocarbon, the original source of which is prehistoric ANIMALS; COAL is a fossil fuel, the source of which is ancient, carbonized PLANT life. The relationship is one of *sequence*.

43. **(E)** A PORTICO is a fancy PORCH; a PORTAL is a fancy DOOR. The relationship is one of *degree*.

44. **(E)** A GLACIER is an ice field formed by a build-up and compaction of SNOW; a DUNE is a mound built up of blown SAND. The relationship is one of *definition*.

45. **(C)** A PATIENT is a person who relies on the services of a DOCTOR; a CLIENT is a person who utilizes the services of a LAWYER. The relationship is one of *association*.

46. **(E)** DeCoubertin hoped for nothing more than to establish a framework for athletes of many nations to come together in peaceful athletic competition on a regular, periodic basis.

47. **(C)** The term "free world" is used to apply to non-Communist nations. Many nations which consider themselves independent, (B), have governments which are aligned with the Communist bloc and are thus dominated to some degree. These Communist independent nations are not considered to be members of the free world.

48. **(B)** Politicization of the games here refers directly and explicitly to the use of the games for political purposes.

49. **(A)** A pawn is one that can be used to further the purposes of another. Jesse Owens was used as a political pawn by Adolph Hitler. Hitler dramatized the Nazi dedication to Aryan (white) superiority by ostracizing Owens. Owens was connected with political events, though most certainly not in any active sense. Even though he was black, Owens was not associated with the black liberationist movement, which rose to recognition long after 1936.

50. **(B)** A successful boycott of the Olympics would show only that the free world opposes invasion

of one country by another. The boycott itself is a further politicization of the Olympics, and the regret with which the boycott is called for makes clear the high esteem in which athletics and the Olympics are held.

51. **(B)** There is no doubt that the author is highly critical of today's society. He is opposed to change for its own sake, to shoddy workmanship and to stubborn adherence to old methods when a better way might be possible. Along with his criticism he makes suggestions. Specifically, he suggests that legal remedies be taken against deceptive packaging and that public agencies take over where private enterprise has failed.

52. **(E)** A doctrinaire is a person who tries to put into effect abstract doctrines without concern for the practical aspects. In this passage the doctrinaire myth is an impractical theorist's delusion that private enterprise is always the preferable course and that all that is not private enterprise is socialism.

53. **(C)** The author is discussing the problems of the commuter, of poor construction and of deceptive packaging in order to illustrate his point that change should be related to progress. While some changes, especially in the management of the railroads, should be encouraged and expedited, much "change-for-the-sake-of-change" should be resisted.

54. **(B)** The author can find no good reason for the renovation of Penn Station. He feels that the original structure was very good and that the replacement must be inferior.

55. **(C)** The author is concerned with the public relations aspects of those practices to which he objects. The antidote to the situation would be total honesty of thought, attitude and statement.

56. **(B)** The first sentence of the third paragraph makes this statement. All that follows this statement is further development of the theme. Thus, while it is truly stated that classroom experiences may change attitudes, (C), and that the attitudes of teachers may influence the attitudes of pupils, (D), the all-encompassing theme is that of the role played by teachers.

57. **(B)** The author implies that school is a broadening experience in many ways. In the elementary school, the child first encounters a wide diversity of attitudes in many areas and is first introduced to concepts about which to develop attitudes.

58. **(D)** The passage does recognize that children come to school with attitudes which they have developed outside of school, but it neither states nor implies that these attitudes are based upon the children's treatment as infants.

59. **(D)** The last paragraph warns of the harmful effects of a teacher's personal prejudices upon the development of children's attitudes. Since the teacher is a respected adult, the children will readily adopt his/her attitudes, even if they are unspoken. Hence, the teacher must be especially careful not to transmit attitudes in highly controversial areas.

60. **(C)** Positive experiences may be developed from field trips, visits and books. A resourceful teacher can also manipulate the classroom environment for positive experiences to be derived through units of study and daily interaction.

61. **(B)** The essence of this article is that the tests are not inherently bad and that publishers do distribute guidelines for their use and interpretation, but that users are often irresponsible and ignore the interpretative guidance offered.

62. **(B)** The article is clearly a defense of standardized tests. As such, one can assume that the author would consider the SAT to be generally reliable, especially when interpreted along with other information about the testee. The author states that the reliability of a prediction increases with the amount and quality of information available.

63. **(A)** The selection makes clear that the value of a standardized test is in the interpretation of the results and the use to which the results are put. This is explicitly stated in the last sentence of the first paragraph.

64. **(E)** In the fourth paragraph the passage states that the tests work most effectively when the traits or qualities being measured can be precisely defined. Thus, a test of knowledge of a specific subject would be the most valid; a test of aptitude would be reasonably valid; and a test measuring a nebulous quality such as creativity would have limited validity.

65. **(D)** The author fears that the harsh criticism which is misdirected at the tests themselves instead of at the misusers of the tests, will lead to the abandonment of standardized testing altogether.

SECTION II

1. **(B)** $40\% = \frac{2}{5}$
   $\frac{2}{5} \times \frac{10}{1} = \frac{4}{1}$

2. **(D)** 27 and 51 are each divisible by 3; 17 and 59 are prime numbers.
   Hence, I and IV only.

3. **(A)** Angle DOC = $6 + x$
   Angle AOC = $(6 + x) + x = 180 - 20$
   $6 + 2x = 160$
   $2x = 154$
   $x = 77$

4. **(D)** Let C = the capacity in gallons.
   Then $\frac{1}{3}C + 3 = \frac{1}{2}C$
   Multiplying through by 6, we obtain
   $2C + 18 = 3C$
   or $C = 18$

5. **(E)** $\frac{91 + 88 + 86 + 78 + x}{5} = 85$
   $343 + x = 425$
   $x = 82$

6. **(C)** $12 \times .39 = 4.68$ inches; that is, between $4\frac{1}{2}$ and 5

7. **(D)**

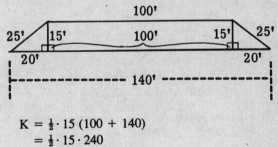

   In the figure above, PS⊥QR. Then, in right triangle PSR,
   $x^2 + 24^2 = 26^2$
   $x^2 = 26^2 - 24^2$
   $= (26 + 24)(26 - 24)$
   $x^2 = 50 \cdot 2 = 100$
   $x = 10$
   Thus, QR = 20

8. **(C)** All terms involving x are 0.
   Hence, the equation reduces to
   $0 - 7y + 15 = 0$
   or $76 = 15$
   $y = 2\frac{1}{7}$

9. **(E)** Let s = number of shirts t = number of ties, where s and t are integers.
   Then $7s + 3t = 81$
   $7s = 81 - 3t$
   $s = \frac{81 - 3t}{7}$

   Since s is an integer, t must have an integral value such that $81 - 3t$ is divisible by 7. Trial shows that t = 6 is the smallest such number,

   making $s = \frac{81 - 18}{7} = \frac{63}{7} = 9$

   $s:t = 9:6$
   $= 3:2$

10. **(C)** rate = $\frac{\text{distance}}{\text{time}} = \frac{\frac{2}{5} \text{ mile}}{\frac{5}{60} \text{ hour}} = \frac{\frac{2}{5}}{\frac{1}{12}}$

    rate = $\frac{2}{5} \cdot \frac{12}{1} = \frac{24}{5} = 4\frac{4}{5}$ miles per hour

11. **(D)** Draw the altitudes indicated. A rectangle and two right triangles are produced. From the figure, the base of each triangle is 20 feet. By the Pythagorean theorem, the altitude is 15 feet. Hence, the area

    K = $\frac{1}{2} \cdot 15 (100 + 140)$
    $= \frac{1}{2} \cdot 15 \cdot 240$
    $= 15 \cdot 120$
    $= 1800$ square feet

12. **(E)** If $1 + \frac{1}{t} = \frac{t + 1}{t}$, then the right-hand fraction can also be reduced to $1 + \frac{1}{t}$, and we have an identity, which is true for all values of t except 0.

13. **(E)** All points 6 inches from A are on a circle of radius 6 with center at A. All points 1 inch from b are on 2 straight lines parallel to b and 1 inch

from it on each side. These two parallel lines intersect the circle in 4 points.

14. **(E)** Let R = 5P and S = 5Q where P and Q are integers.

Then R − S = 5P − 5Q = 5(P − Q) is divisible by 5

RS = 5P · 5Q = 25PG is divisible by 25

R + S = 5P + 5Q = 5(P + Q) is divisible by 5

R² + S² = 25P² + 25Q² = 25(P² + Q²) is divisible by 5

R + S = 5P + 5Q = 5(P + Q), which is not necessarily divisible by 10

15. **(D)** $\frac{1}{2} \cdot h = 49\pi$

Dividing both sides by 7, we get
$\frac{1}{2}h = 7\pi$
or h = 14π

16. **(A)**

$\frac{\frac{3}{7}}{\frac{5}{14}}$ $\qquad\qquad$ $\frac{\frac{5}{14}}{\frac{3}{7}}$

$\frac{3}{7} \div \frac{5}{14}$ $\qquad\qquad$ $\frac{5}{14} \div \frac{3}{7}$

$\frac{3}{7} \times \frac{14}{5}$ $\qquad\qquad$ $\frac{5}{14} \times \frac{7}{3}$

$\frac{3}{1} \times \frac{2}{5}$ $\qquad\qquad$ $\frac{5}{2} \times \frac{1}{3}$

$\frac{6}{5}$ $\qquad\qquad\qquad$ $\frac{5}{6}$

$\frac{6}{5} > \frac{5}{6}$
∴ Column A > Column B

17. **(A)**
$\frac{9}{8} = 1.125$
$\frac{3}{5} = .60$
1.125 − .60 = .525
.525 > .5
∴ Column A > Column B

18. **(B)**
$\frac{3}{5}\% = .6\% = .0060$
.06 > .006
∴ Column B > Column A

19. **(B)**
Let x = the no. of days A & B take working together.
A can do the job in 4 days or $\frac{1}{4}$x
B can do the job in 3 days or $\frac{1}{3}$x
x/4 + x/3 = 1
12 (x/4 + x/3) = 12
3x + 4x = 12
7x = 12
x = $1\frac{5}{7}$ days

2 days > $1\frac{5}{7}$ days
∴ Column B > Column A

20. **(A)**
The ratio between seniors and the total of seniors and freshmen is 1:4. The ratio between seniors and the total enrollment (including sophomores and juniors) would actually decrease.
∴ Column A > Column B

21. **(C)**
Since the sum of the 3 angles of a triangle equals 180°
then, x + x + 60° = 180°
2x = 120°
x = 60°
Therefore, the triangle is equilateral
Hence side m = side n
∴ Column A = Column B

22. **(D)**
The relationship cannot be determined from the information given.

23. **(A)**
(3x − 4)(2x + 3) = 0 $\quad$ 2x + 3 = 0
$\qquad\qquad$ 3x − 4 = 0 $\qquad$ 2x = −3
$\qquad\qquad\qquad$ 3x = 4 $\qquad\quad$ x = $-\frac{3}{2}$
$\qquad\qquad\qquad$ x = $\frac{4}{3}$
The product of the roots $(\frac{4}{3})(-\frac{3}{2}) = -2$
$-\frac{3}{2} > -2$
∴ Column A > Column B

24. **(C)**
4 + 6(−1) ÷ 3 $\qquad$ −1 + 1(−6) ÷ −2
4 − 6 ÷ 3 $\qquad\qquad$ −1 − 6 ÷ −2
4 − 2 $\qquad\qquad\qquad$ −1 + 3
2 $\qquad\qquad\qquad\qquad$ 2

∴ Column A = Column B

25. **(B)**
Since the sum of the angles of a triangle equals 180° then, x + 2x + 90 = 180
3x = 90°
x = 30°
therefore ABC is a 30–60–90 right triangle. In a 30–60–90 right triangle the hypotenuse is equal to twice the side opposite the 30° angle.
∴ AB = 8
8 > 5
∴ Column B > Column A

26. (C)

$\sqrt[3]{125} = 5\,(25)^{\frac{1}{2}} = 5$

∴ Column A = Column B

27. (C)

$(x - y)^0 = 1 \qquad (x + y)^0 = 1$

∴ Column A = Column B

28. (A)

∠b = 130° (vertical ∠s are equal)

∠a = 50° (supplement of 130°)

∠c = 50° (supplement of 130°)

∠d = 50° (alt. int. ∠s of ∥ lines are equal)

∠g = 50° (vertical ∠s are equal)

∴ ∠b + ∠g = 180° and ∠a + ∠c + ∠d = 150°

180° > 150°

∴ Column A > Column B

29. (B)

$xy + 2x - y \qquad xy - 2x + y$

$-1(1) + 2(-1) - (1) \qquad -1(1) - 2(-1) + 1$

$-1 - 2 - 1 \qquad\qquad -1 + 2 + 1$

$-4 \qquad\qquad\qquad\quad 2$

$2 > -4$

∴ Column B > Column A

30. (B)

Since a line from the center of a circle drawn perpendicular to a chord bisects the chord, AM = 3.

If OB = 5

then AO = 5 (all radii in the same circle are equal)

∴ △AOM is a 3 − 4 − 5 right △

$2(AM) = 6 \qquad OM + AO =$

$\qquad\qquad\qquad\quad 4 + 5 \ = 9$

$9 > 6$

∴ Column B > Column A

31. (A)

$15\% = .15$

$.15 \cdot (43.50) = 6.525$

$\$43.50 - 6.53 = 36.97$

$\$36.97 > \$36$

∴ Column A > Column B

32. (C)

$75\% = \frac{3}{4} \qquad\qquad 50\% = \frac{1}{2}$

$\frac{3}{4}(\frac{1}{2}) = \frac{3}{8} \qquad\qquad \frac{1}{2}(\frac{3}{4}) = \frac{3}{8}$

∴ Column A = Column B

33. (E)

$\frac{9}{13} = \quad$

$$\begin{array}{r} .69 \\ 13\overline{)9.00} \\ \underline{78} \\ 120 \\ \underline{117} \end{array}$$

$\frac{13}{9} = \quad$

$$\begin{array}{r} 1.44 \\ 9\overline{)13.00} \\ \underline{9} \\ 40 \\ \underline{36} \\ 40 \\ \underline{36} \end{array}$$

70% = .7

$\frac{1}{.70} = \frac{1}{.7} = \quad$

$$\begin{array}{r} 1.42 \\ .7\overline{)1.000} \\ \underline{7} \\ 30 \\ \underline{28} \\ 20 \\ \underline{14} \end{array}$$

Correct order is $\frac{9}{13}$, 70%, $\frac{1}{70}$, $\frac{13}{9}$

or I, III, IV, II

34. (D)

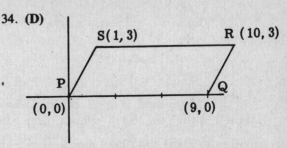

S(1, 3)   R (10, 3)

P

(0, 0)   (9, 0)   Q

Since PQ and RS are parallel and equal, the figure is a parallelogram of base = 9 and height = 3

Hence, area = 9 · 3

= 27

35. (A)

From the figure, in right △PCO,

$PO^2 = r^2 + 4^2$

$(8 - r)^2 = r^2 + 16$

$64 - 16r + r^2 = r^2 + 16$

$48 = 16r$

$r = 3$

Diameter = 6

36. **(B)** Area of wall = $4 \cdot \frac{60}{3}$ = $4 \cdot 20$ = 80 sq. yd.
    Cost = 80 × \$10.50 = \$840.00

37. **(D)** Distance of (4, 4) from origin =
    $\sqrt{16 + 16} = \sqrt{32} < 7$

    Distance of (5, 5) from origin =
    $\sqrt{25 + 25} = \sqrt{50} > 7$

    Distance of (4, 5) from origin =
    $\sqrt{16 + 25} = \sqrt{41} < 7$

    Distance of (4, 6) from origin =
    $\sqrt{16 + 36} = \sqrt{52} > 7$

    Hence, only II and IV are outside circle.

38. **(A)** Let x = the cost.
    Then $x + \frac{1}{4}x = 80$ $\qquad \frac{\text{Cost}}{\text{S.P.}} = \frac{64}{80}$
    $4x + x = 320$
    $5x = 320$ $\qquad\qquad = \frac{4}{5}$
    $= \$64$ (cost)

39. **(C)**

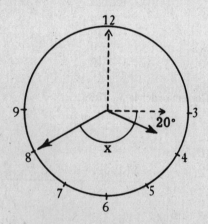

    At 3:00, large hand is at 12 and small hand
    is at 3. During the next 40 minutes, large hand
    moves to 8 and small hand moves $\frac{40}{60} = \frac{2}{3}$ of
    distance between 3 and 4; $\frac{2}{3} \times 30° = 20°$
    Since there is 30° between two numbers of clock
    $\angle x = 5(30°) - 20° = 150° - 20° = 130°$

40. **(B)** Area of sector = $\frac{120}{360} \cdot \pi \cdot 15^2$
    $= \frac{1}{3} \cdot \pi \cdot 225$
    $= 75\pi$

41. **(D)** $\frac{17}{10} y = 0.51$
    Multiplying both sides by 10, we get
    $17y = 5.1$
    Divide by 17
    $\quad y = .3$

42. **(D)** 40% = $\frac{2}{5} \times 50$ = 20 girls attended
    50% = $\frac{1}{2} \times 70$ = 35/55 total attendance at
    dance

    $\frac{55}{50 + 70} = \frac{55}{120} = \frac{11}{24}$ $\quad 24\overline{)11.000}$ = 45.8%
    $\qquad\qquad\qquad\qquad\qquad \frac{96}{140}$
    $\qquad\qquad\qquad\qquad\qquad \frac{120}{200}$
    $\qquad\qquad\qquad\qquad\qquad \frac{192}{}$

    Approx. 46%

43. **(E)** Since $x + 2x + y = 180°$, it follows that
    $3x + y = 180$
    $y = 180 - 3x$

44. **(B)** $\frac{18}{33} = \frac{6}{11} = \frac{\sqrt{6^2}}{\sqrt{11^2}} = \frac{\sqrt{6^2}}{\sqrt{11^2}}$
    $\qquad\qquad = \frac{\sqrt{36}}{\sqrt{121}}$

    Missing denominator is 121

45. **(D)** There are 20 numbers that contain 7 in the
    unit's place. There are 20 more that contain 7 in
    the ten's place. Thus, there are 40 numbers with
    7 in either unit's or ten's place. But the numbers
    277 and 377 must be rejected, and they have
    each been counted twice. Hence, 40 − 4 = 36

46. **(A)** $\qquad (r + s)^2 - r^2 - s^2 =$
    $r^2 + 2rs + s^2 - r^2 - s^2 = 2rs$

47. **(A)** As Q moves from R to S, PQ gets smaller.
    Its largest possible value would be 9.
    Hence, $9 \geq PQ \geq 6$

48. **(E)** Selling price per article = $\frac{K}{8}$

    Cost per article = $\frac{K}{12}$

    Profit per article = $\frac{K}{8} - \frac{K}{12} = \frac{3K - 2K}{24}$
    $\qquad\qquad\qquad\qquad = \frac{K}{24}$

49. **(C)** Analyze this by means of the diagram below

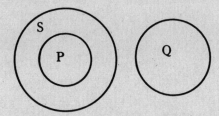

From the figure, we readily see that no P are Q

50. **(B)** The sum of the four numbers is 45 × 4 = 180. For the average to remain the same, the sum must remain unchanged. If one number is increased by 6, then each of the other three must be reduced by 2.

ARCO Books For
College Entrance Preparation

PREPARATION FOR THE SAT—SCHOLASTIC APTITUDE TEST

Brigitte Saunders, Gabriel P. Freedman, Leonard J. Capodice, Margaret A. Haller, and Robert Bailey. Six full-length practice exams with detailed explanatory answers to all questions. Expert review material for both verbal and mathematics sections of the exam. Comprehensive word list.

ISBN 0-668-05898-6 paper **$7.95**

VERBAL WORKBOOK FOR THE SAT

Gabriel P. Freedman and Margaret A. Haller. Comprehensive review for the verbal and TSWE sections of the SAT. Hundreds of graded practice questions for review in each area. Five full-length practice tests with explanatory answers. Progress charts for self-evaluation.

ISBN 0-668-04853-0 paper **$6.00**

MATHEMATICS WORKBOOK FOR THE SAT

Brigitte Saunders with David Frieder and Mark Weinfeld. Authoritative instructional text and extensive drill in all math areas covered on the SAT. Diagnostic tests in each area to spotlight weaknesses; post-tests to measure progress. Three sample tests with complete solutions.

ISBN 0-668-06138-3 paper **$6.95**

PSAT/NMSQT   PRELIMINARY SCHOLASTIC APTITUDE TEST/NATIONAL MERIT SCHOLARSHIP QUALIFYING TEST

Eve P. Steinberg. Four full-length sample exams and extensive practice with every type of examination question. Every answer fully explained to make practicing for the test a valuable learning experience.

ISBN 0-668-06100-6 paper **$7.95**

SAT AT A GLANCE

Ronald G. Vlk. A unique 10-hour study format. Divided into five study units, the book contains an SAT overview, mini-tests, subject reviews, and test-taking strategies.

ISBN 0-668-06464-1 paper **$3.95**

PRACTICE FOR THE SCHOLASTIC APTITUDE TEST

Martin McDonough and Alvin J. Hansen. The essentials of SAT preparation condensed into one compact, easy-to-use study guide that fits into pocket or purse. Complete coverage of every question type, 1000 word SAT vocabulary list, one full-length practice exam with explanatory answers for all questions.

ISBN 0-668-05425-5 paper **$3.50**

For book ordering information refer to the last page of this book.

AMERICAN COLLEGE TESTING PROGRAM (ACT)

Eve P. Steinberg. Four full-length practice test batteries with explanatory answers for all questions. Skills reviews and practice questions in each subject area of the exam. Detailed directions for scoring and evaluating exam results. Valuable test-taking tips.
ISBN 0-668-05957-5 Paper **$7.95**

VERBAL WORKBOOK FOR THE ACT

Joyce Lakritz. Intensive review for the English Usage and Reading Comprehension sections of the ACT. Three full-length sample ACT English Usage Tests with explanatory answers to help candidates assess their readiness for the ACT.
ISBN 0-668-05348-8 Paper **$6.95**

MATHEMATICS WORKBOOK FOR THE ACT

Barbara Erdsneker and Brigitte Saunders. In-depth review of the mathematical concepts essential to scoring high on the ACT. Diagnostic tests in each area, followed by instructional text and practice problems, with re-tests to measure progress. Three sample ACT Mathematics Tests with detailed solutions.
ISBN 0-668-05443-3 Paper **$6.95**

TEST OF ENGLISH AS A FOREIGN LANGUAGE (TOEFL)

Edith H. Babin, Carole V. Cordes, and Harriet H. Nichols. Complete preparation for the college entrance examination required of students whose native language is not English. Six simulated sample tests covering all sections of this important exam. Separate cassette tape available for practice with the listening comprehension section.
ISBN 0-668-05446-8 (book) **$8.95**
ISBN 0-668-05743-2 (cassette) **$7.95**

TOEFL GRAMMAR WORKBOOK

Phyllis L. Lim and Mary Kurtin; Laurie Wellman, Consulting Editor. Intensive review for the Structure and Written Expression section of the TOEFL. Concise explanations of the points of English grammar covered by the test. Diagnostic test to direct study. Three practice tests for review.
ISBN 0-668-05080-2 Paper **$7.95**

TOEFL READING COMPREHENSION AND VOCABULARY WORKBOOK

Elizabeth Davy and Karen Davy. Graded practice in reading comprehension and vocabulary to build these essential English skills. Numerous exercises for practice with a variety of reading materials. Three sample Reading Comprehension and Vocabulary Tests with explanatory answers for all questions.
ISBN 0-668-05594-4 Paper **$7.95**

For book ordering information refer to the last page of this book.

ORDER THE BOOKS DESCRIBED ON THE PREVIOUS PAGES FROM YOUR BOOKSELLER OR DIRECTLY FROM:

ARCO PUBLISHING, INC.
215 Park Avenue South
New York, N.Y. 10003

To order directly from Arco, please add $1.00 for first book and 35¢ for each additional book for packing and mailing cost. No C.O.D.'s accepted.

Residents of New York, New Jersey and California must add appropriate sales tax.

MAIL THIS COUPON TODAY!

ARCO PUBLISHING, INC., 215 Park Avenue South, New York, N.Y. 10003
Please rush the following Arco books:

NO. OF COPIES	TITLE #	TITLE	PRICE	EXTENSION
			SUB-TOTAL	
			LOCAL TAX	
			PACKING & MAILING	
			TOTAL	

I enclose check ☐, M.O. ☐ for $ _____
☐ Is there an Arco Book on any of the following subjects: _____
☐ Please send me your free Complete Catalog.

NAME _____

ADDRESS _____

CITY _____ STATE _____ ZIP _____

Every Arco book is guaranteed. Return for full refund within ten days if not completely satisfied.

NOT RESPONSIBLE FOR CASH SENT THROUGH THE MAILS